AF334058

Sublime Noise

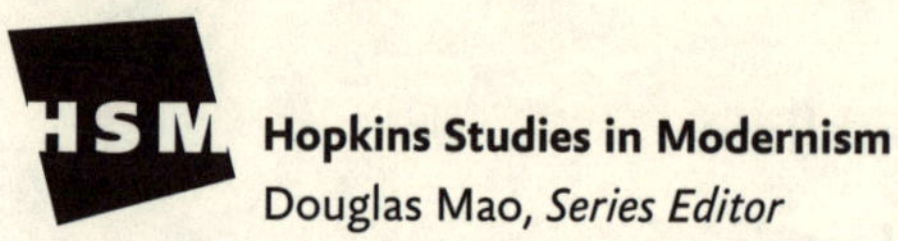
HSM
Hopkins Studies in Modernism
Douglas Mao, *Series Editor*

Sublime Noise

Musical Culture and the Modernist Writer

Josh Epstein

Johns Hopkins University Press
Baltimore

Printed in the United States of America on acid-free paper
9 8 7 6 5 4 3 2 1

Johns Hopkins University Press
2715 North Charles Street
Baltimore, Maryland 21218-4363
www.press.jhu.edu

Library of Congress Cataloging-in-Publication Data

Epstein, Josh, 1981–
Sublime noise : musical culture and the modernist writer / Josh Epstein.
pages cm. — (Hopkins studies in modernism)
Includes bibliographical references and index.
ISBN 978-1-4214-1523-9 (hardcover : acid-free paper) — ISBN 978-1-4214-1524-6 (electronic) — ISBN 1-4214-1523-2 (hardcover : acid-free paper) — ISBN 1-4214-1524-0 (electronic)
1. Modernism (Literature) 2. Modernism (Music) 3. Noise in literature. 4. Music and literature. 5. Music—Philosophy and aesthetics. I. Title.
PN56.M54E67 2014
809'.9112—dc23 2014004991

A catalog record for this book is available from the British Library.

Special discounts are available for bulk purchases of this book. For more information, please contact Special Sales at 410-516-6936 or specialsales@press.jhu.edu.

Johns Hopkins University Press uses environmentally friendly book materials, including recycled text paper that is composed of at least 30 percent post-consumer waste, whenever possible.

Whose silence is our hubbub?

Beauchamp, in Tom Stoppard's *Artist Descending a Staircase*

The rapids were near, and an uninterrupted, uniform, headlong, rushing noise filled the mournful stillness of the grove, where not a breath stirred, not a leaf moved, with a mysterious sound—as though the tearing pace of the launched earth had suddenly become audible.

Marlow, in Joseph Conrad's *Heart of Darkness*

Contents

Acknowledgments

To quote Lina Lamont from *Singin' in the Rain*, if this book brings "a little joy into your humdrum lives, it makes us feel as though our hard work ain't been in vain for nothin'." The hard work of producing this book has indeed been "ours," in the plural (though any remaining missteps are mine alone). To be able to thank the friends, colleagues, mentors, students, and interlocutors who have shared in this work is the foremost of many joys and reliefs of finishing this project.

First, I am exceedingly grateful to know Mark Wollaeger. Without his encyclopedic knowledge and his Carlylean exhortations to sustain courage with work, I struggle to say what this project would look like. I am forever thankful for the guidance of Carolyn Dever, an inexhaustible source of insight and magnanimity; and Joy Calico, an omniscient fount of knowledge and wit, and a lifesaver at those moments where my musical competence started to meet its limits. A 2013 performance of Antheil's *Ballet Mécanique* at the Blair School of Music, which Joy organized and which Mark and Paul Young helped me to attend, provided a spark of energy and morale in the late stages of a long process. Thanks to Paul also for introducing me to Irma Vep; I've never been the same since. Jonathan Neufeld—an improvement on Adorno, Hanslick, and Habermas—helped me, especially in the early stages, to define an inchoate mass of quasi-thoughts. It is impossible to exaggerate how much I benefited from these terrific mentors.

I am forever indebted to Doug Mao, series editor extraordinaire, who has been more patient with this project than I had any right to expect. My thanks also to Matt McAdam, Katie Curran, Helen Myers, and Melissa Solarz for their editorial help, and to Scott Klein for his exceedingly perceptive reading of this work. I always learn something new from Scott, and am glad to have, as a cordial ally, such a luminary in the study of words and music.

Early versions of this work were supported by an ACLS postdoctoral fellowship, fulfilled at the University of California Santa Barbara, and by Vanderbilt University's Robert Penn Warren Center for the Humanities, guided by the inimitable Mona Frederick. Mona and the Warren Center are forces for great good in the world. May they long continue to be so!

The process of composing this text has been aided by a host of genuinely wonderful friends and colleagues. Roy Gottfried and Ellen Levy have offered incisive and helpful readings of my work; Patricia Armstrong was of great support in my transition from grad student to member of the profession; and I want especially to thank Nicole Seymour for her professional insight, her good humor, and her readings of very lumpy draft material. I have valued the camaraderie of many at Vanderbilt: among them, Katherine Fusco, Brian Rejack, and Jane Wanninger have been loyal earwitnesses. While I was at UCSB, Andrew Griffin and Scott Selisker provided helpful commentary, and they, as well as Heather Blurton, Beau Blurton-Donnelly, Brian Donnelly, Faith Harden, and Tess Shewry, made for splendid company. Enda Duffy and Maurizia Boscagli welcomed me warmly into the UCSB modernist fold, and I appreciated the time spent in conversation with UCSB's Center for Modern Literature, Materialism, and Aesthetics and the Southern California Irish Studies Colloquium. At Texas A&M-Corpus Christi, my happiness and work were sustained by the friendship of Jenny Heil, Seneca Holland, Dale Pattison, David Smith, and Rick Smith. I found wonderfully supportive colleagues and friends in Glenn Blalock, Diana Cardenas, Kevin Concannon, Stephen Doolan, Chuck Etheridge, Molly Engelhardt, Shannon Fitzsimmons-Doolan, Elisabeth Mermann-Jozwiak, Nancy Sullivan, and Sharon Talley. In finishing the book I have been very grateful for the welcoming support of new colleagues at Portland State University, including but by no means limited to John Beer, Michael Clark, Bishupal Limbu, Sarah Lincoln, and Hildy Miller, whose insightful questions and confidence in my work have been greatly appreciated. I would have been lost without the guidance of many dedicated staff members and librarians, including Nick Alward, Jennifer Anderson, Becky Flores, Amyl Freeberg, Michelle Harmon, Rose Harris, Shayna Ingram, Galyn Martin, and Raphaëlla Nau.

At meetings of the Modern Language Association, the Modernist Studies Association, New Directions in the Humanities, and "Space Between" Society, I have welcomed occasions to discuss this work with wonderful scholars who—whether they knew it or not—have left deep intellectual imprints on this work. Julia Obert, Wendy Moffat, and Marsha Bryant may recognize their much-appreciated contributions here. I am indebted to Patricia Maguire for helping me navigate the E.M. Forster archives at King's College, Cambridge; though not many archival materials made it into this book, that experience overhauled my thinking about Forster. I also thank the students whom I have subjected to these arguments over the last few years, including those in a TAMUCC graduate seminar on modernism and media, and those in a range of UCSB classes cross-listed in English and Music. They have always been game to join in the madness.

Two journals have graciously permitted me to reuse select materials. Portions of chapter 4 have appeared in an earlier form as "Joyce's Phoneygraphs: Music, Mediation, and Noise Unleashed," in *James Joyce Quarterly* 48, no. 2 (2011), 265–89; earlier versions of material from chapter 3 have been published as "The Antheil Era: Pound, Noise, and Musical Sensation" in *Textual Practice*. I am pleased to extend my thanks to these publications, and to Peter Boxall, Carol Kealiher, Sean Latham, and the peer-reviewers, whose suggestions carried into this book.

And finally, without Richard and Carol Epstein, I would be out of luck in countless ways. I will not be offended if they don't read this massive thing, but I hope they'll at least read this much: thank you.

Introduction

> Who wrote this fiendish "Rite of Spring"?
> What right had he to write the thing?
> Against our helpless ears to fling
> Its crash, clash, cling, clang, bing, bang, bing?
>
> Anonymous letter, *The Boston Herald* (1924)

When modernist writers of the early twentieth century turned again and again to music, what Joseph Conrad calls the "art of arts,"[1] they were not turning solely to Beethoven, Tchaikovsky, Bach, and Mozart. (In any event, Beethoven, Tchaikovsky, and Bach are hardly the docile musical creatures they are made out to be—one need merely ask their contemporaries.) Music seemed to be undergoing a sea-change in the 1910s and '20s: the strident dissonances of Arnold Schoenberg and Alban Berg, the rhythmic shocks of Igor Stravinsky's *Rite of Spring* (*Le Sacre du printemps*; 1913), the syncopations and disjunctive melodic contours of jazz, the introduction of mechanical instruments and industrial noises in concert pieces such as George Antheil's *Ballet Mécanique* (1924), and ballets such as Erik Satie's *Parade* (1917). Of course, these new developments, though startling, by no means came out of nowhere. Stravinsky was taught by Nikolai Rimsky-Korsakoff, and, by the time of the *Herald* letter quoted above, was well into his neoclassical rewritings of the eighteenth-century composer Giovanni Pergolesi (*Pulcinella* [1920]); Arnold Schoenberg's twelve-tone species of atonality was an extension of the intense chromaticism of Mahler, Wagner, and Strauss; Berg quotes Bach's "Es ist genug" in his *Violin Concerto* and Wagner's *Tristan und Isolde* in his *Lyric Suite*; and so on. Music was digesting, not annihilating, its traditions through new rhythms, dissonances, and noises.

But as we know, audiences take it personally when their music seems to be under attack, and figures such as this anonymous doggerelist (writing to the *Herald eleven years* after the *Sacre* had debuted in Paris) readily turn their rhetorical gifts to assaulting it. Reactions to new music develop with surprising constancy, illustrated by the polemical uniformity found in books such as Nicholas Slonimsky's *Lexicon of Musical Invective*, an encyclopedia of nasty and shortsighted music criticism. "New music," whatever that might mean at the time, is noisy (Liszt, Bloch, Strauss), dissonant (Beethoven, Chopin), amelodic (Brahms), "hysterical" (Tchaikovsky), abusive to the audience (Wagner), or not music at all. In response to these annoyingly consistent critical reactions, the American composer Henry Cowell put it succinctly: "If a reviewer writes 'It is not music, but noise,' he feels that all necessary comment has been made."[2]

My study here is well encapsulated by Cowell's epigram, from an essay entitled "The Joys of Noise," about the lazy reviewer who dismisses the "new music" with a vague epithet—"noise." Cowell's claim has a deep resonance with the musical and literary arts of British and Anglophone modernism. Music is not just taken personally, but assumed to be culturally significant; the perceived attack on the "old favorites" is seen as an incursion against cultural order, as we see from the influx of books about the need for classical music to save our souls.[3] As modernist writers take up questions of cultural order in magisterial, occasionally reactionary ways—as in the strivings of T.S. Eliot or Ezra Pound to reconstruct a cohesive "kulchur"—it makes sense that they obsess over the art associated with the pleasures of formal integrity.

What needs more scrutiny is how writers turned to the music of their own time—music often infiltrated with noise—as they rethought the form and the cultural potential of their craft. Cowell knew that the word "noise" could not be applied so insouciantly to the musical world he inhabited—in fact, he put his musical gifts to satirical effect in setting this *Boston Herald* doggerel, along with two other similar verses, in his *Three Anti-Modernist Songs* (1938). Well before Pierre Schaeffer's *musique concrète* experiments with edited tape-recorded sounds (*Cinq études de bruits*; 1948), musicians were composing through the sounds of air-raid sirens, trains, typewriters, propellers, pianolas, recorded birdsong, radio static, and (perhaps most ominously) radio silence. Noise thereby took on new aesthetic and cultural resonances, as a concept and a sonic material. For Cowell, Antheil, Stravinsky, Varèse, and Satie, among others, the musical use of noise could potentially serve a disruptive and a beautiful function in the concert hall.

For these composers, and for the writers listening to them, it became a principal project of modern art to figure out what would "count" as music or noise, and what was aesthetically or culturally at stake in pressing that question. As noise made its way not only into avant-garde efforts to destroy art's sublimity (Dadaist sound poetry, Luigi Russolo's Futurist *Arte Dei Rumori* [*Art of Noises*; 1913], Alexander Mosolov's musical imitation of a factory in *Iron Foundry* [1927]), but also into the productions of what we retroactively call "high modernism," the very boundaries of the autonomous artwork seemed to be building up and decomposing at every turn. As composers put these real-world sounds into dialogue with melody, harmony, rhythm, and (a)tonality, and as writers critiqued or aspired to the musical arts, modernists came to contend with music and noise as interrelated categories of sound, art, and culture. And as audiences reacted vituperatively to new music—as in the riots at Stravinsky's *Sacre*, Antheil's *Ballet*, Satie's *Parade*, and the 1913 "Skandalkonzert" of Schoenberg, Berg, and Webern—noise seemed increasingly symptomatic of a shifting interactive relationship between stage and audience.

Without noise, music, or combinations thereof, little is left of European, Anglo-American, and Anglo-Irish modernism. Without literal or figurative gestures to noise, there is no Duchamp, Kandinsky, or Mondrian, no Brecht or Beckett, no Langston Hughes, no William Carlos Williams. (I stop short of John Cage, for reasons I shall explain.) Without gestures to musical rhythm, syncopation, consonance, dissonance, and tactical silence, there is no Auden, H.D., Toomer, Proust, Lawrence, Yeats, Cunard, Stevens, or Stein (who describes the *Rite* premiere to great effect in *The Autobiography of Alice B. Toklas*). Put more baldly, a twentieth-century world without noise would make it difficult to articulate the value of music. I derive this claim from musicians and writers who use music and writing to reconfigure, or escape from, the noises of a violent modern landscape. I also draw it from literary critics, musicologists, and philosophers who consider "music" and "noise" as fluid sonic and semiotic classifications.

In this book, I argue that noise and music—as mutually informing sonic presences and as aesthetic and cultural categories—shape the writing of the early twentieth century. Modernists imagined music as a mediation of noise: an effort to interpret, orchestrate, sublimate, amplify, or critique the sounds and the affective shocks of industrialization, urbanization, warfare, publicity, and mechanical reproducibility. I argue, in short, that the presence of noise in British, Anglo-American, and Anglo-Irish modernism is the sound of the artwork coming to grips with the failure of its autonomy from social life. Somewhat paradoxically, the more writers and musicians attempt to manufacture this autonomy by repressing or sublimating the noises of politics, history, and publicity, the more they are forced to engage with noise and its implications. In an age of mechanical reproduction and new media, as well, the more desperately artists strive for the ideal of pure music—attempting to detach music from literary meaning and give it a purely formal meaning—the more they leave it open to literary or political misprision.

In showing how noise motivates the modernist text—as a presence to be celebrated or repressed—I contend that modernist writers' oft-acknowledged debts to music are also contentions with music's social purchase, symptomatized by the presence of ostensibly antiaesthetic sounds. Music, Walter Pater wrote in the 1870s, is the art to which all others "constantly aspire," for its unifications of form and content.[4] While Pater's nostrum is often taken as a starting point for literary aesthetics—while modernist writing is read as an effort to approximate music's ineffable aesthetic ideal—I argue that these writers are no less engaged with music as a social and cultural artifact. Modernist literature, that is, grapples not just with the sublime Paterian "condition of music," but with music's cultural *effects*.

Take, for example, a 1918 essay from the *Musical Times*: an instructive document of music criticism from within a decade of Schoenberg's experiments with atonality, Stravinsky's experiments with primitivism and polytonality, Satie's mischievous surrealism, and Antheil's experiments with noise. "Battle Music," an article by a musicologist named Cecil Barber, suggestively takes for granted a point that we may find odd: "That music was only expensive noise," Barber writes, "we knew long before the modern Symphonic-poem had its day."[5] For Barber, music was not just an aesthetic pacification of noise, but an "expensive" variety of it: a way of making it marketable and palatable to good taste. Barber suggests that this intuitive knowledge—music is just noise, except fancier—has been repressed in favor of the pure aesthetic ideal. But the noise of World War I makes it impossible to continue entertaining such a fantasy. In describing the "battle music" of the trenches, Barber synesthetically proposes that even the loudest Berlioz symphony "pales like the stars before the mildest *strafe* on the Western Front." As "the storm bursts, *fffff*" (that's a *fortissississississimo*), the guns "supply a pedal to the frantic exordium; and superimposed on this . . . move notes of lighter calibres, all vociferous however and deadly in their utterance."

If Pater, Stéphane Mallarmé, or any number of other late nineteenth-century aesthetes had idealized music's pleasurable unifications of form and content, Barber recognizes something important: in the noisy, violent, rationalized public life of modernity, that unification *is itself* content. For, as Theodor Adorno wrote, music itself must fight for its right to exist: in a battle-music of a different kind, music must struggle to carve out an autonomous niche for art amidst this "exordium" of violence.[6] The more music disavows its material status as "expensive noise," the more it struggles to claim for itself an inviolable cultural status; amidst such a noise, to assert an autonomy for music requires a kind of willful deafness to the crescendoing hum of modern life, what Emily Thompson has called "the soundscape of modernity."

There is an additional anxiety at work here, which is that music—the voice of the sublime and ineffable—in modernity appears increasingly rationalized and cynical. Modernist writing's aspirations to music had to contend with the fear of music's seductive manipulations of the unconscious, a fear made worse by gramophones and pianolas capable of producing disembodied sounds of their own accord. What does it mean to find oneself singing along automatically to popular music without realizing it—worse, why is everyone else doing it at the same time? Barber, astonished at the "Harvest of Hate" in which men work the "engines of destruction against one another," hears in the "hurly-burly" of war an "astonishing" truth about his kind of music: that it is "both positive and negative—priggish where controlled and brainless where automatic. Yet human heads and hearts are at the back of it! That is the horrible thought!" (25).

Barber's "Battle Music" fantasy is shaped by two coextensive fears of modern mechanization of art, which inform Adorno's critique of the culture industry: the fear that it is idiotic and the fear that it is hyperrational. "The world is not just mad," Adorno says in a 1956 dialogue with Max Horkheimer; "It is mad and rational as well."[7] The reader of "Battle Music" in the pages of the *Musical Times* will arrive there by way of a dry and insular discussion of the "the ancient origin of the major and minor scales and the harmonic potentialities of the unusual scale-degree relations." The juxtaposition provokes the implication that the technical minutiae of (modernized) ancient harmony are but an "expensive" gussying-up of the primitive compulsion to kill. "Controlled" and base, the same heads and hearts that produce sublime art are made complicit in the noise of the battlefield.

Just as modernist music intensified its competition with the battle music of the Great War, as in Leo Ornstein's pianistic imitation of the fighter pilot

(*Suicide in an Airplane*; 1918), the equation of music and noise in wartime is a common trope of modernist writing, limited neither to Barber nor to England. With equally apocalyptic panache, Robert Saint-Loup in Proust's *Time Regained* (1927) indulges in a bit of speculation on "purely musical grounds" as he watches a "constellation" of airplanes in the sky, as if "in obedience to laws as precise as those that govern the constellations of the stars." As he hears the music of the air-raid sirens, imagining a German anthem—a "*Wacht am Rhein*," "with the Crown Prince and the Princesses in the imperial box"—it leads him to wonder "whether they were indeed pilots and not Valkyries who were sailing upwards." "There's no doubt about it," he continues: "the Germans have to arrive before you can hear Wagner in Paris."[8] As Saint-Loup follows the metonymic chain between the real-world noises of invasion and the spectacle of Wagner, the airplanes become a constellation, in Adorno's and Mallarmé's senses of the term: an ordered group of signs which evades the imposition of extrinsic rationality, obeying only the immanent "laws" materialized by its own forms, rhythms, and double-meanings. As Proust's "searchlights strayed ceaselessly to and fro, scenting the enemy, encircling him with their beams," they try and fail to make the constellations of form submit to a stabilizing gaze.

This is the same sort of constellational intuition that shapes, in *Swann's Way* (1913), the constant recollection of Vinteuil's "little phrase" for the violin; the same sort of enthymemic sleight of hand that informs Stephen Dedalus's ruminations on the octave in Joyce's *Ulysses* (1922); the same sort of metaphorical excursion that takes Helen Wilcox, in E.M. Forster's *Howards End* (1910), from the sounds of a Beethoven concert to a vision of goblins marching down the Strand. Could it be that "purely musical" reasoning is the most instinctive literary response to the expensive noise of the early twentieth century—that Proust's, Joyce's, and Forster's obsession with music correlates with the increasingly loud soundscape of modernity? Through cultural history and new close readings, *Sublime Noise* interprets literary-musical collaborations, borrowings, and aspirations as serving a simultaneously formal and cultural purpose. "Noise" and "music" reflect assessments of cultural value accorded to different kinds of sound: to call a sound "music," or a sequence of lines a "poem," represents an argument about what weight that production will be granted.

In using noise to develop a cultural history of musical-literary interactions, I draw on literary appropriations of music and on (relatively light) musical readings, and on the "new musicology" (or, a less partisan term, cultural musicology). An analogue to literary cultural studies, the new musicology draws from materialist, psychoanalytic, semiotic, gender, and other cultural theory to interpret music as freighted with ideology and subjectivity —revealing the historical specificity of "the universal language." It balances a formalist musicological strain with an understanding that musical power grows out of social power and abjection: out of hope and fear, desire and disgust of a deeply historical kind. Chapter six, for example, engages with queer musicology (Philip Brett, Wayne Koestenbaum); chapter two builds on Linda Hutcheon and Michael Hutcheon's suggestive readings of Wagner's *Parsifal* in relation to nineteenth-century codings of the syphilitic body as it strained the limits of moral propriety and ethnic solidarity. The study is buttressed more broadly by Susan McClary's work on how musical form encodes erotic subjectivity. McClary wrote in 1990 that even "scholars who produce work resembling the old-fashioned New Criticism of literary studies still count as radicals in musicology," and thanks largely to McClary's work, that has changed.[9]

This book thus puts cultural musicology into apposition with the "new modernist studies," an ongoing effort to expand literary modernism's chronological reach, blur its geographical boundaries, explode its archives, and dissolve its hierarchies of "high" and "popular." Just as musicology has enriched the study of music as it leaves the (already noisy) concert hall and reenters public debate, modernist studies continues to probe more complex homologies among competing discourses and media. In developing this nexus between musicology and literary modernist studies—two fields seeking ways out of tight "temporal, spatial, vertical," and formal limits[10]—it makes sense to call on noise, which by definition involves the transgression of a sonic, aesthetic, geographic, or social boundary. If noise were found where it belonged, we wouldn't call it "noise"—it would be sound, music, signal, silence, or something else. A concept defined through the effort to abate it, noise speaks loudest when repressed or disciplined.

In joining "new" musicology and "new" modernisms, I work to transform an interstitial space—literary criticism *on* music—that has, for all this, remained intractably formalist. In light of musicology's rich theoretical and methodological blend, which more resembles than differs from literary cultural studies, it no longer makes sense to critique literary treatments of music through Paterian eyes. Similarly, whether or not he would call himself a "new musicologist" as such, Alex Ross's engrossing book *The Rest is Noise* (2007) draws the innovations of Stravinsky and Schoenberg, Britten and

Cage, into dialogue with the "hyper-political twentieth century." Though "it has long been fashionable to fence [classical] music off from society," Ross writes, "that barrier crumbles time and again. . . . Still, even if history can never tell us exactly what music means, music can still tell us something about history" (xiii). Ross twins the fencing off of music as a self-referential niche with the problem of "musical meaning" writ large. Musical meaning is particularly unstable—all the more incentive for literary writers to turn their craft to the task of reappropriating it.

The fenced-off autonomy of music is an aggressively modernist fiction: an extension of Pater and a reaction-formation to the twentieth century's "hyper-political" violence. It represents an effort, that is, to take advantage of the mutable language of music to disseminate cultural politics while cloaking them in the language of sublimity. As Richard Taruskin argues, critiquing Stravinsky's neoclassical doctrines, the rhetoric of "music alone" presents the illusion of a "*cordon sanitaire*, a quarantine staking out a decontaminated space within which music can be composed, performed, and listened to in a cultural and historical vacuum, that is, in perfect sterility."[11] If my account reaches only halfway through the twentieth century, to Britten's and Forster's opera *Billy Budd* (1951), it is because these five decades offer a concerted articulation of the problems of music and history, in a way that has not been sufficiently addressed.

As cultural musicology has made clear, music can perform these mediations largely because it animates the body. *Le Sacre du printemps* is a ballet, of course—an intensely "biological" one, as Jacques Rivière suggested in 1921, in which "the body is no longer an escape route for the soul; rather it brings it back and surrounds it with itself."[12] *Ballet Mécanique* is not a ballet, but calls itself one, as it approximates the noisily ritualistic assaults of modern machinery; Pound heard in it a potential to reenergize rather than exhaust the industrial worker. Much of modern dance, as Carrie Preston explains, "repositio[ns] the expressive performing body as a site combining disparate trajectories in modernism: textual and embodied practices, interests in myth and science, classicism and the machine age";[13] the same can be said of modern music. Though my aim here is not to provide a theory of embodiment per se, each chapter rethinks the body in relation to aesthetic and social categories mapped out by musical and literary form and transgressed by noise. With respect to Eliot, for example, I build on Hutcheon's and Hutcheon's argument that *Parsifal*, among many other operas, lean on "cultural clichés" for disease, exoticism, and other forms of embodied excess or decay. The very notion of the cultural cliché, a public dispersion of anxieties about the body, epitomizes the "difficult" modernist artwork's relation to the trite and ordinary—exactly what poems like *The Waste Land* are about. As *The Waste Land* mediates *Parsifal*, through direct allusion, thematic reference, and formal aspirations to the Wagnerian total artwork, we will see its attempts to sustain a cohesively rhythmic, disciplinary poetic order unraveled by the dissonances, glitching records, disintegrating bodies, and inarticulately yawping voices at its center. In Pound and Antheil, too, we will find a constantly oscillating tension between modernism's classical impulses and the entropic sensations of the flesh. The debt that Edith Sitwell owes to the musical and visual clichés of modern ballet, the exotic moving body served up for collective spectacle, marks the dance rhythms of her poetry, which, in turn, defamiliarize the ballet's stock tropes of empire and race. In Joyce, whose novels obsess over the rhythms of consumption and excretion, the body enables the experience of music as an autonomous epiphanic pleasure, but undoes that autonomy as those bodies reenter the noisy social world. And in the work of Benjamin Britten and E.M. Forster, finally, the figurative and musical drives to consonance reflect, with unsettling consistency, a repression of homoerotic desire.

In particular, I isolate two elements of music, rhythm and dissonant harmony, as efforts to make musical sense of art's social noises. Other features of music—orchestration, tonality, melody, not to mention the literary plots of operas and ballets—will feature as well, but rhythm and dissonance are the elements of modern music most under duress, and most often blamed for music's newfound noisiness. Schoenberg's effort to "emancipate the dissonance," to expand the possibilities of harmonic expression, gave dissonance a particular cultural cachet in the early twentieth century. Adorno's philosophical reflections on dissonance, which should not be conflated with Schoenberg's own program, emphasized its negative critical potential, its ability to expose the false rationality of mainstream systems of knowledge. The literary effort to reproduce the emotional or cognitive effects of dissonance likewise requires the writer to test the limits of representational language, to struggle against too-transparent modes of reading the world.

Rhythm, too, is perceived to have specific kinds of potential for commenting on the noise of modern life, for structuring images, sounds, and harmonies into a communicable narrative. On just these grounds, T.S. Eliot interprets *Le Sacre du printemps* not just as an experiment with "primitive" or folk music, but as a commentary on the modern: "The effect was like *Ulysses* with illustrations by the best contemporary illustrator. . . . In everything in the *Sacre du Printemps*, except in the music, one missed the sense of the present . . . ; but it did seem to transform the rhythm of the steppes into the scream of the motor horn, the rattle of machinery, the grind of wheels, and the other barbaric cries of modern life; and to transform these despairing noises into music."[14] Stravinsky's piece exemplifies what Eliot came to call Joyce's "mythical method," a "continuous parallel between contemporaneity and antiquity."[15] According to Eliot, Stravinsky performs a double transformation: of the "rhythm of the steppes" into all of the "barbaric cries of modern life," and then of those "despairing noises into music." Though Eliot found the trappings of the Russian Ballet dated (he was not alone), Stravinsky's music interprets and "transforms" the dance into the "barbaric cries of modern life," with a "sense of the present" sited in the experience of sound: in those "despairing noises" that serve as material for the mediations of art. Music needs a newly rhythmic language, like Stravinsky's, because modernity has intensified aural experience.[16]

Stravinsky's *Sacre* exemplifies a relation between music and noise, not only because the "rhythm of the steppes" seems to suggest something about modern sound culture, but because the performance event resulted in an outburst of audience pique and, to date, a century's worth of hype, publicity, and rumor about what actually produced the riots at the Théâtre des Champs-Elysées. As with the early reactions to *Le Sacre*, *Parade*, *Ballet Mécanique*, Schoenberg's *Pierrot Lunaire* (1912), Varèse's *Amériques* (1926), and William Walton's *Façade* (1922), new fluctuations in the noise/music boundary were met with audience noise in return. Such sounds of discontent in the early twentieth century, which Neil Blackadder calls the "heyday of the theater scandal," often signified not failure but success, not a crowd of philistines but a critically engaged audience.[17] Trying to reverse nineteenth-century norms of absorbed and "respectable" spectatorship, aiming to unsettle rather than absorb an audience, modern playwrights and producers would capitalize on the scandals at their own performances.[18] Antheil, for example, earned his success not only by using musical noise, but by tirelessly building social networks, appropriating voguish artistic slogans, using the popular press, and disseminating rumors about his works in progress. Russolo's Futurist *Arte dei Rumori*—pursuant to F.T. Marinetti's wish to "destroy the sublime in Art-with-a-capital-A"—was often an art of rumors; the avant-garde interest in noise as a destruction of sublimity was tied to its search for new tactics of publicity and advertising.[19] As Dadaist Tristan Tzara wrote, "publicity and business are also poetic elements"; the efforts of "high modernists" to repress these "poetic elements," in deference to an ideal of organic authenticity, carry the lingering trace of the noise of the market.[20]

Publicity, therefore, is a subtheme of *Sublime Noise*: a character's rhythmic motion through the modern soundscape—think of Bloom's movement through the "GREAT DAILY ORGAN" of "Aeolus's" thumping news presses—is shaped by the production and reception of public discourse. As I discuss in chapter one, the relationship between noise and public discourse, rumor and *rumori*, extends a long way back; its presence in the modern artwork takes advantage of a longstanding rapport between art and the vicissitudes of public relations, scandal, gossip, and advertising. Antheil, the noisiest of the noisy, used the Parisian press to plant the riots at his own premieres—laying ground for Pound, who surreptitiously loved this publicity game, to wax utopian about the modern industrial factory. F.R. Leavis's claim that Sitwell belongs to "the history of publicity rather than poetry" suggests that her work was all rumor and no craft, inassimilable into the sphere of Literature-with-a-capital-*L*.[21]

For if we turn back to 1913—the same year that Stravinsky's ballet premiered to riots—we find Russolo proclaiming noise itself as new musical territory. His *Arte dei Rumori* manifesto asserts that rhythmic and harmonic innovation cannot alone appease the ears of modern listeners, already accustomed to the sounds of machinery and traffic; hence, "*We must break out of this limited circle of sounds and conquer the infinite variety of noise-sounds*."[22] Russolo's collaborations with Marinetti, in continental Europe and in Britain, spread the notoriety of his manifesto and noise-music, played on instruments of his own invention. Aspiring to the condition of noise, modernist and avant-garde musicians swarmed to the possibilities of seemingly nonmusical sounds (planes, trains, sirens) with different timbres and explicit real-world associations.

Though composers such as Antheil, Varèse, and Arthur Honegger (*Pacific 231* [1923]) deny that their experiments with noise are mere imitations of trains and machines, these sounds never lose their real-world associations in the cultural imagination. According to Antheil, the *Ballet*'s "mechanistic" qualities were meant to invoke not machines and factories, but a calculated abstraction thanks to which the audience could perceive new resonances of tone and timbre. The effort to produce a newly intense phenomenology of what Pierre Schaeffer later called "reduced listening"—the hearing of sound without reference to its source, cause, or meaning—resembles Antheil's claims for *Ballet Mécanique*'s purely formal intensification of sound. The problem is that nobody in the 1920s, excepting purveyors of doctrine, actually experienced *Ballet Mécanique* this way. The effort to claim purely phenomenological qualities for sounds with heightened cultural and social meaning was, like Pound's Mauberley, wrong from the start—noise-music addressed the material presence of noise while claiming a nonrepresentational musical function. Building on the *Arte dei Rumori* while claiming his music as a *cordon sanitaire*, Antheil capitalized on noise for both its bracing aesthetic effects and its cultural frisson.

Immersed in the same social circles as modernist musicians, and to varying degrees conversant with the music itself, writers understood the conjunction of noise and music to have its own cultural purchase. In turn, writers heard in the new music the potential to create a buzz, to publicize new cultural, political, personal, and aesthetic agendas. They heard the opportunity both to politicize art—to defamiliarize the material conditions that make music desirable—and to aestheticize politics, to endow the social spheres of life with aesthetic (often totalitarian) order. They heard the possibility both for the avant-garde integration of aesthetics and life praxis, and for the modernist immunization against publicity. The integration of noise, that is, might warn against the threat of noisy mass culture while callusing the modernist reader against its assaults.

This reintegration must either overcome or take advantage of what the Canadian composer (and Pound scholar) R. Murray Schafer terms the "deep-bonded relationship between noise abatement and taboo."[23] Schafer's studies *The New Soundscape* (1969) and *The Tuning of the World* (1977), more recently synthesized in *The Soundscape* (1993), categorize the sonic and tonal properties of acoustic space by mapping out the sources and connotations of specific sounds. The great irony of otherwise ineffectual "noise abatement" campaigns, Schafer insists, is that they provide a litany of forbidden sounds that the composer can repurpose for her own music. *The New Soundscape* begins with a Cowell-like vignette: its author imagines overhearing skeptical audiences of Beethoven, Wagner, and Varèse, each wondering if what they've heard is "music" at all, before Schafer himself proceeds to hear a plane "scrap[ing] the sky" overhead. His own ear tuned to a different frequency, Schafer asks whether this airplane might also be considered music: "Perhaps the pilot has mistaken his profession?"[24] Schafer knew that he wasn't the first to ask this question, and it is instructive that the first chapter of *The Soundscape*, before turning to the primal soundscape of the ocean, frames the sounds of nature with the interventions of modern art—with Proust's description of the sea as "the plaintive ancestress of the earth pursuing . . . its lunatic immemorial agitation" (*Soundscape*, 15). For all the natural nostalgia associated with Schafer's "acoustic ecology," he tunes the soundscape not simply to the sounds of the sea, nor to a quantifiable tone (A = 440 Hz), but to the resonances of those sounds in the measures of Proust and Pound, as well as Antheil, Satie, Honegger, Schaeffer, and Cage. Schafer's ambitious mapping of the rhythms of nature and culture in some respects *had to* be read backward through figures like Pound, glossing in his turn an encyclopedic tradition of poets (Homer, the *Seafarer*-poet) who had turned their ears to the water—and who continue doing so even in a modernity when, as *The Waste Land*'s Wagnerian Thames-Sisters sing, the water is slicked with "Oil and tar." The "meaning" even of a "natural" sound represents a series of mediations among its genetic sources, somatic effects, and inherited connotative legacies. Noise, an interference that destabilizes listening and opens the text's interiority to a range of external pressures, exposes music as a historically concrete mediation of other kinds of sound.

Situating soundscapes in relation to cultural musicology and modernist studies thus returns us inevitably to the problem of signification: what does it mean for music to "mean" anything? For many modernists, I argue, the emergence of new media and the problem of musical meaning are related. Schaeffer's and Schafer's acoustic, musical, and literary insights open up modernist music and writing in complex relation to "aural culture": the technologies, practices, and cultural assumptions circulating around sound and hearing, constantly reconstructing the distinctions between noise/sound, noise/music. To make this case, *Sublime Noise* dips its toe into "sound studies," a budding field of inquiry into listening habits, sonic environments, and social institutions as aesthetic and ideological interactions that "enforce certain kinds of inclusions and exclusions, involving gender, race, class, sexualities, and other formulations of identity."[25] As Emily Thompson shows, one needn't look far to find noise aligned with demographic shifts and porous architectural boundaries, and finds these destabilized further as the radio and telephone reconfigure the experience of space. Sound, a hub of aesthetic developments, new technologies, and any number of "inclusions and exclusions" has proven fertile ground for critics looking to destabilize the "ocularcentrism" of media theory.[26]

The real-world and taboo resonances of noise make it a useful avant-garde complement to modernist narratives of aesthetic autonomy; and a useful theoretical complement to Adorno's conception of dissonance as a feature that gains critical strength by virtue of music's contingent separation from everyday social practices. I draw on various conceptions of noise, the most polemical being Jacques Attali's *Noise: The Political Economy of Music* (1977). Attali argues that music—more and more economically centralized since the advents of musical notation, commercial performance, and recording—sublimates the violent or carnivalesque noises of daily life. On one hand, music makes these noises palatable to systems of power, while on the other hand, it retains its sublimated subversive content. Music thus speaks to the institutional and material political economy that makes it possible, while prophesying noisy real-world upheavals, much as Russolo's *rumori* and Stravinsky's sacrifice appeared on the eve of World War One.[27]

Attali's *Noise* argues that the radical power of music has been tempered as it has grown increasingly centralized, its institutional power increasingly consolidated. Any "theory of power today," Attali argues, "must include a theory of the localization of noise and its endowment with form"—beginning with the apparatuses of eavesdropping and surveillance at the heart of which lie the technologies of "listening in on, ordering, transmitting, and recording noise" (6-7). Through a strange hybrid of Marx, Russolo, Adorno, and Foucault, Attali offers a breakneck "distant reading" of music as it encodes economic and discursive power—attempting, in the end, to reclaim music, and the musical body, from semiotic, technological, and commercial closure. Attali reads music as having progressed through a series of historical stages: (1) *ritual* ("simulat[ion] [of] the social order" as it existed prior to "commercial exchange"); (2) *representation* (the advent of musical notation as performed within the "closed space" of the concert hall); and (3) *repetition*, what we may think of as "mechanical reproduction." Through these stages, he suggests, music has developed from (1) a "simulacrum of the ritual-sacrifice," to (2) an effort to "make us believe," through falsely transparent notations, that social order cannot exist outside of commercial exchange; to (3) an effort to "make us forget," through repetition, the centralization of power to which we have been subjected.

Thus, finally, Attali presages a fourth stage, *composition*, in which we organically compose through unalienated relationships with one another, allowing the composition of music to partake in the experience of lived time, rather than (as for the record collector) "stockpiling" time as commodity. Attali's compositional stage of musical/economic development calls for a music that will no longer "mar[k]" or "produc[e]" the body for discipline or marketing, but will allow the musician to experience and express bodily pleasure in time—producing a new social order through expression freed from administrative reason "to play for the other and by the other, to exchange the noises of bodies, to hear the noises of others in exchange for one's own, to create, in common, the code within which communication will take place. The aleatory then rejoins order. Any noise, when two people decide to invest their imaginary and their desire in it, becomes a potential relationship, future order" (143). The hope here—one at the core of the modernist text—is that music's organic formal development will catalyze newly authentic emotional, erotic, and social relationships. Developments such as free jazz herald for Attali a new order of "music produced by each individual for himself, for pleasure outside of meaning, usage, and exchange" (137). Even if the first instantiations of free jazz were "contained, repressed, limited, censured, expelled," they portend a new "participation in collective play" (140-1), in which we create music freed from what Pound called the "decree[s]" of the "marketplace."[28]

In a way, Attali and Adorno represent a mutually corrective pair: Attali's account of noise is more capacious, Adorno's studies of music more dialectical. If Adorno is proudly narrow-minded, lovingly patient with the music he admires and magisterially dismissive of the music he doesn't, Attali proves trickily unselective, neglecting—for all his rhetoric of liberated composition—the interpretive operations of the specific artwork.[29] If, for Attali, "music" and "noise" writ large stand in for larger institutional presences, Adorno delves into the formal qualities of music as they mediate historical time: "The time that is immanent in music, its inner historicity, *is* real historical time, reflected as appearance."[30] Music is no less historical for its detachment from mass culture; rather, Adorno claims, it re-composes history in a dissonant speculative language liberated from identitarian thought. Adorno's own dialectics themselves may falter as he sweepingly rejects popular music without regard to equally radical musical effects, such as rhythmic syncopation.

For modernist writers, then, the sublime noise of music serves the double function of aestheticizing noise, and of calling attention to the roots of art in lived sonic experience. Literature and music need to be understood as correlate efforts to consider the relation between aesthetic and nonaesthetic forms of sound. In this context, modernist music and literature can be understood as a set of reactions to *noise* conveyed by the textual mediations of *dissonance*, whose movement through time is marked by the often-irregular forward motion of *rhythm*. Musical relationships such as dissonance and rhythm are read by modernist writers, and by commentators on modernism, as mediations of larger social relations, compelling new ways of thinking about the meaning of seemingly ineffable properties of art. Dissonance, I will argue, is heard as an opaque and coded mediation of noise's aural shocks, a dialectical rupture within the artwork that gives voice to an oppositional or critical position to cultural order. Rhythm, rather, comes to be considered as homologous to the patterns of social life: to the flow of the workday, the thump of machinery, and the tempo of the marketplace.

I say "homologous," not "identical." As a scholar recently challenged me, "A novel may have rhythm, but you can't dance to it." True, and all the more reason to consider why modernists find "rhythm" so compelling a metaphor for their work. I am not chiefly concerned with the question of whether music actually does this stuff: in part because I focus less on the Paterian "condition of music" than on its cultural operations; and in part because, as I discuss in chapter one, modernists cast a skeptical ear toward musical mimesis (musical imitations of noise, literary imitations of music), preferring to think more dialectically about art's formal and technological mediations. Even if there is nothing innate about music that makes it a barometer of social change, music is helped to perform this mediating work *in effect* when literary discourses remediate it as (in Attali's coinage) a "channelization" of noise.[31] My aim here is to meet modernists on their own terms, marshaling their metaphors of rhythm and dissonance to show how they imagined the effects of their arts in relation to social noise.

These debates are in many respects familiar. The efforts of some modernists to exaggerate and amplify noise, others to mediate it into blissful Paterian pleasure, recall Peter Bürger's distinction between the avant-garde struggle to integrate artistic experimentation into public life, versus the modernist attempt to cordon off the artwork. Perhaps the interlocking presence of noise and music in modernist culture points to how untenable this distinction has always been. Such tensions are unavoidable in studying figures such as Pound, who railed against Marinetti and Russolo on one hand while cribbing liberally from them on the other; who is so often associated with objectivity, formalism, and neoclassical order, but whose anxieties about labor, capital, and social credit permeated his doctrines; who despised the "market place" while endeavoring, as Lawrence Rainey has argued, to create a new commodity space for modernist art. The modernist emphasis on organic complexity and ironic unity, in these respects, was historical to the core, infused with the noisy public spectacles that it wished to repress.[32]

What, then, can the study of musical noise add to the prodigious accounts of Joyce's, Forster's, and Eliot's musical aesthetics, Pound's experiments with the radio, or modernists' furtive interest in the Futurist avant-garde? By exploring the tension and the integration of noise and music, one comes to see past the well-worn tension between mass media and art, past the idea that music is (to its detriment) mediated by technologies of mass reproduction. Rather, one starts to see music itself *as* a medium, *as* a technology. "Sublime noise" is the phrase used by Forster's narrator in *Howards End* to describe Beethoven's Fifth Symphony.[33] Marshall McLuhan was perhaps first to note that Forster's fiction—in particular, *A Passage to India* (1924)—enacts the "ultimate conflict between sight and sound, between written and oral kinds of perception and organization of existence."[34] As music itself begins to "organiz[e]" not the "existence" of sounds and noises in lived experience, it can be heard, like any other medium, to have a "massage" (to borrow McLuhan's beloved solecism). If the "'content' of any medium is always another medium," as McLuhan argues, then even music with no literary "content" begins to be "about" nonmusical sounds, including, as Attali proposes, the noise of social and economic behavior.

What Forster, Cecil Barber, and Attali recognize in this sublime and expensive organization of sound is that the categories of "music" and "noise" are themselves social. The very concept of noise, "a resonance that interferes with the audition of a message in the process of emission," "does not exist in itself but only in relation to the system within which it is inscribed" (Attali 26). As music grapples with noise, it also redefines it; as audiences grapple with music, they do so in contextual relation to other forms of sound. A novel whose two theses are "Only connect!" (150) and "England and Germany are bound to fight" (52), *Howards End* seems ambivalent about the reparative or exacerbating influences of music on the breaches of class and nation, equally tempted by and anxious about music's propensity to be "broadcast on the field of battle" (28). To be sure, the word "broadcast" had not quite the mass-media resonance in 1910 that it has now. But we can see in Forster an instinct about music's global reach. He shared the understanding, well put by McLuhan and Edmund Carpenter, of the ears as "all-encompassing, constantly alert to any sound originating in their boundless sphere," whereas the eyes are limited to a 180° range.[35] To what degree,

Forster seems to ask, does the "boundless sphere" of the aural faculty, subjected to sound and unable to block it out, make music the right expressive mode for the totalizing aspirations of Empire, pan-German nationalism, or art itself? As Michel Chion writes, due to "the omnidirectionality of hearing" and the diffuse nature of sound, and due to "a lack of any real aural training in our culture, this 'imposed-to-hear' "—our struggle to filter and edit the noise in which we are immersed—sound has "the ability to saturate and short-circuit our perception."[36] Pound, we shall see, shared this concern for the lack of aural training; for him, the decay of a disciplined "kulchur" had caused the modern ear to atrophy, its faculty for discernment short-circuited by the noise of the public sphere.

As Forster, Pound, Eliot, Sitwell, and Joyce engage with the materiality of sound—the same stuff of music and language used to construct our notions of labor, industry, and empire, of the salon and of the closet—they begin to test its formal properties (rhythm, harmony, melody) as technologies, in the basic sense of the word: tools for explaining, critiquing, and manipulating. Take rhythm. Eliot, who claimed that the internal combustion engine forever altered our experience of rhythm,[37] understood that the objective formal structure of rhythm was conceptually inextricable from the beat of technology, just as Pound's imagist ideal of an "absolute rhythm"—the abstract realization of a "form cut in time"—served as one response to the deadening pulse of the work day. This temporal abstraction demands to be reconciled with the rhythmical needs of the body, individual or collective. Henri Lefebvre contends that a "rhythmanalysis" of culture begins and ends with the body's internal rhythms, which serve "as a metronome" for measuring the interpellative rhythms of "dressage" (education, training, discipline), but which also produce the disjunctive "arrhythmias" of sickness, pathology, or an out-of-sync pulse.[38] As I argue in chapter two, Eliot's *Waste Land* offers the sickness of the individual body as a destabilization of culture's externally binding rhythms: the irregularities of his verse, marking the bodily violence that accompanies music, unravels the false macrorhythmic coherence of what Eliot called the "auditory imagination."

For Adorno, the collectively experienced rhythms of culture are always suspect, and thus the promise of modern art relies (contingently) on its autonomy and its dissonance. But one finds more sympathy toward rhythm from critics more optimistic about the collective experience of cultural narratives. For György Lukács, who believes that "*art pour l'art*" represents a solipsistic capitulation, an artwork can communicate meaningfully only if its "rhythm of words" is "set by the rhythm of cultural progress."[39] The late Paul Fussell, whose book *The Great War and Modern Memory* (1975) is invaluable to historicist work on war writing, elsewhere suggests that the rhythms of poetry intensify the physical tempi of the body: "since the beat in most accentual poetry is slightly faster than the normal heart beat," the heart "actually speeds up in an effort to 'match' the slightly faster poetic rhythm."[40] And Raymond Williams, historicizing art on the basis of "ordinary" shared cultural patterns, promotes the power of rhythm to "transmi[t] a description of experience," "not merely as an 'abstraction' or an 'emotion' but as a physical effect on the organism."[41]

Williams's passage has been frequently cited by cultural musicologists; literary critics, who have tended to interpret "classical" music solely in terms of aesthetic doctrine, would do well to revisit it.[42] Brad Bucknell's splendidly insightful *Literary Modernism and Musical Aesthetics*, for example, elaborates musical-literary interactions and doctrine from Mallarmé to Pater to Pound to Joyce to Stein; Daniel Albright's sinuous book *Untwisting the Serpent* traces literary-musical collaborations in terms of "consonance" and "dissonance" among entangled artistic media.[43] If modernist writers appreciated music as an aesthetic condition, they also valued its performativity: as a script to be intoned, a ritual to be reenacted, one strand of many in a collaborative network of poets, composers, artists, singers, dancers, conductors, patrons, and listeners. Albright and Bucknell have opened up the study of music to more broadly materialist accounts of the cultural politics of music.

I by no means discount aesthetics. My focus on modernism grapples with a cultural moment that seems at once driven by, and desperate to repress, the historical pressures of noise, in a way that calls for both distantly historical and closely formal reading. On the more distant methodological end, Hillel Schwartz's *Making Noise* maps out a massive Pound-like cultural history, from Babel to Attali to Mandelbrot, tracing the "larger stories of civilization" that noise has signified. *Sublime Noise*, instead, approaches literary form as a means of understanding and appropriating music's historicity. In both homage and response to Bucknell's treatment of "musical aesthetics," I offer a study of "musical culture": of music itself as a historical artifact, and of the cultural contexts that made noise-music bracing and ripe for literary reinvention.

The work of Adorno largely underpins my attempt to implicate modern music's aesthetic innovations with its ideological work. Adorno provides the most concentrated working-through of my central questions: the historicity of art, autonomy, elitism, mass culture, and mediation. I find him compelling not simply as a theorist of modernism but as an example of it, not just as a commentator on Stravinsky and Schoenberg (nor, certainly, as their equal), but as a modernist fellow traveler with an eccentrically tuned ear for the political valences of music. If music, as Adorno writes, is a language "sedimented from gesture," his opaque philosophical excursions are a language sedimented from modernist art: an effort to "through-compose" the competing tensions and shocks of new artistic experiments.

Yet he will not go uncritiqued. Cultural musicologists, though influenced by Adorno's account of music as an ideological mediation, increasingly resist his (complicated) commitment to the autonomy of art, manifested in strident attacks on popular music.[44] I, too, find much to resist in his narrow-minded elitism. Williams's brand of historicism strikes me as more complete than either Adorno's or Lukács' approach: less prone to make us all victims of Ideology and better able to see art's constructive (rather than solely oppositional) role in culture. Yet I take seriously Adorno's method, not just for its philosophical value, but as an artifact of modernism's desire to seek out (without reifying) broader historical continuities, and to grapple with (without capitulating to) the experience of noise, violence, and fragmentation. To appropriate the parts of Adorno's argument that have held up well (such as his groundbreaking critiques of Wagner's anti-Semitism), while leaving behind the parts that seem tone-deaf (almost everything he said about jazz), would be to rob him of his dialectical energy—to alleviate an ache in the left ear by amputating the right. Richard Middleton, echoing Nietzsche on Wagner, puts it best: to move past Adorno, one must first absorb him.[45]

And for many modernists, to inoculate oneself against the sonic violence of noise, one must compose through it. This effort takes many different forms: some, like Eliot, using the aesthetic seductions of rhythm to sublimate the assaults of noise into an organically ordered artifact; others, like Joyce, turning noise against the aesthetic mediations that would try to pacify it. Noise, then, speaks to modernists' efforts to weigh the artwork's aesthetic merit in relation to its cultural resonance. A study of noise infuses Adorno's method with *more* dialectics: if dissonance unpacks the identitarian thinking of commodity capitalism, noise makes audible the cultural content from which art is sedimented, and amplifies the effects of music's reentry into public discourse. I develop these contours in chapter one, drawing on Adorno, Roland Barthes, and Jean-Jacques Nattiez to account for music's dialogic, interactive dissemination of meaning as it engages with cultural history. My understanding of cultural history is indebted to Williams's account of base and superstructure, which throws into relief the reductive totalizing instincts of various materialist critiques of art: modernist (Adorno's Culture Industry) and antimodernist (Lukács's rejection of modernism as an ahistorical concession to fascism). As ahistorical as the arts they assault, Adorno and Lukács treat their respective ideological villains, mass culture and modernism, as enforced delusions rather than as fluid sets of conventions that undergo, as Williams argues, a "continual making and remaking": producing a "dominant" cultural pattern on which our "reality depends" and that is "built into our living"—a kind of historical rhythm built into the patterns of labor, trade, and urban life.[46]

A study of music in culturalist terms should thus reduce us no more to a totalizing, crudely Marxist view of art than to a totalizing formalist one; rather, it must unpack the specific cultural pressures at stake as they are mediated in textual form. What we see, for example, of Walton's and Britten's efforts to forge a cosmopolitan musical aesthetic, rather than a provincially English one, calls attention to longstanding debates about class, nation, and masculinity circulating around English music (it had long been noted that England's greatest composer, Georg Frideric Händel, was German-born). Williams's account of "hegemony" as something that not only reduces opposition (by naturalizing social relations), but that changes and is changed by the practices of daily life, is reflected in the critical efforts of Walton and Sitwell's *Façade* to play with the naturalizing properties of rhythm, its propensity to insinuate ideology into the pulse. A piece of modernist chicanery often heard as a Sitwellian public relations gimmick, *Façade* is rarely appreciated for its deft, rhythmic defamiliarization of a stolid national-pedagogical tradition that, at the same time, trades on the tropes of empire. As the self-consciously cosmopolitan Sitwell, Britten, and Forster imagine alternatives to the "shrinking island" of British culture, they attempt to stitch and unstitch our sense of Britishness along new rhythmic and harmonic lines.[47]

This study thus enacts competing dialectics in what I call the Adorno-Williams two-step, first exposing the noises made immanent in dissonance, and then mapping out the rhythms to which those dissonances move. As a result, many of the chapters in this book are self-consciously constellational. While I do not aspire exactly to the "theoretical indiscipline" championed by Attali (5), many chapters will have multiple argumentative threads; often, a writer's understanding of noise, rhythm, and dissonance will be at odds even with itself. In Pound, for example, noise signals a range of phenomena:

socioeconomic (usury, broadcasting, publicity), aesthetic (the mud of Wagner, the haze of Debussy, the blunt traumas of jazz), and as with Antheil's machine-like composition, a synthesis of the two. The project will likewise two-step between the holistic synthesis of Wagner's total artwork, and its deconstruction at the hands of Satie and Jean Cocteau, who use modern noise to mock Wagner's Teutonic solemnity. Discussing Eliot and Adorno in concert, too, will require me to stray into several areas (Wagner and the music hall, technology and *The Tempest*) precisely because both figures are willfully committed, like Proust's airplanes, to evading fixed formulations that threaten to reduce phenomenal experience. Each of those musical expressions unto itself stages an anxiety about the "false whole" (see Prospero's "baseless fabric"); as *The Waste Land* synthesizes these wholes in dissonant relation, the result is the noisy breakdown of language and of the body.

Hence the modernist values of ambiguity, irony, and paradox take on additional interest when given new-musicological unpacking: the dissonances inherent to a well-wrought object can be dialectically opened up to performance, audience, technological mediation, and somatic experience. To reanimate the relationships among these problems will require, at times, an openly (I hope not standoffishly) nonlinear discussion. In each chapter, however, I develop a central resonance of noise through close readings of musical and literary form.

Chapter one outlines a method that aspires to be both speculative and thickly historicized, by accounting for the cultural significance of noise; for the cultural and semiotic interpretation of music; and for the use of dissonance and rhythm as homologies for ways of structuring (rather than reduplicating) the real-world noises of modernity. Addressing the social, philosophical, musical, and literary-historical underpinnings of noise, and its often-agonistic relation to the internal logic of art, I offer dissonance and rhythm as two inroads to how modernists articulate their relation to the noise of culture. I address, moreover, debates surrounding noise-music as efforts to consolidate or fray the boundary between music and society. It is no small irony that music used to defend the neoclassical principles of "music alone"—Stravinsky and Antheil—invited sharply violent audience responses; the effort to create a musical *cordon sanitaire*, as Taruskin puts it, merely amplified the sounds of scandal and publicity on which the aesthetic ideals of "high modernism" came to depend.

Chapter two, the longest and most constellational chapter, studies Eliot's *Waste Land*, alongside Adorno, as an effort to understand the aesthetically and culturally binding effects of musical rhythm. What I.A. Richards called the poem's "music of ideas" also represents an effort to articulate the cultural weight of various musical expressions through Eliot's "auditory imagination": the "feeling for syllable and rhythm" that "penetrate[s] far below the conscious levels of thought and feeling." In dialogue with Wagner and Stravinsky, jazz and the music hall, the operatic and the phonographic voice, *The Waste Land* enacts and defamiliarizes the rhythmic pacification of noise. I read the poem's gestures toward these musical artifacts in relation to Adorno's critique of Wagner's total artwork (Gesamtkunstwerk): the synthesis of music, poetry, and gesture into a cohesive artwork aimed at the heart of the *Volk*. While the poem uses "macrorhythmic" structures to bind noise into a Wagnerian whole, its noises, glitches, and "microrhythmic" syncopations unbind music in relation to its cultural patterns. Adorno critiques Wagner and (*a fortiori*) Stravinsky for building up small rhythmic fragments that harden into larger, falsely coherent macrorhythmic "packages"; at the same time, Adorno recognized the revolutionary potential of Wagner's dynamic excesses and of the damaged bodies in Wagner that herald the failure of instrumental reason. The same can be said of the syphilitic and violated bodies that critique the violence inherent in Eliot's "binding," totalizing drumbeats—and can moreover be said of the critical microrhythms of jazz. *The Waste Land* implicitly poses an Adornian critique of identitarian thinking by approximating music's noisy extremes.

Pound, too, saw music and noise as competing yet interrelated components of "kulchur," an idea evolving alongside his interactions with Antheil. As I argue in chapter three, Antheil's music and its reception, including Pound's essay reimagining *Ballet Mécanique* as a factory, bespeak an oscillating friction between two ideals of music: as a sublime, neoclassical modernist experiment with the "raw canvas" of time, and as a noisy material symptom of publicity, industry, and economic alienation. This tension permeates Pound's poetry as well as the radio dramas written with Antheil's help. Pound's contemporaries saw his obsessions with Antheil's noise to bespeak a surreptitious love of sensation and scandal (marked by his oft-denied debt to Italian Futurism), at odds with the rhetoric of neoclassical polish. Antheil's knack for publicity, down to the preorchestrated riots at his concerts, offered Pound more than an aesthetic motivation to sponsor Antheil's music. Rethinking *The Pound Era* (Hugh Kenner's panegyric to high modernism) as "The Antheil Era" (a cheeky abuse of avant-garde doctrine), I suggest that the pressures between music and noise, neoclassical polish and sensational theatricality, belie Pound's disdain for the "decree[s] of the "market place" given expression in "Hugh Selwyn Mauberley" and amplified in the *Cantos*. Pound's poetry strives to negotiate music's abstraction with its emotional and somatic demands, a tension that he focalizes in terms of rhythm.

A principal of the Antheil Era, James Joyce proposed a collaboration with the composer on the "Cyclops" episode of *Ulysses*: an episode that centers heavily on the sonic and rhetorical gestures of political language and the problem of national scapegoating, in a manner suited to the musical treatment of noise. I explain this collaboration before unfolding, in chapter four, the dialectical unleashing of noise throughout Joyce's oeuvre. Joyce's early nonfiction writings and poems, including *Chamber Music*, tend to sublimate or repress noise, but also to acknowledge its lingering resonance; *Dubliners* sets the musical "epiphanies" of its characters against the noise of that music's material surroundings; *A Portrait of the Artist as a Young Man* depicts Stephen Dedalus's obsession with rhythm in his search for an autonomous aesthetic space; *Ulysses* deconstructs the unmediated authenticity of music by considering its relation to ludicrous or mundane noises. This evolution in Joyce's work corresponds with an amplifying awareness of music as a politically engaged, deeply unstable technology. I close with a brief reading of Cage's *Roaratorio* (1979), a mesostic setting of *Finnegans Wake*, as an extension of the effort to unbind the noises condensed into the dubious stability of what Joyce called music's "magical cheats."

The question of authenticity motivates chapter five, on Sitwell's and Walton's *Façade*, the 1922 drawing-room "entertainment" consisting of nonsense rhymes pattered to music hall pastiches. Though hardly noisy in the same way as Antheil or Joyce, *Façade* strives to reinvent the rhythms of poetry to "catch up" (in Sitwell's words) to the "heightened speed" of the city and the changing acoustic functions of the urban cosmopolitan. As it does so, *Façade* preempts Leavis's assertion that Sitwell belongs only to the history of "publicity," by treating publicity and art as coextensive. *Façade* unpacks the aesthetics of social life, while entangling artistic influence with the *rumori* of advertising, media, and nation. *Façade*, to paraphrase Wilde, is a trivial composition for serious people; as such, it pursues the effort aesthetically to remake one's personality. If Williams is put off by Pater's notion that "a man can himself become, can confuse himself with, a made work" (*CS* 168), Sitwell and Williams share the notion that rhythm's appeals to the body can seal the rift between art and social life; rhythm offers Sitwell much in the way of what Shelton Waldrep calls "the aesthetics of self-invention." I explore *Façade*'s debts to the Ballets Russes, arguing that its overdetermined influences lay bare its desire to reaestheticize social life along more cosmopolitan, less insularly English lines, while defamiliarizing the stock orientalist tropes of empire and race. As *Façade* invokes these tropes, inherited from the Ballets Russes, its alienating performative mechanisms expose race—and the social persona *tout court*—as an aesthetic construction: a façade.

The final chapter studies the "sublime noise" in the work of Forster and Britten, examining each individually before considering their collaboration on *Billy Budd* (1951). Throughout his career, Forster uses the term "noise" to register music's indeterminacy and its scattershot potential for effecting social change. In *Howards End*, Forster's narrator hears Beethoven's Fifth disseminating so many inconsistent interpretations that it can scarcely be marshaled for the sake of reform without its main beneficiary (Bast) being victimized by what Attali calls music's "simulacrum" of violence. In *A Passage to India*, Professor Godbole's song (a "maze of noises") signifies the inability of Empire to pin down the colony. For Britten, too, noise represents not just a radical critique of ideology, but the means by which social collectives repress and marginalize through rumor. In *Peter Grimes* (1946), *rumori* is internalized within *Grimes*' ambiguous dissonances; in turn, *Billy Budd* defamiliarizes consonant harmony, and the qualities of nationalism and transparency often accorded consonance, to criticize its structures of prohibition and scapegoating. Reconsidering the effects of dissonance and consonance, rhythm and noise, Forster and Britten rethink the very foundations of culture.

These chapters arc from a focus on often intensely dissonant art (and, to some extent, a constellational mode of argument) to the more accessible idioms of Walton/Sitwell and Britten/Forster. Not incidentally, these represent the few British figures in this study of "British modernism." The relative accessibility of these pieces, I will suggest, represents less a resolution of modernism's dissonant strains than a self-deconstructive reconsideration of how a false consonance like "Britishness" could ever be naturalized.[48] Nation is not my main focus in Eliot, Pound, or Joyce, outliers to the British literary tradition, but the dissonant quality of their texts also reflects an itinerant placelessness. Eliot, upon moving to London, felt assaulted by noise, writing in 1914 that "The noise hereabouts is like hell turned upside down. . . . babies, pianos, street piano accordions, singers, hummers, whistlers."[49] Conversely, Dedalus's niche of "silence, exile, and cunning" in *Por-*

trait breaks down into the antic noises of *Ulysses* and the *Wake*, and seems to bring Ireland and the English literary tradition down with it. If we think of noise as a boundary-transgression, the unresolved "maze of noises" in *A Passage to India* will make the relative consonance of *Billy Budd* seem far from stable. To the question that Lionel Trilling asked of *Howards End*, "Who shall inherit England?,"[50] a consonant resolution, as much as a dissonant one, points to the fraying boundaries of Empire and the discursive muddle of sexuality. The role of dissonance in the first several chapters—critical, constellational, difficult—will expose these same qualities in *Façade* and *Budd*: consonance, too, needed to be "emancipated" from drawing-room "respectability" (Sitwell) and heteronormative masculinity (Britten/Forster).

Large though this book may be, some omissions are inevitable. It will be conspicuous, first, that my emphasis falls squarely on "classical" music; I sidestep uses of noise in electronic music, film music, blues, and jazz. I do this not as a reaction against, but as an extension of, the historical mindset of literary critics working on popular music: Ben Sidran, Alfred Appel, Barry Faulk, Geoffrey Jacques, and T. Austin Graham have parsed the cultural forces at work in popular genres, and such scholarship requires a complementary historicism on modernist writing and "classical" music.[51] I have stated my conviction that classical music is no less mediated than its popular counterparts; there will be little novelty in observing also that genre-bending modernist musicians (Ellington, Milhaud, Weill, Gershwin, Herrmann—and Schoenberg too) made the "high"/"low" split increasingly obsolete. I brush past the experiments of Dadaist sound poetry (though noise as "found object" will at times be an undercurrent), past Beckett's television plays *Ghost Trio* (after Beethoven) and *Nacht und Träume* (after Schubert), or his radio plays (*Cascando*, *Words and Music*, *All that Fall*). And for the most part, I stop short of Cage's experiments with noise, silence, and aleatory. *Finnegans Wake*, and Cage's setting of it, will receive a cursory treatment; like Earwicker, whose circulation through the *Wake* is marked with *rumori*, their antennae point in so many directions as to make modernity's static indigestible.

One might consider this study a prehistory of noise-music in Cage's sense, though Cage is not my *telos*. Rather, I reconsider modernist attempts to order noise rather than yielding to its undecidability. While Marjorie Perloff's *Poetics of Indeterminacy* (1981) has not dictated my choice of writers, it is no coincidence that her main figures (Cage, Stein, Rimbaud) are largely excluded here. *Sublime Noise*, true to its title, focuses on writing and music that preserve a drive, if a hopeless one, toward "organic unity, coherence, indirection, multiplicity of meaning" (Perloff 27) through mediations of noise. The noises of canonical modernism, as they resonate with the shocks of modernity, rarely succumb (thankfully) to Eliot's mythical order, or to Pound's "absolute rhythm"; but the urge to make them cohere as a "music of ideas" must be unpacked.

That unpacking motivates what follows. I aim to account for the cultural anxieties that these noises signify, as they invade (it is so often heard as invasion) the aesthetic spaces of music and literature, which in turn try to digest them. Where do these noises come from? To what historical, economic, bodily, or other material pressures do they speak? What noises, as parlayed in Cowell's remark, do they produce in a listening public? The dilemma is central to modernism's spectacular ruptures. Embracing music's power to shock or appeal to the body, modernist art constantly recalls the material pressures of modernity, and in so doing, aspires to the condition of noise.

Sublime Noise

1 Orchestrating Modernity

Musical Culture and the Arts of Noise

> Accompanied by Mr. Moneybags and by the possessor of labour-power, we therefore take leave for a time of this noisy sphere, where everything takes place on the surface and in view of all men, and follow them both into the hidden abode of production, on whose threshold there stares us in the face "No admittance except on business." Here we shall see, not only how capital produces, but how capital is produced. We shall at last force the secret of profit making.
>
> Marx, *Capital*, vol. 1

Hearing the noise of the marketplace as a symptom of deep economic distress, Marx's Mr. Moneybags leads us, like Vergil leading Dante, from the surface noise of trade into the complex of labor. For Marx, the audible "noisy sphere" of trade resembles a "very Eden" of free choice and self-interested exchange "in accordance with the preestablished harmony of things, or under the auspices of an all-shrewd providence"—a conducting invisible hand. Until, at least, one unfolds the social relations underlying the reification of "labour-power" and the production of surplus value. At this point, Marx contends, the solid fetish melts into air: the "harmonious" myth of the market as a mutually advantageous circulation of commodities is defamiliarized as a baseless fabric, an unraveling theatrical illusion in which we "perceive a change in the physiognomy of our dramatis personae" from mere money-owners into possessors of labor-power. The noise of this "noisy sphere" offers an invitation to probe the material causes of surplus value—the gap between good and commodity, made possible by the mediations of capital—and to double-check the ostensible rationality of the marketplace.

My aim here is not to pose a crudely Marxist reading of music's means of production, although figures such as Pound are concerned with precisely that question. I do, however, suggest that formal properties such as dissonance and rhythm bear a relation, real or imagined, to what Fredric Jameson suggestively calls the "ground bass of material production."[1] The noise of Marx's market invites a closer examination of how value accrues to goods—or to a polished aesthetic object such as *Ballet Mécanique*, which Antheil offered as a polished neoclassical "surface" but which Pound and others heard as a metaphor for material production itself. Likewise, Stravinsky's neoclassical rhetoric of order, tradition, and internal temporality (music, he said to Robert Craft, was the "best means we have of digesting time")[2] might, when confronted by the noises of labor, lead us to ask hard questions about how our time would be structured otherwise.

This chapter elaborates what I see as a necessarily dialectical framework for understanding the material implications of noise, particularly as digested through the temporal and physical experiences of music and writing. I attempt to account for the linguistic interpretation of music; to parse the aesthetic and cultural histories of noise, dissonance, and rhythm; and to explore the relationship between noise and publicity. With both theoretical reflection and brief musical and literary readings, I argue that musical noise, rhythm, and dissonance are conceived of as mediations of history. Noise brings music's formal digestion of time back into tension with its public circulation—with the time-bound processes by which dissonance, rhythm, and music generally accrue meaning and value. Conversely, as noise invades the autonomous sanctum of music, it comes to represent not just a (nebulous) category of sound, but a way of scapegoating sounds as unwanted. The problem is encapsulated by Alex Ross's un-silencing of Hamlet, *The Rest is Noise*, and by the aphorism of Henry Cowell that "If a reviewer writes 'It is not music, but noise,' he feels that all necessary comment has been made." And, I argue, as music and noise accrue cultural meaning, they are readily mapped onto social categories—noise becomes a symptom of abjection, otherness, and subversion. Sublimity-destroying Futurists and "high" modernists alike conceive of seemingly transcendent ways of ordering noise (Schopenhauer's Will, Pound's Great Bass, Russolo's jargon of an underlying "vibration"), which, when performed, technologically mediated, and listened to, are heard to serve material cultural-historical functions, even ones akin to Jameson's ground-bass.

This dialectic is internal to modernist form. Through textual modes of dissonance and rhythm, modernists continually reinterpret noise as a symptom of the artwork's public circulation. Through dissonance, I contend, the artwork is heard to mediate the shocks of noise in discrete simultaneous ("vertical") moments; through rhythm, including the newly jarring off-beats of modern music, it is heard in parallel ("horizontal") relation to the passage of historical time. Debates over the cultural status of rhythm, in particular, diverge, hearing it either as monolithic lock-step conformity (Adorno), or as a constructively communal pattern of living (Lukács).

Though my framework here is materialist, I contest several of these readings—Lukács's insistence that text must lock in with its historical rhythms, Adorno's insistence that the text must maintain dissonant autonomy from them—and I moreover resist Attali's utopian enthusiasm for music's radical potential. What cultural ("new") musicology makes clear is that specific musical articulations, not just music as a general category, are what have cultural resonance; the same applies to rhythm and dissonance, about which there is nothing innately radical or regressive. I find both Lukács and Adorno, likewise, too enamored with a less-bourgeois-than-thou moralizing about art, even despite Adorno's stated commitment to immanent analysis. As this chapter will show, music's fluid, dialogic interchanges between tradition and composer, composer and score, score and performer, performer and audience, audience and composer, effect a complex mediating process in both historical and semiotic terms. This interactive process keeps rhythm, dissonance, or noise from acquiring ossified meanings (though there are continuities in how writers treat them); instead, music's interactive mode enacts what Raymond Williams refers to a "structure of feeling." Such structures are not mere abstractions but embodied performances; and music does not merely imitate or abstract social anxieties but attempts to re-encode them in a new performative language. Indeed, the figures I discuss are particularly resistant to the imitative or mimetic qualities of literature and music—literature should not imitate music, but should be musical; music should not merely imitate the noise of real life, but should reinvigorate it. These arts are endowed with a dialectical status: as mediators of material facts, not merely pale imitations of them.

I therefore argue that dissonance and rhythm circulated as ways for modernist art to enhance the interactive exchange between a text and the subversive or abject cultural presences of noise. Because noise, by definition, never belongs wherever it is (otherwise it would not be "noise"), it readily maps onto subversive social categories which music and literature attempt, with limited success, to contain. Noise is feminized; it is nationalized; it is racialized; it is heard as a symptom of colonial disruption, changing urban demographics, technological intrusion into the home. The process of ordering noise musically, then, takes on the project of hierarchizing it. Echoing a range of traditions, from the Pythagorean monochord to the Wagnerian total artwork, these figures seek to organize noise, as they would organize its homologous social elements.

Material Echoes: Musical Semiotics in Context

The resonances between music and society make audible a concern about the status of a medium that seemed to express something, even as it presented itself as ineffable. Terms such as "resonance" or "echo" offer more than metaphorical value in considering literature, music, and noise as a series of interactions between text and context, and between a text/score and the material apparatuses that perform it. Carolyn Abbate has proposed "echo" and "resonance" as tropes for structural patterns *within* texts and intertextual homologies *among* them—homologies materialized in the "gross physical acoustic phenomenon" of sound "in a particular here-and-now."[3] Thinking of how music and literature echo with each other and with culture stands to energize the new musicology and new modernist studies dedicated to the interdisciplinary, productively dissonant exchanges of art and society. Beyond materialist accounts of a unified Modernism that capitulates to political domination (Lukács), sediments Victorian ideologies (Jameson), or "confesses its complicity with the very social order . . . it seems to escape" (Eagleton),[4] critics are now seeking more specific historical accounts of what Richard Middleton calls the "structural resonance" among "the different elements making up a socio-cultural whole" (9). Middleton's work on popular music resonates with the equally conflicted and equally mediated expressions of "high" culture: not just because music and literature pose two such different elements with both mutual tension and mutual resonance, but also because the warhorses of modernism are cross-fertilized with popular art, jazz, film, and music hall.

As Adorno wrote, "high" and mass art are two "torn halves of an integral freedom to which, however, they do not add up," related but noncomplementary echoes of an unalienated state of being. Adorno, who loathed popular music, nevertheless found it dialectically bound with the internal struggles of "high" music as it unfolds in real time; he admired, moreover, pieces such as Stravinsky's *L'Histoire du soldat* (1918) for laying bare what he saw as the cynical and "shabby" torn half of music that had surrendered to the marketplace. I do not share in Adorno's judgments on popular music, nor accept his Schoenberg/Stravinsky division, nor grant modernist art its autonomy. But I do want to meet modernists—inclusive of Adorno—on their own terms: to address modernist form as an effort to work through sociological hierarchies in an aesthetic terrain. Noise shows us the fractures in the well-wrought urn: places where the internal resonances of modernist form, registered by its dissonant stock tropes of irony, ambiguity, and paradox, give way to the noisy material pressures of labor, war, empire, and mechanical reproducibility. Considering these hierarchies and homologies in terms not just of "structure of feeling," but of structural resonance, brings into focus the materiality of sound.

A brief literary reading may illustrate the textual, cultural, and physical resonances of an echo. The echoes of Forster's *A Passage to India*, for instance, do not simply reduce all of Western Civilization to an "ou-boum," as Mrs. Moore (the novel's resident Christian) imagines; nor do they simply reduce all of *A Passage* to one solipsistic existential crisis, as Lukács would argue; nor do they simply deny any possible comity between England and India, as Edward Said argued. It uses echo and resonance to work through an encounter with the overwhelmingly dissonant and rhythmic landscape that *A Passage to India* calls to mind. I discuss *Passage* in chapter six; here it will suffice to say that the novel produces dissonance, rhythm, and noise through a series of disruptive resonances, both textual and physical, as Abbate suggests. In *Passage*, the echoing "ou-boum" is felt by Adela Quested as rapine assault. The back-and-forth between Mrs. Moore and her disembodied "Indianized" presence as "Esmiss Esmoor," a parody of her name that echoes through the public square, resonates with the wave of imperialism and a counterwave of resistance. And at the end of the novel, when the natural world separates India from England, Forster's voicing of the landscape creates a resonance between the spatial and the temporal decay of empire ("No, not yet"; "no, not there"). Forster creates a resonance between the material of sight and sound—between the waves of light and heat ("The sun settles everything") and those of sound (the echoes that unsettle the settlers). As textual disruptions and as physical and sociological resonances in Abbate's and Middleton's senses, these echoes direct us to the sonic properties of language and song (such as Professor Godbole's song, an arrhythmic "maze of noises"); in the process, the novel gives intratextual resonances a contextual time and place. The Marabar echoes are noisy, not only dissonant, because they call attention to the confused transmission of a message as such. If dissonance offered modernists like Adorno the hope of antagonizing a sterile mass-cultural populace out of its recursive conformity, noise suggested, or threatened, a possibility not just of critiquing the message, but of destroying its transmitting institutions.[5]

Performed and interpreted in real time, the critical potential of noise to disturb music, of noise-music to disturb its social order, is continually felt both as a textual dynamic and as a "grossly physical" effect "in a particular here and now." The creation and perception of those resonances rely on an interactive exchange—and a sort of feedback loop, akin to Stuart Hall's model of "encoding/decoding"—between artist and text, text and performer, performer and interpreter, interpreter and artist. With figures such as Antheil, as I shall show, the disruptive noise of, say, an audience riot is not merely a spontaneous reaction, but a result of careful planning and publicity-campaigning; in return, audience riots tend to encourage rather than silence the artists responsible for them. Hence to inquire into music's, noise's, and noise-music's cultural meanings calls not just for polemic (such as Attali's), but for a nuanced account of musical meaning as such.

Jean-Jacques Nattiez's "semiology" of music, *Music and Discourse* (1987), provides just such an account. Nattiez has little patience for Attali's treatment of music as a mere stethoscope put to history.[6] Instead, Nattiez uses musical history and sociology to unpack the historically specific nature of meaning, which is not only apprehended but actively produced by a "web of interpretants" interacting with a text and communicating its effects to one another: "An object . . . takes on meaning for an individual . . . as soon as that individual places the object in relation to . . . other objects that belong to his or her experience of the world" (9). Thus Nattiez's semiology of music has three elements:

1. Poiesis: the process of producing a work of art, compositional choices that draw on preexisting traditions and material. Thus poiesis can and should be historicized.
2. The "neutral" realm, referred to as the material "trace" of the music. The text, in its material manifestations, realized through performance. Such a text can be interpreted according to its immanent formal properties. The term "trace" refers specifically to the music's physical realization; Nattiez views the text not as a static object but as an interaction of various interpretants. To wit:

3. Esthesis: the act of interpretation and production of meaning, as an "active perceptual process" (12).

Esthesis (a term borrowed from Paul Valéry) thus has a poietic or creative element, and vice-versa: composers and writers are grappling, cooperatively and agonistically, with tradition and with their occasionally rowdy audiences; and, as Roland Barthes puts it in "Musica Practica" (1970), "to compose . . . is *to give to do*, not to give to hear but to give to write."[7] The neutral space of the text represents a contact zone between intention and interpretation, or, as Barthes interprets the "neutral" figure of Balzac's Sarrasine, an atopic "drift" of meaning and identification.[8]

Refusing Attali's sweeping categories, then, Nattiez's tripartite model allows one to question how noise and music are at any moment defined against one another, as the interaction of poietic choices, material realizations, audience responses, and cultural value judgments.[9] Nattiez suggests that within each of these three realms, and in the interaction *among* those three realms, the boundary between noise and music is highly unstable and ever-shifting (fig. 1.1). At any given moment what might count as "music" for the composer might not correspond to what counts as "music" for the audience, let alone what qualifies, on a "neutral" acoustic level, as a periodic (musical) or nonperiodic (noisy) vibration. Indeed, any path that aspires to cross all three "musical" spaces would have to be a narrow one. In the poietic realm, the category of music ever broadens (the line moves down, such that more sounds seem to qualify as music); conversely, avant-gardists like the Futurists push back against the domestication of noise by claiming that " 'noise' *alone* has the right to occupy the musical domain" (Nattiez 49, his italics). The sounds formerly considered musical are no longer "news" for the avant-gardist; the Futurist aestheticizes the invasion of noise into music in almost militaristic terms. The sublime and the noisy are bound to fight.

Nattiez inherits the term "material" partly from Adorno, whose insistent use of the term reflects music's conflicted mediation of its musical tradition and its social situation. Adorno inherits it in turn from Eduard Hanslick's *On the Musically Beautiful* (1854). Insisting on the intrinsic beauty of "absolute" (as opposed to programmatic) music, Hanslick differentiates the "raw physical material" provided by nature from the "represented idea" of the musical composition. For Hanslick, music has its physiological effect in the "material moment" of its realization.[10] Hanslick's argument that musical beauty emerges from immanent "forms" and "sequences," with "no content other

<table>
<tr><th>poietic level
(choice of the composer)</th><th>neutral level
(physical definition)</th><th>esthesic level
(perceptive judgment)</th></tr>
<tr><td rowspan="3">musical sound</td><td>sound of the harmonic spectrum</td><td rowspan="2">agreeable sound</td></tr>
<tr><td rowspan="3">noise
(complex sound)</td></tr>
<tr><td rowspan="2">disagreeable noise</td></tr>
<tr><td>noise
(nonmusical)</td></tr>
</table>

Figure 1.1. Nattiez Chart. Jean-Jacques Nattiez, *Music and Discourse*. © 1990, Princeton University Press. Reprinted by permission of Princeton University Press.

than themselves" (78), establishes the possibility for this neutral sphere of music, in which musical ideas have exclusively musical meanings.[11]

Adorno pursues Hanslick's formalism, but replaces the notion of nature with those of history and politics: rather than a return to nature, the material of music enacts a dialectical series of contradictions and contingent resolutions.[12] Adorno by no means rejects natural beauty, which remains at the heart of aesthetic experience, but asserts, after Marx, its ongoing dialectical mediation: "Natural beauty, purportedly ahistorical, is at its core historical" (*AT* 65). Adorno's commitment to the autonomy of musical material is bound dialectically to material politics: "The composer's struggle with the material is a struggle with society precisely to the extent that society has migrated into the work, and as such it is not pitted against the production as something purely external and heteronomous, as against a consumer or against an opponent."[13] Even as it must fight for its own right to exist, then, music leads the composer into a fight-to-the-death with the historicity of his own musical language. Through this struggle, music takes on its propensity to expose the gaps and injustices within an increasingly rationalized social order. Nattiez and Adorno, each with his own notions of musical meaning and value, share the sense that this material, produced by composers and by interpreters, is a zone into which "society has migrated," to the extent that music itself becomes a performative philosophical development of meaning.

The interpretive aspect is particularly important for Adorno, for whom a critique of music implicates a critique of listening practices. He calls attention to interpretation as a cultural practice, as in his promotion of "structural listening" (concentrated interpretation of musical form as it unfolds) and demotion of "fetishistic" or "regressive listening" (which fixates on atomized melodies and rhythms). Rose Rosengard Subotnik, turning Adorno's critique of instrumental reason (which he associates with Stravinsky) back onto his own privileging of structural listening (Schoenberg), argues that Stravinsky's music calls for different, but no less radical, listening practices than Schoenberg's. Adorno's judgments, Subotnik clarifies, often impede the radical historical specificity he claimed to promote. In an effort to "read Adorno against the grain," Subotnik, Miriam Hansen, and Andreas Huyssen have turned the philosopher's supple resistance to identitarian allegory onto his own prescriptive arguments, and opened his account to different esthesic modes. As Huyssen shows, Adorno's demonization of mass culture as modernism's "threatening other" closes off a precise account of identification "in the *reception* of mass culture" (my italics)—failing to consider whether collective interpretation, not just solitary "structural listening," might help to expose the limits of reification, rather than merely submitting a lumpenproletariat to authority.

Adorno speaks at length about dissonance and rhythm; his addresses to noise are infrequent but instructive. Richard Leppert, contrasting Adorno's ambivalent dialectical approach to noise with Marinetti's and Russolo's openly celebratory (fascistic) one, writes that Adorno engages noise "as an expressive source for articulating a dual critique of domination and bourgeois historicism, the latter an explanatory paradigm serving, ideologically, to define and defend the former."[14] The presence of noise enables a critique of the commodity culture with which music is fighting, and a defamiliarization of "fetishistic" listening habits in which the beat takes over everything. In a 1968 monograph on his teacher Alban Berg, Adorno argues that the composition *Three Orchestral Pieces* (1915) "opens with pure noise and in pure noise it disintegrates like dust; the music in between is an analogy of how music can be wrested from the mute." Thus Berg's music, Adorno suggests, analogizes the process of wresting musical expression from the "extra-musical reality of commodities; the strictest and . . . expressionless form of banality."[15] Digested dialectically through atonal development, Berg's "noises" are heard to critique the joyless march of the culture industry. Rather than foreground noise in the metallic mode of Antheil or Satie, Berg's piece analogizes both the raw material (in the rumbling percussive chaos of the opening) and the enforced conformity (in the startlingly unisonic final brass assault) of commodity culture. The dissonant expressionism of the music in between grasps individual expression both from modernity's inchoate chaos and from its horrifying unisons, what Pound terms "the 'march of events'" ("Mauberley" 1.17).

Harmony and Aural Culture

For all of these figures—Schoenberg, Wagner, Eliot, Stravinsky, Adorno—the development of harmony as a musical problem is imbricated with sound culture more broadly. One cannot talk simply about "music" without considering the twentieth century's new sound technologies, new listening practices, and new conceptions of acoustic space. For example, Emily Thompson's study of "architectural acoustics" in early twentieth-century New York rethinks the relations between sound and space—forever altered by the telephone, telegraph, and radio—and situates them in relation to the "Noise Abatement" campaigns of the urban metropolis. Noise, Thompson argues, had a double function: signaling capitalism's technological progress, as well as its excess, waste, and nervous exhaustion. Music such as Antheil's and Varèse's, capitalizing on the thrills and anxieties surrounding this clamor, were imagined to callus the ears against the real noise of New York. As a woman said to William Carlos Williams, leaving a performance of *Ballet Mécanique*, "The subway seems sweet after that."[16] Jonathan Sterne has likewise argued that for turn-of-the-century sound technologies—the gramophone, the telegraph, the stethoscope—to be produced and marketed, sound and hearing per se had to be physiologically isolated and then culturally disseminated through the conventions of class, of education, and of medicine.

In this vein, the mediating power of technology deserves a skeptical ear, a key modernist version of which lies in Adorno's essays on the radio and the gramophone. The philosopher's work for the Radio Project in the wake of the 1939 Orson Welles *War of the Worlds* scandal, in which he began to assess the "atomistic" listening practices of the modern audience, has made Adorno a poster-boy for the antitechnological modernist. His break with Paul Lazarsfeld over the Radio Project's positivistic research methods, such as the use of focus-grouping and listener surveys, has likewise made Adorno an archetype for the conspiratorial modernist crank.[17] None of this is entirely wrong, but it flattens out Adorno's refusal to ontologize media generally as an evil—even if its use value almost always becomes evil in the end.

While criticizing the tendency of the radio to "trivialize" the whole formal integrity of Beethoven's Fifth, Adorno warns against trying to "save" music from the technology, granting the radio's ability to erase the "drug-like" "surrounding" quality of music in the concert hall. In other words, though radio programming does violence to music, it might also lift music out of narcotized "atmosphere" and into a critical relation to the musical material.

Adorno insists not that radio makes music worse by definition (though that's usually how it turns out), but only that, owing to the presence of static and noise, to the flattening of tone color, and to the contortions of time needed to stay on schedule, the "radio symphony" is a different medium from the concert symphony, and needs to be heard as such. Adorno (like Forster) chooses Beethoven strategically: the master of development, density, and concision whose compositional dialectics presage Schoenberg. For Adorno the medium's potential for mass education is belied by its reduction of Beethoven's sublime noise to atomistic fragments. Adorno has no sympathy for the radio as Arnoldian mass-cultural uplift, in the manner attempted by the BBC's John Reith and later by the BBC Third Programme (the "high culture" program founded in 1946); rather, the radio assumes its critical potential by lifting music out of the surrounding "largeness" of the concert atmosphere. The gramophone, likewise, flattens and ossifies musical performance, but at the same time liberates music (especially opera) from the spectacular "ritual of performance." For Adorno, while records and gramophones themselves become commodity fetishes, they also open up against-the-grain listening practices; in the process of "petrif[ying]" music, the gramophone "rescues the ephemeral and perishing art as the only one alive" (279). The gramophone record, an artifact of modernity's violence, preserves the traces of its critique.

Music and Publicity: Rumor, News, Noise

In these ways, Adorno and other modernists continually struggled to rethink music both as an artistic mediation and as part of the public sphere—as remediated by new recording and broadcasting technologies, as a means of abating or reshaping noise, and as a species of expression made unstable by its resistance to easy description and by its reliance on performance and interpretation. The very difficulty of accounting for music in language makes music appealing to the modernist writer, not just because difficulty itself was perceived as a virtue, but also because music seemed to enable more active modes of interpretation. The interpretation of music on its own terms is difficult enough, the interpretation of a writer's interpretation of music, or, as in *Howards End*, of a narrator's mediation of a character's interpretation of music, more challenging yet. The performativity of music makes its interpretation as vital as it is convoluted, however, and Forster implicates a range of associations by calling it a "noise" (let alone a sublime one). The phrase suggests a complex tension between this music and the often-noisy public that hears and attributes meaning to it. It implies, moreover, a diversity of social and political thinking about that public.

The term "noise" has always been imbricated with the most powerful and threatening manifestations of language: with the productive yet uncontainable force of publicity, rumor, propaganda, and rhetorical violence. These qualities infuse the operatic tradition as well—the "Calumnia" aria from Rossini's *Barber of Seville*, for example, identifies "calumny" as a breeze (*venticello*) that rapidly crescendos into cannonfire (*colpo di cannone*). Perhaps predictably, *Finnegans Wake*, a noisy text threaded with gossipy "nighttalk," puns on this aria by turning calumny into a noodle—"*La calumnia è un Vermicelli*" [*FW* 199.28-9]—whose beginnings and endings are difficult to locate. The signifying powers of noise are embedded in the Latinate elements of English: the French for "noise" is *bruit*, as in Claudius's proclamation, "And the king's rouse the heavens all bruit again, / Re-speaking earthly thunder" (*Hamlet* I.ii.128-9); the Italian, as we have seen, is *rumori*. Rumor and its (or, often, "her") counterpart "fame" are important participants in the traditions on which Eliot and Pound build, down to the Roman epic. Dryden's translation of the "House of Fame" passage from Ovid's *Metamorphoses* offers an acoustics of rumor,[18] using spatial metaphors to think about how news, and lies, are disseminated through the "mart":

> 'Tis built of brass, the better to diffuse
> The spreading sounds, and multiply the news:
> Where eccho's in repeated eccho's play:
> A mart for ever full, and open night and day.
> Nor silence is within, nor voice express,
> But a deaf noise of sounds, that never cease.
> . . . .
> A thorough-fare of news: where some devise
> Things never heard, some mingle truth with lies;
> The troubled air with empty sounds they beat,
> Intent to hear, and eager to repeat.[19]

"Fama" is a figure of excess ("multiply the news," "for ever full"); of "diffuse[ness]" and "spreading"; and of hybridity (a brass house). Fame's effort to "mingle truth with lies" results in a "deaf noise of sound" and a "hollow roar," so much static that a signal can barely get through, too diffuse to be pinpointed and too hybrid to be distilled. Its core is "hollow," its sounds "empty," but nonetheless persistent, communicative, and physical, "beating" the air. In describing the rape of Philomel, Dryden's Ovid may get his information from *fama* herself: "Fame (which I scarce can credit) has agreed,/That on her rifled charms, still void of shame,/[Tereus] frequently indulg'd his lustful flame" (6.559-62). Noise and rumor may be counterpoised against fact and "credit" but are even more ominous when they get things right, or when they threaten the recurrence of events that have already taken place. As Eliot's appropriations of Ovid and Dryden make clear, this is (to borrow Pound's definition of literature) "news that stays news":[20] "And still she cried, and still the world pursues'/'Jug Jug to dirty ears."[21]

Hence noise, and music's mediations of it, need to be considered in relation to the diffuse encoding of information, what might loosely be called "publicity." The association between noise and rumor permeates classical literature through the Renaissance and through the nineteenth century.[22] The idle village gossip surrounding Bishop Myriel in *Les Miserables* (1862) is exposed as "rumours only,—noise, sayings, words: less than words"; noise as anarchic discourse finds its way into Arnold's "confused alarms of struggle and flight," juxtaposed in "Dover Beach" (1867) against the Sea of Faith's "slow, withdrawing roar," an "eternal note of sadness" harmonized by the secular religion of poetry into a "tremulous cadence." The creation of music, or of poetry that aspires to the condition of music, involves the sublimation of these threats to cultural unity.

Perhaps nothing exemplifies this threat better than Eliot's example of noise transformed through rhythm: Stravinsky's *Sacre*, the archetypal *succès de scandale* of modern ballet (or, if we believe Taruskin, the most "appallingly . . . overdocumented" event in modern musical history [*Stravinsky*, 2.1006]). Eliot heard the ballet's music not just as a celebration of myth, but as an engagement with the shrieks of the modern city. And expensive noise is also what Stravinsky's audiences heard—not just the rioters at the Paris premiere, who paid for the privilege of making a ruckus, but auditors more than a decade later, in the spirit of that 1924 letter to the *Boston Herald*:

> Who wrote this fiendish "Rite of Spring"?
> What right had he to write the thing?
> Against our helpless ears to fling
> Its crash, clash, cling, clang, bing, bang, bing?
>
> And then to call it "Rite of SPRING,"
> The season when on joyous wing
> The birds melodious carols sing
> And harmony's in every thing!
>
> He who could write the "Rite of Spring,"
> If I be right by right should swing!

Leaving the composer unnamed, the writer attempts to restore order through his own ostentatious play with consonance and rime, punning "rite" with multiple senses of the words "write" and "right," and suggesting that the composer should, like the victim of Stravinsky's ballet, be sacrificed for the good of the collective "harmony." Speaking on the behalf of "our" collective "helpless ears," the writer banishes the remainder into the noisy inferno: trying to define what about the *Rite* is so offensive (he stops short of saying that his six-year-old could have composed it), he shifts into onomatopoeia, the last refuge of someone who isn't using his grown-up words. When considering Attali's argument that music is a "simulacrum of sacrifice"—a reflection of the "essential violence" that infuses social order—it makes sense that a ballet about sacrificial violence might start calling into question music's encoding of social relations.

It is hard, moreover, to extract the anxiety about noise from anxieties about politics and the marketplace. A passage from Thomas Carlyle's *Frederick the Great*, quoted approvingly in Wagner's *Art and Revolution*, reads the French Revolution as a "Spontaneous Combustion" upon which more will follow: "many-coloured, with loud noises, envelop[ing] the world in anarchic flame for long hundreds of years," akin to the epic scope of Wagner's "music of the future." Wishing to write this history in the midst of an intensifying onslaught of street musicians, organ grinders, carriages, and "clamoring hawkers," Carlyle had constructed a special soundproof study in his house at Chelsea. As John Picker has suggested, this retreat into a private *sanctum* marked also a struggle for "professional differentiation," an "acute fear of effeminacy" (*fama* as feminine incursion), and of course a desire to maintain autonomy from the Mechanical Age: "The world, which can do me no good, shall at least not torment me with its street and backyard noises."[23]

For all of their bravado, modernists never exorcise this anxiety about noise, an anxiety directed not only at the perceived threats posed by the masses, the popular, the marketplace, and so on, but at our reliance on *rumori* as a means of disseminating culture. If literature is news that stays news, that "news" is disseminated and mediated through the functions of publicity, rumor, gossip, and social maneuvering circulating around the artwork. Rainey argues that the Futurist exhibitions in London urged on the creation and marketing of Anglo-American modernism, encouraging Pound, Eliot, and Wyndham Lewis (et al.) to reconstruct an intellectual aristocracy "within the world of the commodity."[24] The Futurists' assault on the sublime compelled modernists to create a market niche for literature, to benefit from avant-garde noise while preserving its pretense to autonomy.

The fear for antimodernists like Lukács, or oppositional modernists like Lewis, is that this noise might be symptomatic of mental fog—that it had made modern thought static, in both senses of the word, devoid of abstract critical distance (Lewis) or humanizing totality (Lukács).[25] Lewis makes a few appearances in this study, as a noise within the larger trajectory of British modernism: the "enemy within" whose pointed critiques of Pound, Joyce, and the Sitwells identified political and aesthetic risks of modernist experimentation. He heard perils, for example, in the many disembodied voices of modernist art—their susceptibility, as Tyrus Miller has suggested, to propaganda and PR. This destabilizing *acousmêtre*, to borrow Michel Chion's term for an authoritative voice that derives its power from invisibility, for Lewis created a mysterious Oz-like effect of disembodied power. Pierre Schaeffer coined the phrase "acousmatic sound" to describe sound without a visible source, desiring to intensify the listener's perceptual appreciation of the sound itself without reference to its cause or origin. Like Pythagoras, who is said to have spoken from behind a veil to focus his pupils' attention to his words, the sound of Sitwell's voice from behind a curtain portended a dissemination of auditory information without visible accountability.

Lewis in general had little patience for music; his *Time and Western Man* (1927) rejects the "time-bound" arts as being introspective to the point of paralysis, and music is the time-bound art par excellence.[26] Lewis preferred the plastic and visual arts as more sharply defined and intellectually discriminating. But he also saw, even before his celebratory *Hitler* book (1931), the potential of music to have an effect, stultifying or stimulating, on a mass public. In his preface to *Tarr* (1918), Lewis proclaims that England must find a way to contend with the "brain-waves and titanic orchestrations" of "Germany's large leaden brain" (9) by finding a more direct path from art to the body. The novel climaxes in an attempted rape and a comically clumsy duel between the German artist Kreisler and the Polish trader Stoltyk, during which Lewis reflects on the possibility of music as pure disruptive violence, what Attali refers to as the "simulacrum of murder" that noise enacts by cutting off a transmission (26): "Words, glances, music are at present as indirect as hands and cannons. Such music might be written, however, that no fool, hearing it, could survive. Whether it throttled in a spasm of disgust or of shame is immaterial" (*Tarr* 319). The duel itself collapses into mutual hand-to-hand "throttling," a noisy concatenation of embodied effects: "'Acha—acha—'a noise, the beginning of a word, came from [Kreisler's] mouth. He sank on his knees. A notion of endless violence filled him. Tchun—tchun—tchun—tchun—tchun—tchun! He fell on his back, and the convulsive arms came with him" (321). Kreisler's descent into the vortex simulates embodied "endless violence," turning his body into a sneezing Gatling gun and substituting linguistic sense for a whorl of action, noise, and convulsion. This is Lewis's music: an assault on the body so direct that it throttles language itself. The potentially fluid and interactive medium of music—which had been coopted, Lewis thought, by bourgeois, Ballets-Russes-attending saps—needed to be brought back to a form of violence if it was effectively to redefine the public discourse.

Lewis's emphasis on sharp edges, Lukács's antimodernist insistence on realist transparency, Attali's noisy radicalism for radicalism's sake, and Adorno's privileging of dissonance and difficulty all have their deaf spots. If Lewis's fixation on spatial perspective fetishizes violence and penetration, Lukács's critique of static modernist temporality fails to acknowledge the critical potential of spatial mapping or thick description within a discrete moment.[27] Viewing all naturalistic interruptions of narrative as solipsistic, Lukács forges too strict, and too thinly historicized, an alliance with conventional macrorhythmic patterns.

Integral Freedom: Lukács, Bartók, and Ahistorical Reading

Both because of the modernist resistance to hearing music as mere imitation, and because of music's interactive semiotics, modernist literary-musical interactions cannot be understood solely as Lukács's naturalistic adversary, nor solely as an Adornian escape hatch from the market, nor solely as (after Lewis) a sharply defined assault on the body. It may literarily be put to any of these effects. But modernist debates over music and noise call for a fluid, new-musicological approach that opens up music to its contexts, rather than closing it down allegorically (like Lukács) or fencing it off (like Adorno). A brief exploration of Lukács's and Adorno's passing consensus over Hungarian composer Béla Bartók—whose place in this project is minor, but who speaks to both philosophers—might help exemplify the benefits of a thickly historicized musicological model.

Lukács's writings on music are isolated and rarely translated into English. According to Robert Lilienfield, Lukács occupies a middle ground between Hanslick (music as an autonomous language with no "content") and Schopenhauer (music as the expression of a metaphysical Will), suggesting that music is mimetic of the language of emotions.[28] Lukács's exemplary musician, and friend and countryman, was Bartók, whose folk and peasant idioms seemed to escape the turning wheels of capitalism.[29] It appears that Lukács, not unlike Attali, heard Bartók auguring a sphere both pre- and post-capitalist in which "composition" occurs spontaneously as part of authentic social ritual—an "integral freedom," in Adorno's choice phrase, wherein the individual composes through an unalienated relationship with the "potentials" of "his own body" (Attali 135). Yet Lukács sponsors Bartók's use of folk idioms not as a precapitalist fantasy, but as a merging of innovative aesthetics with a humane allegorical critique of modernity. In this reading, Bartók exemplifies the emphasis on social interdependence and conflict that Lukács associates with realist narrative, as opposed to the "pseudo-scientific" naturalist emphasis on environmental particulars, or the solipsistic modernist "bourgeois subjectivity."[30] The "basic content of Bartók's objectivity," writes Lukács, lies in the "battle of the humane against the overwhelming powers of the antihumane . . . in the era of the evolution and rise of power of fascism. . . . The antipower living in Bartók is exactly his connection with the people."[31]

Both Lukács and Adorno, then, hear in Bartók a merging of modernist experimentation with humanizing folklorism: a synthesis that helps him to avoid succumbing to Lukács's *bête noire*, modernist self-abstraction from the world, or to Adorno's, a "romantic nostalgia of a 'state of nature' beyond history" (a different kind of abstraction that ignores the formal mediations of art).[32] Adorno resists primitivist music as the naturalization, through rhythm, of an inorganic sense of false order: "In the repetitive rhythms of primitive music the menacing aspect originates in the principle of order itself" (*AT* 52). But in Bartók, Adorno hears the capacity to render collective, folkloric tradition as a compositional struggle with the musical material, a dissonant refusal to "conceal alienation under the false reconciliation of the epic and the modern," instead using folk idioms to fragment the false unity of mainstream art music (Paddison 41). Even in the stridently Teutonic and pro-Schoenberg *Philosophy of New Music*, where Adorno might be suspected of more than mild condescension toward Bartók's folklorism, he understands Bartók's use of non-Western music to express alienation rather than crude "blood-and-soil" nationalism. And he hears in Bartók, as opposed to Stravinsky, a refusal to reduce folkloric materials to positivist pseudo-anthropology or to cynical game-play. Lukács, in his turn, hears in Bartók a historical synthesis of modern technique with the patterns of everyday life, a hope that music's ritualism might draw the individual back into a more organic relation with society.[33]

This drive to find an organic subtension to both art and civilization is where, in my view, both Lukács and Attali falter—the former in his obsession with realism's totalizing syntheses, the latter in a naïve fantasy of collective sublimation, something like an unhinged D.H. Lawrence novel in which everyone composes through his body at the same time. Some of us would prefer not to live through *The Plumed Serpent*, and I am by temperament more sympathetic to Adorno's negative understanding of art as a space to unstitch the false identities of politics and mass media. But this too grows ahistorical without a complementary objective principle: if not positivism, exactly, then a thickly historicized rendering of musical creation, performance, and reception. Two Marxists arm-wrestling for pride of lesser reification, both Adorno and Lukács are strongly dialectical in their ways, but their readings of Bartók reveal the ahistorical strain in each: Adorno as formalist and Lukács as allegorical realist. If Adorno desperately tries to make Bartók a side-story to Schoenberg's Austro-German aesthetics, Lukács partakes in a kind of ahistorical finger-wagging, as he reduces Bartók to precapitalist primitivism. Jameson has aptly critiqued Lukács's tendency to substitute "ethical judgment" for "historical perception," evidenced by his embrace of realism (and, eventually, soviet realism). By failing to posit a connection between realism and "the life of commerce," Lukács naively endorses (in Jameson's words) a "particular—historically dated—mode of reality-construction" as the ground bass of a new communist social order.[34] In his reading of Bartók, Lukács seems equally over-eager to allegorize him according to a "mode of reality-construction" that doesn't line up with the actual music. Bartók cannot so easily be allegorized as prehistorical; pieces such Bartók's *Miraculous Mandarin* (1926), with gestures to the "'stylized' noise" of Russolo and Varèse (Ross 122), show a historically specific interest in the modern soundscape to complement his ethnographic ear for the Hungarian Roma, merging a 1920s machine aesthetic with a primitivist round dance.[35]

And as if on cue, *Mandarin* prompted so much audience furor that it found itself banned in Germany and never again performed until after Bartók's death. Though the brothel-based scenario prompted the controversy more than the noise, one has to wonder to what extent the noise set its auditors' nerves on edge. Either way, a historical discussion is needed beyond the normatively allegorizing and moralizing discourse that would equate Bartók (a musical genius) to Schoenberg (a very different musical genius), or reduce him to Attali (not a musical genius, usefully flamboyant though he is). What is called for is the materialist Adorno-Williams two-step: one, a dialectical reading of form that meets modernist texts on their own formal terrain, to seek out their "nonidentities" vis-à-vis a social situation; and-a-two, a historical fleshing out *of* that social situation. To do this requires a fuller account of how music can mean anything (beyond Hanslick's "purely musical" idea)—an account of the process by which music acquires a relation to its surroundings, and by which writers endow its formal properties with literary or cultural significance.

Interpreting Writers Interpreting Music

The consideration of music with respect to noise, or its homological resonance with social formations, necessarily introduces the problems of analogy, likeness, and mimesis: music might sound like, or particularly *un*like, sounds of the real world. The problem of "imitative music," the relationship between music and mimesis, has long been at the heart of musical aesthetics. As Raymond Monelle suggests, theories of musical meaning have undergone a shift from classical "imitation" to "expression," though Monelle argues that the eighteenth-century imitative perspectives are "much nearer to semiotic theory than the Romantic views that succeeded them" (namely, those of Schopenhauer and Hoffmann).[36] The urge to question the imitative or semiotic features of art is thus put at odds with the urge to understand music's relationship to literary and historical concerns. Peter Kivy disputes the assigning of associative meaning to music, arguing instead that music acquires meaning according to cognitive experience, a perception of "rightness" and profundity. Noise, too, might be subjected to this sort of purely cognitive listening, akin to Schaeffer's notion of "reduced listening"—a purely phenomenological and decontextualized experience of sound.

Kivy uses characters from *Howards End* as signposts for his argument, assessing whether we really experience Beethoven's Fifth as a goblin-ridden noise—implicitly granting that even if we listen to music for somatic pleasure, not literary interpretation, it is left to the written word to elaborate music's cultural potential, whether outlandishly metaphorical (Helen's goblins), sedately Kivyesque (Margaret), or muddled about the whole problem (Forster himself). Kivy's choice of Forster is emblematic not only of the ongoing resonance of Forster's writing (which Zadie Smith reinvents as a Mozart concert in *On Beauty*), but also of the difficulty of describing "music alone" as an autonomous formal space when one needs language to articulate its effects. Forster seems to be testing in real time different modes of individual and cultural reception of music, in a way that reinforces music's performative and esthesic, rather than simply mimetic, mode of reference. Music leads the writer to reflect on the performative nature of language: in the sense both that it hearkens to the stage and that it has the transactional force of a speech-act. For one thing, the very production of music as a sonic object invokes questions of agency, of who or what is realizing a musical/literary "score" into sound. It is not enough, for instance, to note that *The Waste Land* quotes Wagner; rather, the form of the poem begs us to ask where these sounds are coming from, what bodily, technological, or artistic machine is producing them, and in what context. *Façade* is spoken by the poet from behind a curtain: so as to avoid, if Osbert Sitwell is to be believed, the "blush-rose of shame" that the bodily presence of a lector brings to the faces in the crowd.[37] Antheil's *Ballet* was to be performed by sixteen pianolas, Pound's operas performed over the radio, the principal roles of *Billy Budd* and *Peter Grimes* performed by Peter Pears, Britten's long-time partner. Referring back to a performance, a literary representation of music invokes the presence of a body: of the performer, of the auditor, and, in both cases, of an interpreter. Adorno's assertion that the truest way to interpret a piece of music is to play it—thereby experiencing and mastering it as a structural whole—is in this respect a genuinely modernist ideal.

Tethering musical poeisis, esthesis, and textuality to bodily experience, Adorno anticipates Barthes' critique of a static conception of music divorced from the physicality of performance and audition. Like Adorno (and Pound), Barthes suggests that the standardization of music through mechanical reproduction has resulted in the atrophy of musical interpretation. Barthes' essay "The Grain of the Voice" (1972) sponsors an interpretive relation to music that exceeds a simple ascription of an ethos or a description: in "the normal practice of music criticism," a "work (or its performance) is only ever translated into the poorest of linguistic categories: the adjective. . . . The music is *this*, the execution is *that*."[38] Such descriptions, in their insistence on "perfection" and connoisseurship, devalue music's erotic or performative dimensions, a tendency that serves a socioeconomic function by conforming the listening subject himself to "what in music *can be said*: what is said about it, predicatively, by Institution, Criticism, Opinion" (185, his emphasis). Much of Barthes' essay is devoted to promoting one singer (Charles Panzéra) on the grounds that he "patinate[s]" the language with embodied experience; and to demoting Dietrich Fischer-Dieskau for merely "translat[ing]" emotion in ways describable and receivable in those merely adjectival terms acceptable to Institution and Criticism. Fischer-Dieskau fails, Barthes claims, to give a sense of the parts of the vocal tract (throat, teeth, mucous membranes) that accentuate the bodily action of vocal delivery (the lungs are, for him, incapable of "erection" and suggestive only of resonance and empty space). Ultimately music should not be "like" anything, but should produce erotic identification: "I shall not judge a performance according to the rules of interpretation, the constraints of style (anyway highly illusory) . . . , but according to the image of the body (the figure) given me" (188).

Even apart from its literary representation, the body's dislocation from its voice is intrinsic to vocal music. Abbate, for example, coins the phrase "voice-object" to refer to the attention-drawing "autonomization" of the operatic voice once it leaves the singer's body, a concept that Adorno would have adored (he liked opera best on the gramophone, rescued from the costumes and "phony hoopla" of operatic spectacle).[39] The autonomization of voice is a distinctly late Victorian and modernist problem, intensified by the gramophone; in *The Waste Land*, for example, the typist's "record on the gramophone" displaces her own voice into a stream of Wagnerian sound. In the nineteenth-century novel, as Ivan Kreilkamp has argued, the emergence of a disembodied phonographic voice both enables formal innovation and destabilizes "human agency and authorship"; *mutatis mutandis*, the effects of Marconi's wireless radio on modernist and avant-garde writing disperses the radical energies of artistic sound.[40] As new technologies led perfectly conventional sounds to be experienced as acousmatic, the voice dissevered from its bodily origin pervades modernism: Edith Sitwell's Oz-like voice from behind a curtain, Pound's radio-like poetic transmission, or the echoes of *A Passage to India*. This distantiation of voice fragments the modernist text's syntax and form, but also often compels an ultimate *reunification* of body and voice. The seemingly disembodied thunder at the end of *The Waste Land* is manifested in the "blood shaking my heart" (V.402) and the heart "beating obedient/To controlling hands" (V.420-1); the benevolently dictatorial control of a poet attempts to mediate other controlling hands (conductor, pianist, or stage director) without losing the grain of the voice and its bodily patina.

It is here that the problem of rhythm will often come to the foreground: musical rhythm, led by those "controlling hands," makes more palpable the implications of how music, as it mediates noise, indexes a relationship between the voice and the social situation of its embodied sources. Before turning to dissonance and rhythm specifically, though, I wish to consider how noise itself becomes an aesthetic and a cultural problem, to be composed through, or to be abated.

Modernist Vibrations: Russolo, Schopenhauer, and Structuring Noise

In an episode of *Fawlty Towers* ("A Touch of Class"; 1975), Basil Fawlty listens to a broadcast of Brahms's Third Symphony, escaping from his work and daydreaming of a day when his hotel will attract a more aristocratic clientele. (The echoes of *Dorian Gray* in Sybil's and Basil's names are not entirely impertinent here.) His wife Sybil interrupts this fantasy, urging him to go hang up a landscape painting and a stuffed moose's head. "You could have had them both done by now if you hadn't spent the whole morning skulking in there listening to that racket," Sybil snarks, to Basil's incredulity: "'Racket'? That's *Brahms!* Brahms's Third 'Racket'!"

Wherever one sides on this exchange (my sympathies are with the Third), the anxious class politics of Britain have a way of being triangulated through the German sounds of Beethoven and Brahms. To the narrator of *Howards End*, Beethoven's Fifth is a "sublime noise"; to John Ruskin it is merely noise, "like the upsetting of a bag of nails, with here and there also a dropped hammer." Neither Beethoven's goblins nor Ruskin's can save Forster's Leonard Bast, whose efforts to appreciate Ruskin *and* Beethoven leave him depressed and dead. Notwithstanding her summary dismissal of Brahms, Sybil does recognize Basil's false, Bastian desperation for a "touch of class" (as it turns out, the aristocrat staying at the hotel is a con-artist—a racketeer). The boundary between music and noise readily maps onto the conflict between Britain and Germany; the attempt to hierarchize and contain noise often adds up to the effort to consolidate a different boundary.

If one man's music is another's noise, it is also the case that noise is rarely defined except by negation: whatever noise is, it isn't a signal, a silence, a clear sound, or "real" music. Thus, as Douglas Kahn writes, the desire to identify and marginalize noise must paradoxically "explain itself in the face of the possibility that there is no such thing as noise."[41] Identifying a noise, Kahn suggests, imparts the desire to control or suppress it. Alternatively, trying to move the boundary between sound and noise results in the need to reconsolidate that boundary elsewhere, as the artistic, material, and esthesic boundaries continually shift: "We know they are noises in the first place because they exist where they shouldn't or they don't make sense when they should. . . . Suppressing noise only contributes to its tenacity and detracts from investigating the complex means through which noise itself is suppressed, while celebrating noise easily becomes a tactic within the suppression of something else" (Kahn 21). Hence the liberation of noise by figures such as Russolo and Pound justifies itself in terms of "expansion," of a widening circle of aural material from which to choose. For Pound and the Futurists (fellow Mussolinists whose antagonisms are hard to distinguish from their sympathies), this expansion might carry a more sinister implication: the celebration of "noise" may result in the subjugation of something else. To define "music" or "poetry" is by exclusion to define "noise," to decide what should or shouldn't lie within that expanding sonic circle.

Such a question calls attention to art's material basis: according to Kahn, "Noise can be understood in one sense to be that constant grating sound between the abstract and the empirical" (25). Thinking about the oscillation of noise between the abstract and the empirical serves as a reminder that a similar oscillation is taking place *within* aesthetic form between the ideational and the material. These resonances internal to the artwork seem to grow louder the more self-contained a status one claims for it. Rather than let music amplify noise's internal resonances by suppressing its external ones, Russolo's *Arte Dei Rumori* promotes a "special acoustic pleasure" from breaking down the boundary altogether. Attacking the sublime autonomy of art, Russolo desires to draw music back into the sphere of daily life—while, however, disavowing the imitative component of noise-music.

Though part of Futurism's assault on aesthetic aura, Russolo's argument is made primarily on aesthetic grounds; the grating between music and its surroundings is registered, internally, as dissonance. The way to reinvigorate the orchestra is to listen more attentively, and more collaboratively, to the wider range of sound to which our ears have acclimated:

> Let us cross a large modern capital with our ears more sensitive than our eyes. We will delight in distinguishing the eddying of water, of air or gas in metal pipes, the muttering of motors that breathe and pulse with an indisputable animality, the throbbing valves, the bustle of pistons, the shrieks of mechanical saws, the starting of trams on the tracks, the cracking of whips, the flapping of awnings and flags. We will amuse ourselves by orchestrating together in our imagination the din of rolling shop shutters, the varied hubbub of train stations, iron works, thread mills, printing presses, electrical plants, and subways. (26)

Russolo poses a murky relation between the increasing range of noises present in modern life and the increasing range of harmonies available to the modern orchestra. His chief concern is wideness of range, sonic or timbral, as it affects the sensorium. Conventional orchestras can no longer excite the senses, now that our ears are now accustomed to the noise of modern life:

> In order to excite and stir our sensibility, music has been developing toward the most complicated polyphony and toward the greatest variety of instrumental timbres and colors. It has searched out the most complex successions of dissonant chords, which have prepared in a vague way for the creation of MUSICAL NOISE. The ear of the Eighteenth Century man would not have been able to withstand the inharmonious intensity of certain chords produced by our orchestras (with three times as many performers as that of the orchestra of his time). But our ear takes pleasure in it, since it is already educated to modern life, so prodigal in different noises. Nevertheless, our ear is not satisfied and calls for ever greater acoustical emotions. (24–5)

Focusing on timbre, or tone color, Russolo goes on to state, "Futurist musicians should substitute for the limited variety of timbres that the orchestra possesses today the infinite variety of timbres in noises, reproduced with appropriate mechanisms" (28). The limited range of timbres have left music to "flounder," calling for the introduction of new categories of sound: "*We must break at all cost from this restrictive circle of pure sounds and conquer the infinite variety of noise-sounds*" (25, his italics). While the complexity of modern orchestras has trained the ears to accommodate new kinds of "inharmonious intensity," the variety of timbres available to an orchestra is still too limited. "Do you know of a more ridiculous sight," Russolo asks, "than that of twenty men striving to redouble the mewling of a violin?" (25).

His efforts to expand the circle of musical language lead Russolo to relate noise and the "complex successions of dissonant chords." As he praises increasingly dissonant orchestral music only to damn the limitations of the orchestra, Russolo thus advances a relatively conventional argument about musical evolution: dissonance is pushing music into "noise-sound," much as the late Romantics pushed chromatic tonality to its limits and prompted Schoenberg to abandon it. At the same time, poietic uses of dissonant or chromatic harmonies may sound like "noise" to an audience. Nattiez cites Luciano Berio's assertion that the Tristan Chord (the functionally ambiguous opening chord of Wagner's *Tristan und Isolde* [1865]) would have sounded in its time like noise, indecipherable by virtue of its unclear structural function and context. Similarly, Russolo writes that the ears are ready for "bigger acoustic sensations" and timbres. The slippage between the "ears" and the "arous[al]" of "emotion" indicates that Russolo, though refusing to imitate noise, still means to benefit from its affective resonances. Russolo's and Marinetti's Futurist exhibitions were performance pieces, after all, and their musical noises, like Wagner's, were intended to serve a theatrical function, if not a musical-dramatic function in the Wagnerian sense.

By relating dissonance to noise, Russolo argues that extramusical sounds can function within already acceptable musical syntax: dissonances, he writes, move "ever farther from pure sound" and "have almost attained the *noise-sound*," the noises produced by conventional instrumentation. The logical outgrowth of this tendency is "*the addition and the substitution of noises for sounds*" (28, his italics), starting with the invention of his own *intonarumori* (noise-makers), which produce particular noises that can be orchestrated and reproduced. Russolo offers not a neat distinction between "pure sound" and "noise," but a continuum. For the avant-garde there existed a constant back-and-forth between sound and noise both "from the perspective of music," and "within the sphere of extra-musicality" (69)—both within and without the "circle" from which Russolo wants to break.

That circle motivates much of the avant-garde and modernist efforts to intensify sound, or to exclude and abate it. What Kahn calls the "monochord"—a relic of the Pythagorean cosmology, in which astronomy, mathematics, and music resonate as the overtones of a single vibrating string—shapes the "neo-Pythagorean" experiments with synesthetic arts in the late nineteenth and early twentieth century. The monochord is seen to create a harmonic system that serves a double function, to which I will return often: an "intensification and a reduction, an inclusion of everything and a boundary against much" (Kahn 74–5). The monochord, that is, excludes noise as a "powerful nemesis," identifying and barring whatever counts as noise (consonants, aperiodic sounds) and intensifying what it includes; one perhaps already sees how such categories could be allied to social or demographic ones. Incumbent on this intensification was the establishment of new proportions among different art forms, each with its own "vibrating" resonance: these "synesthetic systems," the Wagnerian total artwork chief among them, were to create "proportionate relations" among various "perceptual and affective registers" (74). In the next chapter I read the vocative "O" in *The Waste Land* as precisely such a intensification of sounds and noises—arranged, constellationally, according to a range of affective resonances, experienced in real time.

And experienced by real bodies—the problem for those after Wagner, thinking about music's material impact, is to consider how these vibrations are felt as somatic resonances. In this respect, Arthur Schopenhauer, Wagner's philosophical idol, conspicuously informs modernist aesthetics; it is he who spurred Pater's claim that all art aspires to music. Promoting music as a "direct copy of the Will," Schopenhauer argues that music operates as the metaphysical undercurrent of representation, the "metaphysical to everything physical in the world." Music is a copy not of a thing, but of an underpinning metaphysical drive manifested in bodily action. Pater, co-opting Schopenhauer, celebrates its intensification of the momentary sensation, its propensity to burn with a "hard, gemlike flame" whose content is its catalytic potential for pleasure, materialized in the flame's gemlike form. For Pater, it is not just art but life itself that "aspires" to music: reaching for aesthetic intensity, irreducible to representation, manifested as form, and experienced as ecstasy.

Modernist appropriations of Pater and Schopenhauer emphasize its material qualities as much as its metaphysical ones. Schopenhauer's conception of music as our closest approximation of the Will leads him into a peculiar reflection on the organization of Nature, in which a ground-bass is analogous to "inorganic nature, the mass of the planet."[42] Above these bass resonances, the soprano, alto, and tenor voices

> always sound faintly at the same time, and it is a law of harmony that a bass-note may be accompanied only by those notes that actually sound automatically and

> simultaneously with it (its *sons harmoniques*) through the accompanying vibrations. Now this is analogous to the fact that all bodies and organizations of nature must be considered as having come into existence through gradual development out of the mass of the planet. This is both their supporter and their source, and the high notes have the same relation to the ground-bass. . . . Therefore, for us the ground-bass is in harmony what inorganic matter, the crudest mass on which everything rests and from which everything originates and develops, is in the world. (I.258; ch. 52)

Building "gradations" of "Ideas" on this ground-bass, the overtones of the monochord structurally parallel the "definite species in nature." Wagner discovered Schopenhauer in 1854, after he had composed *Das Rheingold*. *Rheingold* reflects Wagner's pre-Schopenhauerian strain of radical political critique, depicting a cynical series of lies, killings, and broken contracts.[43] Yet the *Rheingold* Prelude suggests that he was primed to accept Schopenhauer's logic of a deep, world-ordering bass, with a rationality beyond politics. *Rheingold*, and thus the Ring Cycle as a whole, opens with a six-minute elaboration of one chord (E-flat major), built on an almost inaudibly deep bass, which produces the world from primordial musical ooze. This ooze needs to be shaped, however, as the Ring Cycle's hammering noises indicate. Wagner's ongoing struggle, after discovering Schopenhauer, was to relate the Will's noumenal bass to its physical overtones, the "bodies and organizations of nature" bound in self-destructive illusion.

This struggle will call for a redefinition of Schopenhauer's idealist categories about the natural "law of Harmony." Whereas Schopenhauer claims that "impure discords . . . can be compared to the monstrous abortions between two species of animals" (258), Wagner conceived of dissonances as indexes of unresolved erotic desire. Categories of dissonance then come to be conceived, in Schoenberg's hands, not as ontological laws but as contingent constraints, such that (for Adorno) the emancipation of dissonance serves a liberating function. The boundaries of dissonance, like those of noise (and, in fact, like those of "definite" animal species) are ever fluid.

One finds modernists, and materialist critics of modernism, appropriating Schopenhauer's aesthetics to redefine the social and economic structure of daily life. Jameson's claim that texts move to the "ground bass of material production" reads as a commentary on modernism couched in the rhetoric of modernism: the materially grounded "absolute rhythm" that drives the modernist's aesthetic self-containment is detectable (if repressed) in narrative form. Even the Futurists, committed to the destruction of sublimity, seem moved by Schopenhauer's pulse. Russolo writes that beneath the new timbres of noise ought to lie a fundamental vibration: "There always exists, as with a pitch, a predominant rhythm, but around this can be heard numerous other, secondary rhythms" (28). While Russolo wants to expand the range of sounds available to the composer, he hears the need for some underpinning structural principle. Russolo reassures us that "Giving pitch to noises does not mean depriving them of all irregular movements and vibrations of time and intensity" (27), but instead means assigning a pitch to a strong fundamental vibration.

More important, for my purposes, are those modernists for whom Schopenhauer's tempting hierarchical musical vibrations are mapped onto culture and politics. In *Guide to Kulchur* (1938), Pound cites music as the grounds for organizing culture and ritual, citing Pythagoras and Confucius; one detects the influence of Schopenhauer, too, on Pound's theories of "absolute rhythm" and the "Great Bass." Recalling Pythagoras's *acousmêtric* voice—the priestlike words spoken from behind a veil—the detection of cultural and cosmic order seemed, to Pound, to demand attentive structural listening, which demanded in turn an orderly and disciplined intellectual training (*paideuma*). Just as Schopenhauer claims that music structurally parallels the natural order, with vibrating bass-notes producing higher orders of life, Pound insists that the establishment of a ground bass motivates the motion of all the other voices, and extends this analysis to social and economic hierarchies. When the aesthetic superstructure is out of key with the bass, the effect is physical noise—a symptom of alienation and distress. Pound does not share Schopenhauer's distaste for "discords"; as I discuss in chapter three, he's not much interested in harmony at all, dissonant or consonant, but in the correctly gauged intervals of time between one chord and the next. When Pound compares the music of Antheil to a factory, then, he concerns himself more with the horizontal rhythmic organization of chords than with their vertical content. Pound might be thought of as part Adorno, resistant to consonance for consonance's sake, and part Schopenhauer, for whom music is one resonance of a deep structural order.

Crucially, for all of these figures—Pound, Adorno, Eliot, Schopenhauer, the Futurists, and so on—the importance of music is structural, not imitative, performed by and calling attention to some cultural, political, or biological organization of material. All three are joined in a strong distaste for the imitative function of music, insisting that music must manifest our aspiration to deeper structures, be they noumenal, transcendent, affective, or social: be they the Will, the Great Bass, or Russolo's "predominant vibrations." If music is Conrad's "art of arts," it seems driven by a singular, invisibly phonographic Immensity, which is still perceptible in politics and history. Conrad's Preface to *Nigger of the "Narcissus,"* a visually oriented mandate to make the reader "see" the "substance of its truth," begins with an implicit invocation of the Paterian-Schopenhauerian line: "A work that aspires, however humbly, to the condition of art should carry its justification in every line" (131). When Marlow, in *Heart of Darkness*, describes Africa as the "dying vibration of one immense jabber . . . without any kind of sense"—the "immense jabber" doubling the "exotic Immensity" of Kurtz's "Report on the Suppression of Savage Customs"—he suggests that the inscrutable sounds of the jungle are underwritten by a teleological drive: a "singleness of intention" (as in the seaman's report), or a "singleness of purpose" (in the *Narcissus* preface), that moves art and history forward.[44] Though nonplussed by the "jabber" of the colony, Marlow persists in seeking an ideal unity underlying the "terrible frankness of that noise"; that meaning coalesces in the "high-strung eloquence" of Kurtz's report. Kurtz is said to have had "the makings of a great musician"—a talent that has burned with too gemlike a flame, collapsing into nothing but a "voice," "grave, profound, vibrating." The dialectic between noise and a fundamental vibration entails violence from both ends, a "choice of nightmares" amplified by the invaders' self-annihilating involutions: "the whisper . . . echoed loudly within him because he was hollow at the core."

Conrad exemplifies how a tightly wound, even musical prose strives not just to describe the noise of its surrounding, but to control noise by drawing it into its ever-intensifying circle of sounds. For Conrad, as for Eliot and Pound, the rhythms of language serve as ways of rethinking both the "aesthetic justification" of art and the deeply material ground-bass that makes it possible.

Modernists inherit much of their Schopenhauer from Freud, who pursued (not uncritically) the philosopher's disarticulation of the intellect from, for example, the death drive (materialized as the rhythmic *fort-da*).[45] We may, however, see the most direct *literary* inheritance of Schopenhauer's "vibration" in the milieu of French Symbolism and decadence, which shared in Schopenhauer's pessimistic *ethos* even when they were not explicitly engaged with his writings.[46] The speaker of Baudelaire's "Man and the Sea" (*L'homme et la mer*; 1857) sees in the "infinite sea" a mirror to the "bitter" "abyss" of the mind—an elliptical relation detectable in the noise/rhythm of the heart:

> You take pleasure in plunging into the heart of your image;
> You embrace it with eyes and your arms, and your heart
> At times forgets its own rhythm [*rumeur*]
> In the noise [*bruit*] of that wild and tameless complaint.[47]

The mirror of the sea effects an interlocking relation between rhythm and noise, the sound of the heartbeat and the noise of a noumenal vibration: the heart is distracted from its own noisy heartbeat (*rumeur*) by the sound of a fundamental "tameless" noise (*bruit*). As Marlow writes, the "sea is always the same," but all the more destabilizing for being "as inscrutable as Destiny." With the word *bruit* Baudelaire presents the sea not as a static object but as a crucible of desire, mirrored by the rhythmic *rumeur* of the body's heartbeat. The speaker accesses this fundamental noise only by surrendering to the rhythms of the body, of the sea, and of the verse itself.

Musical Noise after Russolo

These vibrations—a range of musical resonances locked in with the rhythms of the body and of culture—suggest that as the literary imagination defends music on Paterian lines, it rethinks them along historical and cultural ones. After Russolo, and as modernist writers were increasingly aware, musicians understood music to be bound closely with the sounds of daily life. And in the midst of a number of musical scandals, they also detected much in the noises from the mezzanine. After the premiere of Varèse's *Amériques*, a tribute to New York City from a Parisian in America, a reviewer noted that "jeers and cheers, hisses and hurrahs, made the audience's reception of this radical work almost as deliriously dissonant as was the 'music' itself."[48] Its air-raid sirens aside, *Amériques* pays urbane homage to its pastoral predecessors: it opens, like Debussy's *Prélude à l'après-midi d'un faune* (1894), with an alto-flute solo—one that sounds, in its melodic contours, much like the opening bassoon *ad lib* of *Le Sacre du printemps*. *Amériques* pulls the *Rite* into the city, playing with several of its folkloric motifs, mimicking the syncopated thump of its "Dance of the Adolescents," and climaxing with a noisy collective battery of voices; the audience, like Stravinsky's, responded with no less noisy enthusiasm and rancor.

Varèse describes his conception of *Amériques* as a series of vacillations between the literal and the metaphorical substance of noise: between the soundscape of a city and of what Eliot called the "Unreal City."[49] In writing *Amériques*, Varèse claimed, he was "still under the spell" of his "first impressions of New York": "I heard a sound that had kept recurring in my dreams as a boy—a high whistling C-sharp. . . . As I worked in my Westside apartment where I could hear . . . the lonely foghorns, the shrill peremptory whistles—the whole wonderful river symphony which moved me more than anything ever had before" (qtd. in Thompson 139). A similar impulse can be detected in Antheil's claims that *Ballet Mécanique* originated first in his prenatal experience of industrial Trenton, and later in music that occurred to him in a dream (the precise quality of which Antheil could never again access).[50] While Antheil (more than Varèse) emphasized clarity, precision, and structural unity, in discussing the *origins* of that music he waxes romantic indeed.

Composers such as Antheil, Varèse, and Cowell were developing noise experiments as a way of appealing, through rhythm, to music's unconscious roots in ritual. Cowell develops this claim in "The Joys of Noise," an essay "calculated to undermine musical standards" (250). Pointing out that noise already exists in conventional music, not just in percussion but also in the form of irregular vibrations (e.g., in sung consonants, the strike of a violin bow), Cowell promotes a new "chemistry of sound" of which noise will be an essential element (252). If Pound's *Guide to Kulchur* refers to noise as a "piglike" disease, Cowell associates the "disease of noise," a kind of musical bacteria culture, with the "good microbes" that produce cheese (251). The metaphor may put one in mind of Bloom in "Lestrygonians"—like cheese, perhaps, noise "digests all but itself" (*Ulysses* 8.755). Not content merely to celebrate modern uses of noise, then, Cowell sees noise as fundamental to the other musical elements. His argument that "noise-sounds" reach back to the "primitive" rhythms of music (251) suffuses much of modern writing on music, from Eliot's review of *Le Sacre* through Attali's neo-avant-gardism. Adopting a primitivist jargon that relates the sounds of ancient ritual to the rituals of technological modernity, Cowell suggests that music's "flow of beats" can be broken down into something more elemental yet: the "noise-sound." Subtly "primitive" rhythms, layered over each other, will create an aesthetically pleasing noise (251). Cowell says that of the three musical elements of melody, harmony, and rhythm, noise is most closely associated with rhythm; he argues accordingly that ritual music is motivated by a rhythmic pulse comprising noises rather than pitched tones: "No primitive can sing comfortably without a flow of beats on some drum-like instrument to support him . . . when the same rhythm is marked by tones rather than by noises, the force of the music is immeasurably weakened" (250-1). Whereas Russolo associates noise with dissonance, both pleasingly harsh assaults on the senses, Cowell associates it with a blend of rhythms that lifts the listener into hypnotic ecstasy, in a way both hypermodern and in tune with the past. The performance of these rhythms prompted mechanical innovation: devices such as the gramophone, the piano roll, and the "rhythmicon" (invented by Léon Theremin) would enable the realization of "a harmony of several different rhythms played together." The rhythmicon allowed, Cowell argued, for the performance of "primitive" rhythms too subtle for Western musicians to perform.[51]

The tension between the "primitive" and the technological roots of art saturates debates over jazz in the modern city, often in pointedly racist ways. Opponents of jazz coded it as a variety of noise that, far from modernizing the primitive (à la Eliot on Stravinsky), regressed back *into* the primitive. The rhetorics of primitivism and futurism, as in the critics Emily Thompson cites from the '20s and '30s, merged into an anxiety about collective barbarity: "Jazz was attacked 'not only for returning people to the jungles of barbarism but also for expressing the mechanistic sterility of modern life.' It was perceived to reflect 'an impulse for wildness' even as it was 'perfectly adapted to robots.' It stimulated the 'half-crazed barbarian to the vilest deeds' while simultaneously constituting 'the exact musical reflection of modern capitalistic industrialism'" (131). The racial element in such critiques indexed a larger anxiety about the shifting demography of the city—the larger rhythms of moving populations. Mechanization and racialization were perceived as concomitant "noisy" threats to white middle-class domesticity. Conversely, as Antheil reclaimed noise, he championed jazz as an embodied experience that would salve the wounds of warfare. In his words, "Negro music made us remember at least that we still had bodies which had not been exploded by shrapnel" (qtd. in Kahn 66). Antheil hoped that compositions like the *Ballet*—merging industrial noise and (classicized) jazz—could use the noise of machinery and the "noise" of jazz to recuperate an unalienated body, in the space of a tightly formalized artwork.

The effort to return music back to its ritual elements, and to the unfettered physical body, thus resonates with particular kinds of social discontent, akin to what Peter Stallybrass and Allon White identify as the twin poles of disgust and desire that map readily onto categories of Otherness.[52] To cite one example, Ruth HaCohen has recently argued that Jews, not just socially but musically, were subjected to an "narrated blood libel" scapegoating them as a threat to an ordered social, cosmological, and auditory order. Jewish composers have reclaimed the noise of the synagogue so as to reconfigure Jewish identity amidst hostile conditions (HaCohen cites, for instance, the noisy glissandi in Schoenberg's twelve-tone opera *Moses und Aron* [1933], accompanying the dance of the Golden Calf).[53] The "noise-libel" establishes noise as a potential source of subversive violence and, at the same time, as an "exotic curiosity" associated with the "synagogal soundscape" (HaCohen 15). Along these lines, Antheil's lines, or the racist lines that associated jazz with "half-crazed barbari[sm]," noise asserts itself as the "outer limit of civil life" that becomes newly fascinating—the very act of excluding what is "marked out" as "dirty, repulsive, noisy, contaminating," and "expelled as 'Other,'" ultimately constitutes the civic identity and becomes the "symbolic contents of bourgeois desire" (Stallybrass/White 195). Much as the attempt to repress noise leads to its amplification in textual form, the attempt to erect a boundary between bourgeois respectability and noisy contamination is internalized into a text's symbolic content. Pieces such as *Moses und Aron* or Bartók's *Mandarin*—in their provocative programmatic content and their nudging of the music/noise boundary—pointed out the social and sonic "contaminations" that disgusted and fascinated their audiences. As Attali suggests, a bourgeois subject who identifies the carnivalesque "outer limits" engages in real time with their spectacular physical excess.

Thus if music speaks to Schopenhauer's confrontation with a jabbering, but unifying, Immensity, noise brings us into oscillating repulsion and attraction to the outer limits of social order. If the physical experience of music allows us, as Adorno contends, to engage in a dialectical critique of politics without succumbing to reductive conceptual categories, its relation to noise calls up symptomatic readings of culture. Pound's assaults on noise in *Guide to Kulchur* as a symptom of usury, for example, are entwined with his continual fascination (often at odds with his stated aesthetic program) with scandal and transgression. Inasmuch as Antheil was also trying to produce a sensational scandal, it is worth noting that Cowell's essay is "*calculated* to undermine musical standards": the shock of these noise-sounds, both ancient and futuristic, is calculated both to produce a solid musical form and transgressively to undercut the esthesic noise/music boundary.

By the 1930s, noise was so explicit a conceptual presence in the modernist music scene, and so clichéd a grounds for dismissing new music, that

Cowell composed a setting of *Three Anti-Modernist Songs*, each based on a doggerel making fun of a musician.[54] In addition to the *Boston Herald* broadside against Stravinsky, Cowell sets a 1909 attack on Richard Strauss, "Hark! from the pit a fearsome sound"; and an 1884 poem, entitled "Directions for Composing a Wagner Overture," the last stanza of which slips quickly between complaints about dissonance and complaints about noise:

> For harmonies, let wildest discords pass;
> Let key be blent with key in hideous hash;
> Then (for last happy thought!) bring in your Brass!
> And clang, clash, clatter, clatter, clang, and clash.

The line of the Wagner satire is almost indistinguishable from the clatter of the anti-Stravinsky invective (the goal is solidarity, not originality), though the language of each verse is stylized to match its content (the clash of the two end-rimes, "pass" and "hash," is itself a dissonance). If noise has a technically specific role in Cowell's music, it also has a general salience in popular discourse, where whatever doesn't count as music is cast into the lake of noise, a response turned to poietic advantage by Cowell. In this popular imagination, noise is the intensification of dissonance and ambiguous tonality: "let wildest discords pass," blend "key with key," and your last recourse will be the clatter and clash of percussion, sounds with no meaningful semantic equivalent. Cowell's songs bring noise back to the surface as a presence that the antimodernist doggerelists wish to repress, only to find that articulating *what* they want to repress is almost impossible.

Thus if Russolo and Marinetti used noise to break down Art-with-a-capital-A from the inside out, Cowell used it to advance art's teleology—grounded in "primitive" ritual, headed toward the future—and to thumb his nose at his listeners' esthesic temper-tantrums. Noise served as a way to exacerbate the irregular and shifting boundaries between noise and music, and to take advantage of the (at least) tripartite semiotics of music, which relies on an audience to accrue significance, and which can heckle the audience in return. For both Cowell and Russolo, noise needed to be pulled into relation with properties such as rhythm and (dissonant) harmony in order to serve its critical use: in order, that is, to call attention to the gaps among poietic, neutral, and esthesic definitions of noise, and in order to articulate a relationship between the noises within and without the artwork.

Two forms of aesthetic innovation, dissonance and rhythmic experimentation, represent different aesthetic shocks to the system through which modernists hierarchize music's social, cultural, and physical vibrations. As competing handlings of noise, dissonance and rhythm are at the center of modernist debates over the cultural value of music. If noise often stands in for something like Arnold's "ignorant armies crash[ing]," anarchic *rumori* in need of reshaping, dissonance is often heard as the artwork's mediation of that noise in its own internal, formal laws. Rhythm, in turn, is heard to index the patterns of culture as it orders and transmits shared narratives. While Adorno argues that microrhythmic innovation feeds back into cultural conformity, or subjects the audience to violence and discipline, other modernists (such as Eliot or Sitwell) consider rhythm a way of jolting the audience into a new relation toward its social situation. For Adorno, dissonant music best spoke (for the time being, anyway) against the consonant homogeneity of the culture industry. His is not the only model of dissonance, and not all modernists, let alone musicologists, do or should accept his strict Schoenberg/Stravinsky dichotomy. What they do tend to share is the notion that the perceived "difficulty" of dissonance compels a more critical stance toward harmony in general.

The "Supervention of Novelty": Dissonance and Tradition

Dissonance, like any kind of harmony, relies on the simultaneity of multiple sounds. How, then, do writers approximate the effects of harmony, consonant or dissonant, within the linearity of the English language? The fact that one can scarcely imitate dissonance in poetry is, for the modernist, a point in its favor—rather, the writer needs to channel its esthesic effects. Pound's definition of the image as "that which presents an intellectual or emotional complex in an instant of time" attempts to reconfigure horizontal language in vertical terms: to take syntax and narrative and compress them within the same temporal unit. It needs to be a "complex," moreover: some combination of experiences. Dissonance offers the ability to take sounds that bear a narrative relation to each other, as they unfold in time, and recombine them to surprising or critical effect in "an instant of time." Hence as dissonance serves as a symptom of art's attempt to carve out its own niche (its struggle to exist), it is also imagined to resonate with its surroundings (noise), and with the historical passage of time (rhythm) that it tries to compress.

Dissonance, for my purposes, has three important dimensions: (1) Vertical: a dissonance is a simultaneity of two or more sounds sounding at once. In a broader sense, they needn't even be sounds; Albright, for example, considers multi-generic works in which dissonances exist among words, images, musical sounds, and nonmusical sounds. (2) Horizontal: a dissonance has a syntagmatic function with respect to the "simultaneities" that precede it and follow it; a dissonance needs to be prepared in a certain way, as does its resolution into a new resonance (a consonance or another dissonance). (3) Qualitative: dissonance is granted particular aesthetic, symbolic, intellectual, affective, or social significance. Whatever these qualities are, they are (like noise) generally defined negatively, against consonance, concordance, assonance, euphony. It is from the normative insistence that dissonances ought to resolve into something else that Schoenberg and, for different reasons, Adorno wish to emancipate the dissonance.

Dissonance, then, can be considered both as an isolated shock—a vertical complex that jolts the system—and as a narrative disruption, something that delays resolution. Adorno and Pound, who thought (for different reasons) that an artwork's formal shape needed to emerge organically out of the development of musical material, tended to reject dissonances that were merely vertical. That is, when conceived of as a discrete funky chord—not as a dialectical development of horizontal melody, counterpoint, and rhythm—dissonance struck Adorno and Pound as faddish faux-novelty. Pound contended that any chord could follow any other chord, provided that the right amount of time had passed in the interim; chords were not dissonant or consonant, but well or badly placed. For Adorno, Schoenberg's music attains its radical qualitative dimensions as it unfolds through time; through that unfolding, each particular dissonance calls attention to its constituent elements. The music preserves the specificity of each dissonance rather than assimilating it into a homogeneity. In this way, Adorno writes, dissonance "is more rational than consonance, insofar as it articulates with great clarity the relationship of the sounds occurring within it—instead of achieving a dubious unity through the destruction of those partial moments present in dissonance, through homogenous sound" (*PNM* 49). Condensing the tensions among sounds while preserving their individuality, the dissonant artwork speaks to its own individual alienation, rather than allying itself to the homogeneous listening habits rationalized by the culture industry.

Adorno does not endow dissonance with a stable ontological status that makes it inherently more radical than consonance. Rather, like Nattiez after him, Adorno emphasizes the esthesic, contextual force of dissonance: the extent to which dissonance is radical within a structure that mandates consonance. (As with Nattiez' music/noise boundary, the dissonance/consonance line for the composer will not always line up with that for the audience.) Part of the qualitative force of dissonance lies in a dialectical interpretation —not just by the hearer, but by the performer herself—of the socially situated artwork. For Adorno, the "negative" quality of dissonance, by virtue of its increased autonomy from the marketplace, is music's best opportunity for rendering, in formal terms, the modern subject's sense of futility: "The source of the immense importance of all dissonance for new art since Baudelaire and *Tristan* . . . is that the immanent play of forces in the artwork converges with external reality: Its power over the subject intensifies in parallel with the increasing autonomy of the work. Dissonance elicits from within the work that which vulgar sociology calls its social alienation" (*AT* 15).

Other varieties of dissonance, what Albright calls "dissonance among . . . component media,"[55] also have an important place within modernist music and literature, much of which responds in one way or another to Wagner's Gesamtkunstwerk. Where Wagner aimed to immerse the audience in a fusion of poetry, drama, music, and visual spectacle, modernists (Cocteau and Satie being salient examples) often responded by emphasizing discordance rather than synthesis. By drawing on these internal dissonances among the visual, verbal, and auditory, these modernist texts dialectically unfold a dissonance between the artwork and its context. *Façade*, for example, draws on conflicting musical, visual, literary, and theatrical influences, to illustrate the Sitwells' own sense of social estrangement. The reciter of *Façade* patters nonsense rhymes through a megaphone invented for a performance of Wagner's *Siegfried*, from behind a curtain modeled on Satie's and Cocteau's anti-Wagnerian *Parade*. Its most conspicuous influence, Schoenberg's *Pierrot Lunaire*, is itself a fusion of atonal music, accompanying the *commedia dell'arte* Pierrot figure, expressed through (translated) French Symbolist poetry, intoned in *Sprechstimme* (speech-singing). If each of these components weren't adequate to express social and psychological alienation, the dissonances among them would do the trick. *Façade*, though it has no buzzers or air-raid sirens, loosely exhibits what Richard Grusin and Jay David Bolter call "hypermediacy": the form of "remediation" that "acknowledges multiple acts of representation and makes them visible" (or audible) (34), whereas what Matthew Smith calls the "iconic" Gesamtkunstwerk attempts to mask its means of production (the point that motivates chapter two). Many of the contemporary artworks appropriated in *Façade*, such as *Parade* and Stravinsky's *Petrushka* (1912), are just the kind of rhythmic, pranksterish, folksy work detested by Adorno, producing a post hoc dissonance among modernist conceptions of the social life of music and poetry. Each of these influences has its own history; to invoke them all at once is to create dissonant cultural resonances, and to mime a conflicted relation with artistic influence per se.

In that vein, Adorno and Eliot have different but mutually revealing positions on the relation between tradition and the individual, a question readily framed in terms of harmony (consonant or dissonant) and rhythm. A dissonance for Adorno and Eliot reflects a dialectical struggle with the past (whereas, for Adorno, rhythm reflects an undialectical reduplication of it). Eliot's "Tradition and the Individual Talent," the classic modernist celebration of impersonality, posits a harmonic (not *harmonious*) relation between the poet and the poets before him. While the poet alters tradition through a "supervention of novelty," the order readjusts into consonance: "the relations, proportions, values of each work of art toward the whole are readjusted" to produce a "conformity between the old and the new." In this consonant homeostatic ecosystem, the introduction of novelty is balanced by a "readjust[ment]" into "order[ly]" stability and synthetic totality. Where Adorno emphasizes the need for a "new" artwork to shock the system, emphasizing the dissonant contradictions at the heart of tradition, Eliot emphasizes totalizing resolution and synthesis.

Notwithstanding this distinction, both figures exemplify the tension between the "really new" and the falsely new, as between the organically developed dissonance and the plopped-in funky chord. This tension pivots on the "supervention of novelty" in relation to a broader system of ideas or problems to be solved. Both Adorno and Eliot evaluate the qualitative nature of consonance or dissonance as the site of an ongoing struggle, not only between tradition and talent, but between the artist and his own material—the place where the artist strains against the limits of what he can articulate ("That is not what I meant at all./That is not it, at all").[56] Adorno and Eliot hear music not as ineffable, but as a confrontation with the unspeakable, a reflection of language as it self-destructs. For Eliot, the way to grapple with this tension, and to allow the order to work its magic, is for the poet to "surrender" his personality to "something which is more valuable. The progress of an artist is a continual self-sacrifice, a continual extinction of personality." Rather than a personality, Eliot writes, the poet has a "medium"—a suggestive word implying poetry as a depersonalized transmission of experience, composing through the valuable order into which it seeks entry. For Eliot, the rhythmic movement of an "auditory imagination" further allows the poet to recombine his own emotions, and the tradition itself, so that the dissonance of the order can resolve.

Dissonance, at least the good kind, digests and interrogates the music that came before it. For Adorno, Schoenberg has the related merit of struggling with musical tradition so as to "gain insight into challenges which remain unresolved and which left flaws behind in the music."[57] This is a materialist mediation of what was in fact a more Eliotic notion of tradition. Schoenberg, as Lydia Goehr writes, positioned atonal music in "a continuous relation to the tonal tradition" of Bach, Beethoven, and Brahms, claiming that "this tradition develops logically according to eternal aesthetic laws dictating principles of form, unity, coherence, comprehensibility, and beauty . . . . Atonal music . . . solves all the problems—harmonic, formal, orchestral, and emotional—tonality created" (226). An actively creative reader of Schoenberg, Adorno ascribes historical qualities to the formal innovations of atonality, making the confrontation with tradition symptomatic of music's social alienation. This tendency leads him to refuse the attempts of different musical traditions, in which art does *not* consider itself alienated from the social, to solve musical problems of their own.

Though many musicians would blanch at endowing their dissonances with an imitative or literal meaning, musical theorists and cultural musicologists after Adorno continue to probe the import of specific dissonances in specific historical moments. In a polemical revision of the "decidedly Gentile" realm of historical musicology, Alexander Ringer argues that Schoenberg's assiduous formalism, including his fight-to-the-death with tonality, was a "condition of inner survival" as a turn-of-the-century Viennese Jew. Hence Ringer analogizes Schoenberg's emancipation of musical dissonance to an emancipation of "historical dissonances"—his refusal to capitulate to anti-Semitic political authority or to assimilate culturally.[58] As much as art "seeks an order," dissonance can resist deceptive reconciliation with a mythic integrity or with the ossification of political binaries.[59] As Daniel Melnick writes, quoting Adorno, dissonance is "a key modernist strategy designed to oppose and overcome what he calls 'the deceptive moment' . . . in which the 'self-limited' audience is made to feel 'in accord with all, accepted and reconciled by all,'" and is thereby "trained to consent."[60] For Adorno, the deceptive reconciliation is often marked by rhythmic conformity, the point that will close this chapter. Other modernists believe rhythm to have its own destabilizing power. If dissonance was often imagined to embody an oppositional or opaque relation to mass culture, rhythm was imagined to put that critique, for good or ill, into more legible relation with the passage of historical time. And inasmuch as it points toward the patterns of culture, rhythm opens music up to the sort of cultural history of modernism that I wish to pursue.

The Rhythms of Modernist Culture

Whereas dissonance, oppositional and hard to describe, tends to be talked about in coded terms, rhythm is among the most oft-cited phenomena in modern literary aesthetics. E.M. Forster announces rhythm as a chief aspiration of the modern novel, and Stephen Dedalus declares it the chief formal relation between part and whole. Eisenstein uses rhythm to explain montage, Roger Fry uses rhythm to describe Matisse, Wallace Stevens searches for the "rhythm of this celestial pantomime," and Pound for the "absolute rhythm" of the Great Bass. John Middleton Murry's avant-garde periodical *Rhythm* tries to measure the pulse of post-Impressionist literature and art; precisely such an artist, Lily Briscoe in Woolf's *To the Lighthouse* (1927), experiences the process of artistic creation itself as a "rhythm . . . strong enough to bear her along with it on its current." In Brecht's *Mother Courage and her Children* (1939), Kattrin's drumbeat warning against the invading Catholic armies merges into noises of cannon fire, and of her own firing squad. For Adorno and Horkheimer, modernity is defined by "the rhythm of the iron system."[61] In "Politics and the English Language" (1946), George Orwell critiques "ready-made" phrases as the last resort of those who prize euphony over precision: "If you use ready-made phrases, you . . . don't have to bother with the rhythms of your sentences since these phrases are generally so arranged as to be more or less euphonious."[62] One might even read this as the theme of Joyce's "Cyclops," in which the Citizen's nationalist boilerplate is too easily unleashed. The relation between rhythm and tribal "savagery," an *idée fixe* of "primitivist" music such as Stravinsky's, is detectable in Marlow's confounding of "the beat of the drum with the beating of [his] heart" (and the "rhythmically clinking" line of enslaved Africans) in *Heart of Darkness*.[63] Marlow's auto-auscultation signals both his solipsistic withdrawal and his anxieties about "the conquest of the earth," twin resonances of Conrad's desire to make the literary subject matter audible in the bodies of its characters and in the material of the text. Fascinated by the nervous energies of the modern metropolis, by the imagined energies of the primal, by the creative energies of jazz, ragtime, ballet, and the music hall, modernists constantly interrogate the implications of organizing sounds to a beat, and ask who gets to set the tempo.[64]

Adorno's represents a provocative articulation of the strand of modernist thought that conceives of rhythmic music as obedience or conformity.[65] He fears, among other things, the imitative properties of rhythm, which too easily syncs up with the rhythms of labor or the beat of the culture industry. One can detect such thinking in the "Malthusian Blues" and whizz-clicking conveyor belts of Aldous Huxley's *Brave New World* (1932), rhythms that represent an authoritarian controlling of subversive noises, but that in other contexts produce noise that deadens and assaults the sensorium. In *The Perennial Philosophy* (1944), Huxley describes a modern "Age of Noise"—an "assault on silence" comprising "a babel of distractions—news items, mutually irrelevant bits of information, blasts of corybantic or sentimental music, continually repeated doses of drama that bring no catharsis, but merely create a craving for daily or even hourly emotional enemas."[66] Referring to "daily or even hourly" regularity, Huxley invokes the ritual, "corybantic" music produced on schedule. This is a deeply Adornian passage at heart, especially when read beside *Brave New World*, suggesting that popular music deadens its auditors to the consolidation of power. As Michael Golston details, developing pseudo-scientific discourses associated with rhythm in the early twentieth century became mobilized in the service of racial science. The discourses of rhythm promiscuously migrating among poetry, industry, and science forged "a theoretical means through which to blend psychology and politics—to politicize the body while 'embodying' the state."[67]

Hence rhythm maps a range of anxieties about what the body is, how it moves, and to whom its motive energy belongs; the modernist heard in rhythm a conflicted uncertainty about the broader patterns of historical time. Osbert Sitwell, who heard in the rhythmic musical landscape both an ersatz *joie de vivre* and a nostalgic Wagnerian idealism, echoes Adorno's cynicism toward the fascist reversal of civilization:

> In the evenings the houses of the great squares of London opened their doors; light poured out from the balconies, and with it came the music of the waltz; for jazz only began, with such tunes as "Everybody's Doing It" and "Alexander's Rag-Time Band", in 1910 or 1911. The world anticipated no future but a continued steady progress, although one of the questions most frequently put to a dancing partner was "Can you reverse?" There can, I think, be no doubt that civilization itself is proving triumphantly that it *can* reverse. . . . The old, kindly German of

> Bach and of Mozart is dead, and the Wagner lovers have reaped their reward in the revival of a boisterous and fictitious past.[68]

The promise of constant progress, paired with the fantasy of a holistic past, are made to represent two of the twentieth century's great delusions: the triumph of reason and the speculative search for a mythological origin. "Can you reverse?" is a central modernist question; Sitwell's reformulation of it, like Edith Sitwell's rhythmic *Façade*, pins the violence of modern "progress" to the sped-up heartbeats of music and poetry, giving a physical pulse to a range of speculative historical problems. Can we resist the violent pace of modern progress? Should we? Is progress really "progress"? Can we calculate the pulse of modern machinery to "reverse" to an authentic set of rituals?

What makes rhythm especially useful for many of these figures, portentous for others, is its insidious propensity to naturalize. Hanslick, for example, makes rhythm the "animating principle of music," the only element of musical form that can be traced back to nature; though harmony and melody evolved through compositional theory and practice; the one natural element that music inherits is rhythm: "the gallop of the horse, the clatter of the mill, the song of blackbird and quail," and most of all, "the law of duple rhythm, rise and fall, to and fro" (69). Hanslick refers not only to small-scale rhythms but to a macrorhythmic "co-proportionality of a symmetrical structure" (28)—a means of structuring music's natural material. Such material, Hanslick asserts, can be found in non-Western ritual customs that don't quite rise to his level of musical beauty: "When the South Sea Islander bangs rhythmically with bits of metal and wooden staves and along with it sets up an intelligible wailing, this is the natural kind of 'music,' yet it just is not *music*" (70, his italics). Cowell could scarcely have put it better —in fact, he implicitly moves from Hanslick's natural property, rhythm, to something more elemental yet: noise-sounds, mechanically calculated and "primitive" in origin.

Perversely, then, rhythm seemed *calculated* to make itself seem *natural* (hence Brecht's desire to defamiliarize it).[69] While Adorno replaces Hanslick's notion of natural musical material with the notion of history, of politics dialectically developed in form, he nonetheless finds Hanslick's categories compelling. It is microrhythmic innovation (syncopation) that Adorno finds unsound and "atomistic," whereas the organic, immanently produced structural rhythm of music (as in Schoenberg) enables individual dissonances to assert themselves. Given Hanslick's notion that rhythm is not just naturally sourced but "the earliest [musical element] to develop in children and animals," it is no surprise to see Adorno describe Stravinsky's rhythmic music as childish, or to see *Façade* using Stravinskian music and images to idealize the childlike.[70] Adorno objects to any such search for a prepolitical origin for music, and resents even more the rationalized conceptual (rather than immanent) justifications for its rhythms of choice.[71]

As modernists try to piece together the poietic and esthesic effects of music as it circulates, acquires semiotic meaning, and acquires cultural capital, they find themselves contending with the rhythms of commerce. Adorno is not devoid of paranoia, but he is not inventing things in associating rhythm with the structures of capitalism. An 1896 volume by the Swiss anthropologist Karl Bücher, *Labor and Rhythm* (*Arbeit und Rhythmus*) links the rhythms of poetry and music to the bodily movements of labor. Bücher argued that the "joyous work" of "primitive cultures," which he observed at the 1889 World Exhibition in Paris, was "diametrically opposed to the alienated labor of modern industrial societies."[72] Bücher's critique of Taylorist economics led him to argue that the rhythms of machines needed to match those of the human body: as Golston writes, quoting Bücher, "industrial machinery alienates human labor because it does not operate at a human tempo; on the other hand, large-scale, 'uniformizing' ('einformige') work is of 'the greatest benefit for a person, so long as he can determine the tempo of his bodily movements'" (22). The hope is that the rhythms of man and machine can be synchronized, the joy of work rehabilitated.

Hence when Pound describes *Ballet Mécanique* as a basis for reorganizing the factory, such that a worker's experience of labor leaves him exhilarated, he benefits from a cultural cliché that tries to attune rhythm to the natural patterns of the body. And while Adorno surely did not know Pound's *Antheil* monograph, it may put Adorno's critique of rhythm on firmer ground, relating the pulse of modernist music to the routines of capital. The Pound/Antheil axis represents each of the two, false forms of rationalization that Adorno hears in the rhythms of "primitivism": a positivistic search for the origins of music and, at the same time, a pretext for capitalist domination. Adorno's and Horkheimer's *Dialectic of Enlightenment* (1946) underscores the association of music with the rhythms of labor—a connection that grounds their critique of instrumental reason and of the "culture industry" in the structures of ancient myth: "For the vanquished . . . , the recurrent, eternally similar natural processes become the rhythm of labor according to the beat of cudgel and whip which resounds in every barbaric drum and every monotonous ritual" (21). Thus the "dread" communicated by these rhythms comes to be treated as a permanent state of being, an illusion of fixity on which power relies. As a result, amusement becomes another kind of labor, where pleasure "moves rigorously in worn grooves of association" (137).

Along similar lines, Georg Simmel identifies rhythm as the organizing principle of urban mental experience, under the increasingly violent ebb and flow of commodity culture: "With every crossing of the street, with the tempo and multiplicity of economic, occupational and social life—[the metropolis] creates in the sensory foundations of mental life, and . . . a deep contrast with the slower, more habitual, more smoothly flowing rhythm of the sensory-mental phase of small town and rural existence."[73] Callused by the numbingly static and "telescoping" rhythms of exchange, the modern subject in the metropolis grows "blasé," indifferent, and uncritical. Amplifying Simmel's account, Walter Benjamin's rangy essay "On Some Motifs in Baudelaire" (1939) pursues the use of rhythm to mark the relation between art and context. Drawing on Simmel, on Baudelaire's channeling of Paris's "shocks and collisions" into lyric, and on Proust's rhythmical perorations on mental life, Benjamin insists that film can be marshaled in dialectical critique of its own means of production: that the rhythms of montage, absorbed by an urban audience, can dilate the equally rhythmic pulses of capitalist labor. Benjamin suggests an abiding belief in the ability of politicized mass art to expose the historical rhythms underpinning the fragmentary shocks of urban modernity.

This belief laid Benjamin's account open to Adorno's critique that the essay "lacked mediation": that it failed to account for the internal formal laws of art itself, equating "the pragmatic contents of Baudelaire's work directly . . . to adjacent features in the social history"; and that it remained naïve about the commensurability of the torn halves of "high" and "mass art." For Adorno, overtly political mass art loses its diagnostic potential; marching to the same beat it portends to destabilize, it reinforces the unity between language and concept, rather than unfolding a more constellational temporality. The effort to rediscover that integral freedom through kitschy primitivism was, for Adorno, a new kind of cynical positivism—a childish, and ultimately joyless, musical science project. Rather, a work of art ought to follow its own "structural rhythm" and to acquire a critical "inner historicity" by virtue of its detachment from "the means-end rationality" of daily life; in turn, the critic should surrender to the internal laws and sensations of the artwork rather than subjecting them to rigid conceptual mastery.

Benjamin, however, posits a more transparent rhythmic back-and-forth between production and reception: "That which determines the rhythm of production on a conveyor belt is the basis of the rhythm of reception in a film." This transparency, this sympathy with the potential of rhythm to transmit narrative and to defamiliarize the "shocks and collisions" of the city, corresponds with an optimism about cultural solidarity (whereas the dissonant Adorno fears solidarity more than most anything). For Lukács, aesthetic autonomy produces decadent modernist writing, all noise and no signal: solipsistic monologues and unselective catalogues, without a redemptive narrative drive that accords with the "rhythm of cultural progress." Williams, whose passage on the ability of rhythm to "transmit" narratives is a new-musicological commonplace, argues hopefully that art can be "reintegrat[ed] . . . with the common life of society." These critiques remain challenging; I shall continue to draw on them. Yet there is much to Adorno's insistence—obvious when highlighted, but easily forgotten in practice—that the rhythm of a film is not the rhythm of a conveyor belt, but a mediation of its contradictions; likewise, the noises of art are nonidentical refractions of the noises of culture, mediated by the form of even the noisiest work of art. I now turn to *The Waste Land*—a poem obsessed with the productive frictions among different forms of music, whose drives to "add up" the torn halves of culture are disrupted by noise at every turn.

Beating Obedient, Thinking of the Key

Adorno, *The Waste Land*, and the Total Work of Art

DA
Damyata: The boat responded
Gaily, to the hand expert with sail and oar
The sea was calm, your heart would have responded
Gaily, when invited, beating obedient
To controlling hands

Eliot, *The Waste Land*, V.418–23

The whole is the false.

Adorno, *Minima Moralia*, 50

If Eliot, Stravinsky, Wagner, Marie Lloyd, Irving Berlin, Prospero and Ariel, and the writers of the "Shakespearian Rag" (Gene Buck and Dave Stamper) all walked into a bar, the result would be something like *The Waste Land*: the Grail Legend of which could have come straight from Wagner, which quotes "high" and popular music with abandon, and which misses no opportunity to gesture to the soundscape. Eliot's poem offers my opening exploration of how dissonance and rhythm, in mediating an array of musical allusions, give voice to contradictory social formations—how music, to requote Eliot, can seem to "transform the rhythm of the steppes into the scream of the motor horn, the rattle of machinery, the grind of wheels, and the other barbaric cries of modern life; and to transform these despairing noises into music." Eliot's urge to structure the modern soundscape, to resolve it back into homeostatic order, leads him to "surrender" to a unifying pulse or vibration, "beating obedient/To controlling hands" of "expert" authority—of a conductor, a composer, an authoritarian Prospero figure who polices illusions of wholeness.

Without pulse, there is no compulsion—the same root propels them both. This, in a phrase, is my argument about Eliot's *Waste Land*. As the poem's final lines accumulate to a series of rhythmic incantations (DA DA DA; Shantih Shantih Shantih; Give, Sympathize, Control), Eliot's final downbeats, like an orchestra conductor, keeps everyone rowing at the same time and propels them forward. Eliot's effort to find rhythmic and harmonic resolution continually reveals itself as, indeed, a compulsion: a neurotic exertion of power, whose rhythms try to insinuate themselves as natural. Eliot's compulsory rhythms continually unbind and revise themselves as they encounter the noises, dissonances, and broken-down bodies subjected to control.

Rhythm, as I have suggested, has a range of contradictory cultural functions: Adorno hears it as the sound of hegemonic discipline; Williams as the physical performance of cultural patterns, which transmits experience "not merely as an 'abstraction' or an 'emotion' but as a physical effect on the organism." As I have also suggested, rhythm is heard to make patterns of speaking, singing, and living seem natural rather than violently historical. We see this in Antheil's call to how jazz recuperates the body "not yet exploded by shrapnel," in Hanslick's excavation of rhythm as music's natural source, and in Adorno's critique of how rhythm naturalizes patterns of labor. Adorno claimed that Wagner formalized this problem in his "phantasmagoria": a term borrowed (after Marx) from the magic lantern shows, which projected optical illusions and ghostly images in darkened theaters (cf. Prufrock's nervous "magic lantern" and screen).[1] Wagner's total artwork, Adorno argued, strove compulsively to mask his means of production: to hide the mechanics of the total artwork by darkening the lights and making the orchestra invisible. Through the binding macrorhythms of his dramas, Adorno further contended, Wagner presented his total artwork as a state of nature rather than as the technological, massively expensive production that it was. The central contradiction of the phantasmagoric total artwork, as Matthew Smith puts it, is that the "more it aims to realize nature, the more it must utilize the machine" (*Total* 35).

This point applies no less to Eliot's return to the Ganges at the end of *The Waste Land*, a site of healing that allows the ailing Fisher King to "set [his] lands in order." The poem merges this holy healing site with Wagner's Rhine, Eliot's Thames, and Conrad's Congo: producing both a flowing sonic monochord that hierarchizes different categories of sound, and a dissonant destabilization of Wagner's chthonic mythologies. If Wagner and Eliot propose natural solutions to the violence of modernity, Adorno helps us to see these solutions as illusory compulsions: efforts to make the contingent and political seem permanent and ontological. Through immanent analysis that unfolds into cultural history, I will argue that the poem's own sonic practices —its disjunctive rhythms, poetic dissonances, and noises—fragment this naturalizing "phantasmagoria" and expose its historicity.

In *The Waste Land*, rhythm serves on one hand to consolidate and bind: to create an aesthetic totality, to approximate the teleological Will, to hierarchize sounds within a monochord, to produce a self-enclosed "record" archiving the vast panorama of noises. On the other hand, rhythmic syncopation serves to disrupt and unbind: to precipitate the noises sublimated into totality; to destabilize the sublime vibrations of the Will and the autonomy of "high" art; to indicate skips in the poem's archival record. The poem's hope is that rhythm, even as it disciplines mind and body, can pull us into an interactive, authentic, and liberating relation with the stage/text: that by surrendering ourselves to sympathy with a performer, we enter into a more critical relation with his or her cultural frame. The same rhythms that discipline noise into art can enable its performative reinvention; if rhythm, like Ariel, polices us, we can at least (as the poem's original title suggested) "do the police in different voices."[2] What Eliot called the "auditory imagination"—an excavation of the historical resonances of sound through dissonance, rhythm, and noise—seeks an illusion of healing wholeness, only to see it unbound into an Adornian constellation: a range of experiences that resist being reduced to a singular identitarian concept.

I thus offer *The Waste Land* as a rhythmic assertion of the "new musicology" *avant la lettre*. I present less a singular reading of the poem than a constellation of its resonances with Adorno and Wagner, figures who share in Eliot's anxious compulsion to yoke into musical shape the raw sonic material of the world. I thereby consider, in relation to Eliot's musical landscape, what cultural implications those yokings might have. Keeping in mind Williams's embrace of rhythm as a transmission of cultural narratives, I argue that the poem unpacks what Hutcheon and Hutcheon call music's "cultural . . . mathematics" (69): the shared social knowledge that conditions our responses to sound, that helps us to form and to recognize cultural clichés, and that helps us to parse music from noise, Wagner from Stravinsky, and good (if tame) versions of ragtime (Berlin's "That Mysterious Rag") from bad ones (Stamper and Buck's "Shakespearian Rag").

There are, moreover, as many different Wagners as there are performances of Wagner. In a poem like *The Waste Land* where the same line is spoken/sung many times in many contexts, we hear "resonances" in Abbate's sense—as moments where "intertextual echoes" are realized in the "assaults [on] our senses in a particular here-and-now," such that these same echoes, put to a rhythmic pulse, dialectically constellate what Middleton refers to as homologous "forms of social organization."

That music is *The Waste Land*'s organizing principle is not news. What I.A. Richards called the poem's "music of ideas" permeates early New Critical responses to the poem; in different form, it shapes Juan Suárez's media-centered account of the "discourse network" triangulating the sounds of opera, the music hall, poetry, thunder, birdsong, street noise, and the other "barbaric cries of modern life." And David Chinitz has cagily shown how Eliot's interest in music destabilizes the too-strict High/Low cultural divide retroactively attributed to him.[3] In Edmund Wilson's judgment (which I share), even the reader least prepared for Eliot's intellectual flamboyance is likely to be seduced by the "new personal rhythm" in his language, which "lent even to the words of his great predecessors a new music and a new meaning."[4] In Clive Bell's view (which I do not share), Eliot's abstract poetic intellect was corrupted by jazzy impudence. Eliot even suggested that the chorus of his melodrama *Sweeney Agonistes* (1932) could be accompanied by "light drum taps to accentuate the beats, especially the chorus which ought to have a noise like a street drill"—a suggestion almost as well suited to *The Waste Land*'s choric explosions.[5]

The Waste Land can be heard not only to put the noises of modernity to a beat, but to have an internal grating among its dissonant component parts. I take it as exemplary that Adorno's *Aesthetic Theory*, a grating text in many respects, uses a noise metaphor to explain how art's critical value grows out of its internal fractures: "What crackles in artworks is the sound of the friction of the antagonistic elements that the artwork seeks to unify" (234). In particular, Wagner's total artwork, attempting to unify discontinuous narrative, musical, dramatic, technological, and embodied elements, exemplified a drive to total artistic integration that could not help but crackle as its discontinuities inevitably revealed themselves. *The Waste Land*, though seeking to unify these antagonisms, likewise bristles with mediated noises and rhythmic jolts that are not quite pacified. *The Waste Land* mimics not only Wagner's drives to totality and holism, but its contradictions—in particular, the total artwork's phantasmagoric masking of its means of production as it creates an illusion of natural prehistory.

The Waste Land anticipates, moreover, Adorno's belief that modern art's utopianism lies not in its sublimity, but in its "stigmata of the repulsive and loathsome" (*AT* 32-3)[6]—in the recognition that true reconciliation is impossible under the commodity logic that reduces lived sensations to packaged wholes. This paradox is made palpable by Wagner's and Eliot's shrieking voice-objects and damaged bodies, the "barbaric cries" that the poem tries and fails to pacify. Mediating these shrieks through its dissonances and syncopes, *The Waste Land* stages the jarring bodily responses subjected to these forms of discipline. Just as Attali calls noise the symptom of "essential violence," Eliot, in moments of crackling sonic rupture, defamiliarizes the intrinsic compulsions of artistic creation.

Eliot's music of ideas cannot simply be packaged either as ineffable music or as one cohesive idea. To call *The Waste Land* a Gesamtkunstwerk is reductive only if one buys into the phantasmagoric logic of organic holism—not if one attends to what these total artworks have signified in theory and practice. The total artwork, understood through Eliot and Adorno, mediates a range of contradictory resonances: a return to nature ostentatiously produced by technology; an embrace of autonomous high art in the service of a unified culture; a critique of the urban marketplace underwritten (as Rainey argues) by an effort to create a commodity space for art; and a search for an idealist theatrical illusion, for "fear in a handful of dust," that is grounded in the hard facts of the body. Fascinated with the potential of musical sound to mediate the noise of its surroundings, aware of both the allure and the threat of embodiment at the heart of music, *The Waste Land*'s urges to control its materials leave it without any form of sound, musical or otherwise, that is not tinctured by violence.

Constellating *The Waste Land*

This chapter maps several functions of rhythmic "binding," as the poem transmits the fragmentary experiences of music and noise, while luring us into a narcotized illusion of wholeness. I resist the critical inclination, identified by Rainey, to give the poem a unified Aristotelian narrative. This ambivalence motivates my resistance to a linear argument in this chapter, both because I agree with Adorno that there is something toxic about the worship of wholeness per se; and because the conflicting cultural mathematics of *The Waste Land* make Eliot's new illusion untenable, exposed as a contradictory artifact of history and not as a timeless Traditional order.

Rather, Eliot's use of music unpacks what Adorno called the compulsion of self-sameness (*Identitätszwang*): the "will-to-identity," a compulsion to reduce experiences to integrative concept-based thinking that corresponds to the rigid limits of the bourgeois ego. For Adorno, the bourgeois subject, seeking stable identification with a stable artwork, is driven to reduce away the artwork's contradictory experiences and social practices, at the expense of exactly what remains unthinkable to instrumental reason.[7] Eliot likewise seeks a form of art that, rather than reaching for stable identitarian allegories, transmits the dissonant experience of shock in real time—rhythmically, as Williams would have it, "as a physical effect on the organism."[8] As *The Waste Land* denaturalizes its own rhythms and renders them contingent, it also defamiliarizes Wagner's effort to mask his own artistic technologies; it in turn defamiliarizes the false unity of the bourgeois subject.

For Adorno, the false whole of the total artwork, an artifact of the bourgeois subject's reifying boundaries (and, as Smith argues after Habermas, of the nineteenth-century decline of the public sphere), was a phantasmagoric illusion attenuated by the dramas' ubiquitous noise and decay. Adorno, in the content of his analysis and in his negative-dialectical method, wished to unstitch the ostensibly self-sufficient formal properties of Wagner's music dramas—rhythm, leitmotif, harmonic modulation—in an effort to demystify their magical spell. It is this same spell in Eliot that calls for constellational unstitching; Eliot's total artwork is riven with Wagner's internal contradictions. *The Waste Land* may strive for Wagner's magical creation of the ideal inner world; but Eliot, like Wagner, knew that to pull off such a feat required massive technical chops. Thus while Margaret Dana writes that Eliot would have been interested in the Wagner of leitmotif and chromaticism, not the "manipulator of grandiose stage effects and hypnotic illusions,"[9] the cultural resonances of these illusions permeate the poem, in constellational arrangements, and are inseparable from the musical techniques that Eliot found compelling.

I assemble these constellating ideas through speculative close reading. Though conversant in materialist accounts of the poem that eschew close reading in favor of institutional histories, I maintain that the poem teaches us a species of immanent analysis through which music's formal patterns unfold social contradictions.[10] Such formal analysis—musical or literary, New Critical or deconstructive—unpacks, as Raymond Williams writes, the "forms of (changing) social organization" mediated by art. Art, Williams notes, gives us not "objects but *notations*," which must be "interpreted in an active way. . . . The relationship between the making of a work of art and its reception is always active, and subject to conventions, which in themselves are forms of (changing) social organization and relationship" (*CM* 47, his italics). Williams wanted none of Adorno's totalizing paranoia about the culture industry, but he shares with Adorno an urge to liberate the artwork: not just from commodification, but from a crudely Marxist model of production and consumption. By rendering noise in the artwork, by marshaling dissonance as a site of the artwork's internal contradictions, and by tracking rhythm as a transmission of cultural meaning, Eliot, Adorno, and Williams put the work in the "work of art," making it not just a created thing but an ongoing labor subject to historical shifts in production, performance, and reception.

I will begin by framing my categories for reading *The Waste Land* against Adorno: Eliot's attitudes toward the rhythmically totalizing auditory imagination, and Adorno's critique of Wagner's binding rhythms. The poet's auditory imagination, using rhythm to reconstruct a deep historical continuity, calls us to internalize the dissonances, rhythms, and cacophonies of music and poetry, and to understand them as part of a constantly readjusting order. In different ways, for Adorno and Eliot, these totalizing rhythms are destabilized by microrhythmic flux, damaged bodies, and textual dissonance, which can be detected from the poem's first lines.

I then proceed to the elements of this textual constellation through which Wagner's, Eliot's, and Adorno's false wholes are bound and unbound. I open with the matter of the high/low cultural divide, which frames much of the critical anxiety about both Adorno and Eliot, and which is too reductive for either. While Adorno's and Eliot's faith in art is tinged with skepticism about its commodification in the hands of the middle class, this skepticism is not limited to popular music. Adorno is terrorized by the fear that cynically manipulated music is being internalized as natural; for him and for Eliot, this problem applies no less to Stravinsky or Wagner. Indeed, for Eliot the music hall throws the passive digestion of music, "high" or "low," for a jolt. The too-strict allegiance in Eliot criticism to categories of high and low is troubled by the poem's merging of Wagner and the music hall; and troubled by the contradictory cultural politics of each of these figures unto itself. Wagner, autocratically binding and liberatory, and Marie Lloyd, a master craftsman who holds her *Volk* in thrall, together suggest that Eliot is exploring how music's illusory aesthetic hold is bound to its contradictory social elements. The poem's core example of popular stage music, a misquotation of a corny Ziegfeld Follies number ("The Shakespearian Rag"), shows not just Eliot's curiosity about mass culture, but his desire to rethink its reception in the hands of an audience.

To digest music actively, Eliot and Adorno both suggest, calls for a submission to its aesthetic experience, one that is forced to confront its critical aporia. Hence my second and perhaps most important claim is that while *The Waste Land* urges a "moment's surrender" to the "controlling hands" of rhythm, the poem ultimately denaturalizes rhythm, taking the natural ebb and flow of music and revealing it as fundamentally historical. The pseudo-organic false wholes within the poem—as in its gestures to *The Tempest*, woven into the holistic fabric of Madame Sosostris's prophecy—first create and then unbind the phantasmagoric total illusion of nature. A tapestry of false wholes, *The Waste Land* speaks to the artwork's phantasmagoric illusion of natural wholeness, and (as with Philomel's "Twit twit twit") punctures that illusion in disruptive moments of noise. In particular, Madame Sosostris's prophecy denaturalizes Schopenhauer's condition of music: an underlying noumenal truth that she articulates in grossly corrupted and hypermediated form.

Third: this noumenal illusion, materialized by musical rhythm, asserts a grip on the body. As *The Waste Land* quotes Wagner's *Götterdämmerung*, for example, it also adapts his *Stabreim*: a two-beat alliterative accentual measure (akin to Anglo-Saxon verse) that best approximates the "sound-language" (*Tonspräche*) of our linguistic roots, binding music and poetry to the third sister-art—bodily gesture. (Recall Fussell's assertion that accentual verse compels the heartbeat to keep up.) But the presence of illness, decay, and damage in Wagner's dramas, and in *The Waste Land*, herald the destruction of this binding rhythmic order, all the more so as these sites of disease resignify according to changing cultural mathematics. At multiple points, the poem's drive to "bind" minds, bodies, and cultural productions encounters the damaged life at its own center: violated and decaying corpses given sonic form by a constellation of dissonances, syncopes, and cacophonies. At these moments, the illusion of music as a natural rightness breaks down—binding *Stabreim* unbinds into noise—and we hear it instead as a manifestation of essential violence.

Finally, I will suggest that Wagner's "voice-objects" (Abbate's phrase) prepares an uneasy relationship in *The Waste Land* and in Adorno between the motions of the body and the grain of the recorded voice. Eliot binds Wagner's disease-ridden Schopenhauerian illusion to the typist's "record on the gramophone," tying the sublime choric imitation of Wagner to the concrete material that archives it.[11] The record, encoding noise, preserves the autonomy of each mass-reproduced record without reference to its authentic performative source—the operatic performances from which Adorno wished, in any event, to rescue the music. If the phonograph is a symptom of rationalized violence, Adorno suggests, it also archives that violence, as (in his analogy) a herbarium archives fossilized life. This archive becomes valuably disruptive as the mechanism of the gramophone starts to glitch and its crackling noisy static becomes audible. At these moments, the objective whole—the disembodied voice etched into wax, and the commodity fetish itself—starts to melt into something newly interpretive: into a script rather than an object. Friedrich Kittler has suggested that the phonograph made it possible for writing to exist without a subject; *The Waste Land* animates this contradiction by archiving the false holism of music and the decay of the subject coextensively.[12] As the record itself starts to skid, it unbinds the contradictions at its own center; it can "connect/Nothing with nothing" (*TWL* III.302).

These contradictions must be preserved to appreciate the full, fleshly resonance of Eliot's poetry. Reading Adorno and Eliot against each other, and against Wagner, tends to destabilize the poem's final reconciliation, defamiliarizing it as the false "promise" of a "new start" (*TWL* III.298). Eliot and Adorno both interrogate the categories of culture not as fixed allegorical concepts, but as the fluid transmission and reception of competing cultural narratives (and, in stage music, competing media). James Martin Harding identifies Adorno's own "penchant for totalizing concepts," such as the culture industry model, which deafen Adorno to the diverse cultural energies of jazz. Such concepts might well be destabilized by Eliot's more ecumenical ear.[13] Just as Adorno helps us to see Eliot's Wagnerian contradictions, Eliot's jazz clarifies where Adorno forgets his own skepticism of totality. For both Eliot and Adorno, music is fighting for its right to exist: fighting with the cultural and technological landscape, and with other music. This discussion begins with Eliot's writings on music and poetry, which begin to unfold his thinking about how the sounds of music (or musical poetry) carry meaning in dissonant relation to other cultural productions.

Eliot's Dissonances: "The Music of Poetry" and the "Auditory Imagination"

Eliot shares in Adorno's embrace of organic rhythm: the notion that the individual, figural rhythms of the text should add up to the "whole rhythm" of a form. In "The Music of Poetry" (1942), Eliot suggests that poems should create a "rhythm of fluctuating emotion" between individual "passages of greater and less intensity." Eliot tentatively differentiates poetry from music, suggesting that "We can be deeply stirred by hearing the recitation of a poem in a language of which we understand no word; but if we are then told that the poem is gibberish and has no meaning, we shall consider that we have been deluded—this was no poem, it was merely an imitation of instrumental music" (30). "We" may mistake the phonemes of words for poetry, or we may learn that their lack of semantic content identifies them as imitations of music, calling to mind the distaste for the imitative model of musical meaning. Eliot suggests that being "deeply stirred" is not a critical response; music structures "fluctuating emotions" into a whole, rather than merely describing them, but needs also to help the reader absorb meaning. For Eliot the music of poetry creates consonances or dissonances not only of sound but of association: "The music of a word . . . arises from its relation first to the words immediately preceding and following it, and indefinitely to the rest of its context; and from another relation, that of its immediate meaning in that context to all the other meanings which it has had in other contexts, to its greater or less wealth of association"[14] (32–3). Art should aspire not to an imitation of music, but to a musical organization of meanings *and* sounds—to the "music of poetry."

Eliot claims that "dissonance, even cacophony, has its place," that all-too-common merging of dissonance and noise (32). No gesture here is made to what dissonance might signify (the question of signification is largely avoided). But the associations that accrue to a cacophony is sure to test the tightly bound limits of the text, what Adorno calls the "unshakably self-assertive form" of a total work of art. To understand that wealth of association, in other words, is to become well-versed in different kinds of cultural mathematics. Importantly, Eliot wishes to avoid "an imitation of *instrumental* music," not of opera; perhaps something like Wagnerian leitmotif, in which music is directly associated with gestural, verbal, and symbolic meaning, would suggest a poetic "figure" as well as a musical one. For Eliot, poetic rhythm (both micro- and macro-) creates and transmits effects of consonance and dissonance, but in Eliot as in Wagner this produces a figure in the artwork that can just as easily shake the externally binding whole as submit to it.

Eliot's conflation of dissonance and cacophony bespeaks (by his own admission) a limited technical knowledge of music, but it is not unprecedented—one finds the same conflation in Russolo. Eliot's technical uncertainty is matched, moreover, by his poetic engagement with the sounds of culture, which the rhythms of language have absorbed. As he puts noise into play with the dissonances and cacophonies of language, he calls on cultural clichés: commonplaces that reveal what meanings our music and language have taken in, and inform how those meanings recirculate. Dissonance and cacophony, cliché and novel formulation, all draw language into a deeper historical awareness in what Eliot, in an essay on Matthew Arnold (1933), calls the "auditory imagination": "the feeling for syllable and rhythm, penetrating far below the conscious levels of thought and feeling, invigorating every word; sinking to the most primitive and forgotten, returning to the origin and bringing something back, seeking the beginning and the end. It works through meanings, certainly, or not without meanings in the ordinary sense, and fuses the old and obliterated and the trite, the current, and the new and surprising, the most ancient and the most civilized mentality."[15] The auditory imagination, described, like his celebration of *Le Sacre*, as an interpenetration of ancient and modern, calls on a rhythmic movement through aesthetic, historical, and cultural meaning, excavating also what has been "obliterated." For Eliot, Arnoldian disinterest, taste and authority fail to "go deep enough" in their inability to hear history in the rhythms of language; without this imagination, Arnold was "so conscious of what . . . poetry was *for*, that he could not altogether see it for what it is" (111–2, his italics). Rather, the symmetrical rhythmic structure of art (also Hanslick's "animating principle" of music) allows poetry both to probe the unconscious and to map out what it is that makes culture alive. Like Wagner, who uses rhythmic gimmicks like *Stabreim* to excavate a "primitive and forgotten" unconscious, the auditory fusion of experiences requires not just access to Arnold's "best that is thought," but movement to "beneath the thought," an ear for the physically and psychologically naturalized experience.

The Waste Land's clichés are reanimated by, but highly resistant to, Eliot's Wagnerian attempt at totalizing aesthetic and auditory "fus[ion]." Cleanth Brooks noted in his seminal 1937 reading of the poem that it takes the "mass of *clichés*" representative of Christianity in modern life and "renew[s] and vitaliz[es]" them through "violent and radical" ironies and complexities (210, his italics). We needn't resurrect and re-bury Brooks, like Eliot's Hanged Man, to find this point both fundamentally clarifying and in need of a historical jolt. The poem, in its expansive auditory and musical range, seems to me intensely self-aware about how its clichés invite formal and historical modes of reading working at productive cross-purposes. Eliot's effort to run the currents of irony, paradox, and complexity through musical clichés opens itself up to a two-stepping dialectic between Adornian and Williamsian modes of reading, noting both the larger cultural patterns at stake, and the tensions that result from their dialectical mediation into art. Such a two-step also echoes the alternating forward and backward motion that animates *The Waste Land*, and that makes the poem resistant to being critically asserted with a pin. The cultural clichés that Hutcheon and Hutcheon associate with disease and embodiment are integrated into complex relation with the poem's allegories of spiritual healing; yet they also reassert themselves as inarticulate disruptions of the poem's drives for rhythmic reintegration.

If Eliot's essayistic use of the term "dissonance" here is a bit tentative, his poetic dissonances are subtler, as in *The Waste Land*'s opening:

> April is the cruellest month, breeding
> Lilacs out of the dead land, mixing
> Memory and desire, stirring
> Dull roots with spring rain.
> Winter kept us warm, covering
> Earth in forgetful snow, feeding
> A little life with dried tubers. (I.1-7)

Without being too literal in moving between musical and poetic sound, I suggest that these lines offer effects of verbal dissonance to match its effect of cognitive dissonance (between the Chaucerian April and the cruel Eliotic one), the most jarring being the fourth and seventh lines: the words "dried tubers" clash sonically, as well as cognitively, with the expected resolution. Eliot mimics the form of a musical period (an antecedent cadence followed by a consequent one), both of whose cadences end in dissonances. The limping trochaic rhythm of the lines merits attention as well, beginning on strong syllables and ending on weak ones, suggesting a pattern of retreat rather than resolution. Both sonically and semantically, those infamous participles intensify the anticipation of a resolution—ultimately, an anticlimactic one, as the "period" ends with desiccation.

Michael Levenson has read these opening lines as the artifact of a fluid consciousness—in particular, of a decaying corpse—suggesting that the stability of the ego itself is under duress.[16] Much as Adorno suggests, bodily decay threatens the stability of the healthful total package. In the opening lines, even before the disease has gotten ugly, the total artwork opens in a sensory abyss, marked by visual confusion (a "heap of broken images") and auditory death (a "dry stone" that offers "no sound of water"). In the "hyacinth girl" passage, the quiet intimacy of the opening implodes into abysmal silence, punctuated with Wagner:

> I could not
> Speak, and my eyes failed. I was neither
> Living nor dead, and I knew nothing.
> Looking into the heart of light, the silence.
> *Öd und leer das Meer*. (I.38–42)

From the "dead land," the poem offers the sound of water in the form of an allusion to *Tristan und Isolde*, "*Öd und leer das Meer*" ("The sea is empty and desolate"). Having nothing to say, this zombie sings a line from Wagner, but the music that emerges out of this abyss amplifies its disillusionment. Music-drama does not cure the "heap of broken images," but piles Wagnerian sensory excess onto it. Just as the most memorable portions of *The Waste Land* are those that illustrate rather than redress nihilistic fragmentation, Wagner leaves one stunned into silence: Eliot replaces a heart of darkness with a "heart of light," a "silence" that collapses Wagner's visual and sonic streams.

Eliot's search for a primal auditory imagination presents the dark and desolate Wagnerian sea (from 1865) as an auditory-imaginative analogue to Arnold's "Sea of Faith" (1867), "retreating" with a "long, withdrawing roar" ("Dover Beach," l. 21–5). In a gesture to "Dover Beach" ("The sea is calm tonight"), *The Waste Land* closes by embracing the heartbeat's subjection to discipline and control: "The sea was calm; your heart would have responded/Gaily." Confronted with anarchic chaos, *The Waste Land* reaches back to the abysmal seas of Arnold and of Wagner, perhaps even to Baudelaire's "Man and the Sea," seeking a primal source of poetic feeling, not merely Arnoldian "certitude." Eliot does not dismiss the Arnoldian moral purchase of art, but tries, like Baudelaire, rhythmically to insinuate it. Eliot transmits two dissonant seas that cope differently with the loss of certainty ("and I knew nothing") and binds them, not erasing their distinctions: as the opening dissonances establish a communicative fault line ("I could say nothing"), they establish competing resolutions both through the unconscious auditory imagination and through conscious belief in the secular religion of art.

As with any invocation of Arnold (or any monochordal corralling of noise), the question is how Eliot's order takes on hierarchical values, in the drive not only to erect an order but to naturalize it and urge our surrender to its beat. How does *The Waste Land* differentiate among the trite and the ordinary when trying to orchestrate them into objective shape? These contradictions are internal to the figure of Wagner himself. If *The Waste Land* betrays ambivalence about the categories of high and low by letting Wagner and Lloyd share the stage, it is no less ambivalent about the relations to class and commerce signified by each individually. "Torn halves of an integral freedom to which . . . they do not add up," popular art and "high art" gesture to the same illusion of cultural-aesthetic wholeness that, when pasted back together, crackle in apprehension.

Adorno, Wagner, and the Cultural Divide

Accompanied by the Prelude to *Das Rheingold*—the opening elaboration of one single chord that mimics the creation of the world—a 2010 Levi's ad ("Go Forth to Work") shows a scene of postrecession Braddock, Pennsylvania, reemerging out of the soil. A child's voice instructs us: "A long time ago, things got broken here. People got sad and left. Maybe the world breaks on purpose so that we can have work to do." The choice of Wagner is provocative and unsettling. It speaks, at least, to Adorno's suspicion that Wagner's "mystic" music was well suited to advertising, though he had the atomized leitmotif, not the amorphous *Rheingold* prelude, in mind. The notion of a world broken by technology, and yet *needing* technology to recuperate the "dead land," reveals the contradictions at the heart of Wagner and Eliot. For us, as for Adorno and Eliot, a Wagnerian TV ad that promises to restore the broken world with blue jeans invites salutary questions about the health and wholeness of music itself under the baton of Mr. Moneybags.

Ambivalence, Adorno states in his essay "Wagner's Relevance for Today," is "a relation towards something one has not mastered";[17] it is also, writes Chinitz, "the one mature response to most of the cultural phenomena of the modern world . . . which are themselves full of contradiction, never monolithic, and seldom coherent."[18] Using "ambivalence" as a historicist update of William Empson's "ambiguity," Chinitz savvily rethinks Eliot's cultural politics along less monolithic lines. By the same token, *The Waste Land*'s ambiguous aesthetic uses of Wagner—the chromatic "endless melody" that makes his music so appealing, the layered archetypes that make his function in the poem so polyvalent—mark an ambivalent *cultural* status. Wagner himself is among the most intensely contradictory figures in Western art: a figurehead of High Autonomous Art and a spokesperson for the *Volk*; a proto-fascist reactionary and a Bakuninite anarchist; a Feuerbachian-turned-Schopenhauerian whose Dionysian pessimism drove the early Nietzsche to rapture and the late Nietzsche to despair; a Romantic prophet of the return to nature and a master craftsman of expensive theatrical technology. Eliot would have understood, at least in cribbed form, what was unusual about Wagner's chromatic, leitmotivic technique; he would have also known its political resonance, as in Bernard Shaw's influential socialist reading of the mines in *Rheingold* as "a whitelead factory, or a chemical works, or a pottery, . . . or any other of the places where human life and welfare are daily sacrificed."[19] At least, Shaw contends, until Wagner discovered Schopenhauer, at which point his radical materialism gave way to idealist disillusionment with worldly politics. Yet Wagner's idealism never loses contact with the fleshliness of the body, and in Eliot's hands, Schopenhauer's deep bass—a teleological pressure to which we might surrender—is never steady. These cultural contradictions mark themselves on the sonic textures of Eliot's poem and on the corpses that walk the stage.

Wagner, too, fancied himself not a "grand opera" composer but the champion of an organic *Volk*, temporarily at the mercy of capitalism and commerce, but ultimately integral with German blood and soil. Music may have been the basic "loam of feeling" underwriting his productions, but for Wagner, we had advanced to the precarious state of needing more technology in order to excavate the natural elements, a dialectical-materialist *mise en abyme*. Wagner thus embodies Eliot's ambivalent ironies, a weaver of holistic creation myths and a figure for the horror of mass-cultural assimilation. As Huyssen argues, Adorno's writings on Wagner, more than the "modernist triumphalism" of the pro-Schoenberg *Philosophy of New Music*, bear the fractures of an integral freedom torn in two directions, of a "fierce struggle between tradition and modernity, autonomy and commodity, revolution and reaction, and, ultimately, myth and enlightenment."[20] For Adorno, Wagner's efforts to identify music with the liberated individual through leitmotif end up "corporate" in function; Wagner's musical mastery is bound to a neurotic desperation for control.

Huyssen's against-the-grain reading of Adorno exposes the philosopher's uncertainty about the effects of the modernism/mass culture dialectic on ego-formation: on one hand, his embrace of the individual subject as the outer limit of what the culture industry can control; on the other hand, his argument that "the hardness of the epistemological subject" is a compulsion hammered (through leitmotif) into allegorical rigidity. Poking at this tension,

Huyssen retorts that commodity culture might be tested by mass art—by intersubjectivity and collective action—and not merely by a hypostasizing "self-identical" ego. Adorno never accepts this hope, but Eliot and Williams are willing to consider it. Eliot likewise resists treating the unified subject as the only resistance to "the human engine." As Levenson shows, the poem develops overlapping principles of continuity, continually tempting us to identify a single speaker only to undercut that stability idiomatically and thematically: a breakdown of the subject and of the *Identitätszwang*. As Eliot denaturalizes rhythm, he denaturalizes consciousness, perspective, and ego as fluid and self-reinventing processes—tenuously constructed by modernity's barrage of sensory and conceptual echoes.

Adorno critiques the total artwork as a totalizing negation of the individual, in which the "formal premises of an internal logic are replaced by a seamless external principle in which disparate procedures are simply aggregated in such a way as to make them appear collectively binding."[21] The total artwork's consonant totality encloses us from the outside in, Adorno argues, rather than through the organic rhythms of fluctuating emotion. Its external binding quality enforces a rhythmically inflexible structure: "The giant packages of his opera are divided up by the notion of striking, of beating time. The whole of the music seems to have been worked out first in terms of the beat, and then filled in; over giant stretches, . . . the time seems to be a kind of abstract framework" (*Search* 22). In his critique of Wagner, Adorno begins to resemble Lukács, suggesting that Wagner's art presents a political capitulation in its motivic recapitulations: "Wagner's aesthetic weaknesses spring from . . . the idea that 'This is the way things are, and always will be; you don't escape, there is no way to escape'" ("Relevance" 599). In the drive to self-referential totality, suffering and pathology become, as Lukács suggests, an inescapable "*condition humaine*"[22] rather than a condition of history; they become naturalized through rhythm and iteration, forestalling real musical development through compulsive repetition. Adorno, writing after the Holocaust, seems to compare the binding rhythms of Wagner to the experience of a labor camp.

Or, as *The Waste Land* protests, "Thinking of the key, each confirms his prison." Eliot's line urges a break from solipsistic materialism, a surrender of trivial passions to the controlling hands of authority. But if Eliot tries to restore the contingent into the timeless consonance of an overarching "key," the musical aesthetic of wholeness also acts as a rhythmically repetitive and consonantly enforced prison. If we think of rhythm as a kind of poetic technology, a reading licensed by Eliot's claims about the internal combustion engine and the street drill (if not by Adorno's equation of rhythm and domination), we may hear it with more ambivalence in Eliot's Gesamtkunstwerkian poem. Just as Wagner's return to nature requires a vast technological apparatus, *The Waste Land*'s efforts to sacrifice the artist to tradition requires the discipline of an individual rhythmic pulse—one which continually and disruptively reasserts itself—to a larger order.

For Adorno, Wagner's music moves not to an organic rhythm but to the artificial, externally imposed rhythms that bind the total artwork. These rhythms rely on a conductor whose beating of time enacts the music's violently gestic quality—mimicked, as I discuss in chapter four, in the "anvil motif" that marks the noisy hammering throughout the Ring Cycle (Alberich's mines in *Rheingold*, Siegfried's forging of Nothung in *Siegfried*). Adorno's disciplinary "fascist conductor," beating the time of Wagner and Stravinsky, finds his body disciplined by the very authority that the music has granted him. Adorno likewise argues that the small blocks of rhythm in *Sacre*, divorced from the "structural rhythm," force the conductor to "walk a tightrope for the sole purpose of using convulsive blows and shocks . . . to hammer into the dancer and the audience an immutable rigidity" (*PNM* 117). Dancer, audience, and conductor alike are subjected to immutable battery.

While Adorno critiques the inescapable quality in Wagner's music—rationalized further, he argues, by Stravinsky—he also acknowledges the way in which Wagner's music offers critical points of entry, laying bare the "cracks" in the façade of its own totalizing mythology. For all his frustrations with Wagner, Adorno casts him as the first "to draw the consequences from the contradiction between traditional forms . . . and the concrete artistic tasks at hand," a tension materialized both in the musical form and in the mechanics of the production ("Relevance" 588). Despite Wagner's emphasis on allegory and *Weltanschauung*, Adorno argues that Wagner's is a horizontal art in which "the figure in its concrete, elaborated reality" threatens "any kind of scheme or externally imposed form." This musical "nominalism" allows for composition according to the demands of the music, not to the norms of "tact" and "taste" (*PNM* 48). These norms, Adorno suggests, motivate Stravinsky's "stuffy" bourgeois distaste for Wagner.

Therefore the musical material itself renders the progressive decay of one social order, and the regressive consolidation of a new one. Wagner's music presents (rather than *re*presents) violence as the "decisive truth" of modernity, which "breaks through as the same law that it was in the prehistoric world," impeaching its own "mythological" pretenses: "when . . . violence expresses itself in pure form, unobscured, in all its terror and entrapment, then the work, despite its mythologizing tendency, is an indictment of myth, willingly or not" ("Relevance" 589). These incidents of violence enter the text as what Adorno calls "noise": dynamic excesses in which Wagner marshals "pure sound" in opposition to the "moderate cultural consensus," producing music that "cannot be listened to with delectation" (595). (Pound found Wagner distasteful for his excess of noise that *lacked* a clearly binding rhythmic structure; these arguments say as much about Pound's, Adorno's, and Eliot's esthesic faculties as they do about Wagner.)

In exposing these cracks in the edifice, Adorno draws also on the language of injury and disease—bodily breakdowns realized in *The Waste Land* by disruptive microrhythms. As Karin Bauer writes, quoting *Dialectic of Enlightenment*, "It is the decaying form and the injured subject that give expression to the nonidentical" and "give rise to the new and the different by revealing . . . the 'trace of something better.'"[23] It is not in compulsory wholeness, but in aporia that bear the traces of "integral freedom," that art expresses its utopian drives. In Adorno's words,

> whatever makes Wagner better than the social order (to whose dark powers he aligned himself) owes itself to decadence, to the damaged subject's incapability of playing sufficiently by the rules of the existing social order. In this way he fails to meet the expectations of health, cleverness, communication, and mutual understanding, and turns silently against the power in whose service his language stands. It is not the unshakably self-assertive form, but rather the decaying form that indicates the coming of the new.[24]

In Eliot's Wagnerism, the binding of the subject to an "existing social order" produces a damaged figure whose rhythmically repetitive failure to communicate ("Why do you never speak? Speak") leaves a seam in the whole form of the total artwork. As I discuss later, the violated and syphilitic specimens occupying Eliot's stage continue, in various ways, to signal decay in the rules of language itself. Philomel's "Jug Jug," a reinvention of the Elizabethan nightingale's song, serves as an "inviolable voice" and a sonically disruptive source of *fama*. When Verlaine's choric reflection on Wagner's *Parsifal* ("*Et, O ces voix d'enfants*") is yoked with Philomel's guttural noise, Eliot indeed produces music that "cannot be listened to with delectation," turning Philomel's damage against the "power in whose service [her] language stands."

Eliot's decoding of birdsong offers a good example of "natural" expression exposed as historical—and a core example of Wagner's Romanticism making rich and strange a phenomenon of nature. Attali, with characteristic hypervigilance, marks birdsong as a fundamental moment at which sound meets power: "Among birds a tool for marking territorial boundaries, noise is inscribed from the start within the panoply of power" (6). Adorno is more nuanced, treating birdsong as a sublime moment of aesthetic pleasure that, at the same time, unstitches the auditor's faith in a stable concept of nature. Any self-respecting aesthete, Adorno writes, would find birdsong beautiful; nevertheless, "something frightening lurks in the song of birds precisely because it is not a song but obeys the spell in which it is enmeshed" (*AT* 66). Nature's spellbinding quality over the auditor has become part of its content—the terror "lurking" in the perception of birdsong is that human reason can only begin to master the spell exerted by the natural world. "Wherever nature was not actually mastered, the image of its untamed condition terrified," Adorno writes; "The progress of civilization, however, easily deceives human beings as to how vulnerable they remain even now" (65). For Adorno, then, the experience of natural beauty is apprehended as "the trace of the nonidentical in things under the spell of universal identity"—as the aporetic gestures to "what is unutterable in the language of nature," which destabilize the effort to master nature through the self-sufficient linguistic concept. By attempting to copy something like birdsong in aesthetic form, the artist responds (at worst) by falling into fascist neo-Romantic holism (at most mediocre) by reducing it to kitsch, or (at best) by defamiliarizing natural categories: "Natural beauty is ideology where it serves to disguise mediatedness as immediacy" (66).

Eliot takes on a similar logic, pursuant to the role of birdsong in Wagner. In *Die Meistersinger von Nürnberg* (1868), Walther auditions for a guild of Renaissance "mastersingers" with a remarkable, rule-breaking song ("Fanget an!"); "shoemaker and poet" Hans Sachs, the Meistersinger also quoted in Pound's Canto LXXV, compares Walther's music to birdsong. The stuffy Beckmesser (a satire of Hanslick) rejects the song for its lack of melody and ornament, and another declares it "vain ear-abuse" (*Eitel Ohrgeschinder*), but Sachs hears it as the voice of one "who heard a bird singing and, carried away by madness, imitated its song." Sachs suggests surrendering to the immanent logic of this birdsong: "If you wish to measure according to rules something which does not agree with your rules," he cautions Beckmesser, "forget your own ways, and first seek *its* rules." (Sachs's noisy hammering frequently interrupts Beckmesser's prolix master-singing.) Walther's birdsong signals the cracks in an art form that has grown stale, much as birdsong in *The Waste Land* serves less as a symbol of natural beauty than as a diagnostic of the sterile modern mechanization of ritual.

Also apposite is the moment in *Siegfried* where the eponymous hero, having tasted the blood of the dragon Fafner, is able to interpret birdsong and to detect the true meaning of speech; he thus detects the lies told by his foster parent Mime. This scene invokes dramatic and musical problems in Wagner, whose solutions both Joyce (in Stephen's forging of Nothung) and Sitwell (in borrowing Wagner's stage-devices) will explore. In a passage of particularly fine dramatic writing, Mime thinks he is telling Siegfried to drink a reviving broth, but Mime's voice(-object) lets slip his intention to poison Siegfried. So Siegfried kills him, calling him a "loathsome babbler," and resumes chatting with the bird's sublime music (which next leads Siegfried off to Brünnhilde). For Walther and Siegfried, the gesture to birdsong is both an inkling of the sublime, and an attempt to puncture the duplicitous artifice of language. In *Siegfried* it also serves as a sonic scapegoating—an effort to kill off Mime's interloping into Siegfried's (incestuous) bloodline.

To hear noise, as Attali suggests, is "a little like being killed" (28): an exposure to unmediated sonic violence with a provisional inkling of natural entropy not yet subjected to ritual order. To understand birdsong in Wagner and *The Waste Land* relies on a material strength (the forging of Nothung) and the killing-off of "loathsome babble." Eliot's birdsong acquires its force not only by approaching the terrors of nature, but, paradoxically, by declining the pretense of having identically reproduced nature. As birdsong becomes a rhythmically pestering noise, it renders both the attempted dominance over nature in trying to unify it aesthetically (the futile effort, for example, to imprison Philomel in a framed "sylvan scene"), and the lingering perseverance of those aspects of nature that can't be aptly articulated ("Jug jug jug"). Like the birds in Pound's *Cantos*, Eliot's birdsong produces nature as a state of resistant disintegration.

The Waste Land's treatments of Wagner thus mimic not just a return to Nature's sublime and terrifying unity, but an Adornian gesture to nature's entropic disintegration. Eliot's attitudes toward the stage share in Adorno's concern with the relationship between music and staged embodiment. Wagner's better (torn) half, Marie Lloyd, suggests for Eliot a figure whose critique of the middle class's illusion of salutary wholeness is at risk of being mechanized out of existence.

Making It Personal: The Music Hall and the Ballets Russes

In his essay on Marie Lloyd, Eliot contrasts the liveliness and audience interactivity of the music hall to the middle-class's impending death "from pure boredom." This essay reveals much about Eliot's fascination with both of Adorno's torn halves of high and mass art. Eliot's echoes of Stravinsky and Satie, and in turn their appropriations of jazz, ragtime, music hall, and the popular, attenuate the "high"/"low" boundary. Rainey argues that *The Waste Land*'s efforts to set its lands in order are destabilized by "modes of cultural production" that "thrive on wild exaggeration, hyperbolic repetitions," and "a grotesque machinery of extremism" that "undermines the modes of connectedness (repetition, narrative) that the poem elsewhere takes pains to assert."[25] These contradictions between Wagner and his disjointed mirror image in *Parade* can be heard as internal to Wagner: the leitmotif, for example, represents a method of connected repetition that binds together hyperbolic extremes and theatrical mechanisms.

In the music hall, as in Wagner, Eliot believed this machinery to have a broad moral purpose, drawing the lower classes into a more interactive and more educative relation to the stage. The music hall, for Eliot, breaks down the walls between actor and spectator, as individuation begins to crumble, and mimesis is discarded in favor of communal identification: "With the decay of the music-hall, with the encroachment of the cheap and rapid-breeding cinema, the lower classes will tend to drop into the same state of protoplasm as the bourgeoisie. The working man who went to the music-hall and saw Marie Lloyd and joined in the chorus was himself performing part of the act; he was engaged in that collaboration of the audience with the artist which is necessary in all art and most obviously in dramatic art."[26] Eliot treats the trip to the music hall as a pilgrimage, guiding the *Volk* into a more authentic interchange with music, and thereby into a higher state of moral reflection. Conversely, Eliot associates "the decay of the music hall" with the mechanization of music and culture, and the concomitant degeneration of the working class into bourgeois "protoplasm." He proceeds to suggest that "when every theatre has been replaced by 100 cinemas, when every musical instrument has been replaced by 100 gramophones, . . . when electrical ingenuity has made it possible for every child to hear its bedtime stories from a loud-speaker," the entire "civilized world" will "rapidly follow the fate of the Melanesians" (174), the ancient civilization that allegedly died from boredom.[27] Thomas Edison did in fact claim, in 1876, that the phonograph would one day teach a child to sing and then put him to bed;[28] the question asked by Thomas Eliot is whether "the civilized world" will be taught to sing and then put to sleep in its turn.

Eliot, unlike Adorno, fears not popular music itself, but its commodification and reliance on technology, which threaten to sterilize the ritual functions of art. This seems no less than an anticipation of Benjamin's concept of the aura, but unlike Benjamin, mourns the loss of aura as a cultural deadening. Eliot, like Adorno, believed that both "high" and popular art, increasingly reproducible, were susceptible to unreflective appropriation, one example of which was the new "primitive art and poetry." As Eliot writes in "War-Paint and Feathers" (1919), reviewing a collection of American Indian chants that have "burst into the drawing room," these primitivist experiments could "revivify the contemporary activities," but could just as easily fall into trendiness and camp.[29] Eliot moreover critiques, as a version of corrupting mass-reproduction, the bourgeois tendency toward unreflective name-dropping. In a letter from July 1919, Eliot cites the Ballets Russes, "liked by people who know nothing of the art," as one of many fashionable "contemporary tastes" that people "assimilat[e] . . . without making them personal" (*Letters* I.317). For Eliot, culture requires "something personal: one book or painter made one's own" (317). While music can promote a shared language, it can also become an inauthentic jargon brought willy-nilly into the drawing room. Adorno hears a similar unsedimented citationality both in Stravinsky's primitivism and in his neoclassical rewritings of Pergolesi in *Pulcinella*. Adorno's problem with Stravinsky resembles Eliot's problem with Stravinsky's *audiences*: if the beat is good enough, a middle-class audience will swallow it uncritically. For Eliot, without a charismatic figure such as Lloyd to offer the artwork an aesthetic and moral center, the audience will start consuming art out of habit—a recipe for death-by-boredom.

Eliot's attempts to negotiate the individual artist's relation to culture, the attempts to "make art personal" while submitting to an impersonal tradition, enter into the rhythmic flux of his poetry. Eliot's speaker in "Portrait of a Lady" (1917), for example, draws on imagery from the ballet. As a street piano, "mechanical and tired/Reiterates some worn-out common song" (ll.79–80), and as he suffers the stale conversation and oppressive hyacinth smell around him, he feels compelled to

> borrow every changing shape
> To find expression . . . dance, dance
> Like a dancing bear,
> Cry like a parrot, chatter like an ape. (109–12)

Trying to forge authentic connections not just to the people around him, but to their tastes, their "ideas, right or wrong," and to the "things they have desired" (82–3), the speaker is unable to "make personal" this "mechanical," "worn-out . . . song." Instead, he can only repeat the sounds and gestures of words, or dance to their whims; the tired mechanism of the piano leads him not to structure his own experiences but to imitate the experiences of others, even if (as is no doubt the case for a parrot) some cognition sinks in of what is being imitated. These images recall *Petrushka*, Stravinsky's fairground tableaux for the Ballets Russes, in which dancing bears and puppets (modeled on stock circus and *commedia dell'arte* characters) seem to jeer at the seriousness of balletic decadence. *Petrushka*'s mechanical hand organ, resonant with Eliot's street piano, is compared by Adorno as "the shock of an already-lapsed modernism, degraded to the childish," a claim to which Stravinsky would probably not have objected (*PNM* 111). Eliot's speaker takes on bodily performances that Adorno associates with the crudely mimetic gestures of Wagner and Stravinsky: as Martin Puchner explains, "what stands behind [Adorno's] critique of Wagner and Stravinsky is a critique of a primitive form of mimesis that reminds Adorno of the acts 'android apes perform in the zoos'" (4). His claim that *Le Sacre* makes the conductor "walk a tightrope" suggests that the performer as well as the auditor is disciplined into a mimetic circus act. As with Eliot's hearing of *Le Sacre*, modern music transforms the auditor; in this case, however, it transforms him into an emptied-out echo of what he hears—into a sort of dancing gramophone.

At the close of this chapter, I read the dancing gramophones of the Ballets Russes' *Parade* as a homology to the poem's emptied-out singing bodies. Eliot seems to share Adorno's hunch that the imagery of the Ballets Russes was best served for fashionable "borrowings," the "changing shapes" of subjects emptied of volition. The repetitive patter of the mechanical piano (the villain, also, of Pound's "Mauberley") marks an anxiety about a middle class that likes a good beat, but doesn't know what to do with it, and simply becomes a group of what Adorno and Eliot see as uncritical puppets, dancing bears, and gramophonic parrots repeating what they are told.

Eliot's anxiety about mimetic "android" primates shapes his effort, in *The Waste Land*, to find a "rhythm of fluctuating emotion" that naturalizes rhythm without merely becoming an "imitation of instrumental music." This fear applies to "high" and mass culture alike, and underlies his search to tape these torn halves back together—his search, to put it more tendentiously, for the underlying pulse of stable cultural authority. Indeed, as Barry Faulk suggests, Eliot's gestures to the music hall served to consolidate his own connoisseurship and cultural authority—allowing him to produce reviews like "Marie Lloyd" that doubled as quasi-ethnographic social critique.[30] As Eliot makes overlapping appeals to different masses (Wagner's *Volk*, Stravinsky's rite, Lloyd's music hall), his search for a unifying pulse renegotiates the relations that music (and, especially, theatrical music) has to its own public, and that Eliot has to his.

What "Portrait" hears as an "out-of-tune" violin becomes, in *The Waste Land*, the "pleasant whining of a mandoline" (III.261), an appealing twang amidst the noisy "clatter and . . . chatter" of the fishmen in a public bar (l. 262), the vibrancy of which Chinitz aptly contrasts with the poem's indifferent middle class.[31] Wagner's Rhinemaidens are "bashful fish" whom Alberich wants to capture (I.i); in *The Waste Land*, accordingly, music-hall bleeds back into Wagner, as the pleasantly whiny mandolin transitions directly into Eliot's Thames-daughters. To choreograph this reintegration, Eliot adopts Wagner's *Stabreim* ("The river sweats / Oil and tar" [III.266–7]), setting the Rhinemaidens' diatonic music to Wagner's duple meter, and to the "beating oars" moving down the Thames (III.280). Yet these lines break into the Rhinemaidens' "Wallala leialalas" (III.290–1), the consonant prelinguistic music of unfettered nature, moving us not just between Wagner and popular song, but also between language and pure sound. Eliot footnotes these inarticulate sounds to *Götterdämmerung*, where they also reprise the opening scenes of *Rheingold*, in which the Rhinemaidens (in *Stabreim*) ridicule Alberich's "toad-like form" (*Krötengestalt*) and "croaking voice" (*Stimme Gekrächz*) (*Rheingold* 1.1). Reading backward from *The Waste Land*, one might say that the Rhinemaidens engage Alberich in a seductive music hall act, titillating the "lustful beast" [*lüsterne Kauz*] while keeping him at arm's length. Eliot's ululations pull at once toward the allegorical return to nature at the end of *Götterdämmerung*, and toward titillating mockery; we hear both

Marie Lloyd's efforts to tease a cohesive community, and Wagner's efforts to return to primal sound.

These Wagnerian resonances, while underscoring Eliot's efforts to bind together different cultural productions, amplify the poem's warnings about sexless boredom. While *The Waste Land* begins with "memory and desire," moves through a series of sterile or rapine sexual encounters, and ends with a direct appeal to the "obedient" heartbeat, the Ring Cycle as a whole tries to rekindle desire through a negative-dialectical motion, marked by the repetition of these ululating noises. After the Rhinemaidens heckle him in *Rheingold*, Alberich renounces love altogether, allowing him to acquire the Rhine's gold and hammer it into shape. (*The Waste Land* offers many such Alberichs who renounce love for material "prudence.") By the end of *Götterdämmerung*, the last of the Ring dramas, this renunciation of love is transmuted into—and, through leitmotif, bound with—Brünnhilde's refusal to give up the Ring, at which point she immolates herself ("Burning burning burning burning" [*TWL* III.308]). Brünnhilde's self-immolation at the end of *Götterdämmerung*, counteracting Alberich's cynical renunciation of desire, is a valuably Adornian double-negative: Brünnhilde renounces the renunciation of desire, in the process destroying Valhalla, and herself, with the ring that Alberich has worked so hard to produce. As a result, her body and the materialistic Valhalla of "profit and loss" (*TWL* IV.314) go up in flames (along with all the "Falling towers" of "What the Thunder Said" [V.373–4]), while the Rhinemaidens ululate at the return of their gold to the depths. It is through renunciation and negative critique—the Adornian refusal of commercial cynicism and the Schopenhauerian unraveling of representation—that the order's violence to desire is revealed and destroyed. Binding the beginning of the Ring to the end, these "leialalas" are a call to the triumph of the artist, who has inserted all sorts of profit and loss into his own drama, asserting his own mastery over them, and seeing mastery itself threatened by natural entropy.

Eliot hears in the Rhinemaidens' guttural ululations a critical noise—perhaps just the disruption needed to revivify the protoplasmic middle class. The poem invites us to contemplate our own binding to a falsely macrorhythmic form of desire ("the human engine" of an "age of prudence"), and to defamiliarize our neglect of real desire ("The awful daring of a moment's surrender / Which an age of prudence can never retract"). Like Brünnhilde's ultimate surrender of her own body, Eliot's effort to stimulate us out of our cynical, jaded boredom is a negation ("never") of a "retraction": a litotical approximation of desire that cannot be reduced to a static positive concept.

Rhythms such as the two-beat of *Stabreim* seem to hierarchize and organize sound in historical relation, to pull them into a total order which may or may not hold up under its own weight; which may, by decaying, give voice to a new (possibly equally totalizing) one; and which may find its source in a conductor, a dictator, or another staff-wielding master. When bound to a cultural whole, as in Wagner's or Marie Lloyd's mobilization of the mass, the effort to rekindle "obedient" desire becomes dictatorial—a form of compulsory love. As rhythm binds a heart obediently to a larger order, naturalizing historical dominance, it finds itself confronted by the syncopations, dissonances, and noises of that order's ultimate decay.

Corrupting Prophet/Profit: Madame Sosostris's Condition of Music

As *The Waste Land* celebrates the heart's obedient surrender, its integrations into a totalizing order meet with considerable resistance. One sees in Eliot's gestures to *The Tempest*, for example, a self-conscious uncertainty about the ephemerality of aesthetic integration. Like *The Tempest*, Eliot seems alternately to naturalize and to defamiliarize an aesthetic order rooted in human knowledge and power. It may help to consider Prospero as the Adornian artist-conductor, whose struggles for control and integration ultimately implode. The "compulsion toward disintegration," Adorno argues in *Aesthetic Theory*, moves the artist "to set aside the magic wand as does Shakespeare's Prospero, who is the poet's own voice. However, the truth of such disintegration is achieved by way of nothing less than the triumph and guilt of integration" (45). Prospero's desire for mastery and control is so tightly bound that its "triumph" is inextricable from its "guilt"; the urge to master Nature, an isle "full of noises," leads the total art work into grating disintegration. A form of rationalized clothed as natural—a "rough magic . . . To work mine end upon their senses" (5.1.57-60)—Prospero's narcotizing "heavenly music" includes, and is disrupted by, the "strange and several noises/Of roaring, shrieking, howling, jingling chains,/And mo diversity of sounds" (5.1.264). In *The Tempest*, as in *The Waste Land*, we see an anticipation of Adorno's skepticism about music that presents itself as a natural element, rather than a dialectical working-through of a damaged subjectivity. As Shakespeare's Alonso perceives, "These are not natural events" (5.1.291).

As *The Waste Land* itself is exposed as a false whole—a monument of fragments "yoked by violence together" (as Dr. Johnson said of Eliot's beloved Metaphysical poets) in a simulation of coherent knowledge—we come to see music as a phantasmagoric illusion, suggesting that even our unconscious urges have been subjected to "an age of prudence." Ariel's dilemma in *The Tempest*, which Eliot's poem re-voices beautifully, is his status as both an agent of Prospero's musical order and a herald of its collapse. In Sosostris's prophecy, too, Ariel's disembodied voice speaks to his place in a series of orders beyond himself: an (Eliotic) historical order; a (Shakespearean) textual order that can be licentiously cited; a commercial order that can mechanically reproduce his words (on a gramophone); and a series of decaying bodies that herald these orders' collapses. Madame Sosostris's citation of *The Tempest* speaks to the instability of citation per se, a problem amplified by the presence of the gramophone, which dissevers music from its time and place.

Sosostris's merging of these textual orders speaks to her urge to illusory totality, even when she doesn't fully keen its significance. I propose that she gives voice to one particular order—Schopenhauer's condition of music—in corrupted form. Her prophecy produces the illusion that she, in spite of herself, is aligned to a deep, ineffable Bass, even as the rhythmic textures of Eliot's verse expose cracks in that illusion. Sosostris can only grasp for this deeper truth with an inescapable, and incurably infected, physical presence: a corrupted body that needs to burn away worldly desire, but which is too locked into the commercial order of representation to do so. Sosostris embodies a range of urges toward rhythmic integration, and of anxieties about that integration's limits; her prophecy has an internal logic that the rest of the poem historically dilates.

My equation of Sosostris and Schopenhauer in "A Game of Chess" is not entirely fanciful, given the gesture in *The World as Will and Representation* to the "phantasmagoric" "game of chess." Schopenhauer's phantasmagoria metaphor lacks the politics of Marx's, but each emphasizes an illusion (worldly experience, the commodity fetish) that requires denaturalizing. In Schopenhauer, the game of chess metaphorizes the phantasmagoric illusion of life, brought to light only once we have denied the "threads of willing which hold us bound to the world" in "constant pain." Having un-"bound" himself from worldly illusion, Schopenhauer claims, the "phantasmagoria of this world" reappears, neither living nor dead, as "indifferently as chess-men at the end of a game. . . . Life and its forms merely float before him as a fleeting phenomenon, as a light morning dream to one half-awake" (*WWR* I.390–1). In Eliot's treatment of a blasé and mechanical illusion, the "fleeting" Representations (broken images) of urban modernity, keep each subject in the thrall of "constant pain." To defamiliarize this Simmelesque puppet show as a phantasmagoric "ghostly pantomime" requires a visionary poetic prophecy, and an audience to make that prophecy personal. The "awful . . . surrender" of oneself to music may, as in Wagner's Ring, catalyze a reconciliation with the Big Rhythm—the Ground Bass of the Will and of the earth itself—but one will eventually find this reconciliation illusory.

Among the poem's most cryptic figures, Sosostris calls on the line from Ariel's song as she cycles through a "wicked pack of cards":

> Madame Sosostris, famous clairvoyante,
> Had a bad cold, nevertheless
> Is known to be the wisest woman in Europe,
> With a wicked pack of cards. Here, said she,
> Is your card, the drowned Phoenician Sailor,
> (Those are pearls that were his eyes. Look!)
> Here is Belladonna, the Lady of the Rocks,
> The lady of situations.
> Here is the man with three staves, and here the Wheel,
> And here is the one-eyed merchant, and this card,
> Which is blank, is something he carries on his back,
> Which I am forbidden to see. I do not find
> The Hanged Man. Fear death by water.
> I see crowds of people, walking round in a ring.
> Thank you. If you see dear Mrs. Equitone,
> Tell her I bring the horoscope myself:
> One must be so careful these days. (I.43–58)

Even as her "bad cold" (a Great War euphemism, McLuhan points out, for venereal disease)[32] suggests her damage and unsettles her authority, she seems to foretell the poem that follows, down to the "Death By Water" that picks the Phoenician's bones and the "Hanged Man" who materializes at the poem's end. Ariel sings the song in front of Prospero's cell, "thinking of the key" to his own prison, whereas Sosostris is "forbidden to see" the blank image of what the merchant is carrying, let alone of the Hanged Man. Like Ariel, she is both empowered by knowledge and subject to its limitations; she understands only those parts of nature that she can buy or sell, but she disseminates her wisdom anyway. As she passes this privileged wisdom along to "Mrs. Equitone," she makes clear that her insights, right down to the tribal ring, are (as in "War-Paint and Feathers") easily bought and sold. If Attali suggests that music's essential ritual functions have been mediated by the advents of representation (ossifying music into written signs), performance (singing for money), and reproduction (recording and stockpiling music), Sosostris gives voice to all of these corruptions at once. Much as Sosostris compresses the entire trajectory of the poem into one vaguely ludicrous fantasy, she mediates the Plantagenet history of England ("Equitone" an echo of "Aquitaine" [l. 529]) into an "equitone," a technology that makes everything sound identical. It is worth remembering the initial title of "A Game of Chess," "In the Cage," as a call to Henry James' telegraph girl, both precociously eidetic and sexually neurotic.

As vulgar as her readings of these horoscopes may be, the constellating signs take on a prophetic internal logic that, like the auditory imagination, plunges below the conscious resonances of sound. Sosostris's reading is not wrong, but thin: she has naturalized the rhythms of her prophecy but is not fully alive to what they mean. Even the "men walking round in a ring" resonate not only with the cycling atrophy of the city, a spinning record, but with Wagner's Ring and the tribal circle-dances of *Le Sacre*, Eliot's fellow crafters of an auditory order. Working for profit, trying to rationalize the irrational, she reifies the Tarot deck's static symbols, predicting resolutions (Death by Water, the Hanged Man) that will be produced whether or not she knows why.

Sosostris's gesture to *The Tempest* ("the pearls that were his eyes") emerges in "Game of Chess" as the mediation of "that noise" (the wind) into music (the "Shakespeherian Rag"):

> "What is that noise?"
> The wind under the door.
> "What is that noise now? What is the wind doing?"
> Nothing again nothing.
> "Do
> "You know nothing? Do you see nothing? Do you remember
> "Nothing?"
> I remember
> Those are pearls that were his eyes.
> "Are you alive, or not? Is there nothing in your head?"
> But
> O O O O that Shakespeherian Rag (II.119–128)

"What is the wind doing?" is an odd question, but it suggests that this woman, like Sosostris, is attuned to noise as a symptom of an underlying, entropic disorder of which she is a part, just as for Pound the noise of wind is part of what he calls "the process," a fundamental but irregular passage of time. Her auditor, shell-shocked and barely paying attention, is traumatically trying to restore that order in art, in Ariel and in the Shakespearian Rag, with mixed results.

Before turning to the Rag, I would point out how Eliot unites these torn halves of culture into dissonant relation, an internal whole that constellates its external venues. If, as Levenson argues, the poem's first section emerges from the porous consciousness of a corpse, that corpse too undergoes sea-change as it enters into the urbane settings of the passages that follow: the closed car, the beer hall, and the music hall ("The Shakespearian Rag" was written for the 1912 Ziegfeld Follies). Eliot's Ariel gives way to a public bar on the Lower Thames, as if to unpack the social and aesthetic relations reified in the form of the monochord/record/o:

O City City, I can sometimes hear
Beside a public bar in Lower Thames Street,
The pleasant whining of a mandoline
And a clatter and a chatter from within
Where fishmen lounge at noon: where the walls
Of Magnus Martyr hold
Inexplicable splendour of Ionian white and gold. (III.259–265)

This self-enclosed noise-music—some kind of popular song merged with the clatter and chatter of an organic and participatory working class—excludes, as Chinitz points out, the speaker himself, who responds by idealizing it into a Valhalla, a hall of "white and gold" that sits atop the Thames/Rhine/Congo. Like The Ring Cycle, in which the phantasmagoric Valhalla burns to the ground, "The Fire Sermon" ends by burning away the earthly trash that would cut off social connection, and the earthly desire that forestalls our reconciliation with the Will.

It seems clear to me, then, that Eliot is less interested in hierarchizing "high" vs. "low" art than he is in gauging their reintegration with a vibration that resonates both aesthetically and culturally—producing a phantasmagoric macrorhythmic unity, albeit one that is exposed by its own microrhythmic hiccups. And indeed, *The Tempest*'s invisibly sourced music gives way to a range of other poems and songs that pursue and destabilize the play's integrative, unifying impulses.

Oh, *That* Shakespeherian Rag: Popular Music as Mediating Midwife

Mediated by the neurotic voice of "A Game of Chess," *The Waste Land* takes us to the rag by channeling noise, first, into Ariel's (now Sosostris's) song—"the wind under the door" (l.116) into "pearls" (l.125)—and then into the empty head of the "Rag's" auditor ("Have you nothing in your head?") (l.126). That auditor does have something in his head—something quite catchy at that:

O O O O that Shakespeherian Rag—
It's so elegant
So intelligent

"What shall I do now? What shall I do?
"I shall rush out as I am, and walk the street
"With my hair down so. What shall we do tomorrow?
"What shall we ever do?" (ll.128–34)

The syncopations of "What shall I do now? What shall I do?" contrast with the loose pentameter of the following line, suggesting that the auditor is shaping the speaker's voice to the rhythms in his own head. The meter then unbinds back into disorder, moving, like the speaker, unevenly in relation to the beat. In this exchange the poem vacillates between two types of neurosis: one fixated on one manifestation of culture industry, another with no sense of culture at all. Eliot's exchange between a free-verse line and a (loose) pentameter line mimics the back-and-forth between ignorant anarchy and compulsory integration. This vacillation dilates from the contracted present of "It's so elegant" to the extending future of "What shall I do now? . . . What shall we do tomorrow? What shall we ever do?", mirrored by the verse's rhythmic expansion and contraction. The auditor, immersed in the rag, shapes his experience of the present to a song; the neurotic speaker, however, obsesses over what it "shall" do at the expense of what it is doing now, or what is being done to it.

Take "The Shakespearian Rag." (Please!) Heard backward through *The Waste Land*, "The Shakespearian Rag" is disappointing: unadventurous at its most memorable, and clumsy at its most adventurous. If the "neurotic woman" exhausts through emotional codependency, the song (used as escape) doesn't do much better: if she seems desperate to be amused, the song is no less desperate to be amusing. Its melody pounds away at the tonic; its laugh-lines are all pounded on strong beats. The song refers to "syncopated lines," but its own rhythms are conservative, and its modulations take a lot of wind-up for very little delivery:

But the high browed rhymes, [modulation to dominant]
Of his syncopated lines,
You'll admit, surely fit,
any song that's now a hit,
So this rag I submit.

That Shakespearian Rag— [return to tonic]
Most intelligent, very elegant,
That old classical drag
Has the proper stuff
The line, "Lay on, MacDuff"

As with Sosostris's unconsciously insightful reproduction of Ariel's song, Eliot seems amused by the perverse notion that someone saying "Lay on, MacDuff!" might be quoting Stamper and Buck rather than *Macbeth*, though it is at least possible that the speaker has made this lousy song personal.

But the mechanics of how Eliot introduces the Rag mitigate against allegorizing it as "low culture" *tout court*, either in elitist mockery or in populist recuperation. A gesture to the sonic landscape, the Rag also becomes a figure for mediation and miscitation—in Williams's terms, it becomes not an object (not a "rag," as such) but a process of reinvention that infiltrates the speaker's "memory" of the song with his "desire" to perform it. There is no "o o o o" in the original, and no hiccup in "ShakespeHErian."[33] These are inserted by Eliot's silent auditor, a spontaneous pick-up note to the cited text. The tmetic disruption of "ShakespeHErian" adeptly imitates the syncopations of ragtime; it also inserts "hear"ing (in sound, not in spelling) into an otherwise tone-deaf number, and into a character who lends his ears desultorily to his surroundings. Eliot ironizes the "elegance" and "intelligence" of a song that has little of either, but he does not seem to dismiss ragtime itself; in fact, his version out-rags the original.

The contrast to Berlin's "Mysterious Rag" is illuminating—as an example of (tamed) ragtime whose ostentatious wit has been made personal, it is not farfetched as a source for Eliot. A popular hit in its own right, Berlin's song features in Satie's *Parade*, softened into affectionate parody.[34] The lyrics and the Shakespeherian hiccups of "That Mysterious Rag" do seem much closer than Stamper and Buck to Eliot's mark:

> Are you listenin'?
> Are you listenin'?
> Look! Look!
> You're whistlin'
> That mysterious rag
> Sneaky, freaky ever melodious, mysterious rag

Aside from the "Look! Look!" that Sosostris sings in her Ariel costume ("Those were the pearls that were his eyes! Look!"), Berlin and Eliot hear in popular music something both mysterious and serious, "freaky" and "sneaky," something unconsciously persistent, as if Schopenhauer's noumenal Bass were a stride piano. Berlin's infectious tune instructs us to listen to the song that we're already unconsciously whistlin'. Eliot's "Shakespeherian Rag" seems to merge the Stamper/Buck song with Irving Berlin's, whose verbal mastery gestures at unconscious mystery.

Thus if Madame Sosostris, as Christina Hauck suggests, is the poem's resident abortionist and/or midwife, delivering and withholding knowledge, popular music may perform the same dual function: cutting off authentic expression (if not made personal), or allowing it to reproduce itself.[35] Clive Bell's "Plus de Jazz" (1921), published in *The New Republic*, eroticizes jazz as the thin legs of the cabaret dancer, racializes it as a black presence, and domesticates it as Eliot's poetic midwife—a case study in the High Modernist feminization of mass culture.[36] Bell regrets that "genuine artists" have been inspired by jazz, and predicts and delights in the impending death of the "Jazz spirit" (94). His two examples are Stravinsky and Eliot, whose "syncopations flou[t] traditional rhythms and sequences and grammar and logic," and "whose agonizing labors seem to have been eased somewhat by the comfortable ministrations of a black and grinning muse" (94).[37] To Eliot's agonizing labors, jazz serves as a "midwife," rhythmically aiding the birth of poetry; jazz helps give birth to Eliot's "demurely irreverent" and "primly insolent" "attitude," and to Stravinsky's "note of defiance" (94). Bell's concern extends beyond jazz's sneering syncopation, to its lowbrow social settings, "dancing palaces and hotel lounges" that cut off the "intense and passionate thought" required of a critic: "Thought rather than spirits is required; quality rather than color; knowledge rather than irreticence, intellect rather than singularity, wit rather than romps, precision rather than surprise, dignity rather than impudence, and lucidity above all things" (96). When Bell suggests that jazz, "like short skirts, . . . suits thin, girlish legs, but has a slightly humiliating effect on gray hairs," he laughs at dilettantes like Eliot who pretend to enjoy it. Bell, who associates jazz with dance halls, seems to fear that jazz makes the delivery of art too "irreticently" easy.

Bell reiterates his preference for the term "rag" over the term "jazz," asserting that jazz "rags everything," a set of "tricks of self-advertisement" appealing only to dilettantes (93). The Stravinsky pieces to which Bell is likely referring—*Ragtime for Eleven Instruments* (1920) and *L'Histoire du soldat* (1918)—marked Stravinsky's "final break with the Russian orchestral school," as he put it, and a shift into neoclassicism, using jazz as the medium of intellectual "lucidity" (qtd. in Taruskin, *Stravinsky*, 1.1301). Yet Bell performs major rhetorical prestidigitation by equating rag and jazz, especially with respect to Stravinsky, for whom jazz and ragtime have very different salience. As Taruskin suggests, much of the rhythmic writing in *L'Histoire*, the rag-inflected chamber piece, "might even be called 'anti-jazz'" (2.1311). Adorno heard *L'Histoire* as one of Stravinsky's few genuinely dialectical pieces, satirizing the puerility of "light" music, much as the Marx Brothers crash down the sets of "high" opera. When Bell hears Stravinsky's rag rhythms as narcotic, he misses the denaturalizing friction used to revitalize the clichés of both classical and popular music.

Eliot's use of the "Shakespearian Rag" seems like a strange amalgam of Adorno and Bell, one that distracts the auditor from his own pain while acting as a "midwife" that births an engaged interpretive response. So much of the landscape in *The Waste Land* is stillborn that any birth is welcome, though Eliot seems skeptical of figures, like Sosostris, who too easily birth right-sounding things without understanding whence their rightness. If Sosostris's prophecies tell us to "look" to Shakespeare, they lead us first to the "Shakespeherian Rag," a song being performed unconsciously in a neurotic and diseased laquearia. The "Rag" poses a site of friction between two songs, one whose desperation to be clever never makes its source material personal, and one that makes itself indispensable, worming its way into the unconscious so effectively that it almost births itself.

This automatic hum, the unconscious naturalization of rhythm, is exactly what Adorno and Bell fear most; Eliot, with a more ecumenical ear for the popular, tries out that naturalization and butts heads with its failures. As Ariel leads us to Prospero, the "Shakespearian Rag"—even if it provides a rhythmic burst of new life—draws us straight back into the nagging authoritative thunder of the barkeep, punctuating a conversation about stillbirth:

> HURRY UP PLEASE ITS TIME
> If you don't like it you can get on with it, I said.
> Others can pick and choose if you can't.
> But if Albert makes off, it won't be for lack of telling.
> You ought to be ashamed, I said, to look so antique. (II.153-7)

The poem offers several versions of "Portrait's" "public clocks," such as the "dead sound" of 9:00, the viole[n]t hour that brings the typist home. More than any of these, the barkeep's repeated "HURRY UP PLEASE ITS TIME" offers what Eliot calls a "rhythm of fluctuating emotion," organizing and midwifing this abortive conversation. The repetition of this cry marks time *within* the passage, and between various moments in the speaker's and Lil's pasts. These pasts are associated with Philomel's: the lines "it won't be for lack of telling. / You ought to be ashamed to look so antique" (II.155-6) recall the "antique mantle" re-"telling" Philomel's rape. *The Waste Land*'s compulsion to prove leads backward into repetition and re-telling; thus, Adorno might argue, the seeming progressivism of rhythmic play marks a regression. Recall Osbert Sitwell's Wagnerian query: Can we reverse?

The rhythmic intensification of the speaker's gossip about Lil and Albert is itself aborted mid-sentence, giving way to the closing downbeats of its conductor:

> And they asked me in to dinner, to get the beauty of it hot—
> HURRY UP PLEASE ITS TIME
> HURRY UP PLEASE ITS TIME
> Goonight Bill. Goonight. Goonight May. Goonight.
> Ta ta. Goonight. Goonight.
> Good night, ladies, good night, sweet ladies, good night, good night. (II.167-172)

Eliot's ungrammatical "ITS" effects an additional ambiguity in the barkeep's call. This ideogrammic condensation reinforces a submission to the noumenal conductor: "Hurry up, please, it's time" has become "Hurry up, please its time," a masochistic submission to a disembodied order. "Game of Chess" uses the syncopations of the Shakespeherian Rag to defamiliarize the false illusions of health and wholeness, and to show us its fractures: its rhythmic syncopations and its crumbling bodies.

In showing us the corrupted female bodies from which these births do not happen, "The Fire Sermon" tries to find compensatory forms of rhythmic binding and dilation, naturalizing and denaturalizing them in turn. If Sosostris is Schopenhauer's unwitting agent—a mediator of the ineffable who can approach it only through citation—"The Fire Sermon" pursues a similar Schopenhauerian logic, urging us (after Buddha's "Fire Sermon") to detach ourselves from fleeting desire, or (after the ghostly game of chess) to refuse the phantasmagoria of linguistic representation and aspire to music instead. Where "A Game of Chess" defamiliarizes our slavishness to a false whole, compulsory and corrupted, "The Fire Sermon" offers a bound monochord, which attempts to keep at bay the distracting noise of the city, only to find its musical sublimity distorted.

"O City City": "The Fire Sermon's" Monochord

Rhythmic binding is a master trope of "The Fire Sermon." We are bound to the rhythms of a mythic pilgrimage and a circular Ring. We are bound to desire; texts are bound to other texts, and to their own constituent parts; the totality of art is bound as a monochord—a mediation and an exclusion of noise, rendered as the vocative "o" that dots the poem's textual surface. Eliot introduces these noises in the feminized incursions of *fama*, of a marred body, of a colonized space, giving voice to the damaged lives subjected to this whole. In this way "The Fire Sermon" binds together the anxieties swirling around Wagner himself: labor, culture, and (after Schopenhauer) the abdication of worldly desire in the service of a noumenal order—making the rhythms of urban life no more "natural" than the illusions of puppet theatre. The "o" that unites the urban horns and motors, the Shakespeherian Rag, and Verlaine's "*voix d'enfants*" becomes a monochord, a unifying intensification of sonic overtones, that is also a palimpsest: a cross-media layering of meanings, hierarchies, textual echoes, and cultural mathematics.[38]

Much as Eliot earlier binds the unlikely Schopenhauerian combo of Conrad and Wagner—"Looking into the heart of light, the silence / *Öd und leer das Meer*"—here he performs the dual interpenetration of the Thames with the Congo and the Congo with the Rhine. Eliot binds the literal streams of the Rhine and the Thames together in monochordal unity, perhaps as they feed into Wagner and Arnold's seas. Wagner's primal stream and the Thames, Marlow's "dark plac[e] of the earth," symptomatize the decay of Arnoldian Culture, and of the empire itself. The songs of Thames Sisters and the center of the now-fracturing Empire are reduced to inarticulate Wagnerian ululation, "Weialala leia," which itself is bound to the "terrible frankness of that noise" heard by Marlow on the Congo. "The Fire Sermon's" pastiche of Wagner's *Stabreim*,

Dame Sun
sends down her rays of light;
night lies in the depths:
once they were bright,
when safe and glorious
our father's gold gleamed there.
Rhinegold!
Lustrous gold!
How brightly you once shone,
majestic star of the deep!
Weialala leia,
wallala leialala.

which Eliot transforms into a journey down the Thames,

        The river sweats
Oil and tar
The barges drift
With the turning tide
Red sails
Wide
To leeward, swing on the heavy spar.
The barges wash
Drifting logs
Down Greenwich reach
Past the Isle of Dogs.
        Weialala leia
                Wallala leialala

is at the same time a recasting of *Heart of Darkness*, in which "the tanned sails of the barges drifting up with the tide seemed to stand still in red clusters of canvas sharply peaked, with gleams of varnished sprits" (103). *The Waste Land*'s song of the Thames cross-fertilizes the Romantic loam of Wagner's Rhinemaidens with Marlow's self-annihilation in the "dark places of the earth."

If the way back to the loamy Rhine is to sail down the Thames, we may as well be swept into the Congo, or the colonized Ganges that projects (as in Forster) the disembodied voices of landscape:

> Ganga was sunken, and the limp leaves
> Waited for rain, while the black clouds
> Gathered far distant, over Himavant.
> The jungle crouched, humped in silence.
> Then spoke the thunder. (V.395-9)

The concentrated immanence of the Rhine—the pure tone of the Rhine-maidens' "Weialalas," and the material gold mined by Alberich—diffuses into the "far distant" transcendence of "What the Thunder Said." The Rhine-maidens' ululating thus serves as the boundary of a monochord—the enclosure of pure sound distinguishing authentic nature from industry—only to find that boundary all too permeable. At the same time, the Rhinemaidens' glossolalia acts as a disruption (though a musically consonant one) of syntax, which does violence to the industrialized order of the Thames. As Juan Suárez argues, this glossolalia draws us into a realm of "pure externality" as "at once message and massage—content *and* tactile stimulus that seems to skip sense and logic and caresses the ear and skin" (135). It acts as a glitch in the record that nonetheless bears the physical grain of the voice. As aural stimuli that mirror the inarticulate "Twit twit twit" of Philomel's violation, these "Weialalas" also mark the limits of the body, the boundary between the Rhinemaidens/Thames-Sisters and the streams of water/sound.

The poem's descent into inarticulacy manifests not just the onset of neurosis, but the breakdown of that great British totality—Empire—indexed by a near-plagiarism of *Heart of Darkness*. Eliot excised the epigraph from Conrad ("The horror! the horror!") on Pound's advice, but he claimed still to find the passage "elucidating." Perhaps it is more elucidating for being excised; Eliot gestures not just to *Heart of Darkness*'s decaying empire, but to the ineffable condition of music that underlies it. Conrad's Preface to *Nigger of the "Narcissus"* associates the Schopenhauerian aspiration "to the condition of art" by "carry[ing] its justification in every line" with a "single-minded attempt to render . . . justice to the visible universe," giving the formal unity of art a driving teleology. According to Mark Wollaeger, Conrad's Schopenhauer antedates Eliot's "panorama of futility and anarchy" (the phrase of Eliot's "*Ulysses*, Order, and Myth") as "noumenal reality . . . by making the phenomenal world available to the individual consciousness as an ordered whole" (34-5). Conrad's Kurtz, a *quondam* musician who abandons the "art of arts" for the violent unifications of empire, pursues the artist's single-minded aspiration to order with a "singleness of purpose" (*HD* 127). Conrad's Schopenhauerian teleology pulls the rhythmic shocks of his African jungle into relation with the noumenal vibrations of the Earth: "The monotonous beating of a big drum filled the air with muffled shocks and a lingering vibration" (171).

The irrational undercurrent of a hyperrational modernity, Schopenhauer's noumenal Will gives a "singleness of intention" to Conrad's world. Eliot shares with Conrad, or at least with Marlow, this infectious desire for totality, as he reduces the violence of Empire to the psychological narrative of Margate Sands. The cries of the Thames sisters, bound into music, *Stabreim*, "singleness of intention," become overtones of psychological disorder: "I can connect/Nothing with nothing." And as Wagner's music dissolves into incomprehensible noise, "intention" and disorder conjoin in the same sonic stream, which, like the Thames, "run[s] softly" till the speaker ends his song. With or without the epigraph, the poem manifests an "echo of [Kurtz's] magnificent eloquence" (*HD* 179).

The effort to align the modern soundscape to a primal vibration thus gives illusory order to the full range of musical productions. As Eliot's typist, putting a record on the gramophone, tries abandoning herself to the music of *Götterdämmerung*, and to the irrational urgency of the Will, she rematerializes Eliot's anxiety about the fluidity of the female body. Her journey down the sonic/liquid stream of the Thames flows into a ballad on Mrs. Porter, interpolated into the same O:

> But at my back from time to time I hear
> The sound of horns and motors, which shall bring
> Sweeney to Mrs. Porter in the spring.
> O the moon shone bright on Mrs. Porter
> And on her daughter
> They wash their feet in soda water
> *Et O ces voix d'enfants, chantant dans la coupole!*
>
> Twit twit twit
> Jug jug jug jug jug jug
> So rudely forc'd.
> Tereu (III.196–206)

A rewriting of Marvell's "To a Coy Mistress" ("But at my back I always hear/ Time's winged chariot hurrying near"), the lines resonate with Eliot's "transform[ed] rhythm of the steppes into the scream of the motor horn." Eliot stretches Marvell's tetrameter into blank verse: moving from constancy ("always") to contingency ("from time to time"), he slackens the meter and diffuses Marvell's concentrated *carpe diem* into distracted, self-amused patter. Eliot bowdlerizes the ballad "Mrs. Porter," which originally "had the word 'cunts' instead of feet,"[39] but leaves a lingering connection to Wagner's quest for liquid relief. Whether seeking a cure for venereal disease or attempting a return to a primal birth canal, Wagner and the Porters are integrated into the same sonic stream, which runs through the ballad, through Verlaine's meditation on *Parsifal*, and into the inarticulate utterances of the violated Philomel: discrete, repetitive shocks to the aural illusion.

Eliot links the ballad and the line from Verlaine by means of the monochordal o, on which he also perorates before the "Rag." The o is semantically empty; visually, it is a whole and a hole, a Ring and a spinning record from which mediated sound is broadcast. Sonically, it is pure vowel: unstopped sound, which transforms and mediates other kinds of sound. Wagner argued that vowels were "purely auditory," whereas consonants were related to "visual rhythm and gesture, 'the eye of hearing' [*Das Auge des Gehörs*]" (Puchner 44); *The Waste Land* the vowel comes into dialectical tension with consonantal noise. One might again consider Kurtz's final words, which Marlow hears as an "eloquent" coding of what he hears as Africa's irrational noise, riding the waves of a "dying vibration of one immense jabber" (*HD* 153). That vibration is encoded in a word that is almost entirely vowel ("horror"); like Wagner's "eye of hearing," like Lil (who has lost and refuses to replace her teeth), and like the landscape's "carious teeth that cannot spit," Kurtz's hollow final utterance is quite literally a word that has no teeth, producing merely the echoes of his own corrupted music.

Eliot's ambitions to Schopenhauer's noumenal vibration are clarified in an earlier version of the "O City City" passage—when *The Waste Land* still had Kurtz's last words as its epigraph:

London, the swarming life you kill and breed
Huddled stunned between the concrete and the sky
Responsive to the momentary need
Vibrates unconscious to ~~their chords of~~ its formal destiny
Knowing neither how to think, nor how to feel,
But lives in the awareness of the observing eye[40]

These unconscious responses give order to the "swarming life" of the city's "momentary" spasms, first as musical "chords" and then as a "formal destiny," an irrational Schopenhauerian drive manifested as ineffable Paterian form. So ineffable that the entire passage needed to be excised—it reveals, however, Eliot's pressure to unify the "huddled" masses of *The Waste Land* ("phantasmal gnomes," as the draft calls them) in keeping with a vibrating structure and an "observing eye." As he says momentarily in this apostrophe to London (also excised), this formal destiny strives to

> Record the jerky motions of these pavement toys
> And trace the ~~painful, ideal meaning~~ cryptogram which may be curled
> Within ~~this penumbral consciousness~~ these faint perceptions of the noise[.]

The puppet show is being recorded, the fragmented "jerky motions" of "pavement toys" made part of a larger "ideal meaning . . . curled" into, and accessible only to, the unconscious. Even the "splendour" of Magnus Martyr has grown out of the "~~Inviolable music~~ Inexplicable splendour of Corinthian white and gold." These are, I think, strong verses, but too philosophically explicit (Pound singled them out as "bullshit").[41] The gestures to the Will's noumenal music, the "penumbral consciousness" on which "the noise" has recorded its impress, needed to be induced rather than described. The public bar, Chinitz notes, is inaccessible to our "observing eye"; we are exposed only to the sounds that escape it, forced to supply a "painful, ideal meaning" to these phenomenal sounds. The "~~inviolable music~~" that would have resonated with Philomel's "inviolable voice" suggests that the City's most sacrosanct artifacts (the fishmen's bar that we can't see; the splendor of Magnus Martyr) remain "inexplicable" (the Rhine's "Weialala"; Philomel's "Twit twit twit").

The "despairing noises" and "barbaric cries" of Philomel's consonantal utterance struggle to be bound into this monochord, interrupting the o-like stream of Verlaine's, Kurtz's, and Eliot's poetic sounds. Verlaine's line, itself about singing voices, makes the juxtaposition with Philomel's guttural cries all the more poignant: what noises are being dissolved into choric sublimity? The voice is inviolable only because its somatic source is so readily violated; the "painful, ideal meaning" that gives order to the city cannot, for Eliot, overwrite the pain experienced by the actual organism.

Syphilitic Schopenhauer: Un-binding the Illusionary Body

Hence Eliot seems at once to be naturalizing the auditory imagination—assembling its rhythms into fictitious coherence—and denaturalizing its pretenses to health and wholeness as it descends into noise. If the poem's civilizational collapse fixates on (for Eliot) the terrorizing fluidity of the female body, it also represents a "rhythmically grumbling" effort to transmit these bodily traumas in a communicable narrative. Turning Adorno's dialectical ear for form onto Eliot's illusion of unity starts to unravel these binding rhythms, allowing us to see how they come to seem natural. Consequently, turning historical musicology onto Adorno produces a fuller sense of their specific historical resonances, liberated from Eliot's and Wagner's efforts to resolve and bind them. The problem of venereal disease, for example, motivates Eliot's and Wagner's anxieties about embodiment, enabling a critique of the false ideologies of public health.

Hutcheon's and Hutcheon's study of *Parsifal*, an opera suffused with anxieties about syphilitic infection, puts the characteristic disease of *fin-de-siècle* Europe at the center of an allegorical pilgrimage of sin, redemption, and cleansing. *The Waste Land* shows that the logic of totality is driven by disease and neurosis, through recycled images from *Parsifal*; Verlaine's *Parsifal*; the Fisher King (the equivalent of the wounded Amfortas in Wagner's opera); Baudelaire's *Fleurs du Mal*; bawdy sailors' ballads about women who wash their genitals; a rape scene from Ovid (transmuted into the "sounds of horns and motors"); and a fortune-teller with "a bad cold." While we don't get all of what Eliot calls the "second-hand machinery" of Baudelaire's "prostitutes, mulattoes, Jewesses, serpents, cats, corpses" ("Baudelaire" 233), we do get a recombination of cultural clichés pointing to the diseased corruption of body and mind, woven into Eliot's "Unreal city" (a pastiche of Baudelaire's "Sept Vielliards") and into Sosostris's unwittingly pertinent prophecy.

For Eliot, Baudelaire gave poetry a new moral edge that compensated for his dated imagery, a battery of clichés ironized in the Philomel passage. Through his "command of words and rhythms," and through his dissonant post-Metaphysical metaphorical yokings, Baudelaire "was at least able to understand that the sexual act as evil is more dignified, less boring, than as the *natural*, 'life-giving', cheery automatism of the modern world. For Baudelaire, sexual operation is at least something not analogous to Kruschen Salts."[42] Like Marie Lloyd, Baudelaire denaturalized the "cheery" and passive automatism of sex and art, calling the audience to a newly intense way of living while confronting the breakdown of the body, and of the self-delusions of commodity culture.

Parsifal, in particular, merges "Christian redemption and Schopenhauerian negation of will (and desire)" in a way that "returns us to the sexual and even to the syphilitic," and to a complex of the "mythic" and the "medical" (Hutcheon and Hutcheon 85). These anxieties exemplify Wagner's fixation with cultural healing, neurotic to the core: Wagner's obsession with totality is manifested as nostalgic scapegoating of noisy Others. Wagner's toxic anti-Semitic writings, for example, are infused with complaints about Jews' "nonsensical gurgling, yodeling, and crackling," manifested in the fear of "loathsome babble" associated in the Ring Cycle with Alberich and Mime.[43] Eliot's own anti-Semitism is well known, and I shan't belabor it, except to say that *The Waste Land* is bound with the ideological and aesthetic sicknesses of organic holism that suffuse Wagner and Wagnerism. *The Waste Land*'s music of ideas is, in a word, infected with the disease of the total artwork.

In *The Case of Wagner* (*Der Fall Wagner*; 1888), Nietzsche argues that Wagner *is* a disease: an illusionist whose stimulation of the nerves is coated with the deceptive gloss of a spiritual calling. "Illness itself," Nietzsche writes, "can be a stimulus to life, but one must be healthy enough for such a stimulus!—Wagner increases exhaustion . . . he attracts the weak and exhausted to him. Oh, the rattlesnake joy of the old Master precisely because he always saw 'the little children' coming unto him!" The children's chorus from *Parsifal*, filtered through Verlaine and Eliot, marks a fear that Wagner's musical-dramatic decadence attracts the exhausted and, "stimulating tired nerves," only exhausts them further—drowning dull roots with spring rain.

Disease, as cultural critics have come to understand, is a social as well as a medical artifact—a notation and not just an object. Syphilis registers an entire hierarchy of moral, civilizational, social, and neurological side-effects and contaminations. According to Elaine Showalter, Victorian syphilophobic discourses centered on a pronounced misogyny and fear of female sexuality. A site of social anxiety as well as medical confusion, the search to cure syphilis was also a quest to identify a culprit; representations of the disease tended to spotlight a contaminating racial or sexual presence. One finds sailors and soldiers often blamed for the introduction of syphilis to Europe, blame that they share with homosexuals, prostitutes, and women generally. Yet by the end of the nineteenth century, the disease did not signify moral turpitude so much as satirize the ethos of "conjugal obligation."[44] Syphilis represented both "an abyss of contamination" and an "ideal of a regenerate sexuality"—serving as a scapegoated contamination and as a dissonant critique of false health.[45]

Both the reactionary and the radical meanings of syphilis echo in *The Waste Land*, particularly as it pulls Wagner into the drawing room. Hutcheon and Hutcheon spotlight *Parsifal*'s Kundry, the wild woman whose vaguely Arabian qualities mark her as an overdetermined exotic symbol—a surrogate for both Mary Magdalene and the Wandering Jew. The decadent opening of "A Game of Chess," a pastiche of Baudelaire's morbid decadence, likewise sets apart the female body as alien, framing the mantle of Philomel and the "bad nerves" of the first speaker as neurotic and erotic scapegoats. The "burnished throne" on which she sits reflects "the glitter of her jewels rose to meet it," an uneasy metaphor for the "unstoppered" diffusion of female sexuality, "Unguent, powdered, or liquid—troubled, confused." The section begins with rich Symbolist synesthesia, a "confused" profusion of sense impressions, from which the sense of hearing is temporarily absent. Baudelaire's hypocrite reader, Marie Lloyd's audience, and the spectator on the "burnished throne" are all implicated in esthesic sin; sound enters "A Game of Chess" in a moment of violence that in turn calls on the ears of its audience:

> by the barbarous king
> So rudely forced; yet there the nightingale
> Filled all the desert with inviolable voice
> And still she cried, and still the world pursues,
> "Jug Jug" to dirty ears. (II.99–103)

The syphilitic body and the violated Philomel share the stage as damaged lives whose "inviolable voices" threaten to awaken the poem's chess-zombies to their illusion. The beginning of the second section, like the "heart of light, the silence" (I.41), silently frames the aural "change of Philomel" with a visual offering of the body: Philomel's "inviolable voice" is depicted (or filled in by the speaker himself) in ekphrastic depiction. The use of a visual frame to clarify sonoric experience, a dynamic of operatic theatre (Wagner's "eye of hearing"), is no less important to music of the drawing room, a point that clarifies Sitwell's reworking of ballet imagery for the in-home performance of *Façade*. Richard Leppert, analyzing of the surfaces of pianos and harpsichords, explains that "sight acts as an organizer of musical semantics" and "connects sonoric phenomena with the social."[46] The visual and verbal inscriptions on women's pianos of hunting and violence, of sexual seduction and of the power to dominate nature (Orpheus's lyre) make "force and imputed violence the agents of art" (128), and make music "the sonoric analogue to her imprisonment" (122). Philomel is imprisoned by the music that seems to emanate from the frame, a gramophonic logic as well as a pianistic one; her "inviolable voice" engendered by violence disallows us from hearing nature in the poem as separate from domination and seduction. As Philomel and the "neurotic woman" are made alien, the boundaries among the senses are "troubled, confused"; the passage travels an unlikely path from the eye through the nose to the ear, the "odours" of candles and "synthetic perfumes," before reaching the tongueless victim. The battery of sensory assaults seems not just to exhaust this woman's nerves but to keep her in a state of inarticulate exhaustion. Whether or not she is expressly syphilitic, as Sosostris is, she carries the clichés: coded as "exotic," repressed, and internally afflicted by some kind of fire, which "Spread out in fiery points / Glowed into words, then would be savagely still."

Thus Eliot's syphilitic clichés take both sonic and visual form. Hearkening to the infections of *Parsifal*, to the children's chorus mediated by Verlaine, to the hyperstimulated Wagnerian theater, and to the mythic structure of the Grail Legend, he implicates the musical-medical-mythical totality by which women's bodies are assaulted and imprisoned. Yet those same sites of disease and sonic rupture are what implode their false wholes. Eliot's cure for neurotic emotion is the "extinction of personality" and its assimilation into the order—as he writes in "Tradition and the Individual Talent," "only those who have personality and emotions know what it means to want to escape from these things"—but this attempt to purify the body leads only to a different neurotic noise. Matthew Smith argues that Kundry's guttural laughter and "hysterical gestures" puncture the drama's somatophobia by "forcing" the "crisis of corporeality . . . to neurotic extremes," making the Wagnerian orchestra a "gramophone *avant la lettre*" as it enacts this crisis.[47] This problem permeates Wagner's most Schopenhauerian dramas (*Tristan* and *Parsifal*), which betray, as Abbate suggests, a "deep uncertainty about the origins of voice and its natural association with the human or material."[48] Eliot hears in *Parsifal* a grasping for the sublime that tries to sever voice from body, only to find itself anchored to those bodies' lingering materiality.

Philomel's cries, like Kundry's laughter, question the authority of a poetic whole desperate to identify women as hysterics and abstract their voices. As *The Waste Land* amputates the voice from its diseased corporeality, producing what Abbate calls a "voice-object," it compensates by binding voice to a nondecaying materiality: the painting of a nightingale or the material surface of a gramophone record. If *The Waste Land* pursues the Schopenhauerian logic of *Heart of Darkness*, it all the more pursues what Kreilkamp calls Conrad's "phonographic logic," a fascination with the disembodied whisper of a hollow man. Like Eliot's "rapid-breeding" gramophone, the phonograph threatens the authenticity of the theater with technological violation, but preserves, as an artifact of that violation, the inviolable voice of the damaged subject.

Walking Phonographs: Mediation and *The Waste Land*'s Glitch

The gramophone enables Eliot, like Adorno, to interrogate the relationship among the sound produced by the musician, the sound produced by the machine, and the social setting in which that musician and that machine appear.[49] The o-shaped exhalation of what Kittler (quoting *Tristan*) calls Wagner's "world-breath"—the exploration of acoustical excess *as* acoustical excess—makes of music a technological objectification of the Will, but also a disruptive mediation of its formal unity. *The Waste Land*'s gramophone (like its monochord) rhythmically gestures to, and destabilizes, the medium's false illusion of wholeness. The poem's merging of the gramophone with the human body tries to redress the poem's "torn" dislocations of body from voice, of bourgeois subject from nature, of music from pure tone—losses that entreat the compensatory mediation of a technology too flawed to provide it.

These two problems, of false wholeness and of music's bodily (dis)location, are related in ways that I have addressed: Wagner's phantasmagoric invisible orchestra, the distant Schopenhauerian condition to which we aspire, remains troubled by the neurotic corporeal extremes to which Wagner pushes his characters. In *Parade* and *Les Mariés de la Tour Eiffel* (1921), Eliot's balletic contemporaries Satie and Jean Cocteau use "human gramophones" to puncture Wagner's organic holism and extravagant gravitas. The gramophone's materiality, what Adorno calls its "thingness," makes it at once a threatening binding of music to a consumer object, and a source of productive critical deterioration, akin to the decomposing corpses that resist the poem's controlling hands. The record's materiality also leaves it prone to decay—to a glitch that foregrounds the technology's limitations and reopens it to the rhythms of politics and history. As in the total artwork, the more the record player struggles to preserve the illusion of fidelity to its natural source, the more it exposes its own material limitations.

The Rhinemaidens—Wagner's best shot at a "pure tone," but a disruptive fracture in Eliot's language—amplify the poem's Adornian ambivalence about a state of nature that requires (masked) technology to be reexcavated, and prepare the glitchy record that will destabilize the illusion. Much as the Rhinemaidens' ululating acts as a skip in the monochord of "The Fire Sermon," Philomel's "Twit twit twit/Jug jug jug jug jug"—birdsong, citational to the point of cliché, and frantically rhythmic—seems to be wearing down the mechanism that would aestheticize its "sylvan scene." In "What the Thunder Said," likewise, the "Drip drop drip drop drop drop drop" that seems to interrupt the "hermit-thrush sing[ing] in the pine trees" gives us a gradual return to the landscape, but loses control even over its rhythmic alternating; stuck on "drop," it renders the song of nature all upbeats and no downbeat, eroding the solid rock and wearing down its own sonic groove. I will not here pursue recent developments in "glitch music," a neo-Russolian use of technological malfunctions to rescue music from cold, standardized digital recording,[50] but *The Waste Land*'s noise sets up an illusion only to glitch it, to unsettle the record player's illusory pretense to "exactness."

Returning to "The Fire Sermon": a palimpsest of false wholes bound into an o-shaped record, it can be seen to archive the noise of its own production in a productively unstable way. If it serves as a binding whole—an integral physical surface that archives a body of sounds—it also gets stuck at key moments, the citational nonsense of the Rhinemaidens and Philomel unsettling the phantasmagoria. Both the Rhinemaidens and Philomel represent female voices fluidly entered into the monochord and disruptive of its order. In keeping with the trope of *fama* as feminized incursion, *The Waste Land*'s typist, Philomel, and Sosostris, Wagner's Kundry and Rhinemaidens, integrated into a totalized aesthetic landscape, puncture the effort to put an objective veneer over nature, or to mystify nature through phantasmagoric bad faith.

Turning from Wagner to his homologous technology, in Adorno's essay "The Curves of the Needle" (1927), the female voice troubles the phonograph's pretense to naturalization. The essay offers a couple false notes about the gendered voice in ways that resonate with Eliot's oft-noted fear of the female body. Adorno surmises, for example, that "male voices can be reproduced better than female voices," because "in order to become unfettered, the female voice requires the physical appearance of the body that carries it. Only there where the body itself resonates, where the self to which the gramophone refers is identical with its sound, only there does the gramophone have its legitimate realm of validity."[51] As in *The Waste Land*, where the shrillest female voices are detached from their bodies, Adorno sounds the device's limits by ascribing the "shrillness" of the recorded female voice to its distance from her body: the sonoric wholeness of voice requires a visible frame. That "there," "where the body itself resonates," is the irrecuperable vanishing point of her recorded voice, of a voice-object without visible source. Yet this failure to capture her body along with her voice prepares a different, potentially destabilizing moment of failure, when the phonograph starts to fail, and "the exactness one has ascribed to [the phonograph] is exposed as an illusion by the very technology itself" ("Curves" 271). The absent body and the missing performative soul of music reemerge as ghostly presences when the gramophone itself dies.

The threat of the gramophone—its indifference to what Barthes calls the "kneadingly physical" and "lubrificating" liquidity of music—is for Adorno matched by the medium's own materiality, and therefore its propensity to decay. This threat and potential of decay are archived in the material "thingness" of the record. In "The Form of the Phonograph Record" (1934), Adorno (pen-name Hektor Rottweiler) considers the record as a condensation of the "height and the abyss" of music into the two-dimensional disc. The disc's contoured thingness monumentalizes the "herbaria of artificial life" in modernity: "the phonograph records are not artworks but the black seals on the missives that are rushing towards us from all sides in the traffic with technology; missives whose formulations capture . . . the first and the last sounds."[52] The music fades in volume and is distorted in pitch as it approaches the center of the record (the "heart of light, the silence"). As the record kills off the constellational performance of music and binds it to a commodity, Adorno argues, it archives that killing-off in the "scriptal spiral that disappears in the center, in the opening of the middle, but in return survives in time" (280). Poking fun at Nipper, the RCA/Victor puppy who listens to "His Master's [dead?] Voice," Adorno writes that "the artist merely offers him a substitute for the sound image of his own person, which he would like to safeguard as a possession. The only reason he accords the record such value is because he himself could also be just as well preserved" ("Curves" 274). Jonathan Sterne, linking His Master's Voice to Victorian representations of death and mourning, explains that the gramophone offered its consumers the allure of preserving the voices of the dead, a hope that Adorno recognizes as the gramophone's thrall over its owner.[53] The record reminds the auditor of his future dissolution, offering a narcissistic promise of speech after death and a future-anterior archival of modernity's self-destructive "traffic with technology" into an "archaic text of knowledge" ("Form" 280). Though Adorno resents this commodity (like the leitmotif) for ossifying the boundaries of the subject, he recognizes its physicality in a way that resonates with the typist's exhaustion. Like Eliot's

"Dog . . . that's friend to men," which digs up a corpse (I.74) (or like Rottweiler trying to consume Nipper), the record petrifies a voice and exhumes a body: its very thingness "absorbs into itself, in this process of petrification, the very life that would otherwise vanish" ("Form" 279).

In Eliot, the gramophone's violence against music follows on the dispassionate violence of the "young man carbuncular" (another broken-down *soma*) against the typist. The typist cannot by herself produce a song that implicates the dirty ears and voyeuristic eyes of the witnesses to her assault; the gramophone has to do that work for her. As the boundaries between subject and gramophone dissolve, the typist is assimilated into the "human engine": she "smoothes her hair with automatic hand / And puts a record on the gramophone" (III.255-6). Eliot's forced rhyme between "automatic hand" and the word "and," which itself follows on a citation of Goldsmith ("When lovely woman stoops to folly, and") underscores the technology's automatism: robbed of performative gesture, the typist / human gramophone gives equal sonic weight to the jarring imaginative conceit and the conjunction "and," a purely syntactic utterance that can connect anything with anything. The scene is mediated further by Tiresias: "throbbing between two lives" like the "throbbing waiting" "human engine" of modernity itself, but also throbbing between musical expression and noise, nature and technology. Tiresias's vision entangles the technologies of the typewriter and the gramophone with the violent yokings of poetry—and with the human body, which has become a "rapid-breeding" mediator of noise even when it cannot breed new bodies.[54]

The Waste Land's implosion of Wagnerian totality into an unstable multimedia text can be detected not just in the gramophone's breakdown, but in the merging of gramophone and body—an ironic compensation for the gramophone's severing of body from voice. One need merely look to Eliot's balletic contemporaries to see gramophones, noise, and the rhythms of dance pulled together to deconstruct Wagner's controlling hands, and to pierce the authority of the master artist. Satie's and Cocteau's rebellion against Wagner took the form of "*ballets réalistes*," such as *Les Mariés de la Tour Eiffel* and *Parade*, in which staging and music were punctuated with sirens, car-horns, and ads read through megaphones. (Lynn Garafola suggests that the parodic "Managers" of *Parade* may have satirized Diaghilev, the occasionally overbearing impresario of the Ballets Russes.) I discuss these developments in more detail in chapters four, in detailing Antheil's attempted collaboration with Joyce, using the "phoneygraph" to parody the false unities of nationalism; and in chapter five, where Sitwell's campy "poetry of publicity" ironizes Wagner's aesthetic of organic authenticity. The maniacal rhythmic repetitions of *Parade*, rather than leading us back to Wagnerian nature, only get us further from it—and more deeply entrenched in the rhythms of the market.[55]

While Eliot was composing and Pound was midwifing *The Waste Land*, the Ballets Suédois premiered *Les Mariés*, with scenario by Cocteau, music by Satie and the French composers known collectively as *Les Six*. Influenced by fauvism, Futurism, American film, and the music hall, the ballet is narrated by two "actors costumed as Phonographs," whose "bodies are the cabinets, their mouths the horns," and which comment on the action and "recite the lines of the characters . . . pronouncing each syllable distinctly."[56] By absorbing the Futurists, and Cocteau and Satie, Eliot transitively absorbed the music hall acts with which all of these artists were obsessed.[57] Satie and Cocteau aimed to puncture the Wagnerian bouillabaisse with human beings dressed as cubist phonographs—a denaturalization of what Kittler calls "Wagner's media technologies" minus his chthonic illusion. The bodies are cabinets, storing information and disseminating it from the horns; marking time and commenting on it, they dissever music from a translinguistic ideal, producing instead a charmingly antisocial mix of dance and diegesis. If Wagner, as Kittler argues, presages sound media by privileging sound not as dramatic accoutrement but as pure data, Cocteau's talking gramophones and noisy Managers embody the glitchy record: inassimilable presences that yell at you, only to fall apart in exhaustion.[58]

I submit, as the two human phonographs in *The Waste Land*, Sosostris (the corrupted condition of music) and Tiresias (the exhausted prophet whose voice cannot die). Two sickly embodied mediums unfolding the processes of encoding and decoding in real time, both figures occupy the poem's stage and "see" lives beyond it, as they move in and out of their own prophetic visions. The syphilitic Sosostris finds a complement in the blind prophet whose body is wasting away:

> Like a taxi throbbing waiting,
> I Tiresias, though blind, throbbing between two lives,
> Old man with wrinkled female breasts, can see
> At the violet hour, the evening hour that strives
> Homeward, and brings the sailor home from sea,
> The typist home at teatime, clears her breakfast, lights
> Her stove, and lays out food in tins. (III.217–223)

I would link this to the "O City City" passage, with its monochordal public bar: even without the excised lines ("Vibrates unconscious to its formal destiny"), the two passages share a search for a unifying "formal destiny," a vibrating teleology for which Sosostris and Tiresias act as tainted decomposing telegraph-girls in a binding Wagnerian cage. A brief note about Tiresias's "wrinkled female breasts": Wagner's defense of *Stabreim* is couched in the metaphor of the mother's "'nourishing breast' (melody) and her 'milk' (the open tone)" (a "murmur of maternal lamentation" [*TWL* V.396]).[59] As language was "weaned" from its roots in vowel sound, Wagner claimed, it needed to re-forge its origins; *Stabreim* was an archaic artistic mechanism that could distinguish authentic language from "loathsome babble." Tiresias's dried breasts imply a need for a new milk of open tone, however illusory, to compensate for a lack. He may get there in the form of the Rhinemaidens' *Stabreim*, but their sonic and liquid river has been corrupted with "oil and tar," an archaic binding device slicked with the detritus of modernity.

Tiresias, like the gramophone, represents the material petrifaction of subjectivity: his milk dried up, he presents a corrupted *soma* that mediates the mechanized modernity around him. He has "perceived the scene" through sound and intuition (he is blind), and "foretold the rest" in the form of the typist's indifferent sexual encounter. As mediator, Tiresias filters the poem's ambivalence toward the material and ideal capacities of music.[60] Caught between two lives, between two gendered modes of identification, between (in Adorno's strange logic) the reproducible male voice and the irreproducible female one, Tiresias embodies the contradictions of the metropolis. "Like a taxi throbbing waiting," he archives the tumescent rhythmic pulse of the city in conveying its violence against the subject. Not without another gesture to *Tristan* ("the sailor home from sea"),[61] this throbbing back-and-forth between ancient and modern produces the mechanical typist—the object of Tiresias's *ecoutistic* fantasy and the automatic hand who plays more bastardized opera.

Considering Tiresias in light of the typist/gramophone, in light of Wagner's phantasmagoric autonomization of sound (the gramophone *avant la lettre*), and in light of Satie's and Cocteau's ballets (gramophones *dans la lettre*), the poem's mediations of music ironize the prophetic, rhythmic return to nature. Redressing Tiresias's "shrunken dugs" with a series of aesthetic mediations—only to find each new mediation further corrupting the Rhine, and the corpses floating on it—the poem doubles Osbert Sitwell's ironic Wagnerian question ("Can we reverse?") with an equally ironic Cocteauvian and Nietzschean one: Can this possibly be the cure for hyperstimulated exhaustion? *More Wagner*?

Tiresias as "record-player" flattens out historical time and awaits an interpreter to breathe "a little life" back into it. Within the space of Eliot's o-like monochord, Tiresias has become something like a phonograph stylus: confronting the flat record, decoding its material, and encoding it in his own stream of sound, "perceiv[ing] the scene" and foretelling "the rest." The rhythmic back and forth between poetic and technological mediation, tumescence ("throbbing") and passivity ("waiting"), becomes as indifferently relentless as the Will itself, spiraling toward the abyss at its center. These human phonographs reinforce the anxieties about Wagner's music, which consolidates a whole while heralding its own obsolescence; and about the gramophone, which seems to enforce "reconciliation with . . . objects" but whose glitches herald a dissonant irreconcilability. The typist's automatic hand, reified and subjected to the clerk's "assault," allows this encoded script to sing in its spiral of decay: "London Bridge is falling down falling down falling down."

The Waste Land presents a "throbbing" impersonal Will that orders experience, while being materialized in an artifact—the record—that glitches unpredictably. The poem's final rhythmic peals, presenting the image of a total return to a primal maternal "murmur," produce "natural" sound as a hybrid palimpsest of media. The song of the earth is punctuated by visual flashes ("In the faint moonlight, the grass is singing/ . . . / Co co rico co co rico / In a flash of lightning") as Valhalla and its analogues come crashing to the ground:

> Cracks and reforms and bursts in the violet air
> Falling towers
> Jerusalem Athens Alexandria
> Vienna London
> Unreal (V.372–376)

Cracking noise marks the breakdown of a spent order ("voices singing out of empty cisterns and exhausted wells") into fragments that must rhythmically be shored into a new one; the poem's "Tolling reminiscent bells that kept the hours" suggest the inexorable temporal entropy decaying these crumbling Valhallas. Yet the poem's mediations of noise destabilize its fantasy of restored natural purity. The "broken Coriolanus" is temporarily restored by "aetherial rumours"; but if his power is rehabilitated, it will be by the unstable *rumori* of the same populace that he has previously tried to contain. This attempted reconsolidation of order and that of the Fisher King, whose "setting" of his "lands in order" (*TWL* V.425) echoes the curing of Amfortas's syphilitic wound in *Parsifal*, reprises the illusion of "health and wholeness," an illusion whose neuroses have been exposed.

Even Eliot's return to rhythm at the poem's end ("Shantih Shantih Shantih") cannot be presented without a mediating gloss ("The peace which passeth understanding"), which Eliot offers as "a feeble translation of the conduct of this word." The word, indeed, has *conduct*: it conducts, in the musical and the ordinary senses of the term. It beats time, acts out, filters electric energy (DA), and triangulates other languages and media. And rhythmic incantation "passeth understanding" because it works on the body and tries to naturalize itself in the pulse. If Eliot encourages surrender to the controlling hands of Tradition or the Will, *The Waste Land*'s play with noise, dissonance, and rhythm prepares us not to trust transhistorical rhythmic authority, but to constellate the conventions by which that authority means anything. Even while the auditory imagination of *Waste Land*—the dissonant nonrhymes and yoked conceits—tries to integrate the historical record into a mythical totality, the whole is punctured by the "rudely forced" screech of a body in crisis, marked by the hope that "the decaying form . . . indicates the coming of the new."

DA Capo: Coda on *The Waste Land*

In a 1970s experiment known as the McGurk Effect, a film depicts a woman saying "Ka," while a voice on the soundtrack says "Pa." The almost uniform result is that we perceive her saying "Da."[62] We cognitively mediate the position of the tongue to somewhere between the lips (Pa) and the palate (Ka)—between the plosive of "April" with the choking off of "cruel"—landing it on the back of the "carious teeth" (Da). Perhaps there is something more perceptive than expected about Eliot's use of this syllable. If sight helps to organize musical semantics, and if, as Wagner insists, music underwrites the gestural and poetic Idea, for Eliot sight and sound are joined even at the element of the syllable, yoking consonantal noise with the vowel's "eye of hearing." The poem's final resolution into a rhythmic DA could be the palimpsestic dubbing of one medium over another, a phantasmagoria whose sensory, musical, and mechanical technologies are internally at odds. Heard in this light, the Thunder of Eliot's Ganges speaks not as a prehistorical source of unmediated sound, but as a hypermediated site of ironic hybridity.

Even as its hybridity leads us to overcompensate with holistic narratives (the poem is a pilgrimage, a Tradition, a total artwork), *The Waste Land* defamiliarizes the compulsion to reconcile constellational systems of meaning into identitarian ones. Levenson's reading of *The Waste Land* in view of Eliot's philosophy thesis, unstitching monadic subjectivity into multiply mediated interactions with the world, underscores the poem's alienation of our very processes of seeing and hearing. The poem's auditory imagination—like Pound's *Cantos*, unfolding history as a rhythmic process subject to noisy interruption—plays out the contradictory effects of music as a dynamic range of performances, a notation whose reduction to object always leaves something abjected.

I will now largely (not entirely) leave Adorno behind, because *The Waste Land* represents the most distilled concentration of his central dialectics: aesthetic and technological mediation, composition and reception, high and mass culture. But he will remain in the background: without Adorno's ear for the dissonances, fractures, and nonidentities of art, our understanding of modernism's cultural mathematics—or of schemes of "kulchur" such as Pound's—would be much less supple. Poetry, opera, nature, and culture will often show us Ka and sing us Pa. It is our own failing if we keep hearing them say DA.

3 The Antheil Era

Ezra Pound's Musical Sensations

Verity: are you ready to hear it?
In sickness alone is there joy
Life's true stories are tragedies
Louts are the only knights errant
Only in screeches are there melodies
Nor any cool heads but lovers.

Francois Villon (trans. Galway Kinnell), "Ballade"

Because all the air trembled and the shadows trembled as
  with a collapse
        As thunder shaking the rain,
Blazing phrases without sense shot thru the rain,
A grating noise inside the submarine when the beam
  strikes it.
I heard the spirit as if in torture.

Pound, Canto LXXII

Throughout the *Cantos*, Pound speaks to and from the underworld through music, ideogram, and radio, embracing poetry as profane pleasure and as merciless social critique.[1] The endpoint of a man who had long protested his belief in an "'absolute rhythm' . . . which corresponds exactly to the . . . shade of emotion to be expressed," Canto LXXII communes with Marinetti, the militant Futurist antithesis of sublimity, classicism, and everything else implied by the "absolute rhythm"—whose influence on Pound, however, resonates more with every tortured disavowal.[2] Faced with such discontinuities, the question arises: what ideologies are sublated by these formalist "absolutes" or (as in Joyce's "Sirens" episode) by the *Cantos*' contrapuntal structure?[3] The question deepens on examining Pound's collaboration with Antheil, whose doctrines of formal purity are tested by the pianolas, sirens, propellers, and buzzers of *Ballet Mécanique*. What happens when "absolute rhythm" not only serves as an abstract poetic doctrine, but is heard in practice as a machine-like pulse to the grating noise of industry?

This problem, which motivates the next two chapters, I loosely call "the Antheil dilemma," though it is not unique to Antheil and is characteristic of neoclassical modernism more broadly. By claiming to unmoor music from literary signifiers, one paradoxically leaves it more open to being attached to different ones, and thereby makes it susceptible to interpretive abuse. The dilemma permeates Joyce's work as well as Pound's: the more music claims for itself an autonomous status—the more vociferously it tries to sublimate noise away—the more troubled and unstable it becomes. In short, by integrating noise and music, Antheil exposes music not just as an ineffable art, ideogrammic condensation, or "new learning," but as a way of profiting from the material effects that those noises chronicle—industry, publicity, sensation, and scandal—phenomena amplified rather than silenced by Antheil's neoclassical reductions of form.

As in Eliot, it is rhythm that motivates Pound's fascination with music's aesthetic and cultural purchase—its potential, for example, to demarcate social and economic order. For Pound, tightening the text's rhythmic form, far from limiting its social or cultural meanings, makes the text's "circle of reference" better able to define and diagnose the sensational noises around it. If, as Daniel Albright suggests, Pound began around 1924 to deemphasize the fluid yet "absolute" rhythmic arcs of *vers libre* and to prefer discrete, isolatable "hard bits" of rhythm,[4] concurrent with this shift is the entrance of Antheil, who helped with Pound's operatic setting of Francois Villon's *Testament* (1923), who inspired Pound's *Antheil* monograph (1924), and who premiered *Ballet Mécanique* the same year.[5] A proposed soundtrack to Fernand Léger's cubist film, scored for "three pianos, four bass drums, tam-tam, two pianists, seven (or so) electric bells, a siren, three airplane propellers, and sixteen synchronized player-pianos,"[6] *Ballet Mécanique* proved one of the most infamously noisy concert pieces of the 1920s. Despite Antheil's insistence that the *Ballet* should be appreciated independent of any programmatic elements, Pound heard it as a musical factory:

> Three years ago Antheil was talking vaguely of "tuning up" whole cities, of "silences twenty minutes long *in the form*," etc. . . . With the performance of the

> Ballet mécanique [sic] one can conceive the possibility of organizing the sounds of a factory, let us say of boilerplate or any other clangorous noisiness, the actual sounds of the labour, the various tones of the grindings; according to the needs of the work, and yet, with such pauses and durées, that at the end of the eight hours, the men go out not with frayed nerves, but elated—fatigued, yes, but elated.[7]

In tension with the solitary artist meme of "Hugh Selwyn Mauberley," closer to the drift of Pound's "totalitarian treatise" *Guide to Kulchur* (1938), Pound's musical workshop posits a formal immanence to the workday: hierarchically organized, but shaped by an organic relation between the sounds of labor and the material "needs of the work."[8] If in "Mauberley" the pianola "'replaces'/Sappho's barbitos" in a thanatotic march toward cultural suicide, in the *Ballet* it powers a rhythmic factory that produces "hard bits" with maximum efficiency. For Pound, *Ballet Mécanique* transmits not just a condensed ideogram, but an unalienated workshop in which no sound or energy is wasted.

Pound's description of *Ballet Mécanique* as a Lawrentian industrial merry-go-round, expanding the orbit of its "circle of reference," betrays, first, the poet's deep fascination with Antheil's "bad boy" celebrity; second, his conception of music in relation to the structures of labor; and, finally, his conception of music not just as something mediated or mass-reproduced, but as a medium in itself: a way of remediating cultural programs. In "Mauberley" (Pound's first poem to use the word "usury"), the pianola figures a kind of alienated labor that upsets the link between a poet/singer and her instrument.[9] According to Tim Armstrong, the player piano bespeaks music's status not as an auratic artifact mediated by technology, but as a technology per se, which "*already* carries the notion of redeemed time later attached to the gramophone."[10] Pound considered Antheil's music not just an abstract "form" that "the performing musician cuts . . . in the air and in the time flow," but a species of mediated materialist critique.[11] *Ballet Mécanique*, Pound would come to argue, pulls music "into a wider circle of reference," "out of the concert hall," and into "a phase of life not hitherto tackled by musicians and freighted . . . with reference to already existing musical reference."

Antheil's *Ballet Mécanique*, and Pound's reactions to it, are emblematic of a set of cultural anxieties over musical form as a mediation of noise. Antheil and Pound model a "grating" back-and-forth between two understandings of music—one, as a sublime, purely mathematical expression of form; the other, as a way of understanding the temporal structures of public life. Accordingly, Pound's desire to keep lines distinct, demarcations pronounced, and rhythms absolute and "calculated" always has to be negotiated with his desire to honor the institutions of material production, the contingencies of artistic production, and the sensations of the flesh. In trying to negotiate the objective form of art with the needs and limitations of the body, Pound uses rhythm to test and expand art's circle of reference in relation to noise. Pound's rhythms, whether imagined as "absolute rhythms," "hard bits," or "fundamental irregularities," seek out an ethical and an aesthetic organizing principle, while furtively nurturing his need for sensation and spectacle. Music, for Pound, is both fluid and solid, ordered and entropic, sensational and coldly formal.

I pursue this argument first by detailing Antheil's rise to stardom, the use of outlandish publicity stunts to craft his "bad boy" celebrity (an argument that chapter five makes, in different form and with much less noisy music, in relation to Edith Sitwell). I then consider how *Ballet Mécanique* resonated as an allegory for industry: Pound himself imagined it as an energizing rhythmic arrangement of time that might valuably remake the workday, and a cartoonist for the American Marxist journal *The New Masses* reimagined Antheil as a captain of industry. Scrutinizing Antheil's piece and Pound's responses to it, I analyze how Antheil's "mathematical" objectivity might give rise to (reductive) Adornian or Lukácsian allegories of his music as a naturalization of labor. Pound's contemporaries, namely Wyndham Lewis, considered Pound's responses to the *Ballet* as positive proof that his new classical aesthetics were a cover for sensationalism—a reading prepared by the piece's cold formalism as well as its mechanical noise.

Hoping that these cultural resonances undermine any pretense to a purely aesthetic ideal, I parse Antheil's and Pound's doctrines concerning the materiality of musical time—its "plasticity," as Antheil refers to it. These doctrines speak to Antheil's conviction that music *sans* literary programme could interact with the "universal laws" of temporal order, an underlying pulse extending from the primitive to the futurist; and to Pound's conviction that music could lock in with the fundamental irregularity of human history, a continuity both ordered and entropic. Rhythm—as it maps out both the internal structure of music and its external relation to social noise—imbricates these dual understandings of music's internal order and external reference, twinning (for example) Antheil's ice-blocks of rhythm with the rhythms of labor. Pound's celebration of rhythm as the prime mover of art, with harmony a mere epiphenomenon, shapes his desire for "clear demarcation" both within the artwork, and in line with the fundamental irregularity of the Great Bass. For Antheil and Pound, the more one tightens the calculated rhythms of the artwork, the more the artwork is able to diagnose—or is left open to—the material noises with which it is engaged.

Having considered both the cultural resonances and the abstract ideals of Antheil's music, as both he and Pound understood it, I close the chapter with a brief reading of selected late *Cantos*, in which his search for more humane temporal organizations of art and commerce manifests in a search for the formal ratios internal to the artwork itself. Michael Golston persuasively reads the voice of the late *Cantos* as "a mechanical apparatus for measuring the inaudible rhythms of a speaking body as its language begins a trajectory of decay" (96). The focus on rhythm as a mechanical apparatus that must, as in Eliot, contend with the decay of body and word is reanimated by Antheil's interest in music that "vibrates" in the "human organism," and by Pound's attendant interest in situating that music's cultural frequencies in sync with universal laws. A similar dynamic resonates in the figure of Francois Villon, whose bodily decay Pound's *Testament* marks with noise and attempts to render permanent through rhythmic reinvention. Villon's presence alongside Antheil in Canto LXXIV speaks to the composer's contradictory function in Pound's career: as a quirky "bad boy," and as an objective correlative for the "absolute" rhythmic form that will give music its fullest resonance with the body and with "kulchur." I contend, finally, that Cantos LXXIV and LXXV (the latter of which comprises a musical score) renegotiate music's public circulation—its propensity to be broadcast, to match up with a historical order, to liberate an imprisoned subject—through sharper rhythmic definition. Antheil's appearance in LXXIV along with his fellow travelers in the Antheil Era (Joyce, W.B. Yeats, Ernest Hemingway, and, honorarily, Villon himself) speaks to the oscillations between the disordered mechanical noise of modernity, and its ordering vibration.

I do not offer here a sustained political reading of Pound in relation (for example) to the ground-bass of C.K. Douglas's theories of Social Credit or Leo Frobenius's ethnographic "paideuma" (the effort to reconstruct a cohere texture of ideas that permeates art, culture, and economics). My account of the *Cantos* themselves may seem breezy. Nevertheless, it will unpack some of what was socially resonant in Pound's discussion of Antheil's expanding circle of musical reference. Having diagnosed the pianola as the symptom of usury in "Mauberley," Pound's late *Cantos* use radio-like disembodied voices to bemoan the material alienation of "usura," thanks to which there "is no clear demarcation."[12] If the move from pianola to radio seems licentious, it had a real payoff for Antheil himself. Collaborating with the actress Hedy Lamarr, who had read his tract *The Shape of the War to Come* (1940) and his user's guide to "glandular criminology" (*Every Man His Own Detective*; 1937), Antheil used the player-piano roll to develop and patent a new radio-guided "frequency-hopping" technology—hopping among eighty-eight different frequencies in order to stymie enemy efforts to jam the signal.[13] This technology aided the defeat of the "Totalitarian State" presaged in *The Shape of the War to Come*, and paved the way for wireless communication technologies, akin to what Timothy Campbell calls the "information network" of the late *Cantos*.

Pound himself refers, in Canto LXXVII, to L'Abbé Rousselot's acoustic experiments with the phonetics of *vers libre*, which led to the development of sonar (he "fished for sound in the Seine / and led to detectors").[14] In different but oddly commensurable ways, Pound and Antheil found their aesthetic intuitions—that the rhythms of poetry and music might concretize the ethereal—matched by the insight that aesthetic temporality might detect more conspicuously material forms of sound.

Antheil's desire to transmit information pervades his work—including the message of not having a message: "My original title for the work," writes Antheil, "was 'Message to Mars.' Considered from the purely euphonistic point of view, it is, of course, a much worse one than 'Ballet Mecanique'; moreover it implies all kinds of moralistic and mystic things which would certainly be allergic to the ice blocks of its music" (*BBM* 139). Antheil saw that the original title's "messages" would undercut his desire to fashion music as an ice-cold, neutral formal canvas. But once out of Antheil's hands, the piece became fodder for Pound's moralistic cultural programs. Moreover, Antheil's music, and Pound's fascination with it, looked to Lewis, among others, like an ongoing publicity campaign for two avant-gardists selling themselves as neoclassicists.[15] As Lewis wrote, Pound's clandestine Futurism and his neoclassical troubadour act were but two sides of a "sensation-loving" personality.

"Sensation" is a deeply embodied term, and strikes to the heart of Pound's classicist rejection of fin-de-siècle music that assaults the "nerves and sensorium"[16] while offering no clear structure to interpret it. Likewise, if rhythm served as Pound's means to negotiate intellectual structure with the material needs of culture, it also threatened this formal integrity by indexing the political "march of events" and the battery of the industrial factory. Pound's and Antheil's rhetoric of formal purity is troubled by their interactions with the spectacles of Futurism, speaking to an internally conflicted hopping between the self-contained modernist artifact and the avant-garde integration of music into daily life. The incessant formal patterning of Antheil's music—defended as "music alone," but turned into a public sensation and esthesically reimagined as the machine-like pulses of industry—threatened to expose the sublimity of music as a mere slogan for the modern aesthete. This dilemma shapes not only the *Cantos* but earlier poems like "Mauberley," in which a credulous "marketplace" reduces "the 'sublime,' in the old sense," to a mass-reproducible catch-phrase.

As Antheil's rhythms resonate with the noises of industry and publicity, then, they help to give a more materialist thrust to studies of Pound's music and poetics; for example, to Kenner's account of Pound as the great collocator of objective poetic particulars; and to Marjorie Perloff's study of Pound's "vortex," the poetic node "through which . . . ideas are constantly rushing" (Pound's phrase). As Perloff convincingly details in *The Futurist Moment*, Pound imagined this "vortex" to be produced by "disjunctive speech rhythms," presaging the polysemous "objets trouvés" of his late *Cantos*.[17] With Antheil in mind, the Pound of Kenner, Albright, and Perloff—a figure of synthetic concretion—can be opened up as a constellation of cultural resonances. Antheil, as his name appears in Canto LXXIV, comes to be an objet trouvé unto himself, a concrete object accruing meaning through juxtaposition, and a personality amassing cultural capital through social spectacle. Alongside Perloff's study of Pound in relation to the Futurists, and Kenner's ideogrammic *Pound Era*, I posit "The Antheil Era": a grating back-and-forth between modernist formalism and the avant-garde assault on the sublime. Specifically, Antheil offers a form of noisy and rhythmically intense music, both calculated and sensational, that tries to appeal both to the material—the structures of labor, the primitive needs of the body—and to the abstract universal laws of pattern and form. Antheil expanded music's circle of reference not just because he abstracted music from message, but because his ear for the formalist jargon, combined with his knack for the publicity gimmick, enabled him to move through the circles of Pound and Joyce.

I recognize that it is an eccentric bird who considers Antheil a major figure on par with Pound; Pound's judgment that Antheil was superior to Stravinsky, or even Varèse, has not held up well. But their contemporaries felt differently: Pound was at times seen, even if he was not in fact, to be hitching *his* wagon to *Antheil's* star. I wish to clarify, additionally, that this is a study of resonance and not of influence. I think it unlikely that Antheil much shaped the distinctive prosody of Pound's poetry. How Pound might have thought anew about the cultural *effects* of rhythm is a different matter. Contending with Antheil's brash new idiom, which seemed to invite a new way of thinking about sound within and without the concert hall—and faced with Antheil's publicity savoir faire—Pound intensified his focus on music as a wedge into cultural politics, embracing the formal abstractions of art not for their own sake but as a way to lend additional historical leverage to the small-scale bodily sensation.

A ubiquitous player in the Pound Era, a relentless self-publicist whose performances were major social events, Antheil's association with canonical modernists makes him an intriguing figure for cultural study. His wide-ranging career culminated in a popular autobiography, *Bad Boy of Music* (1945), suggesting that his enfant terrible persona was entirely self-conscious. He collaborated with Yeats on the masque drama *Fighting the Waves* (1929), and with Joyce on an operatic treatment of "Cyclops." Pursuant to Joyce's "mythical method," perhaps, Antheil composed *Transatlantic* (1928), a Weimar-influenced opera retelling *The Iliad* as an oil baron allegory. He published in the *Little Review*, *transition*, *Der Querschnitt*; assisted Nancy Cunard with the musical portions of the *Negro* Anthology (1934); composed film scores for Cecil B. DeMille; and under the pseudonym Stacey Bishop, wrote *Death in the Dark* (1930), a breathtakingly unconvincing detective novel published with the editorial approval of T.S. Eliot.

This lapse in taste aside, Eliot's editorial aegis—in particular, his 1953 edition of Pound's *Literary Essays*—is responsible for giving many of us the Pound we know best. As Michael Coyle contends, while Pound never thought art autonomous from economics, from Eliot's volume we inherit the more tractable Imagist who promoted concision and stylistic economy, realized in "the sequence of a musical phrase." Eliot's volume, Coyle argues, resolves the "modernist ambivalence over choosing an intractable political world over a potentially perfectable aesthetic one" by withdrawing literary criticism altogether "from the arena of immediate political contest."[18] As a result, accounts of Pound's musical praxis emphasize a formal notion of surface and depth in which the material is immanent but condensed to an objective textual space.[19] Such accounts, though not unaware of Pound's politics, reinforce an aestheticism truer to Eliot's editorial mediations than to Pound's social consciousness or love of sensation, scandal, and the avant-garde publicity game. Arguing, for example, that Antheil's music served as a "revivified exemplification of Vorticist ideals," William Hoffa writes, almost as an aside, that by 1923 Pound sought a new American "in need of his polemical skills,"[20] Eliot no longer needing his promotion.

I take this aside as a pivotal point: modernist aesthetic doctrines offered a means of publicizing modernist personalities. If some critics ignore Antheil's orchestrations of publicity at the expense of aesthetic doctrine, and others ignore the music itself in narrating his celebrity, in the Antheil Era music and publicity were inextricable. Satie, one of Antheil's idols, adapts the experiments of Futurism and Dada in *Parade*, which accompanies the noisy Managers of a circus (dressed as Cubist gramophones) to the sounds of typewriters and sirens. For Satie, Tzara, and the Dadaists, as for Antheil, "publicity and business are also poetic elements"; and much as *Ballet Mécanique* integrates noise and music, Antheil orchestrated publicity down to the riots at his own premieres, producing himself as the bad boy of modernism.[21]

As Antheil's noise-music tautened its own formal canvas, then, it expanded its circle of reference—an expansion that resonates with Pound's efforts, in his radio operas, to produce an ethical space of "heightened listening."[22] The circumference of this "circle," the broadcast range of modernist art, continues to motivate media-centered accounts of Pound.[23] As Mark Goble has argued, the presence of noise or "interference" in modernist art confuses the "fantasy of perfect communication between form and content" found throughout both the productions of High Modernism and the found objects of Dada.[24] As in Eliot's Wagnerian gramophone, the haunting noise of "repressed materiality" disrupts the pretense of the object's fidelity and formal autonomy. The condition of music that equates form and content serves, for Pound, as an archive of industrial capitalism and, once unarchived, as a historical pattern of material and aesthetic production.

For Pound the presence of noise is a symptom of social dis-ease, of an alienated disjunction between superstructure and base/bass. Pound, though cautious of the usurious waste signaled by noise, suggests in *Guide to Kulchur* that only by confronting noise can one delve into its cause:

> It appeared to me impossible that any clean form of teaching cd. lead a man, or group, to cause that damnable and hideous noise and inflict it on humanity in the vicinage. . . . Vigorous anticlerical phase ensued. NOT based on noise itself but on the states of mind necessary to induce that gross and piglike tolerance of infamous sound. . . . The effect of a "trifle" like the noise wd. have been effaced

> had I found any contrary evidence, i.e. of any health or cleanliness in British religion. But for the noise I shd. not have been started investigating. What I *found* was disgusting. (300–301, his italics)

If Pound here marginalizes noise as corruption and social disease, he also posits music as a taming of noise. "The function of music," he writes, "is to present an example of order, or a less muddied congeries and proportion than we have yet about us in daily life" (*GK* 255). Noise signified doubly in the 1920s—modernity and progress on one hand, inefficiency and waste on the other—and Pound (like his contemporaries William Strunk Jr. and Melville Dewey ["Dui"]) recognizes both effects, diagnosing "infamous sound" (*fama*) while trying to reduce the static in language with ideogrammic "cds." and "shds." Emily Thompson savvily connects Strunk's dictum "Omit needless words!" to the cultural fear of noise pollution, an effort that becomes all the more self-defeating when reduced to such abbreviated extremes. Owing to the tension between noise on the level of form, and noise on the level of esthesis, abbreviations like Pound's—meant to reduce noise at the level of the word—will only waste the reader's time: as Strunk observed, the reader encounters "the abbreviation *tho* and mentally supplies the missing letters, at the cost of a fraction of his attention."[25] Like the noise of thunder "shot thru the rain," the drive to reduce and intensify may try to counteract the external symptom of noise, but may also amplify noise: either by integrating (like Antheil) noise into music; or by involuting the noise-addled esthesis of an audience.

Pound uses the term "noise" to probe causes and solutions for the atrophying ear. His attitudes toward noise vary, but consistent is his fear that mismanaged noise debilitates active hearing, making audiences unable to discriminate among sounds without rhythmic signposts. Pound hears noise also as a symptom of usurious or inefficient labor management; as the resonance of rhetorical "old lies"; and as a productive invitation for better poietic management through (as in Antheil's musical factory) mathematical calculation. Antheil's music seemed to train the ear by expanding music's circle of reference to include noise, while keeping it rhythmically ordered so that these noises could be diagnosed. Pound's sense that music orders noise, that noise operates as a diagnostic of material distress, or that the aurality of radio might rematerialize the grating echoes between abstraction and physical embodiment, mandates a noisy assault on the senses, given form by the rhythms of music and poetry.

In navigating the tension between musical form and embodied musical sensation, Pound's rhetoric often sounds deeply Futuristic. I have recounted Rainey's claim that Pound, distancing himself from Italian Futurism, adopted publicity techniques from Marinetti himself; the 1912 Futurist exhibitions in London ushered Pound away from "self-referential discourse" and archaic troubadouriana toward the embrace of "art as a public practice." Pound's rejection/embrace of the *Arte dei Rumori* made rumor part of the arsenal: as a reviewer for the London *Times* put it, Marinetti had to "put up with a rude reception from a gallery which seemed fully qualified to give him a lesson in his own 'Art of Noises' "; yet nothing, Rainey writes, "could have made plainer" to Pound "the value of a concerted polemical onslaught, the formation of a collective identity buttressed by theatricality and publicity" (*Institutions* 29). A decade after *Blast* claimed Futurism and impressionism to be the "corpses of the VORTEX," and even as Pound continued to disavow the Futurist influence, he was cribbing liberally from Russolo's proposal to reimagine the "hubbub of train stations, iron works, thread mills, printing presses, electrical plants, and subways." Echoing Russolo's assertion that "*We must break . . . from this restrictive circle of pure sounds*," Pound expands the monochord, breaking out of the "concert hall," out of the self-referential universe of Music-with-a-capital-M, and into the "wider circle of reference" that encompasses public life.

Producing the Bad Boy: A Sensation Materializes

The noises of *Ballet Mécanique* thus precipitate questions about the autonomy of modernist art, questions perhaps amplified by the suspiciously literary qualities of Antheil's autobiography. Like the opening description of the Verrières nail factory in Stendhal's *Red and Black* (Antheil's favorite novel, recommended to him by Joyce), *Bad Boy of Music* romanticizes the aural life of his youth, even claiming his birth "across the street from a noisy machine shop" as a "prenatal influence" on his musical love of noise (*BBM* 13). As a child living across from the Trenton State Penitentiary, Antheil writes, he had not yet been conditioned to hear noise as unmusical; he was "still too young to know that factory districts, broken machinery, sand pits, smokestacks, and all that sort of thing, could not possibly be beautiful." At the same time, the music from the two women next door, pounding popular songs on pianos, had instant real-world effects; this "incessant piano playing" was "a cover for the noise of digging an underground tunnel from the cellar of the house next door to the prison yard." Thus these "old maids" enabled "one of the most sensational prison breaks in the history of Trenton Penitentiary" and, in the process, fostered young George's love of piano music (14).

After a high school career that saw him expelled for editorials that "exceeded the bounds of propriety," but eventually reinstated, Antheil received a "severe theoretical training" from a Philadelphia musician named Constantin von Sternberg, an acolyte of Franz Liszt (Whitesitt 4). A conservative but rigorous teacher, Sternberg influenced Antheil's career in important ways: first, by referring him to Ernest Bloch, under whose tutelage Antheil produced his first symphony; second, by referring him to Mary Louise Bok, a music lover on whose financial generosity Antheil repeatedly drew. "Mrs. Bok's" patronage, Bloch's free instruction, and six months' free rent in the home of Margaret Anderson enabled Antheil to focus his energies on composition (*BBM* 19). Though Mrs. Bok did not approve of Antheil's musical style, she believed in his talents strongly enough to fund his 1922 trip to Europe to the very noisy tune of $6,000; Antheil would give a series of piano concerts in London, Budapest, Berlin, Vienna, and Paris (Whitesitt 7). Antheil found the Germans maddeningly insular, patronizing of or oblivious to the efforts of composers outside of Germany, Austria, or Hungary, but it was in Berlin that Antheil met his hero, friend, and rival Igor Stravinsky.

Stravinsky invited Antheil to Paris in 1923, a move that enabled the composer to immerse himself in the avant-garde terrains of music, literature, and visual art. Living above Sylvia Beach's bookstore, Antheil interacted closely with Joyce, Pound, Man Ray, Hemingway, Picasso, and Léger, and benefited from the ascendant influence in 1920s Paris of Dadaism and of the Futurist "art of noises" (Whitesitt 14). The experiments of Futurism had a marked influence on Antheil's early piano pieces, including the "Airplane" Sonata, and *Mechanisms*, which, Antheil insists, inspired the proposed collaboration on *Ballet Mécanique* (though Léger of course insists that his images came first).[26]

If the noises of Antheil's childhood were aestheticized retroactively, à la Stendhal, the riots at his premieres were largely predetermined; Antheil learned quickly that noise and music, self-promotion and art, could enhance one another. A riot at the Paris premiere of his piano music in 1923, which made the concert a publicity success if not a musical one, turns out to have been a stunt prearranged for Marcel L'Herbier's 1924 film *L'Inhumaine*, in which Joyce, Picasso, Ray, and *Les Six* "riot, scream, yell, jump up on the seats" in response to the "inhuman" opera diva played by Georgette Le-

Blanc. Antheil continues: "I naturally asked Margaret Anderson about it, not without a grin of appreciation. She said yes, it had been a *sort* of plot at that, but a plot in which she and Georgette had been sure I would greatly profit. (How right they were!)" (*BBM* 136, his italics). Antheil exaggerates when he writes that "Paris hadn't seen such a good time since the premiere of Stravinsky's 'Sacre du Printemps'"; the premiere of Satie's *Parade* was another such "good time," and in fact Antheil recalls Satie rioting at this very concert, his "shrill voice saying, 'Quel precision! Quel precision. Bravo! Bravo!'" while "clapping his little gloved hands" (133).

These events fueled Anderson's belief that a public incident would be to Antheil's "profit." In Antheil's case, it must be said that these scandals were plotted, framed, and orchestrated in advance: using publicity as the material of art (L'Herbier) and the means of art to circulate publicity (Satie and Anderson). Another example may illustrate the point. Spurred by this filmed "success," Antheil went to work on *Ballet Mécanique*, culminating in a performance of three player-piano "rolls" to a private audience including Joyce, Beach, and Elliot Paul; then a 1926 public performance at the Théâtre des Champs-Elysées. Once more, Antheil's friends in the press would not leave the piece's fame to chance. One Bravig Imbs, a fellow American expatriate, used the Paris *Chicago Tribune* to spread a story that Antheil had been lost in the Tunisian deserts, nearly eaten by a lion, and rescued by the French Foreign Legion.[27] At the infamous performance, the noise-making electric fans created such a breeze that several audience members began brandishing their umbrellas; Pound, ever the diagnostician, leapt to his feet and shouted, "*Vous êtes tous des imbeciles!*" (Imbs 101).

Antheil suggests that the *succès de scandale* as a mechanism for publicity was specific to Paris, where audiences assumed that the noise of a riot suggested real innovation—that "where there is smoke there might be fire." The attitude in New York, however, was "There is too much smoke, let's get out of here, it has a bad odor" (*BBM* 133–4). So Antheil feigned no surprise when the 1927 Carnegie Hall premiere of *Ballet Mécanique* was "a pale carbon copy" of the scene at the Théâtre des Champs-Elysées (133). The New York premiere was panned as a humiliating anticlimax, crystallized by the evocative *New York Evening Post* headline: "Expected Riots Peter Out at George Antheil Concert—Sensation Fails to Materialize" (Oja 35). Yet the performance was certainly a sensation, if not a good one. The air-raid siren couldn't be shut off, and many in the audience left holding their ears; the flop was made more noisome yet by the giant painted backdrop, which

Antheil's manager Donald Friede described as "a cyclorama with a futuristic city of skyscrapers as a background; and in the foreground a series of noise-making machines: whistles, riveting machines, airplane propellers, spark plugs, excavating machines." This "gigantic, rather tasteless curtain," as Antheil called it, "gave an air of charlatanism to the whole proceedings" and sent him crawling back to Europe (*BBM* 193).[28] A Parisian audience may have responded better (i.e., more violently) to the backdrop: Picasso's painted backdrop had been one of the defining markers of Satie's equally raucous *Parade*. The innovation of the "backdrop," as we shall see, made it to Sitwell's drawing room (her eponymous *façade*) as a new way of rethinking poetic authority and voice.

Antheil's premieres were indeed productions, and if audiences could object to what they considered "noise," the artist could anticipate that objection and turn it to his advantage. So when Peter Yates writes that the *Ballet* "was most successful in its headlines" (qtd. in Hoffa 59), he may mean more than he says: Antheil's ambitions shaped audience responses well beyond the sphere of its "concert hall." Antheil reveals that the musical text, however taut its rhythmic form, is always material and never neutral: an object loaded with social and economic implications, made salient by the interventions of active, very noisy interpreters. Pound's attack on the "imbeciles" in the audience, who (he thought) were reacting to rather than intellectually digesting what they had heard, is consistent with his fear of the indiscriminate mob.

Odd though it may now seem, at least one fellow American in Paris credited Antheil for Pound's fame more than vice-versa. In *Confessions of Another Young Man* (1936), Imbs writes that the treatise "was an excellent stroke of publicity for Mr. Pound, for stocks on George were doubling daily, but it gave the average reader the idea that George was more of a pathological case than a composer." Antheil represented not only a talented aesthetic sensibility, nor an empty vessel for Pound's Vorticist bloviating, but an artistic celebrity whose stock was rising: "It was a pity, I thought, that such writers as Ezra Pound had jumped on his band wagon. . . . He always felt grateful to Pound for the latter's opus, but I thought the gratitude should be the other way around. Pound . . . did not write a line of praise about George until he was absolutely certain . . . that George was a sure fire genius. Then, in his confused highly personal idiom, he attempted to explain the meaning of George Antheil's limpid highly personal idiom" (21). Imbs blames Pound for attaching "pathological" associations to Antheil's music; Antheil agrees, claiming that Pound didn't have "the slightest idea of what [he] was really after in music," but merely used him as a cosmopolitan cultural cudgel against "all those who disagreed with him, particularly Anglo-Saxons." For Pound's promotion of an anti-Romantic modernist ideal had long since been won and "superseded by the equally cold neoclassicism" (*BBM* 119–20). Antheil admits that Pound helped him access the "tight-as-a-drum" salons of France, but recognizing Pound's fall into disfavor, claims to regret allowing him to publish the *Antheil* monograph at all.

Antheil's cold "neoclassical" period, usually thought to have begun in the late 1920s with *Transatlantic* and the *Piano Concerto* (1927), has both intellectual and aesthetic roots in the *Ballet*'s cold, anti-Romantic blocks of sound (made more so in Antheil's openly conservative rescoring of the piece in 1953). But the *Ballet*'s noisy sonic aggression turned those streamlined rhythmic structures into a visceral assault on the urban body. From the start, Antheil's "ice-blocks" were engaged with the noisy sensations of culture—"calculated," as Cowell says of his own music, to "undermine" old standards and create new ones.

The Sensations of Labor: Antheil in the Boiler Factory

Pound understood *Ballet Mécanique* as an intervention into the wider circle of urban industry—the temporally managed daily grind of labor interpreted, as in Russolo, in terms of musical aesthetics, organized according to the proper "silences . . . *in the form*." The reading of Antheil's music as a factory was not unique to Pound. Only two months after Pound had recycled his praise of Antheil's factory in the American Marxist periodical *The New Masses*, the same magazine reprinted a cartoon by Isidore Klein (fig. 3.1), the Jewish cartoonist who cocreated Mighty Mouse. The cartoon depicts an upper-crust audience looking out over an assembly line, each laborer with his own music stand: "This Antheil is a genius," one spectator states; "since introducing his theory of orchestration into the boiler factory, our profits have almost doubled." Though Antheil tended to write about noise with a light touch, saving his heavy lifting for the neoclassical rhetoric of formal precision, Klein, like Pound, associates the piece with a "boiler factory" gearing up for the war to come.

Much as Pound's modernism is entangled with Marinetti and Russolo, Klein's aesthetic imagines Antheil's music as a futuristic glorification of technology, invoking anxieties about the onset of fascism. It associates the "mechanical ballet" with the "dreamt-of metallization of the human

Figure 3.1. Klein Cartoon. Courtesy of the Estate of Peter Antheil.

body" through which fascism, Walter Benjamin will argue, "attempts to organize the . . . proletarian masses without affecting the property structure which the masses strive to eliminate."[29] Here, the property structure has been transplanted *into* the concert hall and organized in the service of bourgeois aesthetics. Klein creates a visual divide between the factory-concert and the audience, and a visual parallel between the female spectator and the tacky angel sculpture, inculcating the spectator into her surroundings as seamlessly as Antheil inculcates the laborers into theirs.

Klein shares Pound's contempt for the well-dressed "aesthetes" eagerly consuming the noise-music of the factory, romanticizing labor from the mezzanine in the name of their own profits. Pound had written in *The New Masses* that, with the *Ballet*, "for the first time we have . . . the germ and start of a music that can be applied to sound regardless of its loudness. The aesthete goes to a factory, if he ever does so, and hears *noise*, and goes away horrified; the musician, the composer hears noise, but he tries to (?) 'see' (no, no), he tries to *hear* what kind of noise it is."[30]

For the musician there is nothing pernicious about the "loudness" of noise, if one can only stop playing the aesthete for long enough to understand and rearrange it. Once one plunges in to hierarchize these noises (factory as monochord, perhaps), "the eight-hour day [shall] have its rhythm; so that the men at the machines shall be demechanized, and work not like robots, but like the members of an orchestra" (138). Pound extends this embrace of the factory to the "tribal ceremonies" and the "sea chanteys and labor songs" of the "primitive," claiming that "Modern man . . . has a perfectly good right to live in his cities and in his machine shops with the same kind of swing and exuberance that the savage is supposed to have in his forest" (rpt. in *Antheil* 139). Antheil offers the best hope of this exuberance because he allows noise to be *heard*, not passively received, giving a liberating rhythmic order to the noises of the workday are given rhythmic order, including the appropriate rests. To the extent that Pound's reform will by no means emerge from "the masses," but from a top-down "orchestrated" workshop, Klein would no doubt include him as an object of critique.

As would Wyndham Lewis; Pound's wide-eyed embrace of Antheil's musical factory seems directly at odds with his and Lewis's writings in the 1910s, which lampooned the impulse to sentimentalize the machine. In *Blast* (1914), the two Vorticists had spent considerable energy ridiculing Italian Futurism, despite a shared interest in technology and destruction. In theory, the difference between the Vorticist and the Futurist machine centered on the mimesis question: whereas the Futurist imitated the machine, sentimentalizing its brutality, the Vorticist composition was a machine in itself. Russolo denied that he was imitating noises rather than making new ones; nevertheless, Pound and Lewis were eager to amplify small differences with their Italian interlocutors. Dismissing the Futurist's aesthetic glorification of machinery, Pound argued that the very existence of a machine is "already an expression of his own desire for power and precision"; thus aesthetic representation *of* a machine becomes redundant: "A painting of a machine is like a painting of a painting."[31] For Pound it is music, not painting, that provides the appropriate medium for "mechanistic" expression, since the machine's raison d'être consists in "movement and energy" and not in form, requiring an art that moves through time and not simply through space. Hence Pound celebrates Antheil's rejection of musical "architecture," a conventional metaphor, in favor of musical "mechanism," which suggests movement and energy as structural constituents. The "new vorticist music," Pound insists, "would come from a new computation of the mathematics of harmony not from mimetic representation of dead cats in a fog horn (alias noise tuners)." This music, Pound continues, "was part of the general vorticist stand against the accelerated impressionism of our active and meritorious friend Marinetti" (253).

Pound therefore celebrates Antheil's noisy "mechanisms" not just as imitations of the machine, but as a rhythmic structuring of noise, which would aestheticize the soundscape, energize music, and demechanize the machine-worker. By *Time and Western Man* (1927), Lewis wasn't buying; having dedicated his early years to disowning this "accelerated impressionism," Lewis refused to grant Pound the rhetoric he so clearly coopted from Marinetti and Russolo. *Time and Western Man* assails modernist culture as a loud advertising campaign, mocking the "revolutionary simpleton" who delights in "big and noisy, six-foot advertisers' claims; all the 'Greater than Shakespeares,' the 'Death to the Pasts,' the announcement of the enterprise as that of an absolutely new era, with which you have long been familiar."[32] Lewis cites the "musical factory" passage as evidence that, whatever aesthetic principles Pound attributed to Antheil, he was more interested in public sensation:

> Marinetti is rehabilitated by Pound—music, provençal airs and ballads of Villon, as far as he personally is concerned, taking him paradoxically to the great throbbing, singing heart of the great god, Industry. I should be tempted to think it had taken Ezra a decade to catch up Marinetti, if I were not sure that, from the start, the histrionics of the milanese prefascist were much to his sensation-loving taste. I observe rather that he has not moved from where he was. (41)

Allying Pound with the "great god, Industry" (a wounding accusation, he must have known), Lewis claims that Pound's commitment to a reinvented classicism was a cover for "*disturbance*" and "*action*"—this "is the form [Pound's] parasitism takes" (39). Pound appeared to Lewis as a Marinettian wolf in antique, self-made sheep's clothing: the glorification of the future and the sentimentalizing of the archaic spoke to the same "histrionic" personality, and to a form of sensationalism no less industrial, and no less impressionistic, than the grind Pound heard around him.

Lewis often associated this sensationalism with music, qua time-centered art. And Antheil's truly is a time-centered art. His writings about rhythm as an abstract, calculated medium offer time itself as the integral canvas of musical form:

> My Ballet Mecanique is the new *fourth dimension of music*.
>
> My Ballet Mecanique is the first piece of music on the earth that has been composed *out of* and *for* machines, *on earth*.
>
> My Ballet Mecanique is the first piece of music that has found the best forms

> and materials lying inert in a medium that *as a medium* is mathematically certain of becoming the greatest moving factor of the music of future generations . . . .
>
> In music there is nothing else, except *time* and *sound*, and the physical and psychic *concept* of these vibrating the human organism.
>
> Anything else is literary, and does not belong to pure music. . . .
>
> *Time* is inflexible, rigid, beautiful![33]

Like Pound, Antheil was drawn to the "fourth dimension" of poetry, an "alternative, newly material," "vortical energy" through which to escape noise and effect silence.[34] Also like Pound, Antheil oscillates between the "primitive" and the futuristic—between the "ancient tribesman" and the mission to Mars—though in his associations with *De Stijl*, Antheil prefers the jargon of mathematical inflexibility. Antheil had this manifesto published both in *Der Querschnitt*, a German modernist journal for which he acted as a contributing editor (soliciting contributions from Joyce and Hemingway); and in *De Stijl*, the flagship journal of the Dutch neoplasticist movement of Theo van Doesburg and Piet Mondrian. Even as he distinguished "pure music" from the "literary," then, Antheil saw himself in dialogue with the literary, visual, and plastic arts; his language of mathematical certainty and the fourth dimension speaks to a larger conversation about music's temporal, as well as geographic and artistic, circle of reference.

As Lewis saw it, Pound's celebration of Antheil moved all too quickly from the "inflexible" medium of time into blustering impressionism, whether Futuristic or primitivistic. For Lewis, music threatened an expansion not into a Ruskinian circle of moral "sensibility," but into sensationalism: as Michael Coyle writes, music supported Lewis's charge that the "clamorings of the avant-garde were no less informed by a relentless attempt 'to startle into credulity' than were the ubiquitous slogans of the marketplace" (160), giving the lie to "Mauberley's" self-righteous satire of "mendacities" "[d]ecreed in the market place" (II.7, III.16). Lewis's main objection was to the "Bergsonian" emphasis on temporal flux and subjectivity, whereas Antheil emphasized rigidity and permanence. Lewis admired Antheil's jazzy enthusiasm, but argued that in Pound's hands, the "time art" had become pretext for the same old effort to "startle" its audience; Antheil's ostensibly rigid music had taken on the distracted sensationalism of the "bourgeois bohemian."

The archetypal bohemian for Lewis, as for Eliot, was the Ballets Russes patron, whom *Time and Western Man* assails at length. Pound shared this disdain, as his poem "Les Millwin" indicates, ridiculing the "mauve and greenish"

Millwins who have come to see the decadent spectacle of Michel Fokine's *Cleopatra* (1909); the poem seems equally cynical toward the mob responses of an "undisciplined host of art students," arms crossed "in great Futurist X's." For Pound and Lewis, the Ballets Russes and the Futurists alike were revolutionary simpletons, sentimentalizing musical sensation rather than sheering it down, thereby appealing to the Millwins' middlebrow commercialism. Though Antheil's celebration of formalized time must have struck Pound as a welcome departure from the Ballets Russes' gaudy sentimentalism, for Lewis, it was merely a sensational parasitism on the "great god, Industry."

It is not hard to see how the *Ballet*'s noises resonate with industry, given Antheil's emphasis on the "rigid" materiality of time. A polyglot of jargon, Antheil acclimated to the neoplasticist language of "vibration," and brought his emphasis on the *Ballet*'s materiality into line with *De Stijl*'s search for "the laws which obtain everywhere in daily life" and "take shape in the scientific formula and in mechanized production alike."[35] In this context Klein's and Pound's industrial allegories seem less than farfetched: Antheil reaches for these laws via a metallic organicism ("*out of* and *for* machines"), building a holistic relation among the medium, the idea, and the earth itself. The machine, like the worker, needs to be kept unalienated from its means of production. Antheil reifies his medium, emphasizing that the force of musical time must be rhythmically calculated before it can vibrate in the "human organism": "for our hearts do not feel . . . they *beat*" (790, his italics).

Antheil wishes to realize this physicality through a stiffening of musical form: an intensification and a simplification. He asserts elsewhere that the form of the *Ballet* escaped the "well-known musical formula:—ABA," which would be marked by a shift (from "A" to "B") into a new stylistic idiom (e.g., "Minuet" versus "Trio") or key (tonic to dominant). Instead, Antheil claims, the formula of *Ballet Mécanique* is "AAAAAAAAAAAAAAAAAAAAAAAAA" (hereafter, A[25]), giving voice to these universal laws while leaving the critic unsure of his position relative to where the piece began. Hence music can escape conventional, more conspicuously mediated forms (ABA) within the musical "circle of reference," and draw the listener into a new experience of time itself (qtd. in Whitesitt 105). The A[25] of the *Ballet* should not imply a lack of rhythmic sophistication or motivic development within those twenty-five sections—only that its development does not lead it through conventional cadential departures and returns. The raw material of the piece consists, essentially, of two main themes, each consisting of four pitches repeated and permutated in various ways:

MAIN THEME: (B-D-C#-A): [B-D-C#-B-C#-A]-[B-D-C#-A]-[B-D-C#-B-C#-A] . . . etc.

SECONDARY THEME (C-E♭-F-G): [G-F-E♭-C]-[G-F- E♭-F] . . . etc.

These are the pitches at which the themes are introduced—they are often transposed and, true to the Stravinskian fashion, played in multiple keys at the same time, in various rhythmic configurations, compressed into shorter units of time and protracted into longer ones. In basic terms, the main theme is diatonic (built on the A-major scale), the secondary theme pentatonic (deriving from a five-note scale, commonly found in folk music and used to great effect by the impressionists). The grating back-and-forth between diatonic and pentatonic motifs can be seen to mimic the dialectical (or, less sympathetically, "histrionic") movement between futurism and primitivism, two sides of Antheil's and *De Stijl*'s "universal laws," underpinning the "jungle" and the machine. Late in the piece, while timpani and pianolas pound away at a tweaked version of the secondary theme, two xylophones play a sped-up version of the primary theme, in a crescendoing call-and-response of several minutes. Eventually, Antheil offers a pause; the timpani and pianos stop pounding and rumble innocently in the background for a while (in the image of Pound's factory, the workers get a break).

The tightening and reduction of form as a way of approximating the "pure canvas of time" leads the auditor grasping for referential orientation, which, for Klein and Pound, was found most easily in the image of labor. It can't have escaped Pound that a day in the workshop resembles something very much like AAAAAAAAAAAAAAAAAAAAAAA. *Ballet Mécanique*'s attempts to disorient its audience were thus culturally entangled with industry's need to aestheticize its own temporal organization. If I may be allowed a moment of distant reading: in 1927—the year that Jonathan Crary, after Guy Debord, identifies as the birth of the modern commodity spectacle[36]—we are confronted with Klein's and Pound's musical factories, with Lewis's "throbbing, singing heart of the great god, Industry," and with Fritz Lang's thesis in *Metropolis* that "THE MEDIATOR BETWEEN THE HEAD AND THE HANDS MUST BE THE HEART." In each of these, the abstract heart that "beats" rather than feels seems to mediate the temporal patterns of work.

The associations between labor and rhythm (such as Bücher's *Arbeit und Rhythmus*) often veer into primitivist kitsch, or into allegorical homologies between modern and ancient ritual (Antheil's oil-baron *Iliad*; Adorno's and Horkheimer's culture-industry *Odyssey*). Antheil manifests this dynamic in his celebrations of jazz; Antheil's mechanistic pieces conjoin classicized imitations of jazz with the pulse of machinery, and imagine the temporal structures of labor and the bodily demands of modernity as reinvented "tribalism." The *Ballet*'s musical language hints at this tension by contrasting the diatonic primary theme with the pentatonic secondary motif (the pentatonic scale being frequently associated with racial otherness and folk idioms). Antheil's use of jazz idioms in the 1920s, from *Ballet Mécanique* to *Sonata Sauvage* and the *Jazz Symphony*,[37] offered his music not only a "dynamic and mechanistic significance" but a continuity with the unalienated body that had "not yet been exploded by shrapnel."[38]

This dynamic opened up *Ballet Mécanique*'s formal concentration to what its audiences clearly heard—the programmatic grind of the factory. The music's tight form subjects *Ballet Mécanique* to a range of hyperallegorical resonances of the Lewis/Adorno/Lukács sort. It was *sensation*—musical and otherwise—that served as Lewis's target, both in his penetrative Vorticist mode and in his attack on the time-art in *Time and Western Man*, which ridicules the modernist obsession with temporal flux as the brain-fogging sensationalism of a Bergsonian "time-cult."[39] As Coyle explains, *Time and Western Man* "denounced the Bergsonian glamorization of sensation. . . . The attempt to make sensation the 'exclusive fact' of our existence threatened to engulf 'western man' in the darkness of solipsism" (160). Antheil emphasized inflexibility, not flux; yet the effects of his obsession with the unchanging materiality of time seemed similar to the glamorized, Millwin-like concupiscence (Lewis believed) of the modernist subjectivity. Indeed, one of Pound's terms in praise of Antheil, *durées*, was a touchstone of Bergsonian philosophy, well known to American musical culture in the 1920s.[40] The *Ballet*'s uses of noise seem undialectical, sensations that cloud and are extrinsic to the music's formal development. At the same time, its mechanical beat has a disciplinary effect, shocking the body in a way that, Adorno suggests, naturalizes violence. Read back through Pound and Klein, it is understandable that the *Ballet* would call to mind the nightmare of the culture industry, traceable to the binding total artwork in which "giant packages . . . are divided up by the notion of striking, of beating time" into an "abstract framework." Ossifying small-scale development into "giant packages," rhythm threatened to make the subject unable to enjoy either art or labor while clouding (as Lewis fears) his spatio-temporal perspective.

As we have seen, Adorno—like Klein—gives the fascist conductor pride of place as he enacts the music's gestic striking and beating. The question of the conductor is already complicated with the *Ballet*; the initial, pared-down version for piano rolls was soon replaced by a more fleshed-out concert version, and then in 1953 a significantly tamed reduction (much more palatable to the mainstream aesthete). Antheil himself claimed that the ideal conductor "does not want temperamental players in an orchestra," but instead wants a "mechanical player" who can fulfill the composer's calculated intentions.[41] If the fascist conductor poses one anxiety, having no conductor at all makes it harder yet (as in the Culture Industry, or the *acousmêtre*) to locate a source of authority. Inflexible and inescapable, the piece's rhythmic onslaught can be seen to reify time as joyless mechanical labor. With long passages of pianolas playing in unison, *Ballet Mécanique* evokes, in both its title and its "mathematically certain" form, the panic of automata taking over for human agents. The title alone suggests machines choreographed to patterned movements ("a score for robotic choreography"[42]), producing metallic molds and aesthetic pattern through formal repetition. Pound's claim that Antheil pulls music out of its self-referential circle, into a "new phase of social life," illuminates the composer's dilemma: the effort to cordon off musical and mechanical time from its literary resonances, far from purifying *Ballet Mécanique*, brought it into contact with a range of social anxieties. If the *Ballet*'s motifs are pounded into inflexible molds, its cultural reception quickly calcified into industrial allegories—the ironic cost of Antheil's purely musical formalism.

While it may resonate with Lang's controlled explosions, or the detonation of Germany's "iron core" predicted in Antheil's *The Shape of War to Come*, *Ballet Mécanique* represented for Pound the potential to aestheticize noise—an inevitable, if undesirable, sonic condition of modernity—in a process that would energize rather than enervate its auditors. Hoping to challenge the worker's reification, Pound insists that total form include silence (rest) as well as noise, and that an "objective" form with "absolute" durability does not require the artwork to be static and fixed. Pound argues in "Retrospect" that form has a "'fluid' as well as a 'solid' content" (9), and the *Cantos* endeavor in many respects to give the entropic process of nature a "perdurable" material form (LXXXIII, 553-4). Pound's *Cantos*, moving well beyond the *Ballet*'s formally static A^{25}, try to latch onto the temporal canvas of music while allying it with what Pound came to call the "fundamental irregularity": an entropic yet rhythmically ordered progression of time. The rhythmic organization of noise, the temporal pacing and spacing of sonorities, is heard to give music its shape, to put it in step either with the historical ground-bass or with the cynical and usurious march of events.

"Fundamental Irregularity" and the "March of Events": Pound and Rhythm

Pound reconceives the processes of composition and reception, manifested in the material form of the artwork, as an organically fluid, yet absolute, rhythmic back-and-forth, which will ultimately give voice to the text's relation to a larger historical order. Pound's erratic musical writings, including a variety of essays written (under the name William Atheling) for the socialist paper *The New Age*, do consistently presuppose that rhythm should shape the other elements of music: melodic invention, harmonic invention, and instrumentation.[43] The central problem of Pound's *Treatise on Harmony* and writings on Antheil is the tension between the vertical (harmony) and the horizontal (rhythm) that motivates musical composition. Pound's *Treatise* insists that the worship of harmony for its own sake represents both aesthetic and cultural atrophy. Rather, he believes there to be only one general principle of harmony: "A sound of any pitch, or any combination of such sounds, may be followed by a sound of any other pitch, or any combination of such sounds, providing the time between them is properly gauged; and this is true for any series of sounds, chords, or arpeggios" (10). For Pound the appropriateness of a progression depends not on a functional relationship among chords, but on the proper arrangement of "pauses and durées," an idea that the *Ballet*'s lack of harmonic cadencing satisfies well. The most "interesting" progressions will be the ones "that demand very set and definite intervals" of time between notes, an organic relation between vertical resonance and horizontal pace, compelling precise organization (14). Pound does not wish to obviate harmony (that would be hard to do), but to make harmonic invention a byproduct of meticulous temporal organization, which in turn orchestrates everything else. The heartbeat, to borrow Antheil's formulation, should motivate the idea, rather than letting feeling motivate the beat. Asserting that the inability of the "modern musician" to "hear a melody till it's harmonized" is "utter atrophy," Pound ascribes a particular vigor to the horizontal melodic line, a vigor he believes present in "negroes in darkest Africa" who "from simple beating of their drums . . . can imagine other instruments," perhaps because these rhythms have not yet been alienated from their physical and social rituals (*Antheil* 26, 30).

Rhythm is no less central to Pound as Imagist, the abstract side of Pound's desire to negotiate rhythmic calculation and rhythmic embodiment. As he argues in "Retrospect" (1918), the Imagist's absolute rhythm catalyzes his directness and condensation:

1. Direct treatment of the "thing" whether subjective or objective.
2. To use absolutely no word that does not contribute to the presentation.
3. As regarding rhythm: to compose in the sequence of the musical phrase, not in the sequence of a metronome. (3)

Though poetry cannot have harmony (a simultaneity of different sounds), it can have a "residue of sound which remains in the ear of the hearer and acts more or less as an organ-base"; the rhythm of the verse-line, having shaped the listener's esthesis, allows a sound to linger in the ear and resonate with the ideas to follow (6–7). To make immanent the depth of this Bass requires Pound to rethink the compositional tension between vertical harmony and horizontal melody and rhythm. *Le Testament* is written in just this fashion: not exactly atonal, but (largely) avoiding conventional resolutions. Bucknell's reading of the opera, Pound's "most earnest attempt at connecting music . . . with his theories of absolute rhythm and Great Bass" (80), points out that the lack of conventional voice-leading is merely a way of putting into practice his commitment to the horizontal: the patterns of Villon's language dictate both meter and counterpoint, and, in turn, harmonic relationships.

The third precept constitutes part of Pound's struggle with *vers libre*, which he associates with musical classicism. Pound develops this emphasis on the horizontal absolute rhythm, not limited to the metronome, in his essays on the period instrument-maker Arnold Dolmetsch, whose *Interpretation of the Music of the Seventeenth and Eighteenth Centuries* (1915) Pound champions as the last hope for "a reconciliation between musicians and 'the intelligent.'"[44] Dolmetsch liberates music from excessive notation, returning to the skeletal notations of early music, which require and allow for greater "intelligence on the part of the interpreters" and which also keep the "whole major structure of music" from being "obscured" (47). The performer must simultaneously interpret and create; the composer, no longer able to hide behind the "multitude of ornamental notes and trappings," must create "fixed lines" that nevertheless allow for melodic and contrapuntal invention. This invigorates the music and the musician, preventing interpretive atrophy in the material realization of a score.

In a 1918 essay on Dolmetsch, Pound seeks to "give us a clue to a wider unexpressed feeling for a fundamental irregularity which would have made eighteenth-century classicism, classicism of surface, tolerable to those who felt the underlying variety *as strongly as the first regularizers* may have felt it."[45] Though Pound waxes classical, the "feeling" and "felt" here strike me as important, dissonantly reconcilable with Antheil's insistence that the heart beats rather than feels. A sense of (irregular) order needs to be felt, physically perceived, in order to be given material form. Dolmetsch preserves the integrity of the horizontal melodic line, in the same way that *vers libre* should follow the sequence of a musical phrase, so as to pull it closer to a fundamental ground-bass with a felt "underlying variety"—a resonance not so different from the underlying vibration for Russolo's *rumori*. Pound's endorsement of *vers libre* speaks not to anarchy but to a fundamental irregularity, a suppler version of the universal laws that Antheil (after *De Stijl*) tries to vibrate in the human body.

Pound's defense of the rhythmic line thus pulls in two directions: toward the "absolute," "fundamental" mathematics underlying culture; and toward variety and irregularity. Pound seeks, through rhythmic demarcation, a way of appealing to embodied sensation without enervating the listener, and allowing the interpreter to realize the unobscured "whole . . . structure" of music; he seeks, moreover, a way to make rhythmic repetition artistically permanent without letting it grow static or unfeeling. "Mauberley" shows how the most sublimely "perdurable" phrase, repeated often enough, will harden into cliché—a form of language for which Pound has less sympathy than we have seen in Eliot. One of the poem's tics is an incessant use of quotation marks; these "scare quotes" rethink the gaps between rhetorical cliché and "sublime" allusion, and etch those aporia into granite:

For three years, out of key with his time,
He strove to resuscitate the dead art
Of poetry; to maintain "the sublime"
In the old sense. Wrong from the start—
. . . .
Unaffected by "the march of events",
He passed from men's memory in *l'an trentiesme*
De son eage; the case presents
No adjunct to the Muses' diadem. (1–8, 17–20)

The poem's opening metaphor, "out of key with his time," is a trope of cultural dissonance; if the musical workshop resembles Adorno's darkest nightmare of a consonant grind, "Mauberley" anticipates, in the last throes of *l'art pour l'art* aestheticism, Adorno's faith in dissonant art to remain "unaffected by" the noise of the marketplace. Recalling Pound's endorsement of the horizontal, being in key with one's own time (worshiping harmony for its own sake) threatens to put one's body and intellect out of step with the horizontal continuities of history. Mauberley's developed consciousness thus has to work against the "tawdry cheapness" of modernity, figured by the grind of the pianola; this same grind has flattened the sublime into a scare-quoted catch-phrase, "the sublime," "In the old sense." Claiming that the "pianola 'replaces' / Sappho's barbitos," Pound quotes even the word "replaces," making the pianola as dispensable as its music.

The "march of events" that passes by Mauberley has both a militant and a "factitious" sense, its inexorable repetitive quoting replacing fresh expression with incantation. Yet quotation can effect permanence: as in the *Cantos*, music here adopts the challenge of rendering noise durable through rhythm without letting it atrophy. Internalizing the Sirens' song ("*ἴδμεν γάρ τοι πάν πάνθ', όσ' ένι Τροίη*/ Caught in the unstopped ear") into the cadence of his own testament, Mauberley remains unaffected by this clatter in preserving the aesthetic thrill. Pound's "Retrospect" essay advises poets to internalize the cadences of foreign languages; here the untranslated Greek Sirens song ("we know everything . . . suffered in wide Troy"[46]) provides an "organ-base," a sonic sensation that lingers in the ear and immunizes Mauberley from the grind. The quoted line "*l'an trensiesme/ De son eage*," from Villon's *Testament*, further marks Mauberley's diagnostic cultural repression. As Pound parallels Mauberley, Villon, and the soldiers returning home from Europe to "old lies and new infamy; / usury age-old and age-thick / and liars in public places," he imagines the ears of the public subjected to the *infama* of old lies and usury. Here we have an enforced regularity that is faithless to the embodied "human organisms" being subjected to it. The fundamental irregularity uniting Mauberley and Villon has been obscured by a public square whose structural incoherence is given the veneer of "march"-like regularity—a tension denoted, ironically enough, by the pianola. Even if Mauberley has immunized his mind and body against it, the market's regularized clatter has led into a "wastage" of "Young blood and high blood, / Fair cheeks, and fine bodies," materialized (as in Eliot's toothless landscape) as "an old bitch gone in the teeth."

Pound finds this fundamental irregularity, a liberated but sharply defined horizontal line, to be obscured by an onslaught of noise that exhausts the listener's mind and body and leaves him clinging to any illusion of sense he can find. In "Mauberley" we see this profusion of rumor and "lies" that leaves one searching for sharper demarcations. Pound's sharp critiques of Romantic and impressionist music associate the "enfeebling" effects of musical sensation with the effects of noise on the public square. As Pound evolves his musical sensibilities in the '20s, he joins Antheil's search for an objective "temporal canvas" to give the ear an focus, rather than leaving it defenseless to the sonic "grind."

Plastic Time: Controlling the Grind, Shaping the Impression

Art is not sensation alone, though sensation it cannot do without. For Pound, rhythm is a means of giving form to the sensation, "impression," "emotion," or "plastic" (material) on which music depends, but which (for him) becomes exhausting and stultifying without a horizontal narrative—an exhaustion that leaves the auditor open to manipulation. In his neoclassical admiration of Arnold Dolmetsch, Pound chastises the enervating effects of musical machines: "Our ears are passive before the onslaught of gramophones and pianolas. By persuading ourselves that we do not hear two-thirds of their abominable grind, we persuade ourselves that we take pleasure in the remainder of what they narrate. We feign a deafness which we have not, instead of developing our faculty for the finer perception of sound" (47). The term "narrate" implies a horizontal drive that ought to predominate over, or shape, the mass of sensations; the auditor "feign[s] a deafness" to the musical through-line that he ought to hear, and thus loses his ability to hear it. The neoclassical return to bare-bones notation, in Pound's view, is a means of noise reduction, erasing the hyperstimulated and formless grind of music in a way that allows the performer/auditor to develop her perceptive faculty. Pound alludes also to the grind of Wagner and Debussy, whose efforts to "confuse the spectator by smacking as many of his senses as possible at every possible moment" with noise and with programmatic associations conflict with the "vortical," concentrated "definition of form, of rhythm."[47] Pound hears impressionism, not inaptly, as an offshoot of Wagnerism, evidenced by his discussion in an earlier piece on Dolmetsch:[48] "Impressionism has reduced us to such a dough-like state of receptivity that we have ceased to like concentration. . . . Impressionist or 'emotional' music . . . is like a drug; you must have more drug and more noise each time, or this effect, this impression which works from the outside, in from the nerves and sensorium upon the self—is no use, its effect and constantly weaker and weaker" (38).

Pound associates this Romantic/impressionist "noise" with pure sensation rather than intellectual "concentration," with the degeneration of "receptivity," and even of "the self." This music's assault on the sensorium, manifested in an expansion of the orchestra, makes the listener unresponsive to anything but more noise. In contrast to Russolo, who celebrates noise as the extension of dissonance, Pound uses the term "noise" here to disparage aural pyrotechnics that obscure the musical skeleton, appealing to the nerves and not the intellect. Though a musician must go to the factory and "hear" noise, she must also refine it through composition, so that music's widening circle of reference is given a narrative rather than bullying the auditor into "feign[ing]" a selective deafness.

As R. Murray Schafer points out in his invaluable edition of Pound's writings on music, Pound "felt at home" in the anti-impressionist milieu of 1920s Paris, led by Cocteau and Satie, the great ironists of a post-Wagnerian musical scene that they wished to puncture with cheek, Dada, and a noisily public aesthetic.[49] The same applies to Antheil, whose affinities with Satie were strong. Pound quotes Antheil to have said that all of Debussy's "nuances" were predicted by the obscure composer Ernest Fanelli, and by that great musical prestidigitator, the "juggler Satie" ("Antheil [Retrospect]" 263). For both Pound and Antheil, throughout the '20s, the term "impressionism" signified a lazily sentimental art that bled into an uncritical sensation and into visual mimesis: "can music be 'impressionistic'?", Antheil asks, in Pound's ventriloquizing voice; "is [impressionism] not a term for painting alone?" (263). In contrast, Antheil's "sound vibrations" seemed to allow the composer to structure that sensation into a fluidly tangible "plasticity."

This curious term "plasticity" merits a bit of dilation; it proves crucial both for Antheil's sense of how the "pure medium of time" produces a revitalizing new music, and for Pound's effort to honor, but give rhythmic shape to, the roots of art in somatic sensation.[50] Their shared frustration with impressionism's formless grind led Antheil to seek a calculated mechanical ideal of musical "plastic," and Pound to seek a humanistic ideal (one that motivates the *Cantos*) in which the artist's *poietic* and *esthesic* faculty gives a rhythmic continuity to the plastic sensations of the body.

In a 1927 article written for *transition*, the "little magazine" founded by Eugene Jolas and edited by Elliot Paul, Antheil argues for an anti-impressionist music to strive for "plasticity" above all. Antheil proposes to strip away its harmonic and orchestral excesses and to develop a tonal language that suits the mechanical medium. This new tonal system, Antheil contends, will *not* be dodecaphonic atonality, which for him is merely a new impressionism. He argues that atonality fails to put into clear mathematical apposition the elements of *time*, which is the "canvas of music," and *tone*, which is its material paint. For Antheil, twelve-tone music offers no traction, no "contact 'point-in-space,'" for tone to lock in with the plastic temporal canvas; atonal music leaves time to run among all twelve notes "like quicksilver," with no center to grip. Hence, he argues, the "theory-loving Germans" have to "place an extra-musical literature or mystic idea" onto their music, "to make up for the lack of point."[51] Antheil perhaps knew that tone (in the senses of both pitch and timbre) had been extensively considered by Schoenberg and Anton Webern's *Klangfarbenmelodie* (sound-color-melody: a way of giving timbre, along with melody, horizontal development through time). Yet he argues that their failure to find traction between the passage of time and the tonal stuff of music results in a "muddy-sounding" impressionism. If his own language sounds mystical, Antheil cautions that this is only because "the plastic direction" of music has not yet been realized; we cannot merely project present sounds onto the canvas of the future. The future of music is not "Puccini's music for orchestra . . . cut upon the pianola," but a "plastic" music written for and through the machine.

As the composer's history clarifies, Antheil was sensation all the way down, albeit calculated sensation; his and Pound's rejection of "impressionism" in favor of *Ballet Mécanique* only represses one noise-mass to embrace another. Still, Pound's and Antheil's jargons of "plasticity" represent parallel attempts to articulate how the tight internal temporality of music can lock in with the "canvas of time," how rhythm can shape the impression. As in the *De Stijl* writings, Antheil drew much of this thinking from the visual and plastic arts. Carol Oja situates Antheil in relation to the cubist (not the sociologist) Max Weber, whose essay "Fourth Dimension from a Plastic Point of View" (1910) anticipates Antheil's "plastic time." Weber proposes a "dimension of infinity" reaching from "'Archaic' art" into the mechanical future, a notion that informs Antheil's continuity between the "electricity of the unconscious from the primitive to the mind that dies in the airplane" (cf. Ornstein's *Suicide in an Airplane*).[52] Likewise, as Pound emphasizes the horizontal structuring of noise, he seeks a language that engenders "electri[c]" movement in each word. As he wrote of the ideogram, "Like nature, the Chinese words are alive and plastic, because *thing* and *action* are not formally separated"; the poet's use of sound takes on the dynamic energy of natural material as it vibrates in the "alive and plastic" organism, an idea echoed in the *Cantos'* ideograms of birdsong.

Pound maintains the need for the creative human agent to perceive and to perform the art inside the sensuous material, "the god inside the [plastic] statue."[53] In detailing the "Tuscan" aesthetic of Guido Cavalcanti, the thirteenth-century poet set in Pound's opera *Cavalcanti* (1933) and the speaker of the horrifying Canto LXXIII, Pound suggests that the artist, perceiving an immanent energy in his plastic material, can render dynamic sonic material in a static form while keeping the auditor's intellect discriminately alert. Indeed, one might think of Pound's so-called "Fascist Cantos"—the homage to the Futurist Marinetti in LXXII and the homage to the medieval Tuscan in LXXIII—as twin poles of the "histrionics" to which Lewis was referring: Pound's "milanese prefascism" required a dose both of Marinetti's adrenal noise and of the "burning-glass of [Cavalcanti's] mind's reason." Pound's homage to Marinetti decries empty destruction without creation, while Canto LXXIII depicts ("Singing, singing/with joy") a peasant girl tempting the Canadian army into a minefield. Pound's militant battle music, and his drive for purposeful aesthetic form, chiastically inform one another, magnetically polarized cultural effects of musical sonority.

In his "Cavalcanti" essay, Pound insists that the concept of sonority itself is not adequate to describe the Tuscan aesthetic, because "sound does not require a human being to produce it. The bird, the phonograph, sing" (151). Any old grind can produce resonance, but Cavalcanti heard a latent potential in the raw plastic material of sound for the bestowal of aesthetic proportion. For Pound, Cavalcanti gives proportional form to the impression, rendering nature (*thing* and *action*) concrete, without surrendering to the indigestible noise of formless sensation, or of what Pound calls the "erotic sentimentalism" of "plastic moved towards coitus." The experience of the "fine thing" (the erotic thrill) needs to be given a balanced, demarcated affective or physical form: the Tuscan resists "sentimentality" and establishes a "proportion between the fine thing held in the mind, and the inferior thing ready for instant consumption" (151).

Proportion is always of importance in the *Cantos*, in which both birds and phonographs sing: the "wail of the phonograph" "penetrate[s]" the "marrow" of three clergymen in Canto XXIX, as the "cicadas continue uninterrupted." As unbirdlike chirpers, cicadas characterize the entropically beautiful and disruptive nature of birdsong.[54] In relation to the Tuscan aesthetic, Canto XXIX demonstrates simply that there is nothing innately human, let alone humane, about "singing"; rather, within such raw "exteriorized" material, the artist must find "the residue of perception, perception of something which requires a human being to produce it" (151). As Nattiez helps to explain, within sonic material lies an esthesic potential: sounds contain a "residue of perception," a latent energy to be through-composed by a mind that can perceive its proportion. As in Antheil's factory, where both work and rest preserve the energy of the worker, the Tuscan aesthetic provides demarcation that realizes energy in its best proportion, finding both motion and "silences . . . *in the form*."

Pound sees the modern lack of proportion and demarcation as a symptom of cultural stupidity: Pound seeks, after Cavalcanti, a "harmony of the sentient, where the thought has its demarcation, the substance its *virtù*, where stupid men have not reduced all 'energy' to unbounded undistinguished abstraction" (152). Balancing formal *sprezzatura* and constructive action, the Tuscan neither reduces art to "vasomotor" sensation, nor "stupid[ly]" abstracts energy as a mere "shapeless 'mass' of force" (153–4); rather, the plastic of the poem reconciles material sensation with internal *virtù*, an "interactive force" (152) that is neither "anti-flesh" or "anti-intelligence."

Antheil's and Pound's emphases on the plastic quality of sound convey related searches for demarcated temporal structures of art that will formalize the physical perception and eroticism through which music is produced and experienced. This tension resulted, as Margaret Fisher claims, in the "palpable surface" of the *Cantos*, an effort to sing in a clearly demarcated yet physical idiom. It resulted also in Pound's two operas; *Le Testament*, in particular, is premised on a back-and-forth between brothel and church, between sacred and secular varieties of coition. The music, Fisher writes, "admits the corporeal rhythms" of human bones, "scratches and hiccoughs, physical obsessions and physical limits—nothing that would be admissible to courtly etiquette," a physicality perceptible in Pound and Antheil's calculated "microrhythms" (33).

Pound's interest in the body as the source of music's plasticity, in the "residue of perception" latent in sound, is balanced by his distaste for impressionistic music, all sensation and no shape. A 1921 performance of Debussy's *Pelléas et Mélisande* appears to have irritated him into setting to work on the more bare bones and Dolmetsch-like *Testament*:

> Sat through the *Pelléas* the other evening and am encouraged—encouraged to tear up the whole bloomin' era of harmony and do the thing if necessary on two

> tins and wash-board. Anything rather than that mush of hysteria, Scandinavia strained through Belgium plus French Schwärmerei. Probably just as well I have to make this first swash without any instruments at hand. Very much encouraged by the *Pelléas*, ignorance having no further terrors if that DAMN thing is the result of what is called musical knowledge.[55]

Having substituted a "mush of hysteria" for skeletal rhythm, the "era of harmony" has to be torn up. Exasperated and encouraged by the failures of this era (its grinding noise seems to signal its breakdown), Pound concluded that poetic emotion began with an embodied shock, "the yeowl and the bark," then gradually purified that shock through rhythm: from the "yeowl" into "the dance and into music, . . . and into music with words, and finally into words with music, and finally into words with a vague adumbration of music, words suggestive of music, words measured, or words in a rhythm that preserves some accurate trait of the emotive impression."[56] As for Eliot, the "measured" rhythm does not *imitate* music but rather "adumbrat[es]" it and distills its emotive impulse. The artwork crystallizes emotion into something that is, "first of all, music, and which is capable of being, after that, many things." A work that appeals chiefly to the nerves is consigned to the noise of impressionism; but a trace or "trait" of the impression needs to be preserved through rhythm.

My argument on the *Cantos* pursues just this point: Antheil augments the tension between the "perdurable" quality of art—its calculated rhythmic solidity—and the unstable noises that Pound wishes to diagnose and repurpose. The noises of usury and war, of nature, of Debussyian "flabbiness," and of artistic production itself produce sensations for which Pound seeks rhythmic shape. Aside from Antheil's and Villon's mutual association through the node of *Le Testament*, their shared place in Canto LXXIV speaks to the potential for even a minor bad-boy composer to diagnose something off-kilter in the larger orders of "kulchur." When Canto LXXIV compares Antheil to Barabbas, and then quotes Villon, it relates the artists' rhythmic experiments to their implicit diagnosis of a corrupt, out-of-tune cultural disorder.

The *Cantos* insist that shaping noise rhythmically—finding the god inside the noisy stone—gives it a fundamental irregularity, like that present in Cavalcanti, in Villon, and in the distant tribal past heard as precursor to the modern machine. In a 1928 article for the *transatlantic review*, entitled "Mother of the Earth," Antheil decries the reflexive comparison of his rhythmic music to Stravinsky: "Do we necessarily need to link all new rhythmic experimentation with Stravinsky's 'Sacre'? . . . What about the music from the campfires of a thousand, no! a million years [ago]! What about the tom-toms. What about the neggers [*sic*] down in Africa. . . . . Do you forever have to stilt about in court dress to 4/4 time, or waltz in the evenings to 3/4?"[57] Antheil resents being the off-brand Stravinsky, though the title "Mother of the Earth" could have come straight from *Le Sacre*. Publicity stunts aside, Antheil's African drums here figure an essential rhythmic pulse, producing a body, not "exploded by shrapnel," as an embodied tuning fork, an integral surface that vibrates with rhythmic time.

Pound set to work with Antheil on *Le Testament* in 1921, and here too he attempted to find the heartbeat—to produce a horizontally rather than vertically motivated music, true to the raw physicality and diagnostic potential of Villon's poems; and then to recast this music for public broadcast over the radio. Daniel Tiffany locates a resonant passage in *Guide to Kulchur* in which Pound extends the "'drumming language' that fulfills the ancient dream of telepathy," and the modern dream of radio: "Frobenius forgets his notebook, ten miles from camp he remembers it. Special African feast on, and no means of sketching for the records. No time to return to camp. No matter. Black starts drumming. Drum telegraph works and sketching materials arrive in time for the beano. Culture possessed and forgotten" (*GK* 98). I share Michael Golston's sense that this "drum telegraph," bound to "the rhythmicized body of the dancer," serves for Pound as the core historical continuity underlying the music underlying his *Cantos* (84); music, as a medium or a message (or a massage), beats rather than feels its way into the cultural subconscious. The binding of Frobenius's ethnographic method to the drum telegraph resonates with the twin impulses of futurism and primitivism, identified by Lewis, bubbling throughout Antheil and rematerialized in the late *Cantos*. Both for the impressionists (bad) and for Antheil (good), as Pound sees it, noise has made music material, voicing its social diagnoses and its compositional and performative process through embodied effects and affects.

Turning to the *Cantos*, on their own terms and in relation to *Le Testament*, I contend that the rhythmic tightening of form, combined with the potential of radio, struck Pound as a way of maximizing music's circle of reference; he wished to intensify rhythm so as to give fullest resonance to—to broadcast—the natural disorder and material noise on which his art depends, and to exploit noise's potential to diagnose less "tight" or well-considered formations (usury, currency, lazy art). The *Pisan Cantos*, the poems Pound wrote during his imprisonment for treason in 1945, process these dilemmas. As Pound expands and refines music's referential sphere, his search for the resonances of a never-ending drumbeat, materialized in the plastic of his confined body and mind, shapes his pursuit of a historical and a musical irregularity underlying history, and (more locally) underlying the cheeky publicity stunts of the Antheil Era. Antheil's cameo in the *Cantos* reflects Pound's interest in the small-scale sensation—his "bad boy" publicity gimmicks and his minute rhythmic tinkering—as leverage into history's fundamental irregularities.

"Ill Beat Music": Materializing Rhythm in the *Cantos*

It was between Cantos VII and VIII that Pound set to work editing *The Waste Land*;[58] both Cantos reflect Pound's evolving concern about what undergirds the "old lies" of the public square:

> Another day, between walls of a sham Mycenian,
> "Toc" sphinxes, sham-Memphis columns,
> And beneath the jazz a cortex, a stiffness or stillness,
> Shell of the older house.
> Brown-yellow wood, and the no colour plaster,
> Dry professorial talk . . .
> now stilling the ill beat music,
> House expulsed by this house. (VII, 26)

The "ill beat music" of Pound's Europe, one that leads into homage to Henry James' Lamb House, indicates wasted energy. Graham argues that for Pound, the "'ill beat music" and 'jazz' of modernity are little more than sonic clutter" in the landscape, akin to the "tawdry cheapness" that infects "Mauberley's" pianola (73). Pound is reflecting not only on what we think of as jazz, but on a mass of unbridled sensation that hasn't found its internal Tuscan shape. The resonant noise of James' Lamb House reads differently when one notes that Pound has also associated James (one of Ford Madox Ford's "literary impressionists") with the sensations of Debussy. In his "Retrospect" essay, Pound claims James and Debussy to be among those modern aesthetic tastes to which poetry needs to catch up: "only after a long struggle will poetry attain such a degree of . . . modernity, that it will vitally concern people who are accustomed, in prose, to Henry James and

Anatole France, in music to Debussy" (9). Pound later gives up on Debussy as a sloppy "grind"; here he seems ambivalent. Debussy and James, representatives of a fresh modernity, by the 1920s would come to figure an exhausted worship of the impression, whose stimulation has diffused into a "gassed out" "mock of motion" (VII). Pound admired James' ability to record "impressions of personal tone and quality," but claimed him to be "ignorant of nearly everything else"; James' novels boiled down to so much "fussing."[59] But for all his excesses, James' fuss had analytic potential: "one must depict such mush in order to abolish it" (HJ 324), a different version of the "piglike" noise in *Guide to Kulchur* ("But for the noise I shd. not have been started investigating"). In Canto VII's Lamb House, James's "fussiness" and Debussy's sentiment have worn themselves out, their modernity washed into a "jazz" of ersatz classicism and "dry talk," plastic without *virtù*, vasomotion in need of demarcation; but to diagnose that noise, he must give it a concrete rendering.

Pound's detection, "beneath the jazz," of a "cortex"—the cerebral source of visual discrimination, and a handy rhyme with "vortex"—suggests a hunch that the noisy "rattle" of these rooms must be symptomatic of a deeper structure. A revitalized rhythmic cortex, such as the one in Antheil's factory, will preserve the artist's appeal to modernity without exhausting the performer (laborer) or the auditor into passivity. The emptied out "husks" and "shells" are given shape by "a stiffness or stillness," akin to Pound's search for an irregularly vibrating Bass. Canto VIII, the first of the Malatesta Cantos, opens with the Eliotic call to order ("These fragments you have shelved [shored]"), nodding to another of Pound's protégés while suggesting the institutional, intellectual, and financial discipline to which this jazz, or to which the "wasted time" of artistic production, might be subjected: "So that he can work as he likes,/Or waste his time as he likes . . . never lacking provision" (29). Antheil's talent for time management needed to be reconciled with the creative demands of disorder and idleness; a larger structural cortex will enable the artist to produce without feeling enervated. What Pound needed, in short, was a larger rhythm to predominate so that smaller ones could fit-and-start freely.

Music in the *Cantos* has been read as a fugue, as ideogrammic compression, as a way of formalizing a deep structure underneath the jazz. Radio in the *Cantos* has been read as a "code for action," a strategy for defamiliarizing the sounds of words and thereby producing a script for cultural change; and, alternately, as a "cryptaesthetic" process of mourning that gives way to the fetish object of the image.[60] I would offer an "infantile synthesis" (LXXIV; 448) of these readings. Pound's collaborations with Antheil, on radio operas that were already merging the operatic and the radiophonic voice-object, suggest a kinship between two strains of the *Cantos*: the classical impulse to fashion hard, dry objective correlatives for a Great Bass; and the impulse to call up ghosts of the past. Through rhythm, the *Cantos* seek both to transmit the ghosts of cultural knowledge and to renew concrete somatic sensations.

Canto I, as is well established, initiates a literary *nekuia*—a ritual journey to the underworld, after Homer's Odysseus, that Pound reprises in LXXIV.[61] This *nekuia* is linked to the imagist condensation of motion into "plastic," a process described elsewhere by Pound as a "phantasmagoria": a ghostly apparition given iconic material form in the image. Synthesizing "precise definition and magic, reason and the supernatural" (Tiffany 254), Pound's image (like Adorno's phantasmagoria) reveals the material roots of this "magic" through formal *virtù*. Using music as a corrective to fiscal and aesthetic disproportion, seeking structural continuity between music and its historical spine, Pound needs music to maintain its plasticity in order to "transmit" this phantasmagoric *nekuia* according to a fundamental temporal pulse. If the *cordon sanitaire* of musical form leaves music open to reappropriation, then the search for objective, absolute music allows Pound to detach musical-poetic excerpts from their sources (the Cavalcanti line rehearsed throughout Canto LXXIV, or the Clément Janequin piece quoted in Canto LXXV) and reattach them to his own rhythmic cortex.

The natural place to start a discussions on music in the *Cantos* is Canto LXXV, in which written text gives way to a musical score: Janequin's *Chant des Oiseaux* described as the voice "not of one bird but of many." I will discuss LXXV in brief, but in many respects it is the ideogrammic condensation of the Canto before it—in which Antheil makes a cameo. Canto LXXIV reads history as a sonic singularity, a "bang" out of which a more linear (albeit still irregular) temporal process emerges. This lamentation on Pound's imprisonment begins with an apocalyptic bang ("yet say this to the Possum: a bang, not a whimper,/with a bang not with a whimper"); it dilates (in Abbate's sense, echoes) Eliot's Kurtzian whimper from "The Hollow Men" into a rhythmic account of history, of the process by which historical forces and figures are twice born (DIOGONOS) and "twice crucified" (LXXIV; 44). Pound links culture's moral and economic lessons to the temporal mosaic of the *Cantos*:

the wind is also of the process,
                                        sorella la luna
Fear god and the stupidity of the populace
but a precise definition
        transmitted thus Sigismundo
        thus Duccio, thus Zuan Bellin, or trastevere with La Sposa
Sponsa Cristi in mosaic till our time / deification of emperors
but a snotty barbarian ignorant of T'ang history need not deceive one (445-6)

"The process" of wind and rain, associated with "the Way" of the Confucian order, also tropes the process of rhythm as a patterning of history, a vibrating Eliotic/Schopenhauerian Great Bass that highlights the muddled economic structures by which the poet has ostensibly been victimized. The mention of "T'ang history" reprises the opening of the copper mine in Canto LIII, a poem striped with musical references that accumulate centuries' worth of thinking about dynastic ritual, aesthetic parsimony, and economic distribution. Kung's music-making before his death—"the rest sick and Kung making music / 'sang even more than usual'" (LIII; 273)—is linked both to his strategies of aesthetic compression ("And Kung cut 3000 odes to 300"), and to the onslaughts of warfare proceeding upon his death. Counterpointing military expansion with aesthetic compression ("Swine think of extending borders / Decent rulers of internal order" [274]), Pound attempts an Adornian aesthetic retraction marked by, but not submissive to, the noise of a strained national boundary.

As Pound picks up on this historical pulse in LXXIV, he suggests a historical and aesthetic continuity between Confucian musical discipline and his own imagistic sharpening of the verse-line. Pound suggests an exact rendering of sensation in what Antheil calls the "pure medium of time," transmitted according to "precise definitions." As Fisher writes, quoting a letter from Pound to Mary Barnard, "Voices on radio offered the promise of pure sonic contour in a time-based medium, the opportunity 'to cut a shape in time'" (38). The demarcation of line, "made thick" by usury in Canto XLV and in "Mauberley," must be transmitted "of the process" if it is to be heard as part of the *Cantos*' structural rhythm. Pound's "process" is manifested as entropy: wind, rain, historical conflict, the wasted time of artistic creation itself; but in the large-scale patterns of history, time is not wasted—or, as in Antheil's factory, it is better understood as rest. Hence Canto LXXIV resembles Attali's gestures to the realm of "composition" in which "the labor of music is an 'idleness' . . . irreducible to representation (to exchange) or to repetition (to stockpiling)" (141).

Pound's gesture to "transmission," with its echoes of the radio, amplifies his assault on the "snotty barbari[sm]" that dilutes the function of money, and the clarity of speech:

> so the total interest sweated out of the Indian farmers
> rose in Churchillian grandeur
> as when, and plus when, he returned to the putrid gold standard
> as was about 1925 Oh my England
> that free speech without free radio speech is as zero (446)

Juxtaposing the Indian farmer's ownership of his product with his own access to "free radio speech," Pound implies that the oligarchy over the airwaves is a form of interest, of "sweat[ing] out" speech from the citizen. Pound asserts that the free dissemination of culture relies on free access to its institutions. Pound does not assert freedom *from* institutions, clarified by the claim that Marinetti "wanted to clear away too much / and now we see more destruction than he wanted" (LXXII; 433). Marinetti's antisublime radio noise is heard to "s[i]ng war" where Pound "wanted peace" (433). Rather, for Pound, the processes of mediation, economic (the mediation of labor) and communicative (the mediations of radio), must be susceptible to a third kind of mediation—the mediations of art ("the 'sublime,' in the old sense")—such that they can be kept in "internal order" with a shared ritual pulse. Canto LXXII speaks of

> Confusion of voices as from several transmitters, broken phrases,
> And many birds singing in counterpoint / In the summer morning (436)

a suggestion that mixed signals and multiple voices, including the entropic disarray of birdsong, must be disciplined into counterpoint before they can be "freely" "transmitte[d]."

Birdsong and radio, sensate artifacts of natural and economic freedom, reflect on the sensations through which a cultured mind can produce an orderly paradise while imprisoned. Not through the "artificial" Baudelairean narcotic haze ("Le Paradis n'est pas artificiel"), but through contrapuntally rendered "fragments" of sense experience ("only in fragments unexpected excellent sausage, / the smell of mint, for example") (LXXIV; 458), Pound brings into shape the plastic sensations of his surroundings, realizing the internal *virtù* of the poet ("in the light of the light is the *virtù*" [449]) and the internal form of the poem ("stone knowing the form which the carver imparts it" [450]). An oft-reiterated line from Cavalcanti (*"fa di clarità l'aer tremare"*—"and make the air tremble with clarity") is dialectically and dialectally counterpointed with the voices of Pound's African-American DTC comrades, with regimental "bumm drum and banners" (448), and with Frobenius (the "man who created thunder" ["das Gewitter gemacht hat"]). This counterpoint makes the air tremble with sounds that are at once instances of somatic plastic used as mental reprieve, and artistic monuments etched "in the mind indestructible." As in Eliot, these ordered fragments are underwritten by the flow of water, "with sound ever moving/in diminutive poluphloisboios [loud-roarings]": an ordering flux, a fundamental irregularity, of musical/natural sound (447).

In these respects, Canto LXXIV, in which Antheil reminds Pound of his own imprisonment, can be read as an anacrusis to Canto LXXV's musical score. In Canto LXXV, Janequin's setting of musical birdsong, joined with a reference to the Meistersinger Hans Sachs and to the organ composer Dieterich Buxtehude ("art thou come forth out of Phlegethon?/with Buxtehude and Klages in your satchel") marks his ascent from the underworld. Pound's emergence from the ghostly realm is marked first by another contrapuntal birdsong in Canto LXXIV ("two larks in contrappunto/at sunset" [451]), then by Canto LXXV's musical score, a transcription of Janequin's choral piece transcribed for Olga Rudge's solo violin. As in "Mauberley," the sublime aesthetic thrill of song catalyzes, but is no substitute for, political action. This political engagement reappears in the last of the Pisan Cantos, on the heels of three Cantos' worth of sublime natural energy: "out of all this beauty something must come" (LXXXIV; 539).

But as in Adorno and Eliot, and as with Dedalus's keening of birdsong in *Portrait of the Artist as a Young Man*, the birdsong that draws Pound "out of Phlegethon" is not all forest magic. The Antheil reference in LXXIV suggests that music's powers to rehabilitate the poet are not entirely idealist; the poem betrays ambivalence about the mathematical and the fleshly vibrating appeals of music. Canto LXXIV calls on Antheil and Villon, two producers of the "hard bits" that make music durable under political duress, leading us to LXXV, a solo violin setting of Janequin's choral music: an individual voice that speaks for "many." Pound wished to "chise[l] down" Janequin's piece so that he could "HEAR Janequin's intervals, his melodic conjunctions," unobscured by harmony (*GK* 151-2)—a material metaphor for carving melody out of sensational plastic sound-mass. Hence we see several musical numbers assembled according to the horizontal intervals of an "underlying variety": Janequin's mediated song, Thomas Wilson's bawdy numbers, Villon's *Testament*, Antheil, and the "song of Gassir / now in the mind indestructible" (462)—an Antheilish fantasy of the bards of Africa. Gassir's lute, the African myth transcribed by Frobenius, recalls a story about a warrior who must fight and die in order to hear music, a resonance with Kung's singing to his death, and a bardic parallel to Villon and Pound.

As Pound seeks a rhythmic continuity, the rhythmic fits and starts of his verse link his encyclopedic cultural history to the economic contradictions of capitalism. Pound's "negotiations with the debris of the past," as Douglas Mao writes, are put into line not only with the natural process but with his "distributionist impulse," informed by C.K. Douglas's theories of social credit—an impulse that "subtends the Cantos, that enormous attempt to put to use the productions of the past while . . . continuing the work of new making."[62] This tension between making and distribution can be seen in Pound's rhythmic technique. His anaphoric repetitions, parodying the false accumulations of usury ("as when, and plus when . . . ") and insinuating "the process" ("The wind is part of the process / The rain is part of the process" [455]), suggest both therapeutic and economic functions for his *nekuia*. Honoring Beardsley's dictum that "beauty is difficult" (46), while unfolding the "difficult" processes attendant to the production of a "beautiful" object, Pound calls on the ghostly presences of the Antheil era—Villon (an honorary member), Hemingway, Joyce, Yeats, and Antheil himself—to transmit "the process" of aesthetic creation within a "putrid" political economy, to dramatize the material consequences of musical corruption, and vice-versa.

Pound's gesture to Villon and Antheil is both a personal recounting of their collaboration on *Le Testament*, and an effort to rehabilitate the aesthetic process of his own "radio speech." Pound calls explicitly on these figures, and Gassir's Lute, in the same breath:

> Lute of Gassir. Hoo Fasa
> came a lion-coloured pup bringing fleas
> and a bird with white markings, a stepper
> under *les six potences*
> Absouldre, que tous nous vueil absoudre
> lay there Barabbas and two thieves lay beside him

infantile synthesis in Barabbas
minus Hemingway, minus Antheil, ebullient
and by name Thos. Wilson (448)

The chant "Hoo Fasa" is itself digested contrapuntally throughout Canto LXXIV—"Hoo Fasa / Gassir, Hoo Fasa dell' Italia tradita / now in the mind indestructible, Gassir, Hoooo Fasa" (450)—and later in Canto LXXVII, where it dissolves back into thunder ("k-lakk . . . . thuuuuuu / making rain / uuuh / 2, 7, hooo / der im Baluba / Faasa!"). What we might now call the poem's ethnomusicological cast of mind offers a "tribal hail" as a correspondence to the betrayal of Italy (Richard Sieburth convincingly hears "Fasa" to chime with "fascism").

Gassir's Lute gives way to Villon's "Frères Humains," the chorus of hanged men that ends Pound's opera, here rephrased as "Absouldre, que tous nous vueil absoudre." Pound's melodrama features Villon penning his final testament, having been sentenced to die for resisting the Church. Built on Villon's plea to "Brothers who live on after us" ("Frères humains qui après nous vivez"), this final chorus prays for absolution from the audience as much as from God:

You see us strung up here five, six:
as for our flesh, which we have too well fed,
it is already devoured and rotten
and we, the bones, turn now to dust and ashes;
let no one laugh at our misery
but pray God absolve us all [*Mais priez Dieu que tous nous vueille absouldre*]

This plea for absolution "not from one voice but from many," is recalled in Canto LXXIV's parallel crucifixion scenes. Canto LXXIV ("Absouldre, que tous nous vueil absoudre") leaves God out, materializing him into a "process": absolution for absolution's sake. Barabbas now represents a dialectical "infantile synthesis" of two bad-boy personalities: the hypermasculine (not to say infantile) Hemingway, and the bad boy of music himself. In this brief homage to Antheil, Pound has softened the hard industrial edges of his *quondam* ally into an infantile bad boy persona.

Yet nostalgia remains for the energetic precision through which that persona, and other such personae, have been created. As in the epigraph that frames this chapter, Villon's acrostic makes an ideogrammic signifier of his own name—its visual sign mediating its "screeches" into "melodies";

one might see the citation of Antheil and Wilson serving a similar purpose as their names give shape to their surrounding resonances. The "ebullient" Thos. Wilson, one of Pound's fellow prisoners at the Pisan Disciplinary Training Center, is called on sporadically in the Cantos as a singer of bawdy numbers—like much of Antheil, designed to get a reaction, but recounted "with precise definition" (LXXVII, 489). Juxtaposed against Pound's recollections of the dancer Michio Itō, Wilson's seemingly nonsensical songs seem to fill out a performative mask—a persona crafted "with perfect precision" (489). The actress Isa Miranda follows, in Canto LXXVII, "changed personality/ changing her roles." Pound's *nekuic* travels through memory, coextensive with his obsession with precision and definition, seem to perform an "Imperial ballet" (LXXVI) in which new singing personae can be critically rearranged. I shall make a similar contention with respect to Edith Sitwell, whose nose-thumbing nonsensical verse produces a socially critical persona from the outside-in, through rhythm and form (in Canto LXXXI, Pound exorcises his "vanity" through an extended tribute to the cavalier poet, adopting stylistic homage to purge error). Here, linking Antheil to Barabbas, Pound recalls the cheekily noisy and the ideogrammic resonances of the Pound Era. This crew of "ebullient" brats, "synthesized" into a productively "infantile" yet "precise" mockery of the culture that has imprisoned them, can be read as an Attalian "simulacrum of sacrifice": a bawdy diagnostic of corruption and a reminder of the scapegoating impulses of social order.

Hence Pound negotiates his need for a clear and distinct rhythmic demarcation of a narrative—Villon's poetic clarity and individualism needs to be preserved—with the compulsion to diagnose and repurpose the noises around it. Rhythm is meant to free the consciousness from its time-bound sensory limitations, without forgetting the *soma* (the Tuscan's "residue of perception"). In something like an Adornian negative dialectic in which these bad boys are synthesized as "minus"es—pulled into a form that refuses to be reified into static (commodity-friendly) allegory—Wilson's Villonesque song endeavors to carve the voice out from its imprisonment in bones and flesh, "already devoured and rotten," without abnegating their physicality. As Fisher says, in *Le Testament* the microrhythms, "calculated according to the supposed speech patterns of Old French," are integrated with the body's own rhythmic hiccups and syncopes (33). In Pound's radiophony, the body's decay unleashes the permanent transmission of free radio speech, made beautiful through Pound/Antheil's unpredictable choral idiom.

The harmonic language of "Frères Humains" is relatively tame, though more complex in the 1933 BBC version than in its earlier drafts for performance at the Salle Pleyel. In both versions, with each iteration of "*Mais priez Dieu*," the piece's eccentric harmony and counterpoint is "absolved" at the end of each stanza: in conventional triads (1933; bar 42); open fifths (bar 86); and two complete unisons. Open fifths, lacking the third of the triad (Do-[Mi]-Sol) of common practice harmonies, are conventional in Renaissance pieces such as Janequin's *Chant*. Returning to a harmony motivated by the horizontal needs of Villon's language, rather than forcing them into orthodoxy, Pound seeks a purer and less clotted harmonic idiom to voice Villon's plea for absolution. Villon's language, so candid and so diagnostic of the corruption around him, pares away even the basic internal workings of the triad, as if the voice leadings were merely rendering the process by which Villon's flesh has been "rinsed and cleansed" ("*debuez et lavez*") from the skeleton. A brief percussive "swinging of chains in wind" (bar 19) accompanies the chorus's instruction to the audience of what they (cannot) see: "You see strung up here five, six: / As to our flesh, which we have too well fed, / it is already devoured and rotten." The spiritual debts for which Villon seeks absolution are sonically linked to the material debts that the *Cantos* frantically rail against: "Vai soli / are never alone / amid the slaves learning slavery / and the dull driven back to the jungle" (LXXIV; 451). Canto LXXIV plays with the "transmitting" properties of rhythm, treating both the rhythmic pulse and harmonic resolution as symptoms of a dull "driving back" toward the essential violence of slavery, and back further yet to the unalienated rhythms of the "jungle" that Antheil's factory was to recuperate.

As Pound follows that "drum telegraph," his repetitions start to resemble the small-scale motivic repetitions of *Ballet Mécanique* (though Antheil's piece, stuck in A^{25}, has little of Pound's large-scale development). The prosody of the *Cantos*, an amalgam of Old English accentual verse and quantitative classical verse wielded in the "final heave" against "the pentameter" (LXXXI; 538), is driven by phrasal contractions and expansions that parallel the fits and starts of Antheil's machine. As he recounts the birds on wires in LXXIX—later reading the image as a musical score written "in their treble scale" (LXXXII; 545)—Pound works through a series of quantitative negotiations, a Confucian rebalancing:

4 birds on 3 wires, one bird on one
the imprint of the intaglio depends
          in part on what is pressed under it
the mould must hold what is poured into it
          in
                    discourse
                              what matters is
to get it across e poi basta
          5 of 'em now on 2
          on 3; 7 on 4
                    thus what's his name
and the change in writing the song books
5 on 3 (505–6)

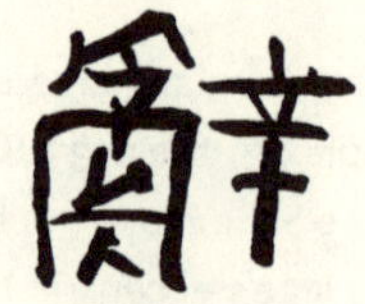

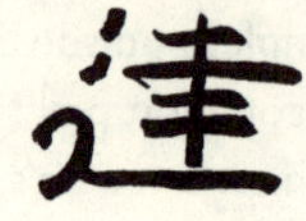

The ideograms at right—the first meaning "message," the second "to apprehend"—formulate the birds as a notated image, the apprehension of a message that "get[s] across" a momentary "sense of freedom" through a calculation of effect. The poem searches for ratios of birds to wires, notes to staff-lines, and words to content ("e poi basta"); the ratio of words to beats remains equally pressing. As the plastic ideograms present the birds' motion and stillness, and as Pound attempts to etch their ephemeral birdsong into a material score, the quantitative measures of Canto LXXIX contract and expand as if to find the right Tuscan proportion.

To manage this requires a negotiation between the technocratic and the liberating demands of art; the musical birds on wires signify both the irregular process of nature and the technical requirements of music. Villon's gesture to the birds that have picked his corpse clean remind us, after Adorno and Eliot, that birdsong represents not a mere expression of pure natural beauty, but a pecking away at the fantasy of an unmediated natural world. As Ellen Stauder writes, Canto LXXV's inscribed score "register[s] a form of production that resists both the personal and institutional follies that imprison the poet,"[63] aspiring for a nominalism in which the particular of the word is rendered, like the Adornian constellation, both plastic and free, material and liberated from the commodity. If musical scoring represents a "spontaneity that can neither be sought nor willed by the poet or captured by the commodity" (Stauder 268), that spontaneity must be preserved and archived for it to become perdurable, but this preservation is not without cost.

In the context of Cantos LXXII and LXXIV, in which Pound's dialogues with Marinetti and *nekuic* cataloguing of names, the song "not of one bird but of many" is an accumulation of efforts to render the flux solid, to concentrate the "sequence of the musical phrase" into hard bits of material. Pound seeks shape in entropy, befitting the plasticity of mental perception:

> This liquid is certainly a
>   property of the mind
> nec accidens est   but an element
>   in the mind's make-up
> est agens and functions   dust to a fountain pan otherwise
>   Hast 'ou seen the rose in the steel dust
>   (or swansdown ever?)
> so light is the urging, so ordered the dark petals of iron
> we who have passed over Lethe. (LXXIV 469)

In his Cavalcanti essay, Pound links the "rose in the steel dust" to the Tuscan's search for a "god inside the stone," for shape in the mass of energy that the scientist is too stupid to see (154). *Guide to Kulchur* links the same phenomenon to Janequin's search for "dynamic form" given to the "immortal . . . concept," which is "like the rose pattern driven into the dead-iron filings by the magnet" (152). The musical-metallic plastic contains an inner form that materializes motion; Pound seeks to etch this form permanently into the mind, while allowing the mind to remain "liquid." Canto LXXIX refers to "the change in writing the song books": Guido d'Arezzo's medieval system of notation, used to inscribe scales into the "mind's make-up" (506–7). He refers to d'Arezzo as "that bastard," though, as Bucknell points out, d'Arezzo is doing exactly what Pound is: forging "a music of vocables" to be etched in the auditor's mind (118). This reduction of music to reproducible elements calls to mind Attali's shift from *sacrifice* to *representation*, from ritual function to alienating notation: "From the moment there was sacrificial ritual coded independently of the musician," writes Attali, "the musician lost possession of music" (135). Pound pays homage to music's lost freedom when it is reduced to notation, even as he knows that such notations are necessary to preserve music in time; his search for a durable formal encoding acknowledges the risk that reducing music to notation alienates it from ritual. Pound, after all, wants us not just reading the score of Janequin's *Chant des Oiseaux* or Antheil's *Ballet*, but singing the *Chant* and hearing the factory's noise for ourselves.

Figure 3.2. Measures 1–5 of *Ballet Mécanique*, by George Antheil. Annotations mine.

Formalized musical calculation is a necessary, but not a sufficient, condition for recuperating music's embodied ritual energy. The microrhythmic organization of Antheil's *Ballet* and Pound's *Testament* relies on a no less calculated "mould" to carry its meaning, even as these works attempt to resonate with bones and flesh. Though the large-scale A^{25} of *Ballet Mécanique* suggests a continuous digestion of time, the irregular small-scale rhythms of the opening bars show a minute calculation of effect, precisely the sort of rhythmic fine-tuning that Adorno decries as hyperrational (fig. 3.2). There would be little surprising about these shifts were the material not boilerplate repetition: the jolt relies on our naturalizing the repeated pitches and expecting them distributed equally over the beat: "5 of them now on 2/on 3, 7 on 4." There is no 5/3 time (unless one were to adopt one of Henry Cowell's eccentric notation systems), so one cannot overliteralize Pound's lines to refer to musical meters; yet when considered amidst Pound's constant fretting over currencies and interest rates ("at 35 instead of 21.65"), the *Ballet*'s first five bars speak to a constant process of negotiation by which an absolute rhythm can be produced.

Pound's effort to approximate the grating oscillation between two understandings of music—as mathematics, as the "'sublime'"—requires both economic freedom and number-crunching, both quantitative and qualitative sensitivity. The line breaks that mimic birds on wires represent a twittering rhythmic flux: an accumulation of total form ("the mould must hold what is poured into it"), scattered and then reconsolidated ("in/discourse/what matters is to get it across e poi basta"), expounding a Strunkian noise-abating economy of expression, which Pound cathects onto birdsong. Pound's reading of the *Ballet* as an effort to integrate noise into industrial and aesthetic economies clarifies his search for a cortex beneath the jazz, dwelling on just the technical calculations needed to materialize such a cortex. Laborious as the process of creation might be, it creates a playful noise, as in Pound's and Yeats's time at Stone Cottage:

> so that I recalled the noise in the chimney
> as it were the wind in the chimney
> but was in reality Uncle William
> downstairs composing
> that had made a great Peeeeacock
> in the proide ov his oiye
> had made a great peeeeeeecock in the . . .

made a great peacock
        in the proide of his oyyee

proide ov his oy-ee
as indeed he had, and perdurable (LXXXIII, 553-4)

Pound dissolves Yeats's tightly written poem "The Peacock" (1914) into a noise in the chimney—itself repetitiously fitting-and-starting, as Yeats tries to get the words just right—only to find that, as in Antheil's factory, this repetitious noise has produced a sturdy object; Yeats's "Peacock" is "nourished" by the "wind-beaten, stone-grey,/And desolate Three-rock." The sounds of Yeats's poiesis (he is also bearing down on a Noh drama) resonate in the solid structures of the stone cottage, becoming integral with the wind and, by extension, with "the process."

"Nec accidens est," writes Pound about the liquid property of the mind—not an accident, but an "element" and a material "agent" of the intellect. Pound's attempted creation of order, as a permanent monument of "kulchur" or a fugal approximation of the process, relies on a mastery of temporal manipulation, verbal repetition, typographical condensation, and other poetic matter that quivers to the emotional and perceptual elements. Antheil, for all of his self-boostering *épatism*, offers Pound's readers the recognition that this intellectual order is at the same time a search for embodied sensation—that the "pure medium" of time needs to "vibrate in the human organism." Pound was licentious enough with Antheil's music that I will allow myself to abuse his trope of magnet and steel: the Pound era of modernism produced itself negatively as a sublime, rose-shaped niche in the sensational masses of Futurism, the material steel dust by which Pound was both repulsed and entranced. The manipulation of time served, for Antheil, to orchestrate the avant-garde sensations of Futurism and Dada, in turn offering Pound a way of rethinking music as objet trouvé. Pound, too, found relief in what Stephen Bayard, Antheil's detective-proxy in *Death in the Dark*, calls the "tricks of time." Bayard, recalling his acquaintance with Satie, proclaims that "Just before his death, Satie wrote a ballet called 'Closed'. . . . So old Satie could walk with his friends and his old umbrella and point to the billboards . . . 'See! they are playing "Closed"'. This is also my principle: I must take advantage of the day, the tricks in time, the speed-limit, Time!" (97).[64] Bayard's detective work merely turns the patterns of life in on themselves; these tricks, like Satie's and Antheil's before him, can unravel the artwork into Dadaist publicity, or can unfold its temporal patterns into social diagnosis. Likewise, what Lewis heard as Pound's relief in the sensations of the avant-garde both shapes the perdurable monument of the *Cantos* and makes it fundamentally irregular. For Pound, as for Dedalus and for John Cage, tightening the rhythms of music opens its forms to remediation and, conversely, digests the very noises that produce a niche for the aesthetic.

4 Joyce's Phoneygraphs

> Gone with the wind. Hosts at Mullaghmast and Tara of the kings. Miles of ears of porches. The tribune's words, howled and scattered to the four winds. A people sheltered within his voice. Dead noise. Akasic records of all that ever anywhere wherever was. Love and laud him: me no more.
>
> Joyce, "Aeolus" (*Ulysses* 7.880–83)

> Empty vessels make most noise.
>
> Leopold Bloom, "Sirens" (*Ulysses* 11.981)

At the first private performance of *Ballet Mécanique*, Joyce remarked that it sounded "like Mozart."[1] The claim offers a continuity with Pound's Feldmarschall Hindenberg, who "Heard for the first time Mozart and asked what the noise was/all this god damned cultural nonsense" (XLI, 204)—but what exactly Joyce meant by it is hard to say. He may have perceived in Antheil's music a kind of classical design consistent with Mozart's aesthetic; perhaps Joyce, like Pound, heard the *Ballet*'s calculated formal clarity. Or perhaps his comment was based more on feeling and mood, on a sense of joy and wit that he reflexively associated with Mozart. *Ulysses* frequently quotes Mozart's operas (usually with libretti by Lorenzo da Ponte), and Joyce attributed to him a "grace and invention" superior to the "muscle-bound" Beethoven; amidst all the noise of the *Ballet Mécanique*, Antheil's sense of humor might have made it through.[2] And perhaps Joyce was just being polite. He knew Antheil personally, having visited his apartment above Sylvia Beach's bookstore and recruited him to attend (uninvited) a few private concerts.[3] Whatever the reason, Antheil was one of the few contemporary composers whom Joyce found congenial. He proposed two collaborations with Antheil, both abandoned: an operatic reworking of *Cain*, Lord Byron's 1822 closet drama, and *Mr. Bloom and the Cyclops*, a four-hour "electric opera" based on the twelfth episode from *Ulysses* (*JJ* 558).

Only a few sketches of *Mr. Bloom* remain, and though Mauro Piccinini and Paul Martin have attempted to reassemble fragments from the opera, we can only speculate about how it would have worked.[4] We can, however, begin to understand the cultural logic of such a project, an effort to experiment with the material force of sound in staging the most explicitly political episode of *Ulysses*. In "Cyclops," the Citizen's nativist rhetoric comes to the reader mediated by parodic interpolations, counterpointing the Citizen's empty clichés with an equally empty, though virtuosic, stylistic play. The opera planned to stage this exchange by using automated instruments, microphones, and speakers to exaggerate the spectacle and sheer volume of the episode's rhetoric. According to Richard Ellmann, *Mr. Bloom* would have included

> for [the] orchestra[,] twelve electric pianos hooked to a thirteenth which played the master roll; on this would be recorded also drums, steel xylophones, and various blare instruments. The score was to be run off at top speed, with crescendos and diminuendos achieved by switching pianos on and off. The singers, seated below the stage and out of sight, would sing into microphones attached to loud speakers on the stage, and a *corps de ballet* would present the action in pantomime. The idea fascinated Joyce, but Antheil disappointed him by turning to other work. (*JJ* 558)

A letter to Pound suggests that Antheil wished to imitate "Picasso's technique of non-coincidence between outline and colors" by having "[o]rchestras and hugely augmented phoney-graphs both play simultaneously THE SAME THING," until "the orchestra stops and one discovers that the phoneygraphs HAVE BEEN PLAYING SOMETHING ELSE. All the combinations to make your belly give up."[5] The opera, while seeming to abstract its physical and verbal artifacts from the singers themselves, establishes a series of cognitive "noncoincidences" among the utterances of the characters, the reproductions of those utterances, and the bodies responsible for producing them. Antheil means to disorient his audience's belly both by means of repetition ("THE SAME THING") and disjunction ("SOMETHING ELSE"). That disorientation would arise only when the orchestra stopped and the audience retroactively discovered what "has been" going on.

Even though it was never realized, *Mr. Bloom* offers a valuable way of thinking about the ideological and rhetorical operations of music in Joyce's writing. His interest in Antheil exemplifies a remarkable curiosity, throughout his oeuvre, about the relative cultural potential of noise, music, and noisy music. Antheil's ingeniously Joycean move is to refer to the phonograph (sound-writing) as a "phoneygraph" (false writing), underscoring the technological aspect of sound while parodying the disproportionately high volume, and false holism, of nationalist rhetoric. The seeds of this critique are planted within the *Dubliners* stories, which seem to offer music as an intensely embodied, psychologically authentic mode of experience, but which also explore music's grounding in the noises of everyday life. Even Joyce's less recognizably modernist writings reveal ambivalence about the work performed by the mediating artifices of music and poetry—a concern that resonates with Stephen's final prayer to an "old artificer" in *A Portrait of the Artist as a Young Man*.[6]

In this chapter I read Joyce's work, from *Chamber Music* to *Dubliners* to *Portrait* to *Ulysses*,[7] as an unleashing of noise, an effort to amplify the noises immanent in music and thereby to reveal music as a material, ideologically loaded artifact. Notwithstanding his gestures to Mozart here, to Wagner elsewhere, Joyce seems as much Antheil as anyone else: I read in him both an interest in the "Musemathematic[al]" (*U* 11.836) condensation of sound into a stable text-object—an Antheil-like effort to calculate music's vibrations—and a destabilization of that text-object back into noise. As Joyce gives voice to the efforts of music and other arts to defend their niche, he gives equal time to the instability, mass-reproduction, and profligate misreading of those autonomous artworks. As suggested by Joyce's relation to Antheil, by his relation to Antheil's forebears (such as Cocteau and Satie), and by his ultimate appeal to John Cage (himself a Satie epigone), to sound "like Mozart" in 1920s Paris is to sound like something much less stable than its classical form may suggest.

Joyce's career speaks to the potential of music, and of "supple periodic prose" (*P* 140), to sublimate the noises of modernity—remaining consistently aware of the materiality of art, and growing increasingly skeptical about music as the ideal of authentic expression. And in keeping with what I have called the "Antheil dilemma," the more Joyce's characters proffer music as an autonomous aesthetic ideal, the more they lay it open to reappropriation. Antheil's contradictory status within modernism—on one hand, as a neoclassicist eager to divorce music from emotional "associations of legend and colour" (*P* 140) and, on the other, as a celebrity with unpredictable cultural capital—illuminates a similar tension in Joyce's treatment of music as both a set of formal relations and a site of social debate and spectacle.

Joyce's thinking about the interrelation between music and its social context evolves in almost schematically dialectical back-and-forths between music and noise. This chapter tracks Joyce from the quiet lyricism of *Chamber Music*, an early cycle of poems that hints at the noises condensed into tightly bound musical form; to the naturalism of *Dubliners*, in which music, as it faces social noise, triggers a withdrawal into silence; to the back and forth between noise and aesthetic "epiphany" in *Portrait*, in which a commitment to music's autonomy leaves it open to esthesic misreading; to the implosion of Stephen's Aesthetic fantasies in the modernist noise-music of *Ulysses* and the maelstrom of *Finnegans Wake*. I shall treat the *Wake* only briefly, largely in relation to Cage's *Roaratorio*. While my main interest here (as with Pound) is in the futile effort to corral noise into aesthetic unity, the vast entropic diffusion of sound in *Finnegans Wake* blows the corral open. Humphrey Chimpden Earwicker's (HCE's) entire persona ("Hush! Caution! Echoland!" [*FW* 13.5]) is the product of *rumori*—noise and rumor dissolved in the static of a malfunctioning radio into a fantasy of *Tristan und Isolde*. Joyce's obsession with music and his obsession with profligate sound have become one with Earwicker himself and with the historical "melomap" (42.15) that Cage renders.

Joyce's interest in sound overlaps conceptually with that of Attali, who, we will recall, argues that music "silences" noise by drowning it out through the bureaucratic and economic structures of "repetition." *Ulysses*, especially, investigates how musical or rhetorical sound can attempt to dilute subversive noises or to marginalize outsiders through mere iteration: of the various literary forms transformed into "Oxen of the Sun," the disingenuous iterations of Irish folk music, and the empty rhetoric of "Cyclops." The distinctive interpolations of "Cyclops," addressing the events in parodic political, legal, and literary discourses, explode the Citizen's nativist cant as so much noise; Antheil's gesture to the "phoneygraph" suggests that the loudest sounds in *Ulysses* are often the most false. The seeds of this critique are planted within *Dubliners* and even *Chamber Music*: texts whose intensely embodied, authentic ideals of music prove to be grounded in social noise. Joyce shows increasing skepticism about musical purity after *Dubliners*, but that skepticism is certainly *present* in *Dubliners*; in "A Painful Case," particularly, the experience of music questions its corrupted material context, and in return the story critiques the solipsistic abstraction prompted by the musical "epiphany."

Whereas *Chamber Music* and *Dubliners* demonstrate the sublimation of noise into music, *Portrait* and *Ulysses* make more explicit their skepticism about the rhetorical and ideological purposes to which music can be put. Moving into the novel, Joyce begins to dilate the process by which music channels noise: *Portrait* and *Ulysses*, in their dialogic and more recognizably modernist forms, question music as one of many expressive and cultural technologies, a means of interpreting the world and also of manipulating it. *Portrait* elaborates on how the sublimation of noise corresponds to a tempting, but untenable, notion of aesthetic autonomy. *Ulysses* precipitates those sublimated noises and then amplifies them as phoneygraphy, foregrounding music as a sonic manipulation of one's material conditions.[8] Many of the interpolations of "Cyclops," specifically, emphasize some kind of sonic resonance, satirizing the relationship between ostentatious rhetoric and meaningless noise as they move from the Citizen's formulaic nativist cant into the interpolation's "booming . . . pieces of ordnance" and "deafening claps of laughter"—a satire ready-made for the media blitz of *Mr. Bloom and the Cyclops*, in which ideological unison is revealed as an illusion. Joyce, with and without Antheil, makes the commonplaces of expression—the orchestra, not just the gramophone—a mechanism of repetitive immersion. For Joyce, the reading of media technology as the corruptor of pure music is too easy: music itself is exposed not as the Paterian aspiration of the arts but as a mediation of cultural experience, a way of assimilating the shocks of modernity, and a manipulative "forging" of sound.[9]

There is a sizable body of work on Joyce's relation to music, with respect to his use of Irish folk song, to his citations of operatic literature, to the musical structure of *Ulysses*, and to the various aesthetic theories articulated by Dedalus and Bloom.[10] Joyce scholarship, like the author's own oeuvre, has begun increasingly to engage with music and noise as related presences. The novel's musicality has been attributed to its multiplicity: of internal structures (Mack Smith reads *Ulysses* as enacting a move from "dominant" to "tonic"), and of semiotic possibilities (Bucknell reads it enacting Barthes' "writerly" text, which throws language into a newly interactive mode).[11] In both ways, the opacity of Joyce's writing resists transparent representation and compels esthesic engagement, by "return[ing] us to its phenomenality, to its presence as something seen and . . . heard, not something seen through and immediately interpreted and understood" (Bucknell 139). In so doing, Joyce's literary use of music has the effect of highlighting its own materiality, as an experience of modernity in tension with the "ineluctable modality of the visible," and as an artifact of textuality itself (*U* 3.01). Joyce's medium, after all, is language and not music; his efforts to approximate music through language, even as they question the fluid esthesic interchange by which music acquires meaning, perpetuate a disruptive effect. As musical pressures push Joyce's language into new territory, they break down the words themselves in noisily destabilizing ways: as Maud Ellmann suggests, "Joyce draws our attention to the noises of language, the acoustic detritus that cannot be assimilated into meaning or intention."[12]

As Antheil helps to clarify, music and noise are subject to those same structures of "meaning," albeit not always in keeping with the composer's "intention." As Joyce imagines and mediates the noises in excess of those structures—the embodied shocks that produce them, and the pains to which musical flesh is heir—his works also unfold the means by which such mediation occurs.[13] For these reasons, Joyce's attention to music as a rhetorical apparatus needs an additional twist, opening up his immanent forms to his noisily musical milieu. Applications of terms like "dissonance" and "noise" to Joyce's work have tended to reaffirm the autonomous musical object. As Jackson Weaver argues in *Joyce's Music and Noise*, Joyce "makes use of a rhetorical and musical use of theme and variation" (4), which, through devices such as chiasmus and retrograde, realizes a Paterian or a "Symbolist aesthetic" in which music and rhetoric are unified (94). Daniel Melnick's application of Adornian dissonance to *Ulysses* convincingly critiques Attali's technocratic indifference to the *immanent* properties of music, which may or may not be radical or "prophetic" (124). Yet the concept of noise opens up Joyce's work in ways that dissonance alone cannot. Like Attali, Joyce attends to the extent to which music is used as a technology for consolidating or resisting power.[14] Noise, like dissonance, can draw out falsities in the seemingly coherent space of the text, while making audible the art object's debts to the material world. It may bear noting, given Weaver's gesture to the Symbolist, that the figure at the front end of Bucknell's study—Mallarmé—is the same figure celebrated by Adorno as the true "materialist"; in his response to Benjamin's "Work of Art," Adorno favors Mallarmé's nostrum that literature is "not inspired but made out of words." For Adorno, the "technical laws" of art "bring it close to the state of freedom, of something that can be consciously made," an assertion that seems to apply to Wagner, Antheil, and Joyce alike. In *Portrait*, for example, Joyce's anxieties about formalized patterns of sound that mystify politics are intertwined with Stephen's faith in the autonomous laws of art, and the rhythmic process of "consciously making" it.

If Joyce merges music and rhetoric as modes of engagement with noise, whether as a retreat (Stephen) or an Antheilesque orchestration (*Ulysses*), he moves not just toward aesthetic unity, but toward a political realization of "integral freedom"—a distant political engagement within the space of the artwork, even from someone who, as Stephen says in "Circe," "detest[s] action" (*U* 15.4414). *Ulysses* seems to recognize that this autonomous cordoning off of music is dialectically inextricable from the noises of politics, of technology, and of mass art. As with Adorno's phoneygraphs, the illusions of technological "fidelity" come alive through glitch and noise—this is true of music even before the phonograph touches it. Like *The Waste Land*, *Ulysses* reveals a Gesamtkunstwerkian musical-mythical spectacle to be a mystification—a phoneygraph—inseparable, like Antheil and Satie, from publicity and politics, and further destabilized with every repetition.

Thus Joyce's allusions to Wagnerian opera can be read not only as fulfillments of a "mythic method," as Eliot put it, but also as efforts to realize the embodied and historical physicality of sound.[15] Joyce's nods toward music share in his fascination both with politics and with bodily movement, gesture, and peristalsis. Kittler's essay "World-Breath" posits Wagner's music-dramas as precursors to modern media, arguing that their "senseless noises and disembodied voices" give a newly privileged status to the "acoustic field" (217). Whereas classical opera abstracts music from the lived experience of sound and occupies only a "symbolic relatio[n]" to the actual "sensory fiel[d]" it occupies, Wagnerian music-dramas "correlate in the real itself to the materiality they deal with," working with sound qua sound and attempting to "reproduce[e] sensuous data as such" (216). Rather than treating sound as an exchange of information or affect, Kittler suggests, Wagner insists on a reciprocal interaction between dramatic events and acoustic data, an interaction initiated (as in "Aeolus") by the exhalation of the lungs and then amplified by musical effects: "Wagner's orchestra has the exact function of an amplifier. This is why his autobiography is repeatedly so fascinated with echoes and feedbacks, with fade effects and acoustic illusions" (224). As Matthew Smith argues, Kittler's essay overstates the case: Wagner's recognition of the total artwork's technological demands was matched by a need to obscure those same technologies (the phantasmagoria effect). Hence modernist responses to Wagner—Brecht's, for instance—recognized the potential of theater (I might add a "theatrical novel" like *Ulysses* or a poem like *The Waste Land*) to unmask the contradictions at the heart of a "totalized" production, even while "achieving a kind of unity through juxtaposition" (Smith, *Total* 79).[16]

Antheil both fulfills and satirizes Wagner's promise, which Joyce found exciting for its dramatic, mythical, and acoustic effects, but which he also found turgid, cultish, and dated.[17] As Piccinini notes, Joyce's and Antheil's plans for this theatrical melee draw heavily from Cocteau's 1921 ballet *Les Mariés de la Tour Eiffel*, with music by the French composers known as *Les Six*, which featured "offstage amplified comments and gramophones" (79). The more notorious precedent for *Les Mariés* was *Parade*, Cocteau and Satie's "ballet réaliste" featuring Picasso's costumes and decor. As I have discussed, Cocteau worked to replace Wagner's total artwork with an aesthetic grounded in everyday modernity; like Wagner's compositions, *Parade* plays with music as a kind of media, using noise to ground music in raw sensory material. And as in Brecht, aesthetic unity is turned inside-out: the interplay between the auditory and the visual creates not a Wagnerian synthesis but a proudly incoherent clash of sensory fields, not to absorb the audience but to annoy it. The captions of "Aeolus," a Cocteauvian antiballet, may be seen also to serve a Brechtian distancing-effect, while implementing Brecht's practice of "complex seeing": quickly alternating esthesic modes of watching, reading, and perceiving the play's generic metacommentaries.[18] In *The Cock and the Harlequin*, Cocteau explains that the *Parade* scenario started as a modern imitation of classical theater, in which "an anonymous voice, issuing from a megaphone, sang a type-phrase" summing up the character.[19] In later versions, that "type-phrase" was linked to advertising, as three managers, "seated in the orchestra, announced through speaking-trumpets, as loudly as posters, the names of advertisements such as Pears Soap, etc., while the orchestra was settling down" (140). "As loudly as posters" is a formulation Joyce would have liked (a bar of soap sings a tune in "Circe"), and much as Bloom believes that the secret to advertising is repetition, *Parade*'s music has a frenetically repetitive quality. The noisy managers would later be transmuted into dance rhythms, weighed down by Picasso's costumes: "The awkwardness of movement underneath those wooden frames, far from hampering the choreographer, obliged him to . . . seek his inspiration, not in things that move, but in things round which we move . . . according to the rhythm of the steppes" (Cocteau 140). *Parade*'s awkward rhythms, matched by the typewriters and sirens of Satie's score, turn modernity into a sideshow characterized by shock, confusion, and aesthetic dissensus. *Mr. Bloom* would have excavated the earlier stages of Cocteau's project: the "noncoincidences" between off-stage voices and orchestra, voices and pantomime, text and paratext.

The scandals surrounding *Parade* and *Ballet Mécanique* suggest that these efforts to rethink music's relation to acoustic and social noise also shifted the relationship between artwork and audience, pulling music (as Pound put it) into a wider circle of reference. In Pound's gestures to Antheil's musical factory, we see shades of "Aeolus," with its "machines clank[ing] in threefour time" (*U* 7.108), where the pulsing rhythmic unison of a well-orchestrated workshop signifies aesthetic wholeness and economic productivity. In "Aeolus," what gets produced is mostly "divine afflatus" (7.774), and yet the episode remains attuned to the materiality of hot air, the concrete materials and dynamic actions through which "A GREAT DAILY ORGAN IS TURNED OUT" (7.84). The episode's movement has little to do with the content being pumped out of the "daily organ" and everything to do with a virtuosic orchestration of sound. If, as Stuart Gilbert suggests, the organ associated with "Aeolus" is the lung pumping out wind, that organ produces the materiality of hot air as an acoustic medium, in Kittler's sense, while it mediates acoustics by playing with visual textuality.[20] "As loudly as posters," "Aeolus" and *Parade* transmute the flatulence of advertisement into theatrical spectacle, marked by the headlines and captions that mediate its already-comical actions. Sara Danius argues that Joyce represents the apotheosis of the modernist total artwork, in a way that bears a "family resemblance" to Léger's mechanization of the visual; *Ulysses* contains as much Antheil as Léger, and its Gesamtkunstwerk obsesses over the social import of sound.[21] Thus while Joyce's qualified appreciation of Wagner contributes greatly to *Ulysses*' "mythic" qualities, as in *The Waste Land*, the iconic phantasmagoria of the total artwork is unraveled, its universal epic scope opened up to deeply historical performance contexts and theatrical mechanics.[22]

If Joyce in theory approached music and poetry as autonomous artifacts, in practice his use of music lays bare a fundamental ambivalence about such autonomy. *Portrait* serves as an important hinge here: Dedalus's final call on an artificer unsettles the efficacy of escaping noise by creating music. For Dedalus, rhythm is the "first formal esthetic relation of part to part in any esthetic whole or of an esthetic whole to its part or parts" (*P* 173). This immanent property of art "dissolve[s]" the Aristotelian "esthetic status" of pity and terror (173) and allows one to "apprehend" the "harmonious" "result of its parts" (178). Yet rhythm is revealed to be set by historical time, as in the movement of the night mail train, which becomes its own Antheilesque music and "dissolves" Stephen's "strange dread" (73): "His prayer, addressed neither to God nor saint, began with a shiver, as the chilly morning breeze crept through the chink of the carriage door to his feet, and ended in a trail of foolish words which he made to fit the insistent rhythm of the train; and silently, at intervals of four seconds, the telegraphpoles held the galloping notes of the music between punctual bars." (73) Stephen's autonomy unfolds itself to its exterior; the passage recalls Lukács's remark that the rhythms of art should be set by the rhythms of history. As an adventure in bildungsroman, the novel recapitulates these small-scale rhythms in constructing the overall arc of Stephen's life. Clearly Lukács (like Lewis) would balk at Stephen's epiphanies, focused on discrete moments of time: small-scale experiences of rhythm that act in a descriptive rather than a narrative manner. In *Portrait*, Lukács might note, rhythm makes the listener a creative agent only in subjecting himself to history. As Joyce's use of rhythm gives the landscape agency in ordering time (the "telegraphpoles held the galloping notes"), it emphasizes Stephen's creative agency as a listener and an utterer who internalizes the shocks to his own body. After Stephen is beaten by a pandybat, his language becomes intensely rhythmical, repeating the phrase "cruel and unfair," "unfair and cruel" six times in the span of a page, in a way that signals his turn inward rather than outward—his rhythmic internalization of physical striking even as he resists it. Joyce's rhythms enact an elliptical process of binding and unbinding, attempting to escape theological and rhetorical artifice by way of tight formal discipline—manifested, as for Adorno's and Eliot's Wagners, in physical striking.

The tension between music and noise can be detected even in Joyce's more contemplative early works, in which noise is channeled into a conventionally lyrical or musical language. In Joyce's early political writings, too, music is heard in relation to political rhetoric. "The Home Rule Comet" (1910), an early essay on Irish Home Rule, uses music as a metaphor for the multivocal sounds of resistance. Addressing the failure of the "people's budget" and the dissolution of Parliament, Joyce writes that a dissident kind of music could be heard beyond the "dense and impenetrable cloudiness" of British parliamentary rhetoric: "Beyond it the orchestral music of the contesting electoral elements could be heard: noble strings agitated and hysterical, the strident bugles of the people and, from time to time, a floating phrase on Irish flutes."[23] While music can sublimate noise into palatable expressions, it can also critique those expressions by piercing the cloudy Dickensian fog of imperial language. This power is attributable not just to the difference between Irish and British factions, but to the differences among the "contesting electoral elements" of Ireland. Joyce suggests even a dissonance embedded in Irish uses of the English language: the Irish, he argues, have assimilated the English language "without being able to assimilate its culture or to adapt itself to the mentality of which this language is the vehicle" (159). Joyce, it should be noted, writes the essay in Italian, from Trieste, making these dissonances in Irish politics easier to observe.

Joyce initially considers art a niche from which he can confront politics anew, by way of escaping repetitive and artificial modes of political rhetoric. Likewise, Joyce resists the use of traditional Celtic "artifices" in Irish poetry, fixated on a particular vision of history at the expense of a new, truly critical voice. These problems manifest the twin pressures of realism and idealism informing all of Joyce's work, particularly with respect to the body: a subject of literary representation and a mediator of noise into music.

"Magical Cheats": Music and Politics in Early Joyce

My argument that Joyce's work unfolds an intensifying skepticism about the musical arts begins with his early poetry and early poems such as *Chamber Music* and "The Holy Office." Though there seems to be little in common between *Chamber Music*, a cycle of meditative, whingy, quasi-Symbolist love poems, and "The Holy Office," a satirical paean to the cloacal, the two works both consider how, and to what purpose, the material of daily life can be channeled into a tightly formalized artistic idiom. There is, as I have suggested, a cultural link between noise and abjection, be it filth or shit or (as in *Le Testament*) human bones; Joyce's early work tries to find a tightly wound poetic containment, but not abnegation, of this material, revealing a latent cynicism about the good faith of that ideal condition of music.

In an early essay on "realism and idealism" in Defoe and Blake (1912), Joyce contrasts Defoe with the musical arts, to the disadvantage of music, by asserting that "Modern musicians, literate or otherwise, would find very little" in Defoe's realism, which "defies and transcends the magical cheats of music."[24] The "magical cheats of music" could be a fine gloss on the Wagnerian phantasmagoria—music gestures to the sublime and masks the substance of the body. Yet Joyce's Blakean desire to annihilate "space and time" by dilating the heart's pulsation—for Blake, every "pulsation of an artery is equal in its period and value to six thousand years because in that infinitely brief time the poet's work is conceived and born" (181)—pulls these magical cheats into clearer focus.[25] As in the epiphanies of Joyce's early prose, such cheats must be prompted by material incidents; Joyce's dedication to realism does not contravene his aspirations to Blakean prophecy and mysticism, but keeps them grounded in materiality. Attention to real matter is more likely to annihilate space and time than are the artifices associated with fin-de-siècle Irish poetry;[26] to find a material equivalent to the formal "universal languages" of music and mathematics, idealism needs to be processed through realism in what Stephen calls "dialectic, the universal language" (*U* 15.4728). This realism is not quite the same as the *réalisme* of something like *Parade*, but there too a celebration of the profane is seen to annihilate temporality, evidenced by the ongoing looping patterns of the music.

Joyce's resistance to poetic artifice, the very quality on which Stephen calls at the end of *Portrait*, drives his ambivalence toward musical "cheats," and his simultaneous recognition that music makes the heart beat faster. For Stephen as for Joyce (as, perhaps, for Mauberley), certain historical images and tropes have, through repetition, become so artificial that they reinscribe imperial subjugation—though as Attali might note, this scarcely nullifies their power. In a 1902 essay on James Clarence Mangan, an Irish poet whose verses Joyce had set to music, Joyce praises Mangan's poetry as the expression of "the rhythmic speech of an emotion otherwise incommunicable";[27] in a 1907 revision of the essay, he claims that Mangan's "extraordinary rhythms and unstudied beauty" are "unencountered elsewhere in English literature" (129). Yet Mangan's inability to extract himself from "the latest and worst part" of his poetic tradition results in a poetry consumed with Celtic Twilight artifices: "plaids and ornaments" which paradoxically become an immaterial "denial of reality" (59). "One who expressed the sacred indignation of his soul in a dignified form," Joyce explains, "cannot have written his name in water" (1907; 136); this kind of rhythmic beauty requires material traction, a body with a heart whose pulse can be stimulated.

The speaker of "The Holy Office," self-nicknamed "Katharsis-Purgative," writes his name in something that is definitively not water, and argues that a critical Irish idiom cannot walk in fear of the body.[28] "The Holy Office" ridicules Celtic lyricism and prudery in a stylistic parody of Yeats's "To Ireland in the Coming Times" (1893) ("Know, that I would accounted be/True brother of a company").[29] Yeats's poem encodes those effects through "rhyme" and transmits them through rhythm meant to effect a public emotional response: "When Time began to rant and rage/The measure of her flying feet/Made Ireland's heart begin to beat" (10-12). As Joyce sees it, however, the elemental force of these "things discovered" are embroidered with extraneous "Celtic fringes," akin to Yeats's "faeries, dancing under the moon,/A Druid land, a Druid tune!" (31-2).

Joyce's broadside, the sort of vulgar genre put to great use in *Parade*, calls on a substance, excrement, that flows to the beat of a body and not of ornamented "dreamy dreams":

> But all these men of whom I speak
> Make me the sewer of their clique.
> That they may dream their dreamy dreams
> I carry off their filthy streams
> . . . .
> Thus I relieve their timid arses,
> Perform my office of Katharsis. (47-56)

Aspiring to a kind of Irish "tune" that gives voice to abject elements, Joyce's speaker champions his ability to deal with the naturalistic detail spurned by the "Holy Office" of his contemporary poets, having been made an outsider to their "mumming company."[30] Drawing on the Aristotelian and Thomistic languages that later motivate Stephen's aesthetic theories, the speaker suggests that real catharsis requires a confrontation with abject bodily material while subjecting it to poetic craft. Joyce showily finds feminine rimes for the words "Katharsis" (arses), "Aristotle" ("brothel"), and "Aquinas," making the assertion of a spiritual and poetic ego resonate with the flesh, to the detriment of "Those souls that hate the strength that mine has/Steeled in the school of old Aquinas" (81-2). Joyce's antecedents, given form in flesh and steel, are matched with the speaker's desire to "do a similar kind of service" "for each maiden, shy and nervous" (61, 60).

The formal and stylistic compression of "The Holy Office," in the service of an aggressively masculine sexual ego, may ultimately unravel into the unleashing of feminine noise in Molly Bloom's monologue, or in the feminized presence of gossip in *Finnegans Wake*. As Christy Burns argues, as Joyce begins to construct women with subjective agency, he increasingly refuses to resort to "containments" of the feminine, preferring to "remak[e] language" in a way that parodies patriarchal codes.[31] And as Julia Kristeva argues, this impulse confronts the filth and waste of the abject, and the materiality of language itself, culminating in a "single catharsis: the rhetoric of the pure signifier, of music in letters—*Finnegans Wake*."[32] My account starts, however, with a tightly self-contained chamber from which this music in letters is unbound—the *Chamber Music* poems whose encoding of bodily functions resonates with the Wagnerian materiality of sound.

Chamber Music Matters

Upon meeting Joyce, Pound wrote to John Quinn that "after the shell of the cantankerous Irishman, I got the impression that the real man is the author of *Chamber Music*, the sensitive, . . . the delicate temperament of the early poems."[33] This may seem counterintuitive; for Joyceans, reading *Chamber Music* can be a labor of love, or just a labor. Joyce's 1907 cycle of lyric poems is everything that his narrative texts are not: clichéd without irony, lyrical without developed introspection, light but not funny, coldly formal but not freshly modern. Yet *Chamber Music* represents a pivotal text for understanding what Joyce saw, or heard, as the material effects of sound and the "magical cheats" of music. Indeed, Pound went on to suggest, the genius of *Ulysses* lay in its "condensation," the "concentrat[ed] and absor[bed]" "registration of realities on the temperament" (153) found in the early lyrics. As *Chamber Music* moves from the elliptical first lyric "Strings in the earth and air / Make music sweet" to the thundering final poem, "I hear an army charging upon the land," its progression seems to condense the development from the sylvan silences of lyric to the polyglottic noise of the *Wake*. *Chamber Music*, in its unfolding lyrical creation of a resonant acoustic and psychological space, gestures also at the material operations of sound, not unlike those one finds in Wagner.

Those realities, expressed with proud indelicacy in "The Holy Office," undergird *Chamber Music*. As Richard Ellmann points out, the title of *Chamber Music* is recalled in the "Sirens" episode of *Ulysses* (232):

> Chamber music. Could make a kind of pun on that. It is a kind of music I often thought when she. Acoustics that is. Tinkling. Empty vessels make most noise. Because the acoustics, the resonance changes according as the weight of the water is equal to the law of falling water. Like those rhapsodies of Liszt's, Hungarian, gipsyeyed. Pearls. Drops. Rain. Diddleiddle addleaddle ooddleooddle. (11.979)

Musical "tinkling" jokes aside, the chamber of *Chamber Music* serves, as David Toop claims, as a crucible for Bloom's acoustic ruminations, which take the form of association and sonic patterning.[34] For Joyce, chamber music bore a relation both to the abstract laws of "Musemathematics," and to the physical interactions of the bodily processes of digestion, nausea, tumescence, and flatulence, which in "Sirens" progress to the temporality of the fugue. The result in both *Chamber Music* and *Ulysses* are streams of language that obey the laws of acoustics, or of Bloom's unreliable bladder, rather than those of English grammar.

A reading of *Chamber Music* prepares not just this allusive link to *Ulysses*, but also an early gesture to Stephen's strained villanelle. "Weary of ardent ways," Stephen (and Joyce's novel itself) will too retreat into the artifice of lyric musicality, while putting a historical stethoscope to modern Irish drama. As the speaker puts it in the twenty-sixth lyric of *Chamber Music*, inviting his auditor to put her own stethoscope to the resonant air,

> Thou leanest to the shell of night,
> Dear lady, a divining ear.
> In that soft choiring of delight
> What sound hath made thy heart to fear?

Joyce's speaker imagines an auditor to his own lyric, and to the wide world, a "choiring of delight" of which, if he is lucky, his singing might be a part. Indeed, the poems find their main continuity in the imagined presence of a silent figure, who seems as much the product of the speaker's poetic sound as its auditor. As Robert Spoo has argued, the poems represent a battle between "two very different confessors—a Capuchin monk and the priest of the eternal imagination—for the ear and soul (and body) of a young woman."[35] Thus there is a fundamental element of deceit, or doubleness, at the core of *Chamber Music*: this music is a persuasive "magical cheat" whose ineffable aesthetic effects can be used to any number of rhetorical purposes.

"Empty vessels make most noise," and in terms of meaningful substance, the *Chamber Music* poems are empty vessels indeed, resonating sonically but signifying little. The cycle begins by imagining an antiphonal orchestra conducted by Love himself:

> Strings in the earth and air
>   Make music sweet;
> Strings by the river where
>   The willows meet.
>
> There's music along the river
>   For Love wanders there.
> Pale flowers on his mantle,
>   Dark leaves on his hair.

All softly playing,
        With head to the music bent,
And fingers straying
        Upon an instrument.[36]

With Bloom in mind we may cast a cynical ear to the "fingers straying upon an instrument" ("Mastabatoom, mastabadtoom, when a mon merries his lute is all long" [*FW* 6.10–11]); and the deceitful doubling of voice previews the internally doubled, two-handed "Diddleiddle doodleoodle" of Bloom's Hungarian rhapsody. One can hear a lot of silences and gaps in this poem—metrical pauses, unnamed subjects, and un-verbed clauses—and the poem derives much of its power from those lacunae. The lyric invites the question of agency, of music's creation and of its effects: in the first stanza music functions as a direct object of the earth's "strings," in the second stanza as a simple existential fact ("There's music"); and in the third stanza (which has no verb or grammatical subject), the word "music" refers to a text being read so that sound can be produced.

Taking seriously Pound's claim that *Chamber Music* offers a formal "condensation," I would suggest that it condenses extramusical forms of sound, the music of micturition, into the auditory aesthetic space of lyric. To this peaceful opening music, *Chamber Music*'s last poem offers a violently choric call-and-response between the speaker's "moaning" and the "whirling laughter" of a Valkyrie-like "thunder of horses":

I hear an army charging upon the land,
And the thunder of horses plunging, foam about their knees:
Arrogant, in black armour, behind them stand,
Disdaining the reins, with fluttering whips, the charioteers.

They cry unto the night their battle-name:
I moan in sleep when I hear afar their whirling laughter.
They cleave the gloom of dreams, a blinding flame,
Clanging, clanging upon the heart as upon an anvil.

They come shaking in triumph their long, green hair:
They come out of the sea and run shouting by the shore.
My heart, have you no wisdom thus to despair?
My love, my love, my love, why have you left me alone?

Myra Russell terms this poem the cycle's one recognizably twentieth-century verse (it was later published in the 1914 *Imagistes* anthology), finally putting stylistic lyricism to modern psychological effect. Having failed in his performance of both confessors, the speaker succumbs to his own role-playing, addressing his plea now to the failed emotional "wisdom" of his own heart. Pursuant to the theme of faulty doubleness, each stanza contains one end-rhyme and one slant rhyme—juxtaposing sympathetic with unsympathetic vibrations, consonance with dissonance. Moving inward from the hushed natural noises of the previous poem—"I hear the noise of waters/ Making moan/***/I hear the noise of many waters/Far below"—Joyce fuses the "flowing" "noise of many waters" (heard again in the *Wake* and the *Roaratorio*) with the imaginary, yet much louder, alien internal entity of his own heart. Doubling silenced anguish with voiced embodied longing, the chamber oscillates not just between the WC and the confessional, but between the chest cavity and the brain, amplifying the resonances of his psychological roar. As Stephen says in "Circe," it is in his head—the "harmonic condenser enginium" par excellence (*FW* 310.01)—that he "must kill the priest and the king." Joyce's protagonists must double themselves as two kinds of confessor, erotic and literary, to kill two kinds of master.

Thus *Chamber Music*'s vaporous idealism, registered by silence alternating with musical lyricism, is knotted with the sounds of the material: these poems work through the novels' same anxieties about the embodied total artworks, theatrical practices, political anxieties, and sound media with which music is imbricated, from Richard's performance of *Tannhäuser* in *Exiles* to the villanelle in *Portrait* to the thumping newspaper presses of "Aeolus" to the thunderclaps and radio silences of the *Wake.* Let us restart, briefly, with Wagner. There are a range of Wagnerian possibilities in the *Chamber Music* poems; the green mermaid-like creatures could easily be Irish Rhinemaidens; the chaotic army, Valkyries. Joyce's later work might invite us to consider the speaker as a Siegfried figure, a motherless hero who returns to forge his sword *Nothung*, and with it the shattered fragments of a racial conscience. With Nothung—the sword that Stephen brandishes (in the form of an ashplant) at his mother's ghost in "Circe"—Siegfried slays Fafner, and then kills Mime after warned in birdsong of his deceits. This scene is rehearsed in *Portrait*, as Stephen's and Cranly's tense conversation on the University College quadrangle is accompanied by the "birdcall from Siegfried whistled softly follow[ing] them from the steps of the porch" (237). As Timothy Martin suggests, Stephen, not yet having forged his sword, "cannot yet understand the bird" and "is not yet prepared for the heroic calling that the birdcall represents" (42). With this in mind, the speaker of *Chamber*

Music could be akin to Stephen (preforging); or, given his rhetorical duplicity, he could just as easily be Mime.

Chamber Music, for all its "emptiness," bears Wagner's fascination with the staging of rhetorical cheats and the embodied materiality of sound, qualities both associated with music throughout Joyce's writing, lyric and narrative—or, as in *Portrait*, narrative unfoldings of lyric. These two forging scenes are bound by the clanging anvils, and linked by a rhythmic clanging anvil motif that persists in both scenes, mimicked by the last phrase of *Chamber Music* (fig. 4.1; *why* have you *left* me a-*lone*). The echoes with *Siegfried* here exemplify Kittler's argument that sound operates for Wagner not merely as accompaniment but as a hard substance: registered by the contact between stone and stone, rooted in the hot air of Siegfried's laughter and the bellows as he forges the sword (and destroys the anvil), climaxing in the octave jump between the two syllables of "Nothung," and underwritten by the loam of the Wagnerian orchestra. Joyce's first line is "Strings in the earth *and air*," both physical and ethereal.

As with Eliot's Thames-maidens, the dimetric verse of *Chamber Music* returns us to *Stabreim*: short alliterative lines meant to merge poetry with music and gesture, and to redefine sound itself. As I have stated, Wagner believed the tensions between vowel and consonant to be akin to the competing "ineluctable modalities" of auditory experience and visual gesture. Wagner's *Ring* rematerializes the monochord, a vibrating string whose overtones delimit the musemathematical range of aesthetic possibilities, marginalizing the noise of consonants and aperiodic sounds. In *Chamber Music*, as in *The Waste Land*, the vowel becomes a ringlike marker of music's boundary against, and its reliance on, historical resonances—moving from the anvil, past the strings of the earth and air, past the drum of the ear, through the body, and into the hermetic chamber of poetic sound. The incessant o sounds of *Chamber Music*—the o itself, and the emphasis in #35 on "moan" and "monotone," "go," "below," "to and fro"—work to abate the noise of consonants, or to tune them to the musical string. Beginning with the consonantal strike of a bow, "*Str*ings in the earth and air," the Joyce cycle ends with the resonant o-vowel of "alone," unifying the material and ethereal in an empty vowel. Joyce's music draws the "noise of waters" into a sonic monochord, the embodied stream of whatever instrument the speaker extracts by the river.

With the exception of Luciano Berio's 1953 *Chamber Music*, musical settings of these poems have been fairly conventional, including Joyce's own

Figure 4.1. *Siegfried*, Act I. Vocal reduction score by Karl Klindworth (1871).

beautiful but slightly pallid setting of "Bid Adieu." (*The Joyce Book*, a 1933 anthology of settings of Joyce's *Pomes Penyeach*, is slightly more adventurous, including Antheil's own setting—not liked by Joyce—of the 1915 poem "Nightpiece.") One can perhaps see the ultimate phoneygraphic deconstruction of the total artwork in Cage's *Roaratorio*: a piece that amplifies and defamiliarizes the latent noise of the music-drama. As R. Murray Schafer and Douglas Kahn both explain, noise-music such as Antheil's and Cage's integrations of noise into music require, first, the distinction between different kinds of nonmusical sound; upon categorizing the sounds of the real world, the "noisy correspondences within music were emphasized as themselves bearing traces of the world of true extramusicality" (Kahn 69). The *Chamber Music* poems inscribe the walls of the chamber with these same noisy traces, leaving marks of the material world within the resonances of lyric. What *Chamber Music* is to *Ulysses*, perhaps, Wagner is to Antheil: with his ear to the shell, Joyce hears not just the elemental loam of music but the clanging anvils of labor.

De-Composing Music: Rhythm, Noise, and "Phrasemongering" in *Dubliners*

Even the soft-spoken *Chamber Music* offers an early glimpse of Joyce's skepticism about the hermeticism of music, and about the rhetorical deceptions of music's magical cheats. Through narrative, *Dubliners* reflects in a similar vein on musical aesthetics and on music's relation to a wider circle of reference by considering whether an epiphanic experience, consummated in silence, can be extracted from the noise of the social. "A Mother," for instance, depicts music as a means of circulating socially, an "accomplishmen[t]" that facilitates Mrs. Kearney's courtship and as a contribution to the Irish Revival (149). Mrs. Kearney's daughter Kathleen is invited to perform at a series of grand concerts because of the "little counter of gossip" causing her name to be "heard often on other people's lips" (150). "A Mother" savages both Mrs. Kearney and her audience: while Mrs. Kearney is satirized for her fixation on drawing-room accomplishments, the audience is accused of having "behaved indecorously as if the concert were an informal dress rehearsal" (153).

Noise is a constant presence in "A Mother," in ways now familiar: murmurs of discontent and (less frequently) content in the audience that augment and (less frequently) counterbalance the mundane practical matters of producing a performance. Mrs. Kearney's attention to the Victorian "accomplishments" associated with music is echoed by her "tact" in "wording" the programme—her knowing, in a manner that presages the *Parade*-like captions of "Aeolus," "what *artistes* should go into capitals and what *artistes* should go into small type" (a different form of phony writing) (150). Much of the audience noise responds to absent or emaciated human bodies, as if the audience has to counteract the inadequate sounds being projected from the stage. When Madam Glynn takes the stage, her "meagre body" and "bodiless gasping voice" produce mockery from the "cheaper parts of the hall" (160). And as Mrs. Kearney prevents her daughter from taking the stage, the "noise of the hall grew more audible" (156), "the noise in the hall grew louder," "the audience was clapping and stamping," the "noise in the auditorium had risen to a clamour" (159). Mrs. Kearney's insistence results in exactly the wrong kind of rumors being spread about Kathleen, as the concert reviewer O'Madden Burke announces that Mrs. Kearney, having acted without a "sense of decency" like a "nice lady," will make no more music in Dublin (162).

Madam Glynn's "meagre body" emphasizes how a musical performance is underwritten by the names and bodies that produce, hear, and review it. (One might be in mind of the dramatic weight loss to which the decline of Maria Callas is often attributed, though Glynn, to put it mildly, lacks Callas's allure.) Bodies become an object around which noises circulate, and a way of mediating those noises for one's own benefit. Mr. O'Madden Burke, writing the notice for the *Freeman*, possesses an "imposing body," which he balances on an umbrella; similarly his "magniloquent western name was the moral umbrella upon which he balanced the problem of his finances. He was widely respected" (158). Burke uses the umbrellas of his body and name to promote Miss Healy, whose bodily "warmth, fragrance, and colour" "appea[l] to his senses" (158). Joyce's critique is as scattershot as the noises of the audience: meager bodies and "imposing" ones all become hubs of absurdity. Burke imposing body, as much as those of the performers', mediates events in order to produce a buzz and to satisfy his pleasures.

Previewing *Ulysses*' clattering trains and presses, "A Painful Case" further speaks to Joyce's intensifying curiosity about music and noise. A chiastic anticipation of "A Mother's" warning against musical simony, an ideal devalued by base materialism, "A Painful Case" delegitimizes music solipsistically isolated from performance. Music is both the villain and the victim of the story; the analogy drawn between music and violence burdens the aesthetic qualities of music with a social and psychological cost. As Allan Hepburn argues (after Attali), music in "A Painful Case" pivots on acts of sacrifice or death, crystallized in abortive physical gestures: Emily Sinico's death is of a piece with the musical repression of noise; and Mr. Duffy's "repudiation of sound" at the story's end, in turn, corresponds to his refusal of human contact when Emily touches his hand.[37]

The autonomy of music parallels the autonomy of Duffy: among the emblems of his social withdrawal at the beginning of the story is his constant presence at his landlady's piano, and the domestic "orderliness" of his mind before he learns of Emily's death is crystallized by the "new pieces of music" that "encumbered the music-stand" in his room.[38] Among the few "dissipations" of Duffy's life are occasional visits to Mozart operas, and his almost-erotic encounter with Emily is fueled by a metaphorical musical resonance: "the music that still vibrated in their ears united them" (109, 111). While music temporarily liberates Duffy from physical isolation, it does not liberate him from psychological isolation: he remains a solipsist and a narcissist, even while music (literally and metaphorically) gives him a language in which to channel these drives.

Duffy's psychological withdrawal is paralleled by the story's structural recursion, which mimics music's dialectical negation-of-a-negation of the material world. He is driven to reflect on his complicity in Mrs. Sinico's death first by the newspaper report of the inquest and then by a goods train "winding . . . obstinately and laboriously" out of Kingsbridge Station; he imagines the "laborious drone of the engine reiterating the syllables of her name" (117). In Duffy's ears, to borrow Joyce's assessment of Antheil, the train sounds like Mozart, giving classical aesthetic order to the world around him even as it temporarily "dissipat[es]" his psychological quandary. The noise of the train becomes solipsistic music ("the rhythm of the train pounding in his ears") while music, the shaping force of Duffy and Mrs. Sinico's interaction, is de-composed into the "laborious" sounds of trade.

As music becomes increasingly material, Duffy's narcissism ceases to be mere abstraction: he stops simply *being* narcissistic and begins *performing* his narcissism. Duffy is fixated on philosophical "exactitude" and on style, preoccupations with social and political implications heightened by his charged interactions with Mrs. Sinico (111). He explains to her that he has ceased to affiliate with the Irish Socialist Party because their "discussions . . . were too timorous," and they "resented an exactitude which was the product of a leisure not within their reach" (111). Duffy's copies of Hauptmann and Nietzsche, sharing space with his sheet music, buttress his authority and license him to abandon a social cause.[39] His abandonment of socialism is not driven solely by "leisure," however; he refuses to write because, he explains with "careful scorn," he resents the "phrasemongers" of "an obtuse middle class which entrusted its morality to policemen and its fine arts to impresarios" (111). Yet as his explanations to Mrs. Sinico become part of the vibrating music that "united them" and "emotionalised his mental life," he begins to fixate on "the sound of his own voice": "He thought that in her eyes he would ascend to an angelical stature; and, as he attached the fervent nature of his companion more and more closely to him, he heard the strange impersonal voice which he recognised as his own, insisting on the soul's incurable loneliness. We cannot give ourselves, it said: we are our own" (111). Duffy is not immune to phrasemongering, and he becomes so enamored with his own language (the product of leisure and "exactitude") that he abstracts his phrases into a "strange impersonal voice." Reading the eponymous newspaper account of Mrs. Sinico's death, Mr. Duffy vituperates against the column's "threadbare phrases" and "inane expressions of sympathy," which he reads as "the cautious words of a reporter won over to conceal the details of a commonplace vulgar death" (115)—journalistic clichés silencing hard facts.

Duffy's final epiphany arises when he merges the noises of his material surroundings (a tram, a public bar, and a goods train) with the narratives that he produces as an interpreter: the repeated utterances of Emily Sinico's name, like his pompous philosophical aphorisms, comprise "the sound of his own voice," but they have been drawn from an autonomous musical sphere and become a kind of noise-music. As the rhythms of her name echo, Duffy "felt that he was alone" (117)—not that he *was* alone but that he *felt* that way, having recognized that being alone is not the only alternative. Duffy's encounters with Mrs. Sinico awaken him to the music of social life, while, conversely, the rhythmic noises of the social world give his "vibrating music" a material weight. The more music he hears, the more he tries to integrate noise with the patterns of his own psychological breakdown; the more noise he hears, the more the illusion of musical authenticity unravels. Pursuant to *Dubliners*' construction and deconstruction of music as authentic, epiphanic self-discovery, the dilemma of *Portrait* is that its musical language constitutes both the means of Stephen's escape and the noise that he wishes to silence.

Noiselessly Devoted: *Portrait* and the Rhythms of Artifice

Portrait of the Artist seems at first to recoil from *Dubliners'* naturalistically social perspective on art, wishing to pull it back into an autonomous sphere of "silence, exile, and cunning" (*P* 208). In *Portrait*, Stephen and Joyce focus on the refined aesthetic object itself, to such a degree that Frank O'Connor parses the novel's "insufferably self-conscious" prose and compares its stylized repetitions to textbook Aestheticism, "as though Walter Pater had taken to business and commercialized his style for the use of schools and colleges."[40] Here, O'Connor writes, "*le mot juste* is no longer *juste* for the reader, but for the object" (374): the aesthetic patterning of the prose suggests a refinement of daily life into a self-contained artifact.

Portrait perorates "insufferably" on the process, associated with rhythm, by which noises are sublimated into art.[41] The discussion of Stephen's villanelle performs a pair of transformations: the composition of art sublimates noise, and those noises are precipitated as art reemerges into public space. As Stephen intones the villanelle in real time, he emphasizes the independent transformative power of rhythm: "He spoke the verses aloud from the first lines till the music and rhythm suffused his mind" (186). Stephen associates lyric rhythm with the poet's ability to "refine" his personality "out of existence," to abstract the temporal experience of emotion from the person of the artist: the "lyrical form is in fact the simplest verbal vesture of an instant of emotion, a rhythmical cry such as ages ago cheered on the man who pulled at the oar or dragged stones up a slope. He who utters it is more conscious of the instant of emotion than of himself as feeling emotion" (180).

On one hand, then, the rhythmic motion of Stephen's language corresponds to an almost imagistic notion of the self-contained artwork. When Stephen-the-artificer enters into private fantasies about his destiny as an artist, his own language becomes musical in both content and manner. Upon rejecting the priesthood, for example, he hears "notes of fitful music leaping upwards a tone and downwards a diminished fourth, upwards a tone and downwards a major third. . . . It was an elfin prelude, endless and formless" (139). This sequence (something like C-D-A#-C-G#) begins to constellate a whole tone scale, the idiom of a "formless" impressionist prelude, and, as Gifford points out, "an echo of the avant-garde aesthetic climate of the 1890s" in which Stephen is immersed (Debussy's *Prélude à l'apres-midi d'un faune* [1894], the most famous orchestral use of the scale, is an homage to Mallarmé).[42] The elfin prelude culminates in a "proud cadence from Newman," but Stephen rejects Newman's proud, "dim image" and, instead, aspires to a condition of aesthetic harmony. Hearing the "phrase and the day and the scene harmonised in a chord," Stephen wonders, "Did he then love the rhythmic rise and fall of words better than their associations of legend and colour?" (140). This formal appreciation of rhythm relies, literally, on an "association of legend"—with Dedalus's own name, which "seemed to him a prophecy" and "a symbol of the artist forging . . . a new soaring impalpable imperishable being" (142). Thus Stephen imagines the rhythms of his art as a transcendence of noise that he can still always hear: he aspires "to hear the noise of dim waves and to see a winged form flying above the waves and slowly climbing the air" (142). Hovering over this set piece is the "artificer," rising above the noise of the world by creating a "winged form" through rhetorical sleight of hand.

On the other hand, Stephen's dissociated notion of art, in which rhythmic form catalyzes Paterian pleasure, does not hold up in *Portrait*; the "Mozart-like" solidity of classical form is destabilized in a variety of ways. For one, the novel reveals that such a "noiseless existence" can be realized only through the creation of even more poetic language, whose encoded noises lurk to be released. Like Mangan, Stephen is too wrapped up in the nightmare of history to awake from it, and the desire to escape the "ardent" noises around him prompts him to compose his villanelle (183). Through his villanelle, Stephen weaves himself into (like Adorno's Mallarmé, "makes out of words") the same nets he desires to fly. The poem's intensely musical qualities, and those of Stephen's self-aggrandizing discourses on his self-exile, suggest that he is reinscribing the nets of artificial rhetoric: much as Jack Duffy's critique of "phrasemongering" results in the production of self-contained, pseudo-Nietzschean aphorisms, Stephen's skepticism about political rhetoric results in pompous Wagnerian declarations about the smithy of his soul. Stephen envisions the "forging" of art as a transcendence of noise, whereas he envisions his friends using "number and noise" as an escapist "refuge . . . from the secret dread in their souls" (142).

And also like Duffy, Stephen's philosophical self-assuredness is reflected in his assertion to Cranly that he does "not fear to be alone" (208). Stephen links the forging of art with the absence of noise: the desire to escape the noises around him prompts Stephen to compose the poem, but at the same time the experience of the poem has historical noises embedded within it. "Are you not weary of ardent ways?", asks Stephen's speaker, suggesting poetry as an alternative to the phoneygraphic rhetoric of politics and theology. It is highly musical poetry at that, structured around complex end-rimes ("heart ablaze" [line 4] and "ardent ways" [1] is nearly a triple rime) and overlapping front-rimes ("Lure" [2], "Your" [4]). Stephen's "weariness," a thematic element and an esthesic effect of an amateurish villanelle, suggests that these "ardent ways" and "enchanted days" have become repetitive and wearying in public speech, and in the exhausted poetic artifice.

Stephen's weariness leads him to reflect on the relation between poem and audience, a relation figured as ardent noise. The novel depicts Stephen intoning and composing the villanelle in real time, and the poem's composition and language emphasizes art's Eucharistic transformations. As a "priest of the eternal imagination," Stephen portends to "transmut[e] the daily bread of experience into the radiating body of everliving life" (186). The means of this is poetry—not only the poem but the act of composing poetry in real time, an act that affects Stephen rhythmically: "He spoke the verses aloud from the first lines till the music and rhythm suffused his mind" (186). When Stephen awakens the next morning, he experiences noises imagined rather than real: "No sound was to be heard: but he knew that all around him life was about to awaken in common noises, hoarse voices, sleepy prayers. . . . Weary! Weary! He too was weary of ardent ways" (186). In a simultaneous recollection and anticipation of noise, Stephen's poetic voice and real voice merge ("He *too* was weary"), and the narrative voice itself begins to speak in rhymes ("common noises, hoarse voices"). The villanelle and the noises that it sublimates are fused into a kind of noise-music manifested psychologically for Stephen and stylistically for Joyce.

Stephen's efforts to escape noise make the sounds packed into his *Chamber*-like poetry and art all the more palpable. The rejected noises of Ireland infuse his aesthetic consciousness: as with *Parade* and Antheil's *Ballet*, the fraying border between music and noise corresponds to an uneasy relation between stage and audience, pivoting for Stephen on Yeats's *Countess Cathleen*.[43] As he moves into a recollection of the play, Stephen experiences the cleansing sublimation of noise through the movement of poetic language: a "soft liquid joy flowed through the words where the soft long vowels hurtled noiselessly and fell away" (*P* 190). The sonic experience of the vowel—uninterrupted vocalized sound—is for Stephen a solipsistic "liquid joy." Yet this abstract experience cannot last: Yeats's vowels repossess their historical resonances as Stephen recollects the performance of *Cathleen* at the Irish National Theater. *Cathleen* is the result of Yeats's aesthetic creation but also the catalyst of the protesters' esthesic energies and of Stephen's hyper-stylized idioms. Prepositional parataxis recursively embeds time, place, and agency into Stephen's memory: he remembers "the scene *of* the hall *on* the night *of* the opening *of* the national theatre," "alone . . . *at* the tawdry scenecloths and human dolls framed *by* the garish lamps of the stage," where "catcalls and hisses and mocking cries ran *in* rude gusts *round* the hall *from* his scattered fellowstudents" (*P* 190, my italics).[44] Despite his desire to aestheticize noise out of existence, Stephen can only dwell on it more obsessively: the rhythms of the artificer unearth, rather than silence, the social noises of the theater.

A GREAT DAILY ORGAN: *Ulysses'* Noise-Music

The fantasy of a noiseless existence in favor of the self-contained rhythms of the artwork is strained in *Ulysses*, which unleashes noise with generic abandon. Here the Antheil dilemma returns as both fulfillment and deconstruction of Stephen's efforts to divorce the rhythms of art from their "associations." As artists unmoor their expressions from specific cultural referents, treating musically patterned sound as form for form's sake, they allow these sounds to be reconfigured for new, often dubious purposes. In "Sirens," these sounds are sung and heard in new contexts with new resonances; in "Oxen of the Sun" and "Cyclops," they are iterated as cultural clichés; in "Aeolus," they are re-typeset, forward and backward; and in "Circe," they are replayed on phoneygraphs, forward and backward.

Coextensively a clumsy ballet, an orchestrated factory, a deep exhalation of the lungs, and a long sustained bad joke, "Aeolus" makes the very process of creating text into a "GREAT DAILY ORGAN": a part of the body and a huge musical instrument. In "Aeolus," Joyce explores the noise-music of the text-factory itself, as musical time drives and is driven by the rhythms of journalism. The episode recapitulates, but also extends, the concerns of "A Painful Case" where the "threadbare" and "inane" rhythms of journalistic prose, mixed with the rhythm of the tram, motivate Duffy's recursive experience of Emily Sinico's name.

The presence of the railway in "Aeolus" binds the production of text to the rhythms of historical time. The episode opens with the caption "IN THE HEART OF THE HIBERNIAN METROPOLIS," using the trams' orchestrations of time, and of sound, to prepare for the musical movements of the galleys at the *Telegraph* office (*U* 7.01-02). The timekeeper of the tram company conducts the opening of the episode, releasing the Aeolian winds and directing their behavior. The trams' "parallel clanging" through the metropolis is patterned like a musical text: "Right and left parallel clanging ringing a doubledecker and a singledeck moved from their railheads, swerved to the down line, glided parallel" (7.10-12). This convoluted sentence builds up a series of parallels that orchestrate sounds as they move through time: right and left; clanging and ringing; doubledecker and singledeck; and "moved," "swerved," "glided." Following on Lenehan's wretched pun about the opera that "resembles a railwayline"—"*The Rose of Castile*"—these syntactic parallels act as musical-metallic "[r]ows of cast steel" (7.513, 7.591), guiding the episode along in dactyls and trochees: *right* and left *par*allel *clang*ing *ring*ing. In fact the only words to disturb this movement are the nouns—doubledecker and singledeck—which are compelled to move, swerve, and glide as the sentence surges forward. The sentence repeats the word "parallel" to announce its own highly constructed quality; a celebration of the orchestrated metropolis transforms into a celebration of orchestration for its own sake, a playful manipulation of form.

These manipulations are further exposed as sublimations of noise, as encounters with textual disruption and nonsense. The episode's opening invocation of "right and left" "clanging" predicts Bloom's later observation of the typesetter who must read backward, from right to left, to set type properly: "Reads it backwards first. Quickly he does it. Must require some practice that. mangiD kcirtaP. Poor papa with his hagadah book, reading backwards with his finger to me" (7.204-6). Comparing typesetting to the reading of Hebrew (and collapsing the processes of text-production and reading), Bloom turns Dignam's name into noise, much as the gramophone in "Circe" reverses "The Holy City" and the one in "Hades" distorts the voice of the dead: "Put on poor old greatgrandfather. Kraahraark! Hellohellohello amawfullyglad kraark awfullygladaseeagain hellohello amawf krpthsth" (6.964-6). Two kinds of materialized language, these phoneygraphs project *Ulysses*' many anxieties about specters, ghosts, and the speaking dead (the haunting presence of Kittler's "writing without a subject"), as well as its attempts to process the glitchy "dead noise" that both disrupts and enables communication, "records of all that ever wherever was."

Intertwining the visual and the auditory elements of language, mediating both through the rhythms of the journalistic machine, "Aeolus" focuses on the gaps and silences—the pauses and durées—that make those rhythms meaningful. Confronted with an ad from Alexander Keyes, Bloom listens to the "racket" of the machines, and watches the foreman feed "huge webs of paper" into their "obedient reels": "Slipping his words deftly into the pauses of the clanking he drew swiftly on the scarred woodwork" (*U* 7.128, 136, 139-40). The foreman must find the beat to understand the pauses: the silences are what become conspicuous, just as the caption explaining Keyes's ad—"HOUSE OF KEY(E)S"—parenthetically isolates the element of his name that makes no sound (*U* 7.141). In the production of text and the morphology of words, the pauses allow sounds to be channeled into sense, yet they also prove disruptive to engaged, occasionally obsessive, readers. Bloom considers asking the foreman about the pronunciation of the silent "g" in the word *voglio*, which he has incorrectly remembered from a Mozart duet, but he defers, preferring to watch the typesetters work: "hearing the loud throbs of cranks, watching the silent typesetters at their cases" (*U* 7.152-3, 162-3).

Much as Joyce's claim that Antheil sounds like Mozart hovers uneasily between a meaningful claim and a clichéd throwaway line, the word *voglio* becomes a figure for the unreliability of textual citation. As Vernon Hall Jr. notes, Bloom mangles the duet "Là ci darem la mano" from Mozart and da Ponte's *Don Giovanni*, recalling Molly/Zerlina's line not as "vorrei e non vorrei," which uses the subjunctive mood, but as *"[v]oglio e non vorrei,"* which uses the indicative (79-80; *U* 4.327). By substituting indicative for subjunctive, Bloom erases Zerlina's uncertain protests against Don Giovanni and acknowledges Molly's infidelity. At the same time, Bloom tries to repress these doubts by fixating on the pronunciation, not the meaning, of his miscitation.[45] Bloom's error also underscores the irony of performing "Là ci darem" extravagantly out of context: taken from *Don Giovanni*'s narrative of sexual seduction bordering on rape, and sung à la carte as a love duet. These iterations of Mozart not only implant doubts about Molly's fidelity, but also question musical citation in general given the ease and profligacy of citation in an age of mechanical reproduction.

Hence the letter "g"—one that seems not to belong in a word that should not even be there—stands as a disruptive noise repressed into silence, a synecdoche for the anxieties of textual production dramatized in "Aeolus." An obstacle to verbal pronunciation, this "g" stands in for the obstacle to textual-sexual fidelity that is the word *voglio*, which, in turn, figures the contingencies of musical performance signaled by the duet as a whole. This then becomes synecdoche for all of "Aeolus": the choreography (dance-writing) of linguistic mediation into a *ballet mécanique*. In the office of the *Telegraph* (distant-writing), the quirky "ORTHOGRAPHICAL" (correct-writing) elements of language, like a silent *g*, are mediated by an "[a]lmost human" technology: "Sllt. The nethermost deck of the first machine jogged forward its flyboard with sllt the first batch of quirefolded papers. Sllt. Almost human the way it sllt to call attention. Doing its level best to speak. That door too sllt creaking, asking to be shut. Everything speaks in its own way. Sllt" (*U* 7.164, 175, 174–77).

By treating an industrial sound as a musical one, "Aeolus" attempts, like Antheil, to unlearn the music/noise dichotomy: what is surprising is not industrial noise itself, but the act of organizing it into cohesion. The "clanking noises through the gallery" are processed into succinct, vacuous slogans, "SHORT BUT TO THE POINT," and then disseminated by the "STREET CORTÈGE" of newsboys, who prompt Lenehan to "mazurka in swift caricature" as he hands them their "tissues" (*U* 7.217, 272, 443, 450). Like Cocteau's managers on stilts, Lenehan is compelled into an awkward dance, as though the slogans were obstacles around which he, and Joyce's readers, must move.[46]

As bodies move through the *Telegraph* presses, functioning as both producers and receptors of sounds, they bridge the naturalistic and the idealistic, noise and music. Professor MacHugh, having dissected the prosody of the word "Ohio," proceeds to make of his body a "HARP EOLIAN": "He took a reel of dental floss from his waistcoat pocket and, breaking off a piece, twanged it smartly between two and two of his resonant unwashed teeth" (*U* 7.367–68, 370–73). Like the clanging trams and the moving slats, Professor MacHugh's nicely parallel teeth produce nicely parallel sounds.[47] Yet Joyce contemplates the violence attendant to the mechanized production of sounds, as Bloom imagines the announcement of Paddy Dignam's funeral:

> Hynes here too: account of the funeral probably. Thumping. Thump.
>
> WITH UNFEIGNED REGRET IT IS WE
> ANNOUNCE THE DISSOLUTION OF A MOST
> RESPECTED DUBLIN BURGESS
>
> This morning the remains of the late Mr Patrick Dignam. Machines. Smash a man to atoms if they got him caught. Rule the world today. His machineries are pegging away too. Like these, got out of hand: fermenting. Working away, tearing away. And that old grey rat tearing to get in. (*U* 7.76–83)

Anticipating Finnegan down the ladder, the tidy self-containment of the newspaper text begins to fray, as Bloom intermingles the "thumping" presses with the "DISSOLUTION" of Dignam's body. In the next line, as the episode promises to tell us "HOW A GREAT DAILY ORGAN IS TURNED OUT," we are reminded that *Ulysses* is organized according to "organs" of the body:

the organ of textual production is turned inside-out, its ruptures manifested as moving bodies onstage so as to disorient the bodies in the audience—to cause the audience's bellies to "give up." As the cryptic Wetherup puts it, the way to earn money is to "get a grip of them by the stomach" (*U* 7.342–43).

These disorientations cause one to latch onto the neat, easy slogans presented by the captions and headlines of "Aeolus," as well as the pat rhetorical moves of the Citizen in "Cyclops." In allying with them—and then watching them dissolve back into nonsense—one processes how phony they are in context. The Citizen's nationalist outburst, "*Sinn fein amhain!*" transmutes into an interpolation celebrating the "hollow booming" of a noisy funeral:

> From the belfries far and near the funereal deathbell tolled unceasingly while all around the gloomy precincts rolled the ominous warning of a hundred muffled drums punctuated by the hollow booming of pieces of ordnance. The deafening claps of thunder and the dazzling flashes of lightning which lit up the ghastly scene testified that the artillery of heaven had lent its supernatural pomp to the already gruesome spectacle. . . . Considerable amusement was caused by the favourite Dublin streetsingers L-n-h-n and M-ll-g-n who sang *The Night Before Larry was Stretched* in their usual mirthprovoking fashion. Our two inimitable drolls did a roaring trade with their broadsheets among lovers of the comedy element. (*U* 12.523, 528, 525–45)

The Citizen's bombast shades into a theatrical spectacle "punctuated" by percussion and by sonic upheaval in the landscape. In the competition between the roaring thunder of the funeral and the "roaring trade" of Irish comedy, the scene tries to drown out its own meaninglessness in a torrent of noise. This noise emerges from a mixing of signals, related to the syncretic Gaelic nationalism being parodied. Introducing the "delegation known as the Friends of the Emerald Isle," the interpolation transforms the Citizen into an Irish sportsman-cum-intellectual, the "Nationalgymnasium museumsanatoriumandsuspensoriumsordinaryprivatdocentgeneralhistory specialprofessordoctor Kriegfried Ueberallgemein" (*U* 12.554, 567–59). In punctuating a long list of Emerald delegates, this word becomes almost unreadable, visually and kinesthetically (to say the word requires a great deal of air): there is so much "heterogeneous" sound packed into the interpolation that it creates a logjam in the stream of information.

The last interpolation of "Cyclops" follows a similar trend, taking a climactic event, which pivots on rhythmical speech, and dissolving it into a soup of letters. Sebastian D.G. Knowles has argued that Bloom's responses to the Citizen follow a waltz-like pattern: "Mendelssohn was a jew and Karl Marx and Mercadante and Spinoza. And the Savior was a jew and his father was a jew."[48] Bloom's rhythmic claim, itself a mystification (Mercadante was definitely a gentile), provokes an immediate physical reaction—the Citizen attempts to "brain" him with a biscuitbox—and calls on what Attali terms the "essential violence" of music (26; *U* 12.1811). Whereas the episode's interpolations describe nonsense in puffed-up language, this act of violence is described dispassionately in what Duffy might call the "inane" and "threadbare" expressions of journalism:

> From the reports of eyewitnesses it transpires that the seismic waves were accompanied by a violent atmospheric perturbation of cyclonic character. An article of headgear since ascertained to belong to the much respected clerk of the crown and peace Mr George Fottrell and a silk umbrella with gold handle with the engraved initials, crest, coat of arms and house number of the erudite and worshipful chairman of quarter sessions sir Frederick Falkiner, recorder of Dublin, have been discovered by search parties in remote parts of the island respectively, the former on the third basaltic ridge of the giant's causeway. . . . The work of salvage, removal of *débris*, human remains etc has been entrusted to Messrs Michael Meade and Son, 159 Great Brunswick street, and Messrs T. and C. Martin, 77, 78, 79, and 80 North Wall, assisted by the men and officers of the Duke of Cornwall's light infantry under the general supervision of H. R. H., rear admiral, the right honourable sir Hercules Hannibal Habeas Corpus Anderson, K. G., K. P., K. T., P. C., K. C. B., M. P., J. P., M. B., D. S. O., S. O. D., M. F. H., M. R. I. A., B. L., Mus. Doc., P. L. G., F. T. C. D., F. R. U. I., F. R. C. P. I. and F. R. C. S. I. (*U* 12.1869–96)

Eloquent prose dissolves into meaningless typography: the actual terms of Anderson's authority become aurally inaccessible and basically unreadable. Similarly, Falkiner's umbrella is marked with a coat of arms and address and with his initials. Just as his heritage has been abstracted into a visual symbol, his identity has congealed into discrete letters and a house number. These antisyntactic interpolations, iterated at loud volumes and exposed as noncoincident with each other, make phoneygraphic textuality itself into a dramatic spectacle. So do the captions of "Aeolus" devolve into alphabet soup: "K.M.R.I.A." (7.990), synthesizing Myles Crawford's response to Bloom, "kiss my royal Irish arse" (7.991). Joyce's headlines, like Cocteau's Managers, say something equally standoffish to the reader.[49]

What would such a scene look like if, as in *Mr. Bloom and the Cyclops*, the action were performed in pantomime and narrated by singers offstage? Like

"Aeolus" and "Cyclops," "Circe" gives us a sense of Joyce's ambitions. In staging a farcical scene of authority and violence with speaking gramophones, pianolas, marionettes, and disembodied voices, it moves playfully between bombastic Wagnerian Sturm und Drang and a Cocteauvian noisy dance. Bloom's psyche, in particular, seems to move to the awkward logic of Cocteau's *ballet réaliste*:[50] physically, as he imagines his grandfather on "*gawky pink stilts*"; spatially, as he "*trickleaps*" around cycles with bells and trolleys with footgongs; commercially, as he recalls ham-fisted advertising jingles; verbally, as he plagiarizes Lenehan's "cast-steel" pun; and musically, as he refers to tram noise as the "music of the future" (Wagner's *Zukunftsmusik*) (*U* 15.2305–06, 196, 1731, 1368).[51]

Stephen brings the Wagnerian undertones of "Circe" to a climax when he threatens the emaciated ghost of his mother with an ashplant. "*Nothung!*" (*U* 15.4242), he sings, naming the shattered sword that Wagner's Siegfried inherits from his mother, reforges, and uses to slay Fafner the dragon in an ill-fated attempt to redeem his half-divine, oddly incestuous ancestry. Taken in earnest, then, the citation recalls Stephen's ambition to forge an aesthetic and racial conscience. One can even imagine his outburst set to the same noisy music that accompanies the reforging of "Nothung" in *Siegfried*—a scene in which, as in *Chamber Music*, we witness the hero "clanging, clanging . . . upon an anvil."

Absent Wagner's music, to poke fun at such a convoluted scenario is barely worth the trouble. For Antheil, and Cocteau before him, one need merely narrate the action as it occurs, and Wagner's aesthetic "coincidences" are immediately exposed as a hyperbolic travesty. The very name of Nothung, meaning "needful" (an echo of *voglio*) and resembling the English "nothing," reveals both the excess and the emptiness of Stephen's fantasy. Stephen's internal and external failure to "kill the priest and the king" is marked by the episode's speedy descent into chaos (15.4437)—if he imagines himself Siegfried, his forging of a conscience and his keening of birdsong only preface the entropy to come. From "Nothung," "Circe" degrades into a spectacle of apocalyptic Gatling guns, hooting foghorns, clanging bells, a barking retriever, a gramophone playing "The Holy City" in reverse; and a series of voices crying "Dublin's burning! Dublin's burning! On fire, on fire!" (15.4660). Dublin, like Wagner's Valhalla, burns to ash, but in a noisy scene of generic parody rather than a purifying immolation: "Circe" reads not as a holy return to the chthonic elements but as a de-composition of music into noise.[52] If Joyce is part Wagner, orchestrating myth and modernity for the sake of audience absorption, he is part Antheil, grounding musical spectacle in sonic rupture. That rupture is exaggerated in *Finnegans Wake*, and Cage's setting of it: the instability of musical signification, further unsettled by noise, is burning away the last remnants of Aesthetic idealism.

Coda: Earwicker's Rumori

In a similarly climactic "Messiagh of roaratorios" (*FW* 41.27), an inauspicious cue to the "Ballad of Persse O'Reilly" HCE's roof falls down around him in shattering glass:

> Arrah, leave it to Hosty, frosty Hosty, leave it to Hosty for he's the mann to rhyme the rann, the rann, the rann, the king of all ranns. Have you here? (Some ha) Have we where? (Some hant) Have you hered? (Others do) Have we whered (Others dont) It's cumming, it's brumming! The clip, the clop! (All cla) Glass crash. The (klikkaklakkaklaskaklopatzklatschabattacreppycrotty-graddaghsemmihsammih nouithappluddyappladdypkonpkot!).

The frenetic storm, "the thrummings of a crewth fiddle . . . , cremoaning and cronauning" (41.23), the perfect background for a "wouldbe ballad" (42.20), sets up a merging between "here"/"where" and "hear"/"heard"—a conflation of sound and place akin to the merging of "Ear-wicker" (Ear and *vicus*),[53] "Echoland," "Environs," and "Everyone," each of which maps the soundscape onto HCE's name. The sound of the crash itself, a "brumming" (a buzz), a "Klatsch" (gossip), a "khlopat" (a clap), and an "appluddyappladdy" (applause, and an apple—a rhythmic clopping to Eve and Adam's), sets up the ballad that turns HCE inside out to the vicissitudes of rumor. William York Tindall associates "cumming and brumming" with an idée fixe of "thundering defecation," conjoining "ear," "erse," (Patrick) Pearse, and *perce-oreille* (earwig) so as to produce Earwicker's persona through noise and abjection. The *Wake*'s "music of the pure signifier" opens HCE's cavernous "harmonic condenser enginium," constructing his identity through noise, rumor, and (feminized) "nighttal[k]" (32). Among his fantasies is that a choice phrase ("with ritual rhythmics, in quiritary quietude") will be redacted into a book of sayings; and although "ritual rhythmics" may be his lasting contribution, they also (as in the "Ballad") lead to his isolation, just as they lead to Duffy's.

John Bishop has argued that *Finnegans Wake* is "one erratically extended sound effect" (281), shaped by the ongoing "otological" process of HCE's "vigilant[ly] sleeples[s]" ears (277). Not unlike Pound, HCE is both a radio receiver and a compendium of musical knowledge, meaning that he not only hears but overhears (to do so is to hear unintentionally and to hear excessively—to *over*hear). According to Joyce, "in sleep our senses are dormant, except the sense of hearing, which is always awake, since you can't close your ears" (*JJ* 546-7), an idea coopted in McLuhan's observation that we don't have "earlids."[54]

Hence though the *Wake* strays a bit from this book's focus on modernism not as diffusion but as (attempted) concentration—an anxiety about noise amplified by the consolidation of form—it seems to unwind the discourses wound tightly into the strings of *Chamber Music*—an echo chamber in which a charging army exists in the same breath "as a finger straying on an instrument"—as it unfolds its protagonist through noise, rumor, and the "disselving" of language. Earwicker's radio, for example, is "equipped with supershielded umbrella antennas for distance getting and connected by the magnetic links of a Bellini-Tosti coupling system with a vitaltone speaker," capable of capturing "skybuddies, harbour craft emittences, key clickings, vaticum cleaners, due to woman formed mobile or man made static and bawling the whowle hamshack and wobble down in an eliminium sounds pound so as to serve him up a melegoturny marygoraumd, eclectrically filtered for allirish earths and ohmes" (309.17-310.1). The "earths and ohmes" of the radio's electric current are prepared by the ingenious joke during the geometry lessons of II.2: "You, allus for the kunst and me for omething with a handel to it" (295.27). Having turned Yeats's overlapping gyres into a "pair of accomplaces," a parody of the "Private Properties" of the vulva (295, 293), Joyce transforms them into art (*kunst*—not the only pun in play here), a *Messiagh* (handel), and into an "omething," a producer of "man made static" with a roaring "handel" on it. HCE's radiophonic "melegoturny," a mulligatawny as well as a melomap of language, uses as its receiver an "umbrella" not unlike Falkiner's, or O'Madden Burke's, or the "parasoliloquisingly truetoned" speech, an umbrella of babble, of the drunk Abelbody (63.20).

Yet any chamber in the *Wake* that is "capable of capturing" anything else is also capable of being pierced. As Peter Mahon suggests in his account of Joyce and Derrida, the attempt to keep one's ears (or text) always open also "becomes that which disrupts hearing" (155), such that noise and "SILENCE," hearing all and hearing nothing, become indistinct:

> —Zinzin. Zinzin.
>
> —Now we're getting it. Tune in and pick up the forain counties! Hello!

—Zinzin.
—Hello! Tittit! Tell your title?
—Abride!
—Hellohello! Ballymacarett! Am I thru' Iss? Miss? True?
—Tit! What is the ti . .?

SILENCE. (500.34–501.6)

As the four travelers try and fail to pick up the voice of Iss (Isolde), the electricity dies and the illusion ends—"Act drop. Stand by! Blinders! Curtain up! Juice, please!" (501.7). The leitmotivic "endless melody" of *Tristan und Isolde* permeates the *Wake*; the four old men, having "smacked the big kuss of Trustan with Usolde" (383.17–8), think they have finally made radio contact, only to find that they, too, have collapsed into Eliot's "heart of light, the silence./*Öd und leer das Meer*."[55] Mutt's "Meldunleize" (Isolde's "Mild und leise"), a characteristically inarticulate/hyperarticulate mangling of the language, has imploded; whether it is with a bang or a whimper may not ultimately signify.

When Cage set passages from the *Wake* in his *Roaratorio: An Irish Circus on Finnegans Wake* (1979), putting mesostic rearrangements of the text to aleatorically composed music infiltrated with the noise of the Irish landscape, he was in a sense merely opening up Antheil's dilemma: using the phoneygraphy of Joyce's language to take advantage of its pretense to neoclassical order. For, as Marjorie Perloff observes, to rearrange Joyce's text vertically is both to preserve its original meanings and, mesostically, to generate new ones from new context: putting the text, as it were, in "quotation marks."[56] It may also be worth noting that Villon's *Testament*, the subject of Pound's opera, includes several acrostic sequences of the poet's own name—not quite the playful opening-up of association as the mesostic, which can capitalize any letter in the word, but another way of shifting the rules of verbal reference by choosing words on visual, not merely auditory or literary, grounds, like a less repressed Mrs. Kearney designing a more open-ended programme. As Villon puts the signature of his own name and body at the front edge of the poetic testament, and as "Aeolus" foregrounds its own noisy textual mediation, *Roaratorio* treats every letter as an instrument of fungible function.

Antheil's great antecedent, Satie, was Cage's as well. *Furniture Music Etcetera* (1980) directs the performer to play selections taken (at her own discretion) from Satie's *Furniture Music* and Cage's own *Etcetera* (1973). An acolyte of Schoenberg and of Cowell, Cage composed several relatively conventional serial pieces before the late 1930s, when he began to "equat[e] the arbitrary distinction between noise and 'musical' sounds in the same light as the historical distinction between consonance and dissonance."[57] Hence Cage's experiments with aleatoric indeterminacy have deep roots in modernist aesthetics—whose institutionalized high-mindedness, however, he resented. With respect to *Finnegans Wake* specifically, Cage objected to the systematic, totalizing analysis of Joyce; he read the *Wake*, rather, as a fellow-traveler with the playful entropy of Dada:

> I think that the artists of the twentieth century who resist our understanding are the ones to whom we will continue to be grateful. Besides Joyce, there is Duchamp. And Satie . . . is no less difficult to understand than . . . Webern. Somewhere in the *Wake* Joyce says: *Confusium hold'em!* I hope that *Roaratorio* will act to introduce people to the pleasures of *Finnegans Wake* when it is still on the side of poetry and chaos rather than analyzed and known to be safe and law-abiding.[58]

"Somewhere in the *Wake*" is about as helpful an instruction as when Marx opens the *Eighteenth Brumaire* by saying, "Somewhere in Hegel. . ."; in this case, Cage is referring to a passage early in the text reflecting a fall out of a pure Irish tongue into a confused linguistic "babel": "The babbelers with their thangas vain have been (confusium hold them!) they were and went; thigging thugs were and houhnhymn songtoms were and comely norgels were and pollyfool fiansees." A "hymn" of Irish reason (Houyhnhnm), confused but also revitalized by its contact with a Babel of tongues, ends in a mangled marriage proposal to the French tongue ("pollyfool fiansees") (15.12–15). *Roaratorio* revels in this confused, polysemous hybridity, both of sound/noise, of words/music, and of the cosmopolitan inroads of avant-garde Dada and high modernism that put Joyce, Satie, Duchamp, Diaghilev, and Cage himself into counterpoint.

A different mesostic setting, the 1982 radio play "James Joyce, Marcel Duchamp, Erik Satie: An Alphabet," clarifies Cage's polysemous liberation of Joyce's sublimely ordered condensations of form. As the three ghosts jump back and forth across the stage, "Alphabet" pays homage to the aleatoric antisublimity of Duchamp, the magical sleight-of-hand of Satie (Antheil's "great juggler" and the Ballets Russes' great ironist), and the McLuhanesque media savvy of Joyce:

he Jumps
with his back tO the audience
for all we know he maY be quietly weeping
or silently laughing or both you just Can't
tEll

now and then niJinsky's ghost
Appears
bringing a telegraM
to JoycE
from marShall mcluhan

wE
heaR
over a radIo
a conversation sticKing

to two wordS
fifty-five And
fifTy-four
It is
an argumEnt
bEtween houdini and satie
about which one of them as a ghost is oldeR
houdIni
sees a cracK

in mathematicS
by meAns of which
aT
fIfty
four and fivE

changE places
satie is delighted and gRateful
now I see he says what people meant
thanK you[59]

In this *nekuic* fantasy of radio contact with the past, numbers, ages, and places become mutable and full of cracKs—as in Eliot, the large temporal order, rhythmically enforced, noisily disintegrate. "What people meant," as EriK puts it, may be a gesture to one of Satie's playful *bon mots*, comically quoted in Antheil's/"Stacey Bishop's" *Death in the Dark*, whose protagonist name-drops every avant-gardist he can think of: "When I was a young man, everyone told me that. . . '*when you are older you will see!'. . . and now I am sixty-five. . . and I don't see anything*" (Antheil/Bishop 97). What the elder Satie now "sees" is not that he needs to behave, but that the magical cheats of art can make mutable the passage of time, in music or in lived experience. The piece opens with the contention that "the subJect/Of/the plaY/is the Curtain/that sEparates them" (55)—in this case turning Joyce's name into the fabric of aesthetic mediation—but rapidly moves the curtain up and down to make that separation baseless, to create instead a *Wake*-like cycle of recurring ages. (I shall soon turn to a different curtain—Sitwell's *Façade*—that creates an equally playful and unstable chain of signifiers.)

Joyce, working at a "roMan bank," runs into Merce Cunningham, the great choreographer (who later worked on *Roaratorio*) and Cage's longtime partner, who "comeS in to cash a traveller's check." Punning on the Viconian cycles of history that govern the *Wake*, the mesostic proceeds: "Just sign/giambattista vicO's name/instead of Your own/and i'll give you Control/of a rEvolving fund" (67). Checks, names, and letters, like Satie's age or Vico's "ages," are at this point involved in a kind of "rEvolving" circulation of empty signifiers. Giambattista Vico's cyclic theory of history, the basis for the *Wake*'s patterning of thunderclaps, seems to have become an inexhaustible "rEvolving fund" of aesthetic pleasure and of semiotic reference, wherein (as in "Aeolus") the discrete letters of a signifier can be detached from one context and realigned to another, any name signed to anyone else's check. Diaghilev and Cunningham are joined in a dance of joyfully licentious empty signification.

Music has, in this respect, finally been emancipated from the Wagnerian Romanticism that links language to a primal *Tonspräche*, and has been instead attached to a cheekily functionalist attitude in which sound is given meaning playfully, randomly, ad hoc. The piece's brief peroration on *Furniture Music*, Satie's "music not meant to be listened to," exposes music as a "fundamentally industrial" accompaniment to daily life, which "creates vibrations" that can "satisfy human needs the way utilities do" (65). Cage liberates Satie's apophatic "K.M.R.I.A." to the sublime from any last residue of Wagnerian idealism, detaching Joyce's already paronomasic language from its already hypermediated context, and putting it into a new melomap. As

Scott Klein argues, Cage's embrace of the Joycean melomap can be considered a radical—perhaps an Attalian—extension of Adorno's faith in the democratizing potential of atonality. Attali writes that while Antheil, Russolo, and other modern noise-experiments never quite managed to "rupture the existing networks" of performance and patronage, Cage more fully destabilized these orders and liberated musical sound from them (136-7). What Klein calls the *Wake*'s "confluence of linguistic and musical effects and its democratizing of the global mind," remediated in a literary telegram from Joyce to McLuhan, decenters the music/noise hierarchy and liberates Joyce's text from the author itself—the final heave of the Antheil dilemma.[60]

Accompanied by a set of sonic objets trouvés—an Irish jig and the shattering of glass that marks Hosty's ballad—the first lines of the *Roaratorio* align the *Wake*'s thunderclaps (Skysign) with "Jiccup/the fAther"—a hiccup associated with the prophetic Joycean author and with the fAther, and perhaps with the hermeneutic laws (of "Judges/Or /deuteronomY") that Joyce's texts had been retroactively made to "watsCh":

wroth with twoone nathandJoe
Á
Malt
jhEm
Shen

pftJschute
sOlid man
that the humptYhillhead of himself
is at the knoCk out
in thE park

Jiccup
the fAther
Most
hEaven
Skysign

Judges
Or
deuteronomY
watsCh
futurE

Later, the scene in which HCE threatens the cad with a pair of watches ("Jurgensen's *shrapnel* waterbury" [35.21]), accompanied by the chimes of "the ten ton tonuant thunderous tenor toller in the speckled church," is accompanied in Cage's setting by the jig, the running water, the noise of a train—the markers, throughout Joyce's work, of time's passage as it wears away at the self-enclosure of textual form. Water, in particular, the great primal symbol of *Tristan und Isolde* (and the Wagnerian cure for "syphilisation" [*U* 12.1197]), takes on a particular importance in the *Roaratorio*, and the eponymous "Messiagh Roaratorio" is cheekily accompanied by Handel's *Water Music*, announcing a palimpsest of Baroque and modern, and a Viconian "recirculation" through Joyce's chamber.

Cage's piece acquires its perdurability not by abating noise but by admitting it: whereas the complexity of the fugue "can be broken up by a single sound, say from a fire engine," the "*Roaratorio* cannot be broken up by a single sound, say from a fire engine" (qtd. in Perloff 216). Cage's "circus" on the *Wake* realizes the final Cocteauvian annihilation of Wagnerian seriousness, producing "a system of differences" among media (Perloff 224) and, through palimpsest and juxtaposition, finally obliterating the music/noise boundary. Cocteau's resonance for Sitwell, as for Antheil, Joyce, and Cage, is the search for something in music other than Wagnerian authenticity. *Façade* pursues the seemingly meaningless arrangements of sound for their own sake—a "music" (or a curtain) "of the pure signifier"—and reveals the critical edge of musical form in the public sphere. My first pair of specifically British artists, whose work thinks about noise in mediated and softened ways, Sitwell and Walton use the unstable resonances of their art forms to inspire critical reflection about the insularity of British music: rearranging the imagery and idioms of the British drawing room so as to defamiliarize their relations to imperial spaces, and so as to suggest an ironically cosmopolitan attitude to the phoneygraphs of art.

5 Performing Publicity

Authenticity, Influence, and the Sitwellian *Commedia*

BEAUCHAMP: If you played my tape on the radio, it would seem a meaningless noise, because it fulfills no expectations: people have been taught to expect certain kinds of insight but not others. The first duty of the artist is to capture the radio station.

DONNER: It was Lewis who said that.

BEAUCHAMP: Lewis who?

DONNER: Wyndham Lewis.

BEAUCHAMP: It was Edith Sitwell, as a matter of fact.

DONNER: Rubbish.

BEAUCHAMP: She came out with it while we were dancing.

Tom Stoppard, *Artist Descending a Staircase*

In February 1922, Edith, Osbert, and Sacheverell Sitwell gave a private performance of *Façade*: an "entertainment" featuring Edith's verse and music by the young British composer William Walton. (For convenience's sake I shall refer to the Sitwells by first name.) In an L-shaped drawing room at her brothers' home at 2 Carlyle Square, Sitwell read her nonsense poems through a giant megaphone ("Sengerphone"), accompanied by eccentric music, from behind a painted screen (fig. 5.1). These private performances would be made increasingly public, most notably at an ill-received June debut at London's Aeolian Hall. Yet Edith exaggerates when she writes, "Never was a larger and more imposing shower of brickbats hurled at any new work."[1] The premiere was met less with vitriol than with bewilderment, and the notion that *Façade* produced a massive *scandale* along the lines of *Parade* or *Le Sacre* is laced with a heavy dose of wishful thinking.[2]

Sitwell's "automythomania" has been well documented.[3] Like Antheil,

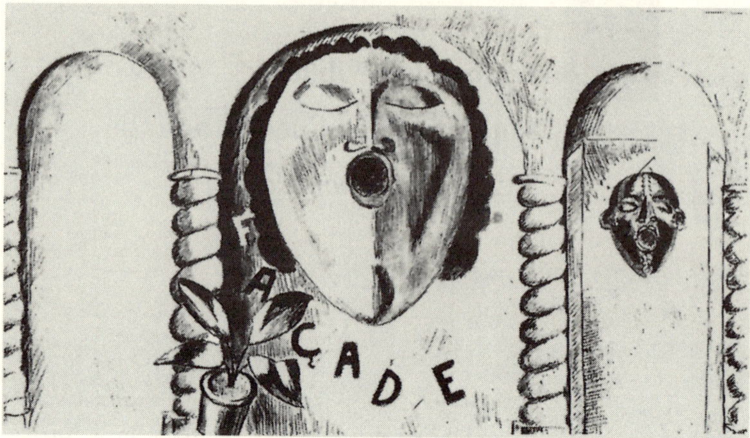

Figure 5.1. Curtain by Frank Dobson from *Façade*, by Edith Sitwell. Reprinted by permission of Peters Fraser & Dunlop (www.petersfraserdunlop.com) on behalf of the Estate of Edith Sitwell.

Satie, and Stravinsky, Sitwell was a relentless self-explicator and very much invested in building up a public persona. For this reason, to write on Sitwell is to contend with F. R. Leavis's assertion that she belongs more to "the history of publicity than the history of poetry." This chapter argues that *Façade* fosters a poetry *of* publicity, in which the two spheres dialectically enhance each other: while social noise compels the Sitwells to seek new poetic rhythms, the pressures of aesthetic influence compel them to reorganize the rhythms of public life. My argument pivots on citation and influence as issues constellating around publicity: as poetic techniques and as ways of circulating poetry and poets. Early in this *annus mirabilis* of modernism, which (as Michael North points out in *Reading 1922*) saw not only the birth of *Ulysses* and *The Waste Land* but the introduction of the first global broadcasting network, *Façade*'s invisibly sourced voice patters out a plea for attention that, at the same time, amplifies those aesthetics of daily life to which our attention has been deadened. If the appropriately titled *Façade* failed, and still fails, to meet Leavisite standards of organic authenticity, Sitwell's "poetry of publicity" is uncritical toward neither of those terms, as it pulls the trappings of publicity—patronage, advertising, public personae—into the artistic comedy of social life.

While the *Façade* premiere was something of a flop, its form reveals it as something more than mediocre poetry cloaked in a silly publicity stunt. In

Façade's form and in its borrowings—English music hall numbers, Schoenberg's *Pierrot Lunaire*, Stravinsky's *L'Histoire du soldat*, the Ballets Russes' productions of Stravinsky's *Petrushka* and Satie's *Parade*, and the imagery of the *commedia dell'arte* that motivates all of these—we see something more complex: a British negotiation with a cosmopolitan aesthetic that at the same time acknowledges its imperial roots. Walton's music, indebted both to Stravinsky's cooled-down ragtime and folk music and to Schoenberg's atonal drawing-room melodrama, strives to move beyond the British musical scene—so insular, to him and the Sitwells, that even *Pierrot* did not receive a British premiere until 1922. The megaphone, another phoneygraph, foregrounds the influence of *Parade*, Cocteau and Satie's self-annihilating experiment in aestheticized advertisement. Many of the same qualities that made the Cocteau/Satie circle appealing to Antheil—its cheeky self-promotion, its inversion and subversion of boundaries among audience, stage, and orchestra—motivate *Façade*'s poetics of publicity, and its dashed hopes at creating a scandal.[4] Finally, the Sitwells draw on a resurgent modernist interest in lowbrow theater (circus, puppetry, pantomime, *commedia dell'arte*) to which the poetry/publicity dialectic is internal. Much of Edith Sitwell's poetry draws on the imagery and the recognizable stock characters of the *commedia* (Pulcinella, Colombine, Harlequin, and Pierrot, the moonstruck clown with a white powdered face). In so doing, I suggest, she draws on a cultural association of *commedia* both with "lowbrow" commercial publicity, and with workaday craft—with an anti-Stanislavskian view of the actor as an artisan, rather than as a "personality."[5] Her appropriation of Pierrot, Schoenberg's "silent dandy of Bergamo," marks them as cosmopolitan participants in a pan-European "commedia cult,"[6] and as practitioners of a self-consciously stylized poetics of self-promotion, in which personality is exposed as artifice. As Raymond Williams reminds us, the word "personality" originally referred to a formed of masked performance—"a mask used by a player through a character in a play and a part that a man acts." The word's "implicit metaphor," Williams continues, "can still haunt us" (*Keywords* 232–3). *Façade*'s rhythmic shaping of the noise of public life, as it modernizes the *commedia*'s masked performances, acknowledges the aesthetic fashioning of the public self, and that tries to extend that aesthetic beyond, as Marsha Bryant writes, an insularly British "respectability." The piece's lack of authenticity and depth, a flat surface play of words, is foregrounded by the curtain: not a Wagnerian absorption, but an effort to make art a mere imprint of the aesthetics of social life, and social life an imprint of art. Like the *encre de chine* referred to in Sitwell's "Something Lies Beyond the Scene," a seemingly pointless sea of orientalist poetic and musical exotica washes back onto the façade: putting the exotic on display, and also putting on display the putting-of-the-exotic-on-display.

Drawing from Diaghilev's Ballets Russes, from Austro-German modernism, from the *commedia* cult, and from Walton's English training, *Façade* is a self-consciously cosmopolitan work. Like many British and Anglo-American writers, the Sitwells found the Ballets Russes refreshing for its aesthetic diversity and its continuous reexamination of its theatrical antecedents. Edith herself wrote two articles on Stravinsky's *Petrushka* for *The New Age* and a book entitled *Children's Tales (From the Russian Ballet)* (1920); on Armistice Day 1918 the Sitwells gave a lavish dinner party in honor of Sergei Diaghilev and Léonide Massine, at which Augustus John, Roger Fry, Clive Bell, Lytton Strachey, Lady Ottoline, Duncan Grant, Mark Gertler, Dora Carrington, David Garnett, St. John and Mary Hutchinson, Francis Birrell, Nina Hammett, D.H. Lawrence, John Maynard Keynes, and Lydia Lopokova "danced in the peace under Diaghilev's watchful eye" (Garafola 335). The Sitwells were thus "in a tactical position to upstage Bloomsbury over their new-found admiration for the Ballets Russes," heretofore unfashionable among the London intelligentsia (Pearson 123-4). The Ballets Russes, therefore, serve *Façade*'s aesthetic needs as well as its public ones.

Leavis's claim that *Façade*'s rhythmic and semiotic play and flamboyant namedropping were mere "publicity" was anticipated by Sitwell's contemporaries, who saw her and her siblings as *enfants terribles* whose main goal was, as Aldous Huxley snidely told his brother, "to REBEL."[7] For the Sitwells, as Huxley saw it, aesthetic rebellion was a form of publicity stunt. The claim is understandable: well familiar with the scandals produced by the Ballets Russes' *Parade* and *Le Sacre*, the Sitwells understood musical and theatrical performance as an chance for notoriety. *Façade* aggressively casts aside Leavisite ideals of authenticity and high seriousness, priding itself as a playfully stylized "entertainment" that drops every name and absorbs every aesthetic influence it can.

Pulling art into the drawing room, *Façade* rethinks the social value of rhythm, reimagining it in relation to the fluid tempi of public debate in ways that test the limits of Adornian critique. As Kate Van Orden argues, music played an important role in the late seventeenth- and early eighteenth-century emergence of the bourgeois public sphere, shaped by norms of communicative reason and critical discourse. Not only did these salons and coffee houses facilitate critical debate about art; the printing of libretti and piano-vocal reductions of opera scores also engendered Habermas's "private made public" by allowing theatrical music to be "played at home, and reintroduced to a public sphere as an element of criticism and discussion" (86). Hence, Van Orden suggests, nineteenth-century debates about opera were "reinforced, if not actually inculcated, in the home through the playing of operatic music on the piano" (87), giving amateurs and connoisseurs a second chance to digest what they may have initially experienced as theatrical frenzy. Though not a "home opera" exactly, *Façade* encourages similar critical activity in the salon, akin to what Axel Honneth calls a Habermasian "process of collective social criticism which would reach the social space where theoretical enlightenment can be politically organized."[8] Habermas, avoiding a pessimistic retreat into purely formal dialectics, attempts to advance Adorno's distrust of "instrumental reason"—skepticism toward reason as domination—into a form of public argument that can be "submit[ted] to the demands of intersubjective verification" rather than merely experienced in philosophical isolation (Honneth 47). *Façade* subjects the boundaries of Adorno's lugubrious individual subject to a bit of ludic defamiliarization: through a mix of English music-hall numbers, rags and foxtrots, the Expressionistic yawp of Schoenberg's Pierrot is revealed as a stylized performance and continually subjected to intersubjective play.

Both the sounds of *Façade* itself, and the noises surrounding its production, circulate around the masked, hidden body. The curtain-and-megaphone setup, both Cocteauvian and Wagnerian, was designed to obscure the figure of the poet and focus the audience's attention on the sounds of the poetry. As Osbert wrote five years later, this setup endeavored to correct the personal embarrassment associated with poetry readings: to "abolish the necessity for the reciter to indulge in gesture, over-abundant vocal accentuation, or to be seen at all," to eliminate the tiresome "infus[ion]" by the reciter "of his own idea of 'charm' " while making it possible for him to be heard distinctly without shouting.[9] The Sitwells' solution was to borrow a Wagnerian stage device: a "Sengerphone," named after a Swedish bass who performed the dragon Fafner in *Siegfried*. A megaphone made of cotton, the Sengerphone was meant to aestheticize the voice by reducing its "metallic tone" ("A Few Days" 31).

Façade's increasingly public performances met with perplexed responses, and understandably so. Between each of Edith's poems, Osbert's voice would intone the title of the next one through the black mask, puncturing whatever illusion Edith's poetry had created. Thus, though the Sitwells repeatedly insist that hiding the speaker would depersonalize its voice and defuse its "charm," it instinctively seems hard to believe that a disembodied voice, intoning and pattering verse through a giant megaphone emerging from the mouth of a Greek mask painted on a curtain, would leave an audience incurious about the voice's origin. As the reviews indicate, if Sitwell intended the Sengerphone to "obtrude" her personality, she failed miserably—one memorably caustic review calls the Sitwells "apostles of *épatism*." If the Sengerphone was intended to shift the audience's focus away from the voice's source and toward the voice's sound, à la Schaeffer's "reduced listening," audiences saw in this design an effort to draw *more* attention to the speaker (namely, Sitwell herself). Her acute awareness of her public persona leads me to discount her word in this respect. In volume five of her periodical *Wheels* (the publication that prompted Huxley's remark), Sitwell writes that "The publication of 'Wheels' is regarded by all right-minded people as more of a society event than a literary one," a passage which Aaron Jaffe convincingly reads as a satire of critical suspicion toward publicity and literary subcultures (159).

Whether *Façade* intended to inspire or to forestall attention to the poet's "personality" has continued to influence debates over how best to perform the piece, and about Sitwell's place in literary history. In Edith's words, *Façade* ought to rid "the work of any personal quality (apart from the personality inherent in the poems and music)."[10] Paul Driver therefore likens the poem to other efforts at modernist impersonality, namely, *Mauberley* and *The Waste Land*. I share Driver's inclination to place Sitwell in the same context as Pound and Eliot (I might add Mr. Duffy's floating "strange impersonal voice"), as efforts to find musical and poetic forms that posture as autonomous but unfold their own mediations of the social world. *Façade* does not eradicate personality, but defamiliarizes it: one might say it replaces identification with alienation. As in Eliot, the rhythms of *Façade* are punctured with awkward glitches—a music too materially engaged, and too self-conscious, to sublate its social noise. Also as in Eliot, the effort to extinguish the artist's presence merely foregrounds her mediatedness—just as Cocteau's human phonographs, Brecht's placards, the headlines of Joyce's "Aeolus," or Cage's mesostic curtain disavow any idea of unmediated expression. Rather than oppress its audience with a domineering reciter, an identificatory focal point, *Façade* perplexes its audience with the overbearing *absence* of a speaker, hidden behind a layered synesthetic spectacle of defamiliarizing mechanisms.

Put otherwise, Sitwell, by coopting a Wagnerian Sengerphone, does more than amplify her voice: she reverses Wagner's Fafner plot, taking the rhythms of daily life and defamiliarizing them, in a sense, as birdsong—as having an aesthetic meaning to which the drawing room has become deaf. Using Fafner's megaphone but dispensing with the overblown drama, and performing the role of a bass through the Sengerphone's softening mediations, Sitwell reenacts Fafner's killing and castrates the ideal of organic cultural authenticity. *Façade* rejects Wagner's *Volk*ish obsession with absorption, framing art instead as fluid public discourse; and also rejects the naturalist theater that proposes art as an "inside-out" discovery of psychological personality, instead embracing an "outside-in" formalization of the persona (mask) through gesture, posture, and attitude.

Sitwell's art rethinks the very concept of publicity by way of rethinking her relation to aesthetic influence. She erects, that is, a façade of modernist impersonality in order to critique the divide between social events and literary ones. Aesthetic influence and innovation, performed to music, become both means and products of publicity, imbricating the form of the text, the context of the performance, and the complex citational web of influence. Cyrena Podrom argues that Sitwell troubles the conventional understanding of poetic influence, focused on "linear, single-source, and unidirectional relationships": Sitwell's overdetermined transformation of Stein, Rimbaud, Apollinaire, and Cocteau results instead in a "distinctive voice" within the "polymorphous fabric of female modernism."[11] This polymorphousness of influence emerges not merely in a written text but within a performative one: *Façade* is a performance document influenced not merely by poetic technique but by theater history and techniques of self-promotion. It becomes, in Williams's sense, a rhythmic performance of changing cultural forms and conventions.

The music of *Façade* is likewise intricately tied to its predecessors, and the theatricality of the *Façade* poems is underscored by their accompanying dance tunes. One number, "I Do Like to Be Beside the Seaside," even had Walton dragged into court for stealing a music hall number by John Glover-Kind.[12] *Façade*'s intensely, perhaps illegally citational music is eminently accessible. Walton is no Schoenberg. But by taking on Schoenberg's *commedic* imagery and Cocteau's stage mechanisms, putting them to a rhythmic blend of Stravinsky and music hall, *Façade* seems to turn Pierrot's expressionist scream against itself: exposing the social world as a psychological horror show (à la Schoenberg), only to subject that horror to a jeer (à la Stravinsky) by refusing (à la Cocteau) to obscure its relationship to the chatter of advertising, or to the imperial aesthetics of the drawing room. Walton is also no Antheil; yet if *Façade* is hardly the noisy composition of the *Roaratorio* or *Ballet Mécanique* sort, it shows a similarly attentive ear for the public resonances of aesthetic sound and, conversely, for the already aesthetic sensations of daily life. Through its mediations of *Parade*, its gestures to publicity, and its effort to accelerate poetic rhythm to match the noise of the city, *Façade*'s "noise like amber softly sliding" pacifies urban life outside the salon into a playful Symbolist patter, while toying with the social implications of its language and music.

The effect of this strange mix of music and verse—impersonal and public, citational and nonsensical, and confounded by the acoustic complications of a megaphone—was one of confused noise, which audiences were left to interpret in light of their feelings about the Sitwells generally. A common accusation among reviews was that *Façade* was intended merely to shock. The "*épatism*" critic acknowledges the Sengerphone's aim to "prevent the personality of the reciter from getting between the poem and the audience," and praises the "gleam of light" thrown by Walton's "clever" (always a patronizing term) use of dance rhythms, but finds the actual poetry irritating for irritation's sake.[13] The news spread quickly: Virginia Woolf had been told that the Sitwells were reciting "sheer nonsense through megaphones";[14] upon hearing the poetry itself, she claimed more tactfully that she "could not judge" the poetry insofar as she couldn't actually hear it. Those who could understand the poetry were unimpressed. One reviewer found Sitwell's poems to work only "on the overtones of words, and just as it is difficult to produce music with bells that are all overtones . . . , so it is difficult to make poetry with overtones alone." The cycle's more successful poems, "Waltz" and "Daphne," added to those overtones some organizing "rhythmic framework." Though decrying the use of the saxophone as a musical "abortion," this reviewer praises Walton's "assurance and dissonance" as an amusing addition to Sitwell's "strain of nonsense." The music, often compared to Stravinsky's, was better received than the verse, though it did not always rescue the poetry or the upper-crust audience from mockery. One critic, Osbert's favorite, entitled his review "Drivel They Paid to Hear." Such reviews inspired Noël Coward to include a scathing send-up of the Sitwells, "The Swiss Family Whittlebot," as part of his revue *London Calling!* (1923). Coward's contemporaries (including Walton) found it funny enough that he published several more parodies featuring the young Whittlebot daughter, causing a lengthy public feud with the Sitwell siblings, who were given to feuding anyway.

The Sitwells' contemporaries, including Coward, found their self-publicizing off-putting and even menacing. Wyndham Lewis, whose thrashing of the Sitwells in his *roman à clef The Apes of God* (1930) lasts some two hundred pages, describes the "Finnian-Shaws" as an "ill-acted Commedia dell'Arte" whose "passion for the stilted miniature drama of average social life . . . had assumed the proportions . . . of a startling self-abuse, incessantly indulged in."[15] In fact, Lewis had attended the private premiere of *Façade* in the Sitwells' drawing room, and liked the piece enough to hear it again at Aeolian Hall. Yet Lewis's later assault on the Sitwells' ill-acted pantomime merges with his loathing for the Ballets Russes, equated by Lewis with the eccentric sensations of "bourgeois bohemian" modernism. As Tyrus Miller further argues, Lewis resented the curtain-and-megaphone setup as a horrifying regime of disembodied public opinion aestheticized by voices broadcast from indeterminate origins—an effort to "capture the radio station," as Stoppard's Beauchamp puts it. Beauchamp, a Duchamp-caricature, insists that his sonic found objects are only for artistic "initiates"; Stoppard's radio play puts the Dadaist art of publicity into dialogue with Lewis, who recognizes the thrall of disembodied sound over the masses, and into a "dance" with Sitwell, who has no more interest than Beauchamp in the uninitiated.[16]

The *Façade* poems read as a simulacrum of sense, a playful chain of supplements that produces an illusion of depth, and as such, Lewis heard the piece not as Habermasian "intersubjective verification" but as the stultifying fog of a culture industry. Though Lewis thought radio a promising forum for artistic patronage, he also found the Ballets Russes to exemplify a "musical society" of decadent dupes. Lewis could not stomach the extent to which 1920s Europe had been "seduced," as James Mansell writes, "by the hypnotism of advertising but even more by music."[17] As it happens, the paterfamilias of PR, Edward Bernays, drew his developments directly from his experience organizing the Ballets Russes' press operations; Lewis's nervousness about the façade of public opinion brings to light an important connection between the aesthetics of the Ballets Russes and the magical cheats of advertising.

John Pearson calls *Parade* the "great precedent" for *Façade*, and writes that the "idea of creating a similar artistic triumph—and issuing an artistic challenge to the diehards and the Philistines in the midst of London—must have been irresistible" (180). *Parade*'s public scandal makes it a case study in the ability of music both to dramatize and to effect new kinds of public discourse. Yet aside from brief nods toward Cocteau's megaphones and a shared ambition to cause a ruckus, the specific cultural import of *Parade*'s influence on *Façade* has not received its due attention.[18] In addition to merging the musical society of advertising and the Futurist aesthetic of noise (two of Lewis's foremost enemies), *Parade* represented the self-conscious theatricality and stylized sensationalism that Lewis associated with the Ballets Russes. For example, through its use of the *image d'Epinal*—a brightly colored wood-cut broadside (later reproduced by lithograph) and a precursor to modern advertising and propaganda[19]—*Parade* previews the kind of public relations state to which, Lewis feared, modernism's sensational fads left us increasingly open.

Façade's and *Parade*'s use of megaphones, curtains, and *image d'Epinal* defamiliarize the PR techniques in which they indulge, calling attention to the stereotypes—the cultural clichés of race and empire, and the technologies of print—on which both art and advertising seemed to rely. The façade of *Façade* merges the Greek mask with Pierrot (white), the African mask with Harlequin (black), and while its poetry may construct race in stock, stereotypical fashion, it blurs these categories of racial and national identification—British, French, European, Eastern, German, and African—and ironizes their artificiality. While a desire to expand the conservatism of modern British music often leads *Façade* into primitivist kitsch, using stock colonial stereotypes to poke fun at Victorian respectability, the piece also turns an ironic eye and ear to the clichés of Empire as it tries to cultivate a European style. As one of *Façade*'s core numbers puts it, "Something Lies Beyond the Scene" of British music; the question is to what extent that "beyond" infiltrates British aesthetics in return.

Even the histories of pantomime, puppetry, and *commedia dell'arte*, as transmuted into British art, speak to an irony of a British aesthetic produced largely through international acquisition, whether cosmopolitan or imperial. John O'Brien, reading the pantomime genre through Adorno's culture industry model, writes that "By the early nineteenth century, pantomime's association with British nationalism had . . . accomplished the remarkable trick of making Continental *commedia dell'arte* characters seem always to have been British."[20] The Sitwells' fondness for stock *commedia* images was noted by Eliot, who (faintly) praised a volume of *Wheels* not for its craft but for its cosmopolitan imagery, the "garden gods, guitars, and mandolines" of *commedia dell'arte*.[21] In mind of the Adorno-Williams two-step, Sitwell's and

Walton's musicopoetic hybrid is imbricated with cultural politics; the internal dissonances among Sitwell's forms register anxieties about, for example, the relative merits of British, French, Russian, and German culture. In a sense this argument mimics Adorno's uncustomary praise of the ironic stylistic tensions in *L'Histoire du soldat*, Stravinsky's hybrid of ragtime and neoclassicism complete with a reciter. If nothing else, *Façade* unsettles Adorno's dichotomy of Schoenberg and Stravinsky, whom Sitwell and Walton found entirely reconcilable.

In *Laughter in the Next Room*, Osbert praises the Ballets Russes' later *commedia*-inflected ballets for their wit, "darkness," and satiric edge; even his description of ballerina Lydia Lopokova invokes a series of qualities equally characteristic of his sister Edith: her "entrancing cleverness," "comic genius," and a "birdlike" face resembling "a mask of comedy" (17). Likewise, *Façade*'s interest in puppet theatre (found throughout Sitwell's verse) ventriloquizes an extensive antirealist tradition—Romantic, then Symbolist, then modernist —in which the puppet represented a retreat from naturalistic acting and an advance into unifying formal synthesis: as an expression of the Will (Jules Laforgue), as a unity of body and soul (for Wagner, the "improviser, poet, manager, and actor all in one"), as a formal depersonalization of that unity (Edward Gordon Craig's "übermarionette"), or as an ironic modernization of all of these (Vsevelod Meyerhold and, in turn, the Ballets Russes).[22] Each of these puppets gives voice to an unconscious reality—psychological, noumenal, or aesthetic—beyond the objective details of his naturalistic landscape. *Façade* redirects the ideal of Wagnerian/Schopenhauerian depth—we are puppets of the Will—into an affect of critical distance, but also connects itself back to the sources that it wants to ironize.

Sitwell's ventriloquism of her literary ancestors is tied to her obsession, detailed throughout her autobiography *Taken Care Of* (1964), with her Plantagenet birthright and with the tyrannies of her father. One such tyranny, the facial brace meant to correct her nose, speaks directly to Sitwell's anxieties about her own appearance. When John Singer Sargent was commissioned to do a portrait of the Sitwell family, Sir George Sitwell suggested that he faithfully render the crook in Edith's nose. Sargent responded by straightening her nose and crooking Sir George's (Pearson 5-6). *Façade*'s attempts to depersonalize poetic voice would, as she saw it, necessitate masking her recognizable face and body—her public mask—and to ventriloquize the ballet's theatrical ancestors in a newly modern way.

By refusing to limit itself to local and national modes of expression, *Fa-*

çade articulates the aesthetic problems of its Plantagenet center with those of the colonial periphery. Some of these poems offer a "parade" of performers and images, many of which are racialized in a similar fashion: "Polka" features Mr. Wagg dancing "like a bear" (line 3) with "whiskers that—/(Tra la la) trap the Fair" (5–6); "Venus' children" (9); "Wellington, Byron, the Marquis of Bristol" (13); "Nelson" (25); and "Robinson Crusoe" who "finds fresh isles in Negress' smiles" (27, 30). The childlike fairground imagery of "Polka" introduces a sea-journey, a military victory, and ultimately, the settlement of an island.[23] The overdetermined cosmopolitanism of *Façade* seeks an alternative to a simply English musical idiom.

Noise itself is cosmopolitan—the noises of Antheil, of Cocteau and Satie, of Pound, Eliot, and Forster, reflect a desire to expand beyond the limits of nation (in cosmopolitan terms), and also an anxiety about that expansion (into the colonies) as it fragments personal or cultural bonds. *Façade*'s softening of Cocteau and Satie's noises into Symbolist poetic vapor, accompanied with innocent dance tunes, reflect a cosmopolitanism grounded in, and eager to pick apart, English poetic and musical idioms, remaking Leavisite ideals of organic authenticity along more stylishly international lines. In *Cosmopolitan Style,* Rebecca Walkowitz considers cosmopolitanism in terms not only of literary style but of "attitude, stance, posture, and consciousness"; though she focuses on the novel, several of her cosmopolitan models apply aptly to Sitwell and Walton.[24] Walkowitz identifies, as a strain of cosmopolitanism, the taking on of "multiple or flexible attachments to more than one nation or community, resisting conceptions of allegiance that presuppose consistency and uncritical enthusiasm"—shifting attachments which often invoke and remake vernacular traditions of consumer culture (9). The resistant or oppositional postures of Aestheticism and decadence also offer cosmopolitans a specific style of productive triviality, consumption, and fluid attachment, one that *Façade* openly adapts (though, Walkowitz notes, this kind of aesthetic of "unbelonging" can also reinscribe imperial values). *Façade* moves among "multiple or flexible attachments" in its very language, which has been read as a shifting Kristevan approximation of the noisy semiotic; and in its use of British and European music hall songs and local dances ironically detached from their allegiances. Sitwell does not disown but proudly reinvents her Plantagenet Britishness as a mask to be crafted; her gestures to *Parade*'s collapsing Managers decenter the authority of an invisible and putatively objective British voice.

Thus even as the voice itself is detached from the personality of its speaker, *Façade* maps out a range of dissonant aesthetic interactions constitutive of the aesthetic personality, many of which were already familiar to the British drawing room. The orientalism of the Ballets Russes, for example, had become so fashionable that it begged for defamiliarization; the same could be said of the kitschy appropriation of African mask. In *The Apes of God*, the Finnian-Shaws are not just fakers, but collectors of Eastern artifacts that they don't even like. As Susan Gubar has written, Sitwell appropriated the "Boomlay BOOM tradition" of racialized music-hall performances (cf. Vachel Lindsay's "Congo" [1912]), but also emphasized racial performance in her poses for portraits such as Stella Bowen's *Le Masque* (1934), which features Sitwell's distinctive spindly hands holding, presumably, an African mask.[25] Much of the recent criticism on Sitwell has focused less on her status in the canon and more on its political work, either, as Gyllian Phillips offers, as a disruption of stable masculine authority, or, as Bryant suggests, as a parody of certain kinds of propriety that, nevertheless, reinscribe the racial stereotypes at the heart of empire.[26]

I do not dispute that *Façade* reinscribes racial stereotypes, nor do I read it as an assertively political text. I do, however, suggest that it treats its own stock primitivist tropes, poetic and musical, with tongue in invisible cheek. Recognizing the poet's construction of a stylized, artificial aesthetic *as* stylized and artificial, *Façade* defamiliarizes its own Boomlay BOOM cultivation of kitsch. *Façade* considers its racial stereotypes to be as citational as everything else in the piece, down to its title. Hence as it pulls toward the Symbolist imaginary that employs images of racialized "darkness" as tropes for the irrational, prelinguistic noise of unconscious desire, *Façade* also treats race as a performative construction of the social persona.

In this respect, *Façade* anticipates a different distancing-effect—Brechtian alienation—as it attempts to take on a "personality" in the original "masked" sense of the word. Much as the Sitwells associated Eastern theatricality with the crafted personality, Brecht in the 1930s would sponsor Chinese theater as an extension of the "theatrical and pictorial displays at the old popular fairs."[27] Brecht's "Alienation Effects of the Chinese Theater" (1935) praises the Chinese actor's consciousness of himself as a representation: refusing Stanislavskian "conversion" into an emotive and "eruptive" character, the alienated actor's performance is "quite clearly someone else's repetition of the incident: a representation, even though an artistic one" (93)—a kind of embodied lithograph. Clearly Brecht's 1935 essay did not inspire Sitwell's 1922 entertainment, but both draw on a shared association of the East with a self-conscious theatricality. The modernist appropriation of *commedia dell'arte* reads, likewise, as a retreat into ironic detachment and self-referential artistry: posing the personality as formalized performance rather than psychological self-discovery.

This self-conscious social performance, linked to an ideal of cosmopolitanism, reveals itself as what Amanda Anderson calls "dandyism," which, after Baudelaire and Wilde, has carried more than a trace of orientalism. Anderson argues that Wilde's dandy figures, as a species of late nineteenth-century cosmopolitanism, reflect ambivalence about the "ethical limit" of critical detachment and irony. The dandy's cosmopolitan ambivalence represents one of many Victorian responses to the "conditions of modernity" that "require certain practices of reflection able to repair the dislocations wrought by non-traditional or defamiliarizing forms of life" (Anderson 13). As Edith herself said, "If one is a greyhound, why try to look like a Pekinese? I am as stylized as it is possible to be—as stylized as the music of Debussy or Ravel"—stylized wit served as a medium to aestheticize her persona.[28] For Anderson, however, the epigram's potently "free-floating" "transferability" from one context to another is also exposed as its limit; the dandy in Wilde's drama is compelled to suspend his ironic detachment and act pragmatically in a given circumstance.[29] We might in a different context think of this free-floating promiscuity as an extension of the Antheil dilemma; an epigram is too good and too tight to be confinable to its original time and place.

Rather than reading Sitwell's abstract, nonsensical language as an Eliotic distillation of poetic emotion, then, I suggest that *Façade* twins the mask of Eliotic impersonality with the mask of a cosmopolitan persona—neither of which (recall Eliot's Ganges) can exist without leaning on the colonies. *Façade* one-ups the Wildean ideal of "epigrammatic detachment": by creating a free-floating surface of clever-sounding words, given an illusion of depth, it exposes social life as a mediated exchange of aesthetic values. The two masks and the multiple personae of *Façade* push poetry and music into a more cosmopolitan aesthetic territory while retaining a skeptical view of imperial expansion.

English Cosmopolitanism: Walton and Modern Music

From the start, *Façade* was situated in international competition. Anxieties about finding a suitable British musical idiom were inextricable from debates over the cosmopolitan and imperial reach of Britain itself, giving *Façade*'s cosmopolitanism a critical edge. Elgar (the English composer unfavorably compared to Beethoven in Forster's *Howards End*) is critiqued by Cecil Gray (1924) as "perfect specimens of that exotic growth called Jingoism which flourished with such tropical luxuriance in this country a quarter of a century ago, and is now, fortunately, almost extinct."[30] Walton himself, even before his introduction to the Sitwell family, had demonstrated a modern musical sensibility that distinguished him from a conservative English scene. Walton was admitted at ten years old to the choir at Christ Church College, Oxford, where his freethinking tutors encouraged him to pursue an unorthodox compositional style, and where he had access to new music through the expansive Ellis Library.[31] He was exposed to several scores, including *Pierrot Lunaire*, and tried to assimilate their techniques without having heard many of them in performance; he played the occasional Stravinsky or Bartók score in piano reduction, but had no training in how to write for a chamber ensemble prior to preparing the *Façade* premiere.[32] Yet Walton made such an impression that Dean Strong admitted him on scholarship to Oxford at the age of sixteen, considering it "unpatriotic of England to let slip such a musical brain."[33]

Walton was badly suited to the academic life and failed his matriculation exams several times over; before he was done failing, he had been introduced to Sacheverell (a fellow undergraduate), and within a year was being referred to as the fourth Sitwell sibling. Through the Sitwells Walton was introduced to E.J. Dent, among the more cosmopolitan English musical figures, a close friend of E.M. Forster (and the putative character basis of Herriton in *Where Angels Fear to Tread*, Forster's melodramatic testament to the attractions of Continental art). Through Dent, Walton interacted briefly with Ferruccio Busoni and the Swiss conductor Ernest Ansermet.[34] Hence it may have been to Walton's good fortune that he never found his way into the Royal College of Music, founded by George Grove (of the *Grove Dictionary*). The founding of the RCM in 1881 represented a British response to the perception that English music lagged behind its Continental competition.[35] According to Walton's second wife Susana, the Sitwells "didn't want him to go to a music college . . . because they thought it turned out composers of doubtful status."[36] Walton later expressed great relief that he had avoided becoming the likes of Charles Villiers Stanford, an important figure at the RCM and at Cambridge—indeed, perhaps the most important musical pedagogue in England, whose students included Ralph Vaughan Williams, Frank Bridge, Gustav Holst, and Herbert Howells.[37]

Walton's relief may have owed less to Stanford's stylistic conservatism than to a preternatural impatience for academic personalities; still, it reflects much of what seemed edgy about *Façade*'s otherwise tame entertainments. Stanford, a born Irishman, was a chief figure in promoting the development a British musical idiom before, during, and after the Great War. His essay "Music and the War" (1916) criticizes the aggressive nationalism of his German contemporaries, while offering a call to arms for British composers to produce better work: Britain's "insular position has . . . militated against foreign recognition of the enormous stride which this country has made in the last thirty-five years" (which would take one back to the founding of the RCM).[38] Stanford attributes the perceived deficiencies of British music not to British provincialism but to German aggression: "the German Press brings its ammunition to bear upon foreign music," creating a "brick wall of insulated prejudice" against which "Art runs its head in vain" (108). Stanford no doubt has in mind Oskar Schmitz's notorious article "Das Land Ohne Musik" ("The Land Without Music"; 1914): a pointed and, if the British response was any sign, a nerve-touching assault on Britain's musical competence. Stanford's essay has its own gripes with British music, chiefly with publishers who reinforce Britain's insularity by publishing music that cannot be exported: English church music, "ephemeral" piano music, and "worthless ballads and part-songs." Stanford believed in the value of folk song for instilling patriotic values, but urged his compatriots not to give in to "Philistinism," or to the "bizarre" experiments of the Germans; nor to follow Germany's suit by infecting music with jingoism.[39] Rather, the English need to match Germany's output with "music of the highest class": "We must do better than they, and gain thereby the respect and confidence of the musical world" (123). In this context, Walton's cheeky music hall numbers suggest that the way for British music "to do better" is to modernize and ironize "ephemeral music," and its civic values, by pulling it into conversation with its European fellow travelers.

Stanford's skepticism about ephemeral popular music is echoed by E.J. Dent, who resists the "intensive culture of folk-song" which, by 1919, had "become a lucrative musical industry."[40] Dent's argument in favor of cosmopolitan music, and Stanford's in favor of an "exportable" idiom, both conflict with the proud provincialism of Ralph Vaughan Williams, who asserts that the origins of music are always national, borne of "the music that is going on at home, in the schools, and in the local choral societies."[41] Vaughan Williams rejects the idea of England as the "land without music," dismissing it as the "cigar theory of music"—the misguided belief that the inability to produce music is as endemic as the inability to produce good cigars—and suggests that the importation of foreign composers (such as Händel/Handel) has caused English musical culture to atrophy. The solution, he suggests, is to produce a more national idiom, for "It is surely as bad to be self-consciously cosmopolitan as self-consciously national" (3).

The Sitwells sided against the provincialism of Vaughan Williams, the imperialism of Elgar, and the moderate nationalism of Stanford, finding Dent's cosmopolitan modernist sensibilities more to their liking. Just as the Sitwells delighted in making themselves outsiders, Walton was an outsider to the musical scene of England, which, in turn, was an outsider to the European music scene. Plunged into the Sitwells' tempestuous social life, and unwittingly embroiled in their social antagonisms, Walton became the fourth character in the satirical pamphlet of Proustian and Pirandellan extraordinaire, C.K. Scott-Moncrieff, entitled *The Strange and Striking Adventures of Four Characters in Search of an Author* (1926).[42] Walton did not share his new companions' thin skin, or their impulse to perform in real-world *commedia*, and stayed at work in his studio. Benefiting from the financial patronage of the Sitwells and their friends (Siegfried Sassoon and Lord Berners among them), Walton was liberated from academic life and moved from his rustic childhood home, outdoor toilet and all, to the drawing rooms of 2 Carlyle Square, where he produced an inventive, occasionally atonal string quartet, "the only English contribution to the International Festival of Music in 1923" (*Laughter* 202). He began work on an unlikely collaboration with Wyndham Lewis, an overture (no longer extant) to *Doctor Syntax*; and wrote the incidental music to Lytton Strachey's "Chinese melodrama," set during the Boxer Rebellion, entitled *The Son of Heaven* (1925). Perhaps his most popular piece, the oratorio *Belshazzar's Feast* (1931), is a witty and melodically memorable rendering of Babylonian decadence, a setting of various biblical texts compiled by Osbert. The most famous anecdote associated with *Belshazzar's Feast* is Thomas Beecham's remark, leading up to the premiere, that Walton should feel free to add as many brass bands as he wanted because the piece would never be heard again. Far from *Façade*'s small-scale parsimony, *Belshazzar* draws on an oversized orchestra and chorus in matching descriptions of Babylonian debauchery with literal accompaniments: "the god of brass" accompanied by brass fanfares, and so on. By this point, at least, Walton had the financial backing to match his artistic ambitions, even as his brash (though still aggressively tonal) music puzzled the conservative sensibilities in British music, including the *Belshazzar* performers who resented having to use the word "concubine." Walton's literary interactions are numerous and understudied.[43] He composed scores for two timely prewar texts: Shakespeare's *Henry V* (1942) and Louis MacNeice's BBC radio drama *Christopher Columbus* (1942), both featuring Laurence Olivier. Like Antheil, Walton's style grew increasingly conservative as his career progressed, pivoting on the *Crown Imperial* coronation march written for George VI. Walton's experience with the Sitwells' patronage and cosmopolitan savoir-faire produced him as a popular composer and, ultimately, an establishment composer, with a national and international audience.

Walton's interactions with Lytton Strachey, though marginal, shed useful light on *Façade*'s pattering *épatism*. The Sitwells, whose relations with the Bloomsbury Group were never comfortable, thought Strachey "exotic" and hyper-stylized in his patterns of speech. As Osbert writes, the "tones" of Bloomsbury conveyed a paradoxical "interest, surprise, incredulity"—a detached cosmopolitan equanimity (echoes of Eliot's Mrs. Equitone), running, like *Façade*, at a very fast clip, "at different speeds and on different gears, and contain a deal of expert but apparently meaningless syncopation" (*Laughter* 18). Osbert subjects this artificial speech to ethnographic parody, claiming that the "Bloomsbury voice" is as "rare and ritualistic outside the bounds of West Central London as the state voice of the Emperor of China beyond his pleasances and palaces . . . .Experts maintain that it originated as an apanage of the Strachey family" (*Laughter* 18). West Central London itself becomes an exotic display, its rapid syncopations defamiliarized as "ritualistic." At the illustrious Armistice Day dance for Diaghilev's Ballets Russes, Osbert continues, a seven-year-old girl—a "precocious mimic" "of real virtuosity"—tried on an imitation of Strachey (who, performing as the anti-Victoria, found the imitation "amusing," but not at all "like.") London speech—as in Strachey's affected tone—sounded no less exotic than a Boomlay BOOM parody of racial otherness.

And the ability of the English language to take on "ritualistic" qualities, by way of absorbing the aesthetics of the East, tracks through *Façade*'s Aesthetic lines of inquiry. A pair of English collaborators to whom Sitwell and Walton are not often compared—Gilbert and Sullivan—specialized in patter-song, a contortion of spoken text into virtuosic rhythmic patterns. Like Sitwell and Walton, Gilbert and Sullivan associate the inauthenticity of this speech with a stylized, dandiacal self-presentation and, at the same time, with an acquisitive exotic aesthetic. In *Patience* (1881), the Wildean dandy Bunthorne, "anxious for to shine/in the High Aesthetic line," confesses that he is an "aesthetic sham."[44] "The meaning doesn't matter / if it's only idle chatter / of a transcendental kind," Bunthorne patters. Such chatter requires an acquisitive aesthetic eye, and part of Bunthorne's fraudulence consists in his affected desire to acquire all things Japanese.[45] A late nineteenth-century craze (due in part to the 1869 Meiji restoration), *japonisme*, *chinoiserie*, and other forms of orientalist appropriation persisted through twentieth-century music and writing; as Glenn Watkins writes, the "conflation" of *commedia dell'arte* theater and orientalist aesthetics "thrived openly from the time of Schoenberg's *Pierrot Lunaire* to the Bauhaus productions of the twenties" (*Pyramids* 49). *Façade*, in spite of its ostensible lack of literary theme, is thus anxious about the problem of what makes an authentic poetic voice, or an authentic English (let alone British) one, or whether there is such a thing. *Façade*'s covetous artistic ear binds its stylistic virtuosity with very material questions about the "exotic" spaces—including England's own rituals—from which aesthetic personae are mined.

The question applies to the Sitwells' own anxieties about patrilineage and blood: Edith frequently cites not only her strained parental relations, but her Plantagenet bloodline and appearance, and occasionally an aristocratic sort of guilt about being a female first-born. In *Left Hand, Right Hand*, Osbert also expresses both a familial and a racial burden, writing that his father had imagined his sons as future "colonial governors and proconsuls, supreme over the wastes and teeming cities of an empire, shining somewhere among his descendants" (4). Even the pianistic title of *Left Hand* suggests a relationship between the marking of time in the left hand—often (fortunately not always) a rhythmic bass-line—and the elaboration of an expressive melodic line or narrative in the right hand. The ground-bass underlying the self-conscious aestheticism of *Façade*, marching along (as we shall see) to the rhythms of "Rule, Britannia!", acknowledges a consciousness of the discourses of empire, the work of the colonial proconsul Osbert might have been.

Façade: From Noise to Rhythm

If *Façade* implicitly links its major musical feature, rhythm, to the forward march of empire, Edith also conceived of it a response to the mechanization of modernity. Richard Greene, her most recent biographer, contends that "Noise was Sitwell's greatest enemy," a source of nervous strain on a preternaturally anxious personality.[46] While writing *Taken Care Of* in the 1950s, she experienced a Carlylean struggle with the sound of a neighbor's electric drill, which led her into a prolonged and exhausting letter-writing campaign, and into the Vice Presidency of the local Noise Abatement Society of London's Mayfair district (Greene 431). Yet artistically, if not psychologically, Sitwell summoned up a defense, similar to Russolo's, for rhythmic innovation spurred by the changing acoustics of the city. Citing the architect Le Corbusier, Sitwell suggests that "as the result of the Machine Age, "the sound of certain machinery" produced a "'noise . . . so round that one believed a change in the acoustic functions was taking place.' It was therefore necessary to find rhythmical expressions for the heightened speed of our time."[47] *Façade* offers these new "rhythmical expressions," applying them to pastoral and domestic rather than urban themes.

Sitwell believed the formal principle of rhythm to be the poetic transcription and mediation of a "dream-like realm." Like Eliot's auditory imagination, which seeks an unconscious historical "feeling for rhythm," Sitwell's invocation of rhythm is indebted to French Symbolism, and to "virtuoso exercises" in musical expression. Even as her neighbor's drill was driving Sitwell to exhaustion, *Taken Care Of* attacks the "rhythmical flaccidity, the verbal deadness, the dead and expected patterns" of Victorian and Georgian poetry, and calls rhythm "one of the principal translators between dream and reality. Rhythm is, "to the world of sound, what light is to the world of sight": something that "shapes and gives new meaning" (140). In a similar passage elsewhere, Sitwell cites Schopenhauer's assertion that rhythm is merely pitchless melody, the purest method of communicating to the body in a manner divested of linguistic sense ("Some Notes," xv). Sitwell's desire to use rhythm to translate between unconscious static and real-world noise is indebted to her longstanding admiration for Verlaine and Rimbaud, whose synesthetic irrationality she preferred to the florid archaisms of the Georgian poets, and to the earnest Victorians parodied in *Façade* as the imperial "Lord Tennyson in laurels" ("Hornpipe," l.3). Sitwell emphasizes the performative and transformative qualities of rhythm—its ability to shape experience rather than to represent it.

Façade rarely invokes noise in the Antheil and Russolo vein (though its main forebear, *Parade*, does), but it is motivated by the search for virtuosic rhythm that will compose through the noisy "world of sound," and that will mediate the pressures of *fama* and *rumori*. Sitwell's search for new rhythms motivates a need for a "transcendental technique," what Liszt had termed *execution transcendant*, to sharpen the skills of the performer and, in turn, to transcend the deadness of "reality." Hence "the poems in *Façade* are virtuoso exercises in technique of an extreme difficulty, in the same sense . . . that . . . studies by Liszt are studies in transcendental technique in music" (140). *Façade*'s acceleration of rhythm to catch up with the soundscape recalls Bunthorne's "idle chatter of a transcendental kind," a diffusion of meaning (it "doesn't matter") in the service of new cosmopolitan style.

Even for Liszt, an effect of transcendental technique was to call attention to the technician: Liszt's *Transcendental Etudes* (1851) privilege virtuosity above all else, to such an extent that the pieces were all but unperformable until he rearranged them in 1852. The aestheticization of the virtuoso performer is not entirely about technique, but also about fashioning a public personality. Sacheverell's book on Liszt notes the composer's extravagant and "magnetic" presence, onstage and in person, suggesting that Liszt's prowess in social life matched or overshadowed his prowess at the piano: "So great were the effects of his personality," Sacheverell claims, "that it is more easy to find accounts of his personal appearance than of his actual playing."[48] Antheil's technically eccentric piano playing likewise drew as much note for his "bad boy" presence as for his knuckle-busting assaults on the keyboard; he was known to perform with a loaded revolver on the piano, lest the audience do anything *too* extreme. Edith loathed Antheil's playing, and resented (ironically) the cultish public presence being groomed for him; she wrote that Antheil played "so loudly and so fast" that between each piece he had to be "be carried out and slapped with wet towels like a boxer."[49] She preferred music of a more dreamlike nuance, wishing to fashion a persona with softer edges.

The rapid-fire rhythms of *Façade*, requiring impeccable enunciation, failed in the first performance to achieve transcendence in projecting anything other than a verbal blur. If the piece seemed to lack sharpness and clarity, it aspired to illuminate the numinous aesthetics of its surrounding space—the drawing room at 2 Carlyle Square. Describing the premiere, Osbert embellishes an ethereal Aesthetic landscape in which the drawing room and the outside landscape bleed together: "Inside, the room, with its tones of pink and blue and white and violet, seemed filled with polar lights from windows and tropic lights from fires." *Façade*'s sounds and pictures, given autonomous agency to wash over the visual scene, actively aestheticize it: "As the strange new sounds shaped themselves under the hands of the rather angry players, the evening outside began to envelop the world in a grape-bloom blue, the lights had to be turned on, and the pictures glowed from the white walls" (*Laughter* 188). Sitwell's florid description suggests that the music awakened a deep noumenal undercurrent refracted from the glass objects inside the room. The lights and sounds themselves are granted an autonomous agency—amplified by the megaphone and curtain, moving across glass and human bodies bristling with affect. Moving to *Façade*'s reception, Osbert suggests that his educated audience, "people of imagination," loved the piece; one Mrs. Mathias, a Ballets Russes patron, arranged for a new performance against the remonstrances of her friends. *Façade* managed to seem transcendently technical, fashionable, and countercultural all at once.

Just as the musical aesthetics of *Façade* work to catch up with the speed of modernity, its visual and theatrical aesthetics are forged from the efforts of other art forms to find a niche—particularly, a niche for the moving theatrical body—in the mechanized landscape. Behind the scene of the Ballets Russes' aesthetics, for example, lie the "biomechanical" theories of Vsevolod Meyerhold, the beleaguered Russian director who reconsidered the form of the moving body along antinaturalistic lines. Meyerhold's "biomechanical" theories, a "Taylorism for the theatre," attempted to discipline the actor's bodily gesture to its utmost efficiency: to produce emotion through a cycle of bodily stimuli, emotional response, and accordingly new bodily stimuli.[50] One finds such theories just as often marshaled as *critique* of or resistance to Taylorist mechanization:[51] in Brecht, for example, or in the *Façade* poems, which could not be less industrial, but which energize rhythm to catch up with the mechanized world. A forebear of both Brecht and the Ballets Russes, Meyerhold rejected Stanislavski's method, preferring a "constructivist" aesthetics in which emotional expression derived from external rhythm and movement rather than from personal inspiration—built "not 'from within', but from without."[52]

Sitwell's desire to respond to the onslaught of modernity by intensifying rhythm tries to make audiences question their relation to their own drawing rooms, bodies, patterns of speech, and national-musical inheritance: to remake personality from the outside in and thereby restimulate its social movement. Sitwell recognizes that art is something other than raw emotional expression; it is cooked emotional expression, shaped by external pressure—a realization that applies not just to the classicized parodies of ragtime in Satie and Stravinsky, but to the alienated Expressionism of Schoenberg's "silent dandy."

Schoenberg's *Pierrot* and the *Commedia Dell'Arte*

Façade, citing the traditions of the *commedia dell'arte*, and perhaps anticipating the Brechtian alienation effects of non-Western theater, calls attention to the performative dimensions of the salon. The Sitwells were well familiar with the *commedia* as it had seeped into modernist theatrical music and the visual arts. The imagery of *commedia* is more gestured at than explicit in *Façade*, introduced in gestures to the "moon-like" gazes of its characters. The mask on the curtain is not explicitly identified as Schoenberg's moon-sick Pierrot, but poems published (sans music) as part of the book *Façade* (1930)—framed by Gino Severini's frontispiece of Pierrot and Harlequin—make it clear that Pierrot is on her mind. The poem "Clowns' Houses," originally written in 1918, presents "Pierrot moon . . . ,/ His face more white than sin." Drawing on the *commedia* imagery in Schoenberg, as well as in Cocteau (anti-Teuton extraordinaire), the Sitwells advertise their work as cosmopolitan in its very lineage. Indeed, the Sitwells advance their international cachet by mimicking Schoenberg's piece before it had ever been performed in Britain. *Façade* matches *Parade*'s hyperstimulating noise with *Pierrot Lunaire*'s introspective scream of internal anguish, to underscore the personal "postures" of their alienated personae. The rhythms of publicity might reenergize the alienated Pierrot as he moves through London's social rituals, both insular and exotic. Coward's *London Calling*, in addition to ridiculing the Sitwells, satirized the Pierrotism of the modern aesthete, offering, in a hit song called "Parisian Pierrot," the eponymous "Pierrot,/ Society's hero" as a figure whose artificial ennui makes him the toast of "Parisians of leisure."

The *commedia dell'arte*'s appeal to modernists lay in what Joseph Kennard in 1935 called its "incongruous humanity"[53]—its odd mixture of intensely colored costumes and masks, classical wit, and broad character types. In particular, the *commedia* actor represented sheer professional competence and craft, rather than "inspired" emotional investment. Stravinsky and Picasso used the *commedia* actor as a model for the neoclassical aesthetic—a figure whose voice represented not an authentic Romantic ideal of character, but part of the actor's professional equipment.[54] Pierrot posed one of the *commedia*'s few claims to psychological authenticity, not least because he was the one figure who wore makeup rather than a mask. In *Façade*, at least in theory, the sincere voice of Pierrot was depersonalized by the masks (rather than his usual makeup) on the screen. For the *commedia* figures who did wear a mask, it was known to give the actor's voice a distinctive sound, focalizing the voice through a small aperture. In the Sitwells' drawing-room, this masked face, likewise with one small opening and some help from the Sengerphone, would amplify the poet's voice while ironizing Pierrot's whingy sincerity—shifting makeup to mask and severing the "unity of actor and type."[55]

A setting of twenty-one poems by Albert Giraud, translated into German by Otto Erich Hartleben, *Pierrot Lunaire* pushes into both expressionism and exaggerated artificiality, both a stylized linguistic *façade* and a subjectivity laid bare. Like *Façade*, *Pierrot* resists easy classification: spoken and sung, ironic and authentic, a revolt against convention and a return to common tropes of the *commedia*. *Pierrot*'s Sprechstimme, a vocal technique that hovers between song and speech so as to avoid either a "*singsong* speech pattern" or a "realistic, natural speech,"[56] prepares *Façade*'s uneasy patter. In his essay "The Relation to the Text" (1912), Schoenberg claims to have composed his piece "intoxicated by the initial sound of the first words of the text without bothering myself at all about . . . what happens in the poem." Giraud's hyperreal Symbolism pushed Schoenberg to meld poetry and speech through sound and association rather than mere literal meaning.

Yet they carry those meanings anyway, and the tensions among music, language, and visual imagery add an ironic dissonance that the Sitwells were determined to exploit. The internal conflicts of *Pierrot* were experienced by both Stravinsky and Adorno. Stravinsky, who attended an early performance of the piece, admired the instrumental music but found the Sprechstimme insufferable, a product of the decadent German *Jugendstil*.[57] At the same time, Adorno contests that Schoenberg's *Pierrot* and *Herzgewächse* (1911) "transcend the *Jugendstil* out of which they arise. For the musical expression assumes an immediacy that . . . consumes the images and speaks directly from within."[58] The piece's ability to consume its old-fashioned imagery derives not only from the music's raw immediacy, but also from Pierrot's dandiacal oscillation between detachment and engagement.[59] The third song of the cycle, *Der Dandy*, depicts "the silent dandy of Bergamo" painting his "waxen" face. Amidst the multicolored landscape, a refraction of moonlight through the "crystal flacons" on his washstand (compare the glass reflectors of 2 Carlyle Square), Pierrot passes on the colors of the East and settles on the ethereal makeup of a "fantastic moonbeam": "He shoves aside the red, and the green of the Orient,/And paints his face in a noble style/"With a fantastic moonbeam."[60] The piano ascends to the word "style" [*stil*], treating it as a mini-climax; this moonbeam—like Sitwell's—consumes the very style that it celebrates, an artificial cosmopolitanism cloaked in Symbolist linguistic surface.[61]

The softened dance music of *Façade* is in no sense expressionistic, but its poetry dabbles in a Symbolist style like Giraud's, bedaubing its own poetic face with makeup. *Façade* attempts to navigate between psychological surreality and presentational self-consciousness. It reimagines *Pierrot*'s stylized subjectivity as a mask of cosmopolitan cleverness, deflecting emotional self-reflection through Expressionism, but inviting social self-critique through ironic amusement. The landscape of *Der Dandy* resembles not just the synesthetic reveries of *Façade*, but Osbert's recollection of the performance setting itself: reveling in the spectacles of patronage and publicity, as "the evening outside began to envelop the world in a grape-bloom blue."

With that point I wish to turn to the Ballets Russes—a source of musical-visual spectacle whose arts had permeated the public sphere and transformed the drawing room. In the background, the cultural resonances of *Pierrot*, and the esthesically nervewracking presence of Sitwell's acousmatic voice, may keep us in mind of an important critical tension between cultural-historical and aesthetic-affective readings of modernist music. Clara Latham's discerning affect-theory analysis of *Pierrot Lunaire* may typify this tension: Latham situates Schoenberg's *Sprechstimme* in relation to the Freudian "talking cure," arguing that the voice's acoustic sonority (heard by the piece's early audiences as "hysterical") evades verbal or cultural signification in deference to autonomous sonic affect moving over bodies, perhaps akin to what Will Scrimshaw, after Seth Kim-Cohen, calls "non-cochlear sound."[62] My contention is that pieces like *Façade* and *Pierrot* expose the false choice between affective experience and cultural history—including the history, convincingly detailed by Latham, of how definitions of "hysteria" came to pivot on the acoustics of voice. For Sitwell, music was not merely an indeterminate emotional fog, but affect shaped through verbal reference, aesthetic influence, and rhythm, and refracted by solid objects found in everyday life. *Façade*'s effort to "depersonalize" her voice redistributes poetic meaning across the social space, trying like Pierre Schaffer to sharpen the perception of acousmatic sound, but not as an end in itself. Rather, like a musical lint brush, the voice of *Façade* picks up the aesthetic and cultural debris of the social space and makes it newly audible, in a way that Sitwell's contemporaries found either compelling, annoying, or (as for Lewis) deeply sinister.

Bernays, the Ballets Russes, and the Aesthetics of Publicity

The Ballets Russes, which had exploded the relationship between onstage, offstage, and backstage noises with *Parade* and *Le Sacre*, developed a close-knit relationship between aesthetics and advertising, as it reconfigured the movement of the body in public life. Edward Bernays, the paterfamilias of institutionalized public relations, attributes his success to the time he spent organizing the Ballets Russes' press operations. As with the Sitwells, the personal dramas and conflicts of the Ballets Russes personae aided the company's ability to create a buzz, even as it put a kink in Bernays's efforts to present a cohesive image: working with the Ballets Russes, he writes, "I had never imagined that the interpersonal relations of the members of a group could be so involved and complex, full of medieval intrigue, illicit love, misdirected passion and aggression."[63] Much as the floating sounds in front of the *Façade* sate the Sitwells' unquenchable thirst for publicity, the advertising campaigns associated with the Ballets Russes conjoined their recognizable aesthetic trademarks with the personal dramas of their main stars and impresarios: Lopokova, Massine, Diaghilev, Nijinsky, and the Diaghilev/Nijinsky/Massine triangle.

In his enviably compact yet detailed glosses on the Ballets Russes' aesthetics, Bernays praises Diaghilev's ability to remake the old "ballet of the Czars," blend it with "Isadora Duncan's modern dance forms," and produce something "startlingly original" (103). He also praises Diaghilev's ease with a range of artists—Stravinsky, Ravel, Richard Strauss, Picasso, Benois, Bakst, and Nijinsky—in creating a Russian-cum-European-cum-"Oriental" aesthetic that "intoxicated his audiences and expressed the new aesthetic freedom of the twentieth century" (103). Discussing Diaghilev's aesthetics as well as his own PR challenges, Bernays emphasizes the blending and unification of heterogeneous elements into a cohesive product with aesthetic and conceptual appeal. Not yet having devised his more advanced techniques of polling target audiences, Bernays had to resort to "hunch" and "intuition"; even so, he was "convinced . . . that the ballet should be projected through interdependent themes. . . . First, we decided to publicize the ballet as a novelty in art forms, a unifying of several arts; second, in terms of its appeal to special groups of the public; third, in terms of its direct impact on American life, on design and color in American products; and fourth, through its personalities" (105–6). To call this a culture industry would be no overstatement.

In America, Bernays claims, this success was the result of an advertising push in which he "bombarded" American newspapers and magazines with "stories and photographs angled to their various reader groups—stories about composers and their compositions for music pages; costume, fabric and fashion design stories for women's pages, etc." (106). The goal was not only to produce an image of cohesiveness within the Russian Ballet —no easy task, given its clashing aesthetics and personalities—but also to make the Ballet consistent with the self-image of "American life." This particular Ballets Russes campaign focused on America, not England, but in both cases the aesthetic appeal of the ballet extended into social life and the world of fashion: "To relate the ballet directly to American life, I persuaded several manufactures to make products inspired by the color and design of the Bakst décors and costumes and arranged for their advertising and display" (108). As Bernays writes, the most publically impressive feature of the Ballet was its "cohesiveness"—an illusion that masked the severe "intrigue, deviant and illicit love, hatred and jealousy," and above all, sex, which "melted lines of demarcation between the hierarchic layers of the organization—business managers loved dancers; men and women . . . , masculinity and femininity" (113). The various divergent elements of the Ballets Russes "melted" conflict into a Gesamtkunstwerkian illusion of wholeness —an iconic phantasmagoric commodity.

Hence the visual and musical aesthetics of the Ballets Russes were dialectically implicated with the aestheticized *rumori* of social life. The innovations of this synesthetic "blend" of auditory, visual, and dramatic elements compelled a similar shift in the daily life of its patrons; conversely, the demands of audiences necessitated that the constituents within the Ballets appear "cohesive." As Bernays writes, "The ballet people were strong individualists," whose relations "were based on intrigue, deviant and illicit love, hatred and jealousy"—and sex, which "melted lines of demarcation" of rank, of marriage, of "varying degrees of masculinity and femininity." Thus the influence of the Ballets Russes was linked as much to its visual and social dimensions as to the music: carrying a set of conflicted attitudes toward (among other things) sex and gender, yet packaged as a cohesive ideal. To make the ballet cohere with American life, Bernays needed to aestheticize life itself—marketing décor and costumes to the public at large.

In Britain, as well as America, the Ballets Russes helped transform the visual aesthetic of the bourgeois drawing room. As Osbert writes in *Sing High!*

Sing Low! (1944), the Russian Ballet motivated an "exotic style" that would replace traditional Edwardian designs:

> The ballet *Schéhérazade* alone was responsible for innumerable lampshades and cushions that blazed in barred and striped splendour from the shop windows; and a more exotic style began to banish the drawing-room wall-papers trellised with roses and water-lilies, and the early Edwardian wood-panelling, that had seemed created as a background for long cigars, or perhaps even fashioned out of the fabric of their boxes. For the rest, in the warm long summer evenings, dance music prospered in the golden air of the squares, and striped awnings rose like mushrooms in the night to shelter the international herds of the rich.[64]

Osbert's emphasis on the orientalist tinges of Leon Bakst's costume and set design shares with Edith's poetry an ambivalence about the relationship between British and Eastern aesthetics. Both within and outside of the drawing room, society becomes a concert hall turned inside out, such that everything seems "fashioned out of the fabric of their boxes." "The international herds of the rich" were exposed to and "shelter[ed]" by a new kind of visual and musical aesthetic, suggesting a cosmopolitan sensibility that is at the same time cynical about aesthetics grounded in imperial acquisition. The passage exemplifies the kind of "witty bricolage" that Christopher Reed has observed of Osbert's writing for the British *Vogue*: appropriating the so-called "Amusing Style," critically aware of the imperialistic undertones of fashion, Sitwell "performs an identity antagonistic to the cultural and political markers of 'respectable' British identity." In a 1924 essay on the Empire Exhibition at Wembley, for example, Osbert presents what Reed interprets as a "jaundiced view of the 'grotesque romance' of a British imperialism that imposes its own customs on 'continent after continent' while making an exhibition of 'the people and customs that it smothers.'"[65]

Façade's Empire

Façade's jaundiced quality toward the imperialist aesthetic inherited from the ballet is given an additional critical edge by the techniques of poetic and musical sound. Pursuant to Le Corbusier's anxiety that new rhythms were needed for the noise of modernity, Sitwell turned these rhythms back onto modernity's geographic and cultural dislocations—against empire, through cosmopolitan irony. The first two songs of the cycle, "Hornpipe" and "En Famille," draw on a stock of images and rhythms both exotic and recognizably British. "Hornpipe," which narrates the sea-journey of Queen Victoria and Lord Tennyson, exemplifies this tendency to ironize the rhythms of nationalism. The words of "Hornpipe" match the rhythmic pattern of the well-known "College Hornpipe," an association that is distinctly English but innocent enough. "Hornpipe" opens with a snare drum beating the rhythm of "Rule, Britannia!/Britannia rules the waves," at which point the melody appears (saxophone and cello) underneath the "College Hornpipe" (in the piccolo) (fig. 5.2). Upon hearing the first words, "Sailors come/To the drum/Out of Babylon," one has the rhythms of the Hornpipe and of "Rule, Britannia!" on the brain. Britannia smoothly merges with Babylon—the "great city" and evil empire of *Belshazzar's Feast*, whose "merchandise" of "gold and silver" (catalogued in Revelation 18) includes the "souls of men."

If the opening salvo of "Rule, Britannia!" reinscribes nationalism in its self-consciously imperial paradiddles, it does so with a smirk. Sitwell's use of Eastern and African imagery, Bryant argues, "unsettl[es] English propriety and imperial unity while simultaneously reinforcing racial stereotypes" (244). Yet *Façade* draws attention to the constructed nature of this East, awakening the audience to the aesthetic of its own drawing room. The sea, the site of naval power, is turned into "the settee of the horsehair sea/Where Lord Tennyson in laurels wrote a gloria free," the site of imperial and poetic authority, but also simply a pretty object on which to sit. Victoria enters next:

> In a borealic iceberg came Victoria, she
> Knew Prince Albert's tall memorial took the colours of the floreal
> And the borealic iceberg; floating on they see
> New-arisen Madame Venus for whose sake from far
> Came the fat and zebra'd emperor from Zanzibar
> Where like golden bouquets lay far Asia, Africa, Cathay,
> All laid before that shady lady by the fibroid Shah. (7–16)

As Bryant notes, Zanzibar provides "more than just an end-rime": the Sultan of Zanzibar had been "made an Honorary Knight Commander for service during the Great War," and that "in the same month that *Façade* was performed privately in 1922, Zanzibar was invited to join the East Africa House for the British Empire Exhibition" (252). The Madam Venus passage (from "Madam Venus" to "Shah") is recited without musical accompaniment, emphasizing the performative Boomlay BOOM quality of the verse: the speaker's voice must both maintain tempo and draw out the appropriate character or tone color without help from the ensemble.

Figure 5.2. Opening bars of "Hornpipe," from *Façade*. "Façade—an Entertainment" music by Sir William Walton, text by Dame Edith Sitwell. © Oxford University Press 1951, 2000. Reproduced by Permission of CopyCat Music Licensing, LLC, on behalf of Oxford University Press. All Rights Reserved.

That Zanzibar provides an end-rime is important, however. The aesthetics of *Façade* are political insofar as they are aesthetic objects ostentatiously forced into a rhyme scheme and the rhythmic scheme of the "College Hornpipe." The image of the Albert Memorial, at the center of the Frieze of Parnassus (with its 169 artists depicted in sculpture), identifies Britain as a site both of political authority and of aesthetic consolidation, both florid ("floreal") and frigid ("borealic"). The College Hornpipe also stands in for a general reduction of local and regional traditions *within* England into one homogeneous form of dance. As Margaret Dean-Smith writes, the "College Hornpipe," a tune "far removed from the traditional hornpipe," attests to "the way in which the variety, rhythmic peculiarities, local characteristics and highly personal skill of the true hornpipe have . . . been submerged by one commonplace tune and commonplace, easy rhythms."[66] In *Façade*'s "Hornpipe," this submergence is ironized as the colonial continents are brought before the "shady lady" who in turn is an object of Victoria's sighting gaze.

The movement across geographic space is under scrutiny in the poem, and the rapid-fire flow of words and the flat stereotypes of race are given the illusion of depth through musical and poetic rhythm: through the parallax produced by the competing pulses of "College Hornpipe" and "Rule, Britannia." The sailors "come to the drum out of Babylon," moving through the ocean to the rhythms of the "Hornpipe." In the process, they spot the fixed positions of foaming hobby-horses, Lady Glaucis on rocking-horses, and Queen Victoria sitting on her iceberg settee accompanied by Lord Tennyson. "Floating on, they see" a variety of colonial figures, which, though fixed on the curtain, are given motion in the poem: Madame Venus is "new arisen," and the image of the lady from Zanzibar has "come from far." Yet the geographical spaces themselves lie in the ocean like golden bouquets. The racialized image of the "shady lady" is likewise objectified as a "good," in the final line, a kind of kitsch used to manipulate and to REBEL. This reduction applies both to Britain and to her colonies: Asia, Africa, Cathay are reduced to "golden bouquets" laid before Madame Venus, the racialized and anti-"borealic" counterpoint to Victoria, who at the end of the poem observes that Madame Venus and the "drinks" of the sea "are as hot as any hottentot and not the goods for me!" (l. 30). To read the final line requires a slight slowing of pace, thanks to the "g" consonant in the midst of an otherwise smoothly-flowing phrase: the word stands out both conceptually and aurally, making it difficult to produce but nevertheless the center of attention. To produce the "goods" in *Façade* is to present an exotic image by way of a difficult and virtuosic production of sound, such that its "consolidation" into the Memorial becomes comically irrational.

The poem that follows "Hornpipe," entitled "En Famille," similarly attenuates the boundaries between the nautical and the domestic. It depicts a conversation among "the admiral red" (Sir Joshua Jebb) and his four daughters, desperate for a sea-journey to the exotic Symbolist landscape, the synesthetic "flowerless rocks of Hell" (8). Whereas the music in "Hornpipe" is dance-driven, the musical accompaniment in "En Famille" is mostly atmospheric—pentatonic and rhythmically and tonally vague—up until the dialogue between the daughters (collectively) and the admiral. The admiral's "only notion" is "of the peruked sea" (5, 7), and his four daughters urge the admiral to cease comporting himself with naval rectitude:

> They said, 'If the door you would only slam,
> Or if, Papa, you would once say "Damn"—
> Instead of merely roaring "Avast"
> Or boldly invoking the nautical "Blast"— (15-8)

Reaching a dynamic climax on "Blast" (likely to have perked Lewis's ears), the music loses its rhythmic thrust and diffuses into an exotic tableau of a barely perceptible "noise like amber" exteriorized in the landscape:

> We should now stand in the street of Hell
> Watching its siesta shutters that fell
> With a noise like amber softly sliding;
> Our moon-like glances through these gliding
> Would see at her table preened and set
> Myrrhina sitting at her toilette
> With eyelids closed as soft as the breeze
> That flows from gold flowers on the incense-trees. (19-26)

The daughters romanticize this Hell as visual spectators peering Pierrot-like at Myrrhina, whose closed eyes confirm her status as an aesthetic object frozen in time—a scenario mirrored in *Façade*'s "moon-like" mask. The admiral, accompanied by an accelerating pulse and occasional strokes of a Chinese block, retorts that Hell is not a decadent free-for-all, but "is just as properly proper/As Greenwich, or as Bath, or Joppa!" (37-8). He remarks that the "turbaned Chinoiserie,/With whom we should sip our Black Bohea," no passive aesthetic object, would "stretch out her simian fingers thin/To scratch you, my dears, like a mandoline" (33, 35-40). Here the chinoiserie is personified as feminine and racialized as "simian," in the name of a "properly proper" respectability, and the young girls themselves become musical instruments at risk of being scratched/played.[67] The "noise like amber softly sliding" suggests that the landscape is being infused with a softened acoustic presence: Myrrhina's own name, the feminized balm of one of the more frugal Wise Men, suggests that she too has slid with a soft noise out of the "incense-trees" of the landscape. The "moon-like glances" gliding through the (almost) silent "siesta shutters" have softened the Admiral's strident Blast into languorous atmosphere, diffusing Lewis's noise (a direct assault on the body) into vaporous decadence of the very sort that Lewis loathed.

To think of this Hell as an analogue to the Sitwells' salon—and to hear "En Famille" as a pun on *infamie*—underscores its embrace of an aesthetic that is both infamous and domesticated, both noisily threatening and "properly proper." The chinoiserie of the salon—constructed as a resonant space for musical performance filled with the orientalist detritus of the Ballet Russes—has attempted to domesticate Eastern aesthetics only to make British aesthetics seem the more unstable. Moreover, "En Famille" implicates the performance of race with the performance of gender: paralleling the masks on the curtain, the reciter must play both British and Eastern types, both male and female. The poem dialectically parodies both the staunch righteousness of the admiral and the easy romanticism with which the four daughters treat the East. The four young voyeuses imagining this decadent orientalist aesthetic themselves become the "mandoline"—a stock *commedia* image—and upon being touched by the Anglicized chinoiserie, will themselves resonate in the soundscape of Hell.

As the poem reinforces racial tropes by way of its vaporous Symbolist metaphors, it transmutes imperial conquest into something essentially harmless: the Admiral's "notion . . . of the peruked sea" becomes a "butterfly poised on a pigtailed ocean." Yet this problematic image serves a playfully critical function. The exoticism of Hell and the voyeurism of the four daughters are parodied as superficial, decadent, and luxurious. Their hair is described as "finer/. . . Than the young leaves of the springing Bohea," their identity fashioned around a chinoiserie aesthetic that threatens to scratch them back. The romantic perspective on the East is cast as frivolous, and the fear of the East as awkward, overbearing, and too "properly proper." This back-and-forth between Britain and the colonies fractures the authoritative British voice that projects this threat; the admiral's voice, like those of Cocteau's Managers, musically collapses on itself, punctuated clumsily with a single drum-stroke. Likewise, in the cycle's final poem, Sir Beelzebub finds his (drunken) authority collapsing as his servants busy themselves with pranking that old scapegoat Lord Tennyson, "Hoping with glory to trip up the Laureate's feet/(Moving in classical meters)." This poem, too, ends in accelerated exasperation: "None of them come!" Both the chinoiserie of hell and the respectable "classical metres" of poetry implode, like *Parade*, unraveling rhythmic authority: "None of them come" to serve the prince of hell his rum.

Here the reference to Tennyson excavates an anxiety about Victorian Britain's relation to Africa, connecting empire with embodied rhythmic sensation. Tennyson's "Timbuctoo," for example, posits a universal "throbbing," a pulsing noise that unifies Africa and Britain. Jason Rudy associates this sympathetic heaving with the development of telegraphy, and its move (as Jonathan Sterne has likewise detailed) from the passive reception of rhythmic electric signals to the actively expert decoding of them. "Like a telegraph clerk" interpreting "long and short electrical impulses," Rudy explains, "the human brain . . . comes to understand the surrounding world through the rhythmic impress of sensation on the body,"[68] a point that gives an additional thrust also to Madame Sosostris's bodily registration of noumenal music in the phenomenal Jamesian "cage." Much as Williams suggests, the physiological appeals of rhythm make it culturally and poetically communicative. "Timbuctoo" links this telegraphic "hum of men" with geographical expansion: Tennyson's "maze of piercing, trackless, thrilling thoughts" makes rhythm a means of unifying disparate spaces in a way that Rudy aptly associates with the telegraphic cable. Such technologies were pivotal in allowing the Empire to dictate and respond to events in the periphery. The innocuous Wordsworth-lite "maze of . . . thoughts" in "Timbuctoo" grew more threateningly public in the "Charge of the Light Brigade" (1854) written as Poet Laureate and recorded for the gramophone (complete with bugle call) in 1890, as Tennyson's death approached. Like the Boomlay BOOM of Lindsay's "Congo," Tennyson's rhythmic assaults, complete with the noise of the recording and the grain of his voice, proved hypnotic for his contemporaries: "The ground seems to shake," wrote Bram Stoker on hearing Tennyson read, "and the virile voice of the reader conveys . . . the desperate valour of the charge."[69]

Edith's and Osbert's impatience for Tennyson ran deep, on both aesthetic and political grounds; *Façade* strives both to reinvent his tired "classical meters" and to cut off his noisy patriotic bluster. Edith argued that the same British nation that had "hunted" Keats and "bullied" Shelley, had "frightened" Tennyson into writing imperialistic dreck.[70] Osbert was even less forgiving. His Cocteau homage, *Who Killed Cock Robin?* (1921), castrates Tennyson's *Enoch Arden* (1864) into "Eunuch Arden"; his bracing essay on "The Edwardians; The Rich Man's Feast" pillages the "convinced and sanguine patriotism" of Victorian poetry. Associating new modern "comforts" of the phonograph, telephone, and telegram with the Victorian "top-hatted poets" "ravag[ing] the country after the Crimean War," Osbert takes aim at the "respectable" poets writing "anthems" for a "virulent and bigoted revivalism." Osbert's mockery of modern progress, discussed in chapter one ("Can you reverse?"), extends to the Victorian "comfortable classes" marching from "triumph to triumph." For him, Tennyson represented both an impotent "Eunuch" speaking a dead poetic language, and an imperialist ideologue.[71] With the help of telephones and gramophones, the Poet Laureate made his acousmatic presence felt, without visible accountability, in the private home.

In this context, Edith's claims that "rhythm is one of the principal translators between dream and reality," and that it catches us up to the intensified sounds of the metropolis, begin to take on political subtext. In light of Edith's association of the unconscious with Africa and the East, and in light of the Oz-like disembodiment that seemed to presage an inescapable PR regime, the patter of *Façade* evokes both a dream-like Eastern realm and a telegraph from the periphery. Tennyson's meters, too respectable for the context of "En Famille," are at the same time incursions into the chinoiserie: the softly exotic "noise like amber" is punctured by a "nautical 'Blast,'" while the virile thump of the Admiral's verse takes up Tennyson's tremulous charge. Here Tennyson serves as synecdoche both for the public figure of the poet, bullied by a nation into bullying other nations, and for an emergent discourse network of "inextricably link'd" media. *Façade*'s disembodied phoneygraph seems to soften and to parody Tennyson's strident colonial triumphalism (not fair to his entire *oeuvre*, as Edith notes), just as *Façade*'s *execution transcendant* breathes new life into the old Eunuch's ghost.

The Sitwells deconstruct the phoneygraphic voice of Tennyson's authority, and defamiliarize imperial stereotypes. In both efforts, *Parade*—the cosmopolitan anti-Gesamtkunstwerk—comes in handy: a convenient rhyme for *Façade*, another *succès de scandale*, and a self-imploding *mélange* of advertising, publicity, and noise. In devising *Parade*, Cocteau shifted the direction of the Ballets Russes from its luxuriant Bakstian decadence toward a more critical, jagged, and recognizably modern aesthetic; while *Parade* blurs the boundaries between stage and audience, it attempts to do so not by "dazzling" or "intoxicating" its audiences, but by pestering them. And, much as the Admiral's bloviating voice collapses at the end of "En Famille," the megaphone-brandishing Managers in *Parade* collapse under the weight of their own persistent salesmanship. *Façade*, after *Parade*, treats the flat and caricatured imagery of race and nation as little more than a curtain, backdrop to a stylized biomechanical trope-factory.

The *Parade* Behind the *Façade*

Francis Poulenc writes that with *Parade*, "For the first time . . . the music-hall invaded art-with-a-capital-A," precisely the terms in which Marinetti spoke. Like the Futurist Variety Theater and experiments with the Arts of Noise, *Parade* seemed aimed at the destruction of the sublime in art. *Parade*, instead of evaporating tensions among dancers, musicians, and managers, dramatizes them. As Albright argues, *Parade* is a spectacle of dissonance among art forms and between "highbrow" and "lowbrow" genres, in which "the component artistic media seem . . . bent on annihilating one another" (*Untwisting* 203). A self-consciously erratic ballet, *Parade* refuses to maintain an artistic balance of power among Cocteau's scenario, Satie's music, Picasso's set and costume design, and Massine's choreography; the ballet depicts rupture of the very sort Bernays wished to paper over. Yet Lynn Garafola notes *Parade*'s debts to the Futurist enterprise and attributes to Cocteau the creation of "lifestyle modernism," grounded in fashion, entertainment, and popular culture: "Cocteau's true genius lay . . . in the ability to appropriate the ideas of the avant-garde for essentially conservative ends. Purged of radicalism, his sanitized art became the stuff of elite entertainment" (100). This may help make more sense of *Façade*, which is hardly avant-garde in the Russolo or Antheil sense, but which represents a kind of lifestyle modernism playing to a self-consciously stylized social identity.

Reflecting on *Parade*'s urban noise, which has mandated new poetic rhythms, *Façade* ironizes the metaphysical significance of rhythm and dance by making publicity its subject matter. Cocteau developed his ballet first as a modernist imitation of classical theater (an equivalent to a mask in the form of a megaphone), then as an experiment with collage and noise, and finally as an experiment with "awkward" rhythmic movement.[72] *Parade*'s

Managers, who introduce the magicians and circus performers, are annoyed to find that the sideshow acts have become the main attraction—true to the avant-garde spirit of the thing, the raw sensations of public life have overtaken the refined formal unity of art. In an essay on the Ballets Russes, Cocteau observes Nijinsky dancing *Spectre de la Rose* in 1910, suggesting that the real force of the ballet lay not in the "flower-Maidens" onstage but in the offstage physical presence of Vaslav Nijinsky: "Instead of going to see the piece, I went to wait for him in the wings. *There it was really very good*. . . . What a combination of grace and brutality! I shall always hear that thunder of applause; I shall always see that young man, smeared with grease-paint, gasping and sweating, pressing his heart with one hand and holding on with the other to the scenery, or else fainting on a chair."[73] The stylized flower-maidens of the Russian Ballet ("the most maidenly and the most flowery") fail to capture the real stress and strain of Nijinsky's exhausted body. In *Parade*, accordingly, the audience focuses on the advertising parade, where the sweat and energy lie, and refuses to buy tickets for the actual event; the Managers collapse and the troupe departs.

While *Parade* passes on the overwrought spectacle of the ballet for the raw physicality of the sideshow, its curtain and the *image d'Epinal* also show how nonsense produces meaning: how the illusion of depth or meaning can be manufactured through a flat, exotic, but nonsensical play of signifiers. The presence of the Chinese conjuror in the ballet brings to light what Christopher Bush has read as an "ideographic" modernist attitude toward the East, a "thought experiment" in "the primacy of the signifier [that] seemed increasingly to characterize the West's own relation to language" (xxiii). The use of *images d'Epinal*, a technology meant to distribute messages to the illiterate, previewed the emergence of abstract networks of flat signifiers in propaganda or advertising, just the kind of rhythmic aesthetic simulacrum that Lewis feared. The music also features mechanical noises—typewriters, sirens, milk bottles—although not to the extent Cocteau wanted: "Material difficulties," he writes, "deprived us of those 'ear-deceivers'—dynamo, Morse apparatus, sirens, express-train, aeroplane—which I employed with the same object as the 'eye-deceivers'—newspapers, cornices, imitation wood-work." Like the "eye-deceiving" *images d'Epinal*, the noises of the Morse apparatus (et al.) would create an illusion of meaning, a Timbuctoo-like inextricability that implodes into an ear-deceiving nullity. Hence much as Sitwell is considered a figure of mere "publicity," Cocteau takes it on the chin for his "awful vacuity."[74]

The rhythmic noise of the Managers' advertisements, sublimated into their awkward rhythms and physical presence, is matched by the flat visual presence of *images d'Epinal*, compared by Robert Pelfrey and Mary Hall-Pelfrey to "today's comic strips and newspaper cartoons" and to "the appeal of the modern technological state": "cheap, easy to distribute, and clear in their propaganda messages to anyone who could not read."[75] In their modern forms, *images d'Epinal* took on national and "exotic" imperial meanings, influencing the flat woodcut aesthetic of Paul Gauguin's painting at the turn of the century, and undergoing a nationalistic renaissance during World War I.[76] *Parade*'s woodcuts reanimate the trivial, such as *images d'Epinal* and advertising chromolithographs, while defamiliarizing how these forms are mistaken for the products being advertised, how the technology of stereotype (e.g., wood lithography) overwrites the thing or person subjected to stereotype. One finds chromolithographs ("chromo for all, crimm crimms") depicting the Crimean War in the museyroom of *Finnegans Wake* (334.24-25); these images open themselves up to semiotic (or mesostic) reattribution as they circulate flattened-out stereotypes of empire.

In their drives to rethink music as a form of cheap advertisement and rapidly spreading information, and to experiment with what Bush calls the "efficacy of the signifier" that flattens out language into an Orientalist play of surfaces, *Parade* and *Façade* flatten the Wagnerian total artwork onto a two-dimensional surface. The dissonances among *Parade*'s multiple auditory, visual, and textual stimuli refuse to produce a Wagnerian illusion of deep historical time, instead treating theatrical performance like advertising or propaganda: a play of signifiers from which an iconic illusion of truth is produced, unless you are acute enough to recognize its mystifications.

Parade's most conspicuous tie to *Façade*, and its principal flattened-out rendering of spectatorship, lies in Picasso's *commedia*-themed stage-curtain (fig. 5.3), which features two Harlequins, a guitarist, and a muscular Moorish boxer, all sharing the stage with—yet staring at—a circus act featuring a unicorn, a ballerina, and a monkey. Inspired by the *Parade* backdrop, Sitwell wanted Picasso to paint the *Façade* curtain (the cost was prohibitive). Sacheverell, in a preface to a book by Cyril Beaumont, contended that the *Parade* curtain represented the "truest atmosphere ever invented" for the Harlequin figure,[77] and the curtain draws less on the primitivism found, say, in Picasso's *Les Demoiselles d'Avignon* (1907) than on the *commedia* and circus

Figure 5.3. *Parade* Curtain. © 2013 Estate of Pablo Picasso/Artists Rights Society (ARS), New York.

imagery of Picasso's Harlequin paintings (cf. *At the Lapin Agile* [1906]). Yet the image of the Moorish boxer produces racial "otherness" as one of many varieties of theatrical spectacle (the boxer, one will remember, was Sitwell's analogy for the brutish Antheil), in the same way that the first movement of *Parade*, "Le prestadigiteur chinois," associates Asia with lowbrow theatrical illusion. The stage curtain features performers staring at performers: as Martin Green writes, the curtain's "theme is theatricality, the pathos of the artist, who can only speak out . . . in performance, and whose best work . . . will always be neglected for the external and superficial" (*Triumph* 7). The *Façade* curtain, much less elaborate in design, deflects that pathos into the social setting of 2 Carlyle Hall: it exemplifies and celebrates the "external and superficial" setting as long as it is seen with freshly aesthetic eyes—and as long as it is allowed, like Sitwell's Myrrhina or Picasso's Moorish boxer, to scratch or stare back.

Façade, through its visual and literary rhymes to Satie's *scandale du jour* and its Cocteauvian imposition of willful immaturity, forces the audience to see its relation to the stage as constructed by a beautiful form of prestidigitation. "Something Lies Beyond the Scene," a title that gestures playfully at its own stage devices, indulges in a mixture of visual spectacle and racial haberdashery:

> Something lies beyond the scene, the *encre de chine* marine obscene
> Horizon
>   In
>   Hell
> Black as a bison
> See the tall black Aga on the sofa in the alga mope, his
> Bell-rope
> Moustache (clear as a great bell!) (ll.1–8)

The "*encre de chine*" on the flat material surface of the horizon gives way to a black figure "mop[ing]" at the bottom of a Symbolist musical sea—one whose "waves in eighteen-eighty bustles" produce a new parade of Otherness: "ancient dames and shames," producing a kind of exotic flea circus ("Chinese as these black-armoured fleas that dance") that performs "a caprice / To the wind's tambourine." As Gyllian Phillips suggests in her essay "Something Lies beyond the Scene (Seen)," Sitwell's approximation of the Kristevan semiotic troubles "the fixing power of referential meaning" by instead producing a synesthetic rhythmic illusion that appeals to "not only written language but also the performing body and subjectivity" (66). The "not only" is important, however, for the *encre de chine* image suggests that this spectacular racialized illusion has materialized into black ink, flat signifier. It suggests, in other words, that the musical-rhythmic "waves" of exotic figures, like the moping "tall black Aga," have washed over the semiotic curtain of words and the physical curtain itself, as if the color of bodies has been aestheticized into a surface of *encre de chine*. As in 2 Carlyle Square, the sounds of words "shape themselves" into objectified color that proceeds to engulf the drawing room. Just as *Parade* shows us the "behind the scene" of a circus that nobody wants to see, Sitwell's "something . . . beyond the scene" is a capricious simulacrum of empty signifiers. The stereotype of the black body, part of Sitwell's Symbolist unconscious, serves as pretext for a musical-linguistic parade of pointless spectatorship.

And as in *Parade*, spectatorship comes under thematic scrutiny as the text invokes the music hall. In "Tango-Pasodoblé," the poem that (as "I Do Like to Be beside the Seaside") created copyright mischief for Walton, Sitwell seems self-consciously aware of her poetry in relation to the racialized contexts of dance and popular song.[78] In discussing *Façade*, Lynnette Gottlieb draws on Abbate's distinction between phenomenal music (heard *as* music by the character—akin to diegetic music in film) and noumenal music (which exists in a separate and disinterested aesthetic realm). In front of the defamiliarizing curtain, *Façade*'s use of phenomenal music (dance numbers identified as such) awakens its audience to the dance of 1920s Europe:

> WHEN
> Don
> Pasquito arrived at the seaside
> Where the donkey's hide tide brayed, he
> Saw the bandito Jo in a black cape
> Whose slack shape waved like the sea—
> Thetis wrote a treatise noting wheat is silver like the sea; the lovely cheat is sweet as foam;
> Erotis notices that she
> Will
> Steal
> The
> Wheat-king's luggage, like Babel
> Before the League of Nations grew ("Tango-Pasodoblé," lines 1–12)

"Tango-Pasodoblé" demonstrates Sitwell's resistance to rhythmic and sonoric "flaccidity," in the digressive patter on Thetis' treatise and Erotis' notices—introduced by a dash, running through a series of internal rhymes, and closed off by three one-word lines that reestablish the tempo. The bandito Jo tricks Don Pasquito into abandoning his wife, who ends up "plucking a white satin bouquet / Of foam, while the sand's brassy band / Blared in the wind" (lines 33–5), apparently entranced by the dance song. An Anglicized version of tango and pasodoble (not really faithful to either), the poem gestures at both union and disorder among national idioms in its references to Babel and the League of Nations; the sand's noisy "blaring" could mark either a tasteless excess of unity or a cosmopolitan dance of disjointed babble.

This dance borders on camp; Gubar's acknowledgment of the racialized "Boom-lay Boom" music-hall rings true. The song "Black Mrs. Behemoth" begins "In a room of the palace," drawing on a recurring concern about racialized musical performance in private domestic spaces (recall "War-Paint and Feathers," Eliot's acerbic critique of Native American kitsch in the English drawing-room). Mrs. Behemoth leads her "court ladies" threateningly through "palace rooms shady." The opening bars and lines of "Black Mrs. Behemoth" draws on stock primitivist tropes, attempting to imitate unconscious primal rhythms by means of an exaggerated ground-bass (here I use vertical lines to indicate measure breaks, and all-caps to indicate accented beats):

In a | ROOM of the | PALace |
BLACK Mrs. | BEhemoth |
GAVE way to | WROTH
and the | WILDest | MALice. |
CRIED Mrs. Behemoth, |

For all of its kitschiness, the poem's idiomatic shifts bifurcate its content. Once Mrs. Behemoth is given voice, and that voice leaves the room from which it emerges, primitivism halts and gives way to what sounds (and reads) like Debussyian Impressionism matched with Symbolism. The poem maps race onto the landscape—the wind becomes a "bud-furred papoose," drawing on the association of racial otherness with an embodied, sexualized, prelinguistic unconscious—what Griselda Pollock (after Cleo McNelly) calls the "dark lady" trope that permeates Western writing (Baudelaire's in particular).[79] "Black Mrs. Behemoth" takes advantage of Symbolist tropes of the unconscious "primitive," but also defamiliarizes them by juxtaposing them so awkwardly with the thumping Boomlay BOOM downbeat. This dynamic is present in the layout of the performance, in which each poem creates an exotically racialized Symbolist landscape, which is then punctured by a voice through the black mask.

Sitwell's cosmopolitan aesthetic, in these ways, traffics in and stylizes race. "Man from a Far Countree," republished in *The Sleeping Beauty* (1924), gives voice to an exotic figure who imagines himself bleeding into the landscape, exotic background to blonde "pretty lassies." In the published version, the song is sung by a "Soldan" imagining a "soldanesse" to "rule [his] far countree." The performed song does not establish even this much—the voice is given no identity at all—and though a plot is gestured at, the poem-song is more picturesque than narrative:

Rose and Alice,
Oh, the pretty lassies,
With their mouths like a calice,
And their hair a golden palace—
Through my heart like a lovely wind they blow.

At this point, Walton introduces a repetitive seven-note motif, each appearance of which enters on a different beat. As such the musical accompaniment does little to establish a metrical orientation or rhythmic drive, but merely, and quite effectively, establishes atmosphere. As Rose and Alice disappear, the soldan is left talking about himself as a figure in a tableau:

> Though I am black and I am not comely
> Though I am black as the darkest trees
> I have swarms of gold that will fly like honey-bees,
> By the rivers of the sun I will feed my words
> Until they skip like those fleecèd lambs
> The waterfalls, and the rivers (horned rams);
> Then for all my darkness, I shall be
> The peacefulness of a lovely tree
> A tree wherein the golden birds
> Are singing in the darkest branches, O!

As he merges into the landscape, the soldan recognizes his own aestheticization; not only his body but his "words" materialize into birdsong, archived in the vocative monochord, "O!" The soldan becomes a dark unconscious "peacefulness," a scarcely visible mediator "feeding" the *encre de chine* of his words to a white consciousness. Like the barely visible Moor on Picasso's curtain, this poem makes its audience both the subject and the object of a racialized gaze of whose source it is not confident.

Façade thus bifurcates race in ways that one has to think ironic. The curtain itself merges the Greek mask with Pierrot (white), the African mask with Harlequin (black). In the song "Four in the Morning," the "allegro negro cocktail-shaker" has a "navy-blue ghost," and this number ends with a Pierrotesque "flattened face like the moon" that is also "rhinocerous black," both Africanized and Anglicized. These decadently racialized tableaux call on several of the Ballets Russes' contradictory aesthetic commitments: the decadence of Bakst, the Meyerhold-influenced fairground aesthetic of *Petrushka* (designed by Alexander Benois), and *Parade*'s noisy *commedic* cubism. "Four in the Morning" gestures to *Petrushka* musically and literarily—here, too, race is ironically forked. In the ballet, as Petrushka's ghost looks over his own carcass, then that of his puppet-master, Stravinsky invokes a now-famous bitonal passage, in which the same melodic line is played simultaneously in two different keys. In "Four in the Morning," the clarinets copy the notorious C-F# bitonalities that mark Petrushka's death and ghostly presence, as the "allegro-negro cocktail-shaker" confronts his "navy-blue ghost." *Façade* pulls its representations of race in both directions: simultaneously, and dissonantly, a constructivist performance and an artifact of the unconscious. As the characters of *Façade* are moved (inside-out) by a racialized dreamlike presence, they expose (outside-in) its formal shape. In this case, the ghost is "navy-blue," suggesting that the racialized unconscious can just easily be recast as the exotic imperial Englishman.

Façade locates its authority not in mimesis or in authenticity—nor, as Lewis anxiously recognized, in visible accountability—but in an ironized stock of musical and poetic tropes. Matching Bakstian decadence with Cocteauvian detachment, *Façade* refashions the clichés of modern dance music to publicize the ironies of social performance—both insular and imperialistic, trivial and sanctimoniously "respectable"—and to catch it up to the vital sounds of the modern *commedia*. If *Façade*'s cosmopolitan style critiques the insularity of British musical culture, Benjamin Britten and E.M. Forster use music to reflect on Britain's contracting imperial power. Like Sitwell and Walton, Forster and Britten use pacified, aestheticized gestures to noise to show how conventional musical elements, such as consonance, are mapped onto the ideological matrix of nation and sexuality. The "sublime noise" serves as a trope in which ineffable music attempts to give artistic form to unspeakable *rumori*—to the ends of empire and to the love that dare not speak.

6 Aristocracy of the Dissonant

The Sublime Noise of Forster and Britten

> Immediately before the conclusion of the first movement of Beethoven's sonata *Les Adieux*, when in a fleeting, vanishing association over the course of three measures the galloping of horses becomes audible as "meaning," this passage, which is more sublime than words can tell, says that this most transient of things, the ineffable sound of disappearance, holds more hope of return than could ever be disclosed to any reflection on the origin and essence of the form-seeking sound.
>
> Adorno, "On the Contemporary Relationship of Philosophy and Music"

Even before Russolo's *Arte dei Rumori* had undertaken to "*conquer the infinite world of noise-sounds*," the narrator of *Howards End* describes Beethoven's Fifth Symphony as "the most sublime noise ever to penetrate the ear of man" (26). And even before Cecil Barber's "Battle Music," Helen Schlegel imagines Beethoven conquering the noises within his own music in a hypermasculine, synesthetic battle scene: "Gusts of splendor, gods and demigods contending with vast swords, colour and fragrance broadcast on the field of battle, magnificent victory, magnificent death!" (28). For the most part, until his collaboration with Eric Crozier on the libretto of Benjamin Britten's *Billy Budd* (1951), Forster seemed to involve himself only cursorily with new music; but even before then he had an acutely modernist sense of the pressures that music exerted on literary form.

My final chapter accumulates to a reading of *Billy Budd*, arguing that the opera, in very different ways from Melville's novel, employs not dissonance but consonance itself to question the values traditionally accorded consonant harmony: stability, solidarity, identity. While Attali describes the "power of dissonance to destroy the faith of those who believe in harmony" (43), Britten's use of consonance reflects a similar unease about the value and the consensual nature of harmony. I should note a potential slipperiness in Attali's phrasing—any two or more notes sounded together produce "harmony," consonant or otherwise. Indeed, a central thrust of Schoenberg's effort to "emancipate the dissonance" is that one cannot equate harmony with consonance. Britten's musical drama suggests that the musical drive toward consonant resolution is not natural but arbitrary.[1]

Commissioned for the 1951 Festival of Britain that was promoted by the British Arts Council as the "autobiography of a nation," *Billy Budd* articulates questions of national identity with those of sexual identity, exploring the extent to which national solidarity relies on the scapegoating and repression of homoerotic desire. Offering both a Forsterian defense of personal relationships and a general lack of enthusiasm for national solidarity, *Budd* refuses to separate the two entirely. As the opera finally resolves into consonance, it refuses to forget the auspices under which Billy and Vere were introduced in the first place, the regimes of violence and impressment that underpin the consonant choral expressions of Budd's ship, the *Indomitable*.

I approach *Budd* from two directions, Forster's and Britten's, investigating it on its own terms and as a reflection on two careers' worth of thinking about music as an encoding of personal and social subjectivity. Forster's *Howards End* and *A Passage to India* reflect a troubled uncertainty about the opacity of music: expressive but semantically unstable and therefore impractical for social reform. These novels' musical/linguistic ruptures speak to the expansion and fragmentation of empire: anxieties about the failure to "connect" nationally and globally, registered as dissonance and noise. Forster's use of music in *Howards End* uneasily entwines his liberal project with his distaste for empire. Helen's celebration of Beethoven's Fifth as a "magnificent victory," "broadcast" onto a transnational "field of battle," suggests Forster's deep uncertainty not only about "who shall inherit England," as Lionel Trilling put it, but about the expansionist impulses germinated by music; if Russolo's noises try to conquer a new circle of music, Forster's sublime noise (as Helen imagines it) marches in like a Carthaginian army of elephants to replace one empire with another. In *Passage*, the instability of Godbole's "maze of noises," or of the caves' confounding "ou-boum," disturbs the colonial order of the British Empire and un-settles the landscape. Forster and Britten's *Budd*, I suggest, negotiates music's emotional instability and semantic opacity with the consolidating and disciplinary uses to which music is put; the opera both critiques the prohibitive structure of sexuality (figured as consonance), and registers the ineffably dissonant resistance to that structure.

From Britten's end: after a brief phase in his early career in which noise-music techniques informed his more politically conscious film scores, his opera *Peter Grimes* (1945) draws on the longstanding literary villain, rumor, as well as mild forms of dissonance and rhythmic irregularity, to show how social order consolidates around scapegoating and repression. As an addendum to Philip Brett's reading of *Grimes* as an "allegory of homosexual oppression,"[2] I suggest that the opera not only establishes Grimes' internalization of a social order, but reflects how that order rebalances dissonantly around the noises it has repressed. In *Budd*, then, Billy is identified as the "beautiful sailor," and scapegoated by word of mouth (Billy introduces himself as "king of the birds"—a sign that things will not end well for him). In this way Britten's noisy consonances suggest that he has been subjected to a deadly mobilization of order, one that Captain Vere, too, has internalized. If Vere's epilogue suggests a dramatic imperative to articulate this open secret, its melodic echoes of early scenes of choric oppression suggest that his sexuality is a product of external prohibitions. Much as Attali suggests, *Budd* defamiliarizes consonant harmony as a regulation of desire.

Britten, along with Schubert and Tchaikovsky, has become a central protagonist of queer musicology.[3] In particular, Philip Brett's groundbreaking work has called attention to Britten's sexuality, long described only in veiled terms. A cartoon by Kate Charlesworth, reprinted in the important anthology *Queering the Pitch* (1994), illustrates the dilemma well, as it portrays a blushing music appreciation instructor explaining Britten's fifty-year relationship with the tenor Peter Pears (who played Grimes and Vere). "Well," the instructor says, "Benjamin Britten and Peter Pears first *met* when they were quite *young* . . . & as they *got on* quite *well*, they decided to go into *partnership* & *work* together. This lasted *quite* a *long time*. When Lord Britten died, the Queen sent Sir Peter a *telegram* of *sympathy*."[4] Pears's "partnership" with the composer had to be identified as more than a footnote, without being explained in anything other than code. Hence Britten, like Forster, "tapped a peculiar characteristic of British society that allows any kind of social deviance and ambiguity so long as it is not named" ("Musicality" 19). Forster, brought into new light by Wendy Moffat's stunning recent biography, has been troubled by the same difficulty. Known by his contemporaries as a gay man, Forster suspected that "much of his writing would forever . . . remain 'unpublishable,'" at least until a posthumous time when his bildungsroman *Maurice* (1914; pub. 1971) could be openly printed.[5] Forster saved any literary record of his sexuality for the archives, recopying his journals by hand while serving as the BBC's voice of ecumenical liberalism.[6]

If the muddled noise of music registers Forster's anxiety about imperial expansion, at the same time, it can be read as the result of having to write one's way around the unnamable "open secret" of the homoerotic. In his essay "Musicality, Essentialism, and the Closet," Brett draws on Eve Sedgwick's and D.A. Miller's concepts of the "closet" and the "open secret" to articulate what was hidden in plain sight: Britten's operas are driven by the sexuality that they are forbidden to name.[7] Brett shows how Britten's sexuality enabled his creative work and social maneuvering: allowing him "to live openly with Peter Pears," to return to the themes of "homosexual oppression" and "bonding," and to collaborate with Forster, W.H. Auden, and Christopher Isherwood (18-9). All this adds to Britten's ongoing attraction to a canon of queer writers including Rimbaud (*Illuminations* [1939]), James (*Turn of the Screw* [1954], *Owen Wingrave* [1971]), Wilfred Owen (*War Requiem* [1961]), Thomas Mann (*Death in Venice* [1973]), William Plomer (*Curlew River* [1964]), and, some would add, William Shakespeare (*Midsummer Night's Dream* [1960]).

The open secret of Forster's career, his unpublished but privately circulated *Maurice*, uses music to mark the development of Maurice's psychological muddle. I address *Maurice* only tactically, but will make two points here. First, the novel pivots, somewhat schematically, on two performances of Tchaikovsky's *Symphony Pathètique* (1893). The first is a pianola record of the 5/4 "waltz" of the second movement, an embodied dance that is a little off-kilter. Forster later claimed that the image of the pianola record "dates" the novel, but this is to the point: Tchaikovsky's music and name signify in time and place, their meanings changing with each iteration. This scene is matched by Maurice's attendance of a Tchaikovsky concert; when Maurice learns that the composer had fallen in love with his nephew, a Tchaikovsky biography becomes his most prized possession. Tchaikovsky posthumously serves Maurice as a gay icon, musically and biographically.

Second, the novel associates homophobia with English norms of masculinity, and homosexuality with cosmopolitanism. Maurice refers to himself as "an unspeakable of the Oscar Wilde sort," daring not to speak the name of his predicament.[8] And when hypnosis fails to "cure" Maurice he is told to move to France, which has adopted the Code Napoléon.[9] So when the lieutenants of Britten's *Budd* attribute to the French "a word which we scarcely dare speak," they are not referring only to the word "mutiny."[10] British Francophobia and homophobia have been deeply interconnected, since the French Revolution (when Melville's novella takes place), throughout the nineteenth century, and well into the twentieth. As Louis Crompton writes in his study of nineteenth-century British homophobia, "Nowhere did English Francophobia find more impassioned expression than in attitudes towards sex."[11] As Brett notes, musicality in Britain has long been associated with effeminacy; even the word "musical" has served as a euphemism for "gay" ("Musicality" 11). And 1954 review of Britten's *Turn of the Screw* in the Paris *Express* marks the first public mention of Britten in the context of homosexuality.[12] Maurice's and Budd's "musicality" makes them outsiders within a matrix of national definition and sexuality: despite their thoroughgoing Englishness, both characters are suspected of being French.

The open secret creates a formal problem as well, which contributes to the vaunted ambiguity of Britten's operas: he and his librettists are forced to compose around the "unspeakable" love at their center. As Lloyd Whitesell succinctly puts it, "One way to gauge the oddity of Benjamin Britten's operatic output is to scour it for love scenes" (637). Likewise, if the muddle of music in Forster's writing voices an anxiety about imperial expansion, it also reads as the result of writing one's way around an open secret. *Billy Budd* questions the foundations of musical and cultural consonance as it explores the opacity of homoerotic ("musical") representation, and destabilizes national solidarity as it coalesces around a scapegoat. The difficulty of articulating a gay identity, or of understanding one's relation to an unstable national space, motivates Britten's and Forster's search for an effective expression with no pretense to linguistic transparency: a sublime noise.

Written in the 1880s but not published until 1924, Melville's *Billy Budd* was still relatively fresh when Britten, Forster, and Crozier set out to adapt it. The novel looks like a logical step, for Britten, from *Grimes*: self-consciously allegorical, anxious about the force of rumor, and skeptical about the transparency of political and narrative authority. The opera exemplifies, additionally, Forster's skepticism about political stridency and his refusal to "believe in belief,"[13] expressed in his collection (also from 1951) *Two Cheers for Democracy*. This skepticism, Britten's pacifism, and both artists' anxieties about the open secret unfold themselves in consonance and dissonance, rhythm, and noise. Just as Forster describes Claggart's otherwise inexplicable hatred of Billy as a "sexual discharge gone evil," the execution of Billy represents sexual paranoia redirected in the name of national unity.

The relationship between national and sexual identity in the opera has been insufficiently acknowledged, even as the correlate relationship in Melville's novel motivates much of Eve Sedgwick's thinking. Sedgwick argues that the "contagion" (Melville's word) of mutiny corresponds to a "surplus of male-male attachment," and observes that while Billy's respect for military hierarchies remains intact, "it remains for the very last moments of the novella to show whether his ultimate effect . . . will be to trigger actual revolt, or . . . to reconsolidate the more inescapably the hierarchies of discipline and national defense."[14] The same is true in the opera, but the emphasis on consolidation and hierarchy takes on a new thrust in the period of Britain's imperial decline. Jed Esty has argued, in *A Shrinking Island*, that late British modernism represents an inward "anthropological turn," a drive toward communal repair rather than expansion and fragmentation. Trying, Esty argues, to re-create a unified history without falling into the crude public rituals of European fascist states, modernists such as Woolf, Eliot, and Forster began turning the anthropological gaze away from the colonies and back onto its own literary, cultural, and religious past, contracting from a global empire to a "shrinking island." Similarly, Whitesell observes that Britten's explorations of queer partnerships lead him to seek settings "at a remove from familiar surroundings . . . adrift on a 'tiny, floating fragment of earth,' [or] away from home and thrown together with unfamiliar company. In each case, geographic isolation creates the crucible-like conditions of a contained culture in which social bonds can be reforged."[15] Forster's collaboration with Britten offered a new chance to explore and "reforge," in a contained environment, the tensions between personal erotics and national citizenship.[16]

In the cultural imaginary, the Britain of 1951 was itself a "tiny floating fragment of earth," the phrase uttered by John Claggart as he promises to kill the "handsome sailor" (I.iii. 137). As Nathaniel Lew writes, 1951 was a banner year for British music, the year also of Ralph Vaughan Williams's *Pilgrim's Progress* and the opening of the sleekly modern Royal Festival Hall—both initially commissioned, like *Billy Budd*, for the 1951 National Festival of Britain, planned for the centenary of the Great Exhibition at the Crystal Palace.[17] The Festival, including a variety of musical performances, pageant plays, agricultural beautifications, and architectural exhibitions meant to demonstrate Britain's recovery from the devastation of World War II, was largely motivated by "exclusivity"; whereas the 1851 Crystal Palace exhibit strove to demonstrate Britain's broad imperial reach, the Festival worked to produce an exclusively British ethos that forswore internal class divisions and external expansionist impulses. "The insularity" of the Festival "echoed the anti-imperial and isolated philosophy of Clement Attlee's Labour Party," modeling a "triumph of . . . central state planning and earnest public education" (Lew 231). The Festival was thus subjected to the contumely of both the radical left and the cultural elite, which (respectively) found its politics milquetoast and its artistic tastes middlebrow. As shrunken as this island may have seemed, Britten wished to shrink it further by producing an all-male opera on an "intimate" scale, one that re-expanded once the actual writing got underway. A number of financial, logistical, and artistic snags kept the opera from being produced during the Festival proper; just as well, perhaps, given the opera's anxiety, marked by disruptive noisy consonances, about nationalism of any kind. Lew elaborates several political readings of *Budd* as a Cold War allegory, anxious both about the loss of the "rights of man" (the name of the ship to which Billy fatally says "Farewell"), and about the threat of war, which "invad[e]s and distort[s] the actions of every character, . . . and engender[s] the brutality of naval discipline" (576).

What Lew admits to understating, in his remarkable study of the institutional and national politics of Britain's and Britten's operas, is the matrix between nationality and sexuality. *Budd* is marked by the moral contamination of military order, which makes good men (Vere) do evil (execute Billy) in the name of martial law. This order is cross-fertilized with anxiety about queer sexuality as it too is subjected to a repressive structure; the fear among the officers that they have been contaminated by "hoppity-skippity ways" elliptically contaminates the male-male bond, whether one reads that bond as an ineffable purity or as a love that cannot be named.

Britten himself would scarcely be associated with Antheil, Varèse, and the like, although he dabbled in noise-music in his early propaganda film scores. Yet his operas reflect an abiding consciousness of music as an ordering of *rumori*, in a way that illustrates the social construction of queer identity. For Attali, music not only reflects but predicts shifts in political economy, "explor[ing] . . . the entire range of possibilities in a given code" and making "audible the new world . . . that will impose itself and regulate the order of things" (11). Music functions as a shifting regulating order, into which "noise," as sonic artifact and as cultural category, is assimilated. Britten's music, whose most consonant moments are often the most terrifying, illustrates just such a consolidation, always (as in Eliot) with a glitch or a stammer: as the "code" and the "order" of things finds a new shape, it exposes the crack in its own façade. In *No Future*, a polemical attack on reproduction- and future-oriented ethics (one that pertains to Britten's killing off of his child characters), Lee Edelman argues that "Queerness . . . is never a matter of being or becoming but, rather, of embodying the remainder of the Real internal to the Symbolic order": not an identity question, in other words, but a way of giving embodied and syntactic form to the excess of *jouissance* (and its better half, the death drive), unnamable desire constantly and resistantly undergoing entry into representation.[18] If one substituted the word "noise" for the word "queerness" in Edelman's claim, I believe one would not have strayed far. The static of unnamable desire permeates *Billy Budd*, particularly at those moments of frictive consonance where music struggles to give this desire representation—where, like Beethoven's "form-seeking sound," the unrepresentable and evanescent are pulled kicking and screaming into a musical code.

Hence the reading of Britten's opera as the allegory of an oppressed homosexual versus "society," and the reading of it as a pacifist allegory about state power, require mutual complication. Britten's blend of rhythmic glitches and mildly dissonant bitonality produces a matrix of national and heteronormative chauvinism: music and language, rumor and rhythm, construct and trouble these categories of sexuality and nation. Britten unfolds a "public," in Michael Warner's sense of the word, as a "social space created by the reflexive circulation of discourse"—a circulation with distinct moments and rhythms that not only describe but create a shared world.[19] As Victoria Joyce Moon's queer reading of Attali contends, *Noise* envisions "composing" not just as aesthetic production but also, as in Sitwell, as the active "composing [of] one's own life."[20] On a larger scale, the public of strangers known as a nation comprises an "imagined community" not just as we picture others with a shared interest, but as we imagine the "inherently limited and sovereign" boundaries of such a community according to the rhythms of daily life and the "ghostly intimation of simultaneity."[21] These limits, as Arjun Appadurai argues, are further destabilized by the "new media order," an ad hoc production of communities in response to a sense of rootless displacement. Michael North argues that Appadurai's attention to late-twentieth-century globalization of both capital and media can be traced back much farther, to the global telegraph cable and the "first modern media network": the BBC (*Reading* 18–9).

While *Howards End*, written in the nascent stages of the radio era, cannot exactly be said to produce what Appadurai calls a "mediascape"—a globalized melomap of "images of the world" through shared "narrative-based" media clusters—Forster does associate music, broadcast over the battlefield, with an effort to map one's place in the global village. And Britten, whose tender melodic imagination is dotted with shanties and anthems of threatening choric solidarity—akin to what Benedict Anderson terms the "unisonance" that "connects us all" (145)—signifies, with his bitonal almost-resolutions, the possibility of an imagined queer community, a shrinking island of counterpublics. Britten has nothing of the activism of Warner's essay "Something Queer about the Nation-State," but his work does suggest similarly that liberal democracy entails "fundamental contradictions on the subject of the abnormal," which produce it as a site of difference and scapegoating, while accommodating it "as the ground of expressive individuality" (218). Through this theoretical "maze of noises," intended to theorize sexuality in Britten and Forster and to approximate their opaque mediations of "musical" subjectivity, I want to suggest their shared interest in aestheticizing the very sounds that discipline their subjects as they produce what might be called a sublime noise. But not without a recognition of the "fundamental contradictions on the subject." The prohibition at the end of *Passage*, for example, in which the "hundred voices" of the landscape forestall the final resolution between Fielding (British) and Aziz (Indian) in a dissonant "half kissing," suspends the unisonance between Fielding's jeering sarcasm about Indian autonomy and Aziz's "awful rage" against the Raj (362).

Democracy deserves two cheers, says Forster in his essay "What I Believe," because it can accommodate diversity; but not three, because only Love the Beloved Republic is capable of real unisonance. "Diversity" of views, in Forster's liberal sense, is impossible in a landscape marked by the reduction of sense to an empty echo: an "ou-boum" that collapses semiotic dissonance/difference. What is therefore needed is not the linguistic sign, but a sublime noise—a complex musical idiom in which counterpublics can map out resistant relations to the prohibitions that inscribe them, down to the prohibitions of harmony itself.

"A Muddle and a Noise": "Broadcasting" Music in Forster

The title of Forster's collection *Two Cheers for Democracy* is taken from its still-resonant central essay, "What I Believe," originally published in 1939 (in the New York *Nation*). Most famous for its statements on personal loyalty, which could easily serve as glosses on *Billy Budd*, the essay asserts, "if I had to choose between betraying my friend and betraying my country, I hope I should have the guts to betray my country" (70). The essay claims that democracy deserves two cheers—one for its tendency toward diversity, a second for its willingness to permit criticism—but refuses to offer a third cheer: "Only Love the Beloved Republic deserves that" (70). *Billy Budd*'s final resolution into B-flat major, as Vere pronounces himself redeemed, illustrates his entry into this beloved republic, as opposed to the republic that has already compelled him to "betra[y] his friend."

Although Forster had written the essay twelve years earlier, its place in *Two Cheers* is important, not least because the book and the opera appeared in such close proximity; the collection, not just the discrete essays, reveals much in Forster's thinking in the early 1950s. Forster calls "What I Believe" the "key" to *Two Cheers* because the essay introduces a section of the book devoted to criticism of the arts. "I have," he writes, "found that the arts act as an antidote against our present troubles and also as a support to our common humanity, and I am glad to emphasise this at a time when they are being belittled and starved" ("Preface" xi). While *Two Cheers* resists assertive political engagement, it claims a "common humanity" legible in art; as such it represents a defense of what we now term the New Criticism. The essay that follows "What I Believe," entitled "Anonymity: An Enquiry" (1925), brushes aside authorial intention in Paterian language: "all literature tends towards a condition of anonymity, and . . . so far as words are creative, a signature merely detracts us from their true significance" (82). True to form, the next essay is entitled "Art for Art's Sake" (1939). In promoting the musical arts, Forster desires to escape from politics and find an antidote for "the noise of the conflict" ahead ("Gerald Heard" [1939], *TC* 25). The book's brief entry into music criticism helps Forster to situate aesthetics with respect to other manifestations of culture, while granting music a space independent of politics.

Within that space, Forster admits the instability of musical interpretation. After a strange tribute to C minor, the key of Beethoven's Fifth ("The C Minor of that Life" [1941]), Forster's essay "Not Listening to Music" frankly admits that "Listening to music is such a muddle that one scarcely knows how to start describing it" (127). For Forster, music was a muddle and a noise: its resistance to description made it a conveyor of multiple meanings, and thereby marked its limitations (for better or worse) for active political engagement. Michelle Fillion argues that "music allowed Forster to transcend the precision of the word and, in his most visionary moments of 'difficult rhythm,' to open the novel to the timeless and the ineffable."[22] "Difficult rhythm," a phrase borrowed from the essay "From the Audience" (1945), represents the moment "when a composition extending through time is suddenly apprehended as a whole" (shades of Dedalus); as Forster imbricates music with class, nation, and sexuality, he offers "a mysterious song of uncertainty beyond the final words of each novel" that keeps it from allegorically hardening (Fillion xviii).

The ineffability of music—its resistance to description, and its disruptive relation to the noisy political melomap—makes it both productively critical and frustratingly inapt for Forster's liberal impulses. Pursuant both to his totalizing "connecting" impulse, and to his deep-seated uncertainty about almost everything, Forster's interest in music speaks directly to the material, yet wavering and tinder, responses of the body. Music in Forster, indeed, "opens the novel" not just to the timeless and ineffable but to a material sedimentation of the "ineffable" in novelistic form—a sublime-ation of noise that recalls music's embodied appeals.

The Beethoven's Fifth passage from *Howards End* merits attention both because of what it suggests about musical interpretation and because of its careful stylistic manipulations. Though Forster's essay on "Art for Art's Sake" proclaims "works of art to be the only objects in the material universe to possess internal order" (95), *Howards End* reveals the value of the artwork's "internal order," what Forster calls its "true significance," to lie in modes of reception and interpretation. The ability of Beethoven's Fifth to "satisf[y] all sorts and conditions" relies on socially emplaced interpretants. The first and most obvious point, then, is that the Fifth is a "noise" precisely because it broadcasts several contradictory meanings at once, rather than a discriminate signal. It therefore requires a mediator, the narrator, to organize its competing resonances—a conductor, as in Eliot, to develop its atomistic motifs coherently:

> It will be generally admitted that Beethoven's Fifth Symphony is the most sublime noise that has ever penetrated into the ear of man. All sorts and conditions are satisfied by it. Whether you are like Mrs. Munt, and tap surreptitiously when the tunes come—of course, not so as to disturb the others; or like Helen, who can see heroes and shipwrecks in the music's flood; or like Margaret, who can only see the music; or like Tibby, who is profoundly versed in counterpoint, and holds the full score open on his knee; or like their cousin, Fräulein Mosebach,

> who remembers all the time that Beethoven is "echt Deutsch"; or like Fräulein Mosebach's young man, who can remember nothing but Fräulein Mosebach; in any case, the passion of your life becomes more vivid, and you are bound to admit that such a noise is cheap at two shillings. (26)

Adorno's writing on hearing Beethoven over the radio may be pertinent: though incapable of the mass-educative potential people ascribe to it (or capable only of very ugly mass education), the radio opens up an interpretive space that could (though probably won't) liberate music from the concert hall and open it up to more active concentration. We don't have radio here, but we do have competing modes of distracted and engaged esthesis; some able to "see the music" as it unfolds; some tapping along (*pace* Adorno) when the atomized "tune" floats by; others distracted (*pace* Adorno again) by the atmosphere of the concert hall. For some, the noise is cheap because the sublime music is more than worth it; for others, the "cheap noise" of frivolous "passion" and clever-sounding shibboleths (*echt Deutsch*) is exactly what has been paid for.

Peter Kivy uses this Forster passage to signpost his inquiry into the "purely musical experience"; for him, Helen, Margaret, and Tibby represent competing hypotheses as to how we interpret music. Kivy sides with Margaret: the purely cognitive experience of "music alone," independent of the programs that a Helen might attach to it, best explains the force of music. Tibby, who likes to hear women singing Brahms, accrues conspicuous social capital as he teaches his friends what to listen for. Helen's fantasy, mediated through Forster's continually refocalizing narrator, projects a *Götterdämmerung* in which the "flaming ramparts of the world" (28) threaten to collapse into a "flood," bringing Tibby's "well-versed" expertise down to earth and washing away Margaret's Hanslick-like ability to "see only the music."[23] If Kivy waxes absolutist about the purely somatic impact of music, Forster seems less sure. Indeed, there is something problematic about the use of such a literary example in defense of music alone: as Kivy articulates the effects of music on the earhole, he seems implicitly to grant that sound acquires new meaning as soon as one person describes it to another (the very fact that enables Nattiez's semiotic readings, and that catalyzes what I have called the Antheil dilemma).

Thus while Forster's treatment of Helen in chapter five is arch, it is not dismissive. If Helen's interpretations seem nonsensical, they are driven by real psychological and cultural imperatives. She mixes imagery of the gothic (goblins), of imperial fantasy ("a trio of elephants dancing"), and, finally, of the authority of the composer himself: having let the goblins run amok, Beethoven "appeared in person" and "made them do what he wanted" (28). With "colour and fragrance broadcast on the field of battle," Beethoven achieves "magnificent victory" over seeds of doubt that he himself has broadcast in the music. The noises of "Panic and emptiness," which Helen hears in the "terrible, ominous" music are no less Beethoven's than is the "tangible statement" of their defeat (28). As Forster tells us two chapters later, the claim that "England and Germany are bound to fight" becomes—is made—more true every time the "gutter press of either nation" repeats it (52); the same could be said of the obsessively repetitive Fifth Symphony, whose battle "noises" can by no means be pacified simply by ending in sublime cadence.

Though Forster and Helen marvel at the creative interpretations enabled by music, they betray an anxiety about music's narratives of expansion. Fredric Jameson uses *Howards End* to exemplify the modernist drive to contain the economies of empire through style; noting Forster's anti-imperial politic, he correlates Forster's "stylistic [and] linguistic peculiarities" with the fracturing of metropolitan place and time. The disorienting fragmentation of modernist writing, Jameson argues, can be traced to the displacement of economic production "beyond the metropolis" and "outside of daily life."[24] Can the same be said of Forster's description of Beethoven's Fifth? Margaret's formal reception of Kivy's "purely musical experience" is underwritten by the narrative offered by Helen: Beethoven's ability to broadcast meanings (i.e., to mediate them) is of a piece with his ability to disseminate the seeds of colonial power.

Helen's use of the term "broadcast" is imperially suggestive. Yet she is taken most by how Beethoven attenuates his "magnificent victory," planting seeds of doubt within the music:

> And the goblins—they had not really been there at all? They were only the phantoms of cowardice and unbelief? One healthy human impulse would dispel them? Men like the Wilcoxes, or President Roosevelt, would say yes. Beethoven knew better. The goblins really had been there. They might return—and they did. . . . Beethoven chose to make all right in the end. . . . But the goblins were there. They could return. He said so bravely, and that is why one can trust Beethoven when he says other things. (28)

Ultimately, Helen hears the Fifth as an act of suasion: an attempt to win over his audience's trust. It is not the symphony's argument, but its willingness to *qualify* that argument, that makes it a persuasive "tangible statement." She recognizes that the symphony's resolution is not a requirement but a tentative poietic choice ("Beethoven chose to make it all right in the end").

Helen is eager to be persuaded, and actively feeds her own interpretations back into the music; where Leonard Bast can't piece the music together without a musical program, Helen creates her own. Helen and Bast are joined by the need to connect music to a narrative; only Helen has the wherewithal to put together a narrative that has any traction. Helen's fantasy is costly, not "cheap." One might note the reference to Roosevelt, for whom the Forsterian impulse to "connect" was often tied to the urge to annex, and on a more narrative level, Helen's desperation to project an authoritative Romantic ideal onto the music resonates with her eagerness to project a similar ideal onto Bast. Beethoven catalyzes the meeting and, ultimately, the procreation between the two, both of them too preoccupied with what the music "means" to keep track of their umbrellas. Helen is so taken with her peculiar fantasy that she runs off with Bast's parasol; in turn, Bast is so distracted by the loss of his umbrella that he finds himself unable to make sense of the proper names of culture: "he might even have heard of Monet and Debussy; the trouble was that he could not string them into a sentence, he could not make them 'tell,' he could not quite forget about his stolen umbrella" (33). As the memory of the umbrella "persist[s], with the steady beat of a drum" (33), Bast's anxiety about his finances and his insecurity about conversing on culture (or pronouncing *Tannhäuser*) make him unable to string names together into a sentence (38), to find a syntactic shape for his muddled reading. As ever, music's lack of transparent meaning compels its auditors to do what they will with its sounds.

The Beethoven set piece exemplifies a modernist focus on the stylistic tropes that might evoke or "broadcast" musical meaning. The passage begins roughly in the rhythm of Beethoven's Fifth, with three short notes and a long elaboration—"It will be generallyadmittedthat . . . ," a pattern that introduces a sequence of stylistic and rhetorical gestures. Like the novel as a whole, which begins with awkwardly casual narratorial offhandedness ("One may as well begin with Helen's letters to her sister"), chapter five begins with an impersonal assertion that speedily moves into a personal one. The opening phrase, "It will be generally admitted," predicts a modest claim but introduces a big one; no such thing would ever be generally admitted, even were it true, but the narrator offers the magisterial upbeat to give false unity and impersonal objectivity to these competing signals.

By the novel's end, the problem of abstraction has taken on a political resonance: in Helen's confrontation with Henry Wilcox, she assails (with the narrator's help) his "complacent" emphasis on the "great impersonal forces" responsible for shaping civilization (155), at the expense of the individual (Bast). In chapter five, the movement from this impersonal expression to more personal ones, to the specific tactics of interpretation associated with Helen and Margaret and Tibby, is couched in a sneaky rhetorical shift into the generic second-person voice ("Whether you are like Mrs. Munt"). The second-person voice offers an affectation of personal contact, but its function is to abstract interpretants rather than to humanize them. The shift turns the Schlegels into more general case studies in "all sorts and conditions" of musical interpretation, just as the Wilcoxes eventually become synecdoches for those who will "inherit the earth" (185). Margaret, for example, reveals herself as an anti-Wagnerian, scornful of the "muddling of arts": "Every now and then in history there do come these terrible geniuses, like Wagner, who stir up all the wells of thought at once. For a moment it's splendid. Such a splash as never was. But afterwards—such a lot of mud; and the wells—as it were, they communicate with each other too easily now, and not one of them will run quite clear. That's what Wagner's done" (33). Margaret describes Wagner as an interference among signals: his attempt to make the languages of painting and music "interchangeable" (32) results not in a universal musical language but in a muddle, akin to Pound's assault on the grinding *Schwärmerei* of Wagner and Debussy. The "noise" of Beethoven's Fifth creates an interpretive muddle that lies in the conflict between its actual sounds unfolding in real time, and the "painted" imagery ascribed to its Romantic German provenance—the Beethoven passage at once abstracts and universalizes its auditors, and muddles the broader social "connection" that it is supposed to catalyze.

And in chapter five, too, Helen's synesthetic fantasy of mythic and aesthetic struggle is Wagnerian to the core: "gods and demi-gods contending with vast swords, colour and fragrance broadcast on the field of battle." *Howards End* refuses, however, Wagner's Schopenhauerian teleology of the Will. With hints of Sitwell's puppeteering ancestors, *Howards End* pokes fun at Helen's willingness to make human behavior a Punch doll for the puppet-master of the subconscious, claiming this to be no less cold and abstract than Henry Wilcox's sermons on the "great impersonal forces" of history. Noting that Wilcox's "voice grew complacent; it always did when he eliminated the personal" (155), the narrator casts doubt on the tendency to abstract the forces of history from their specific participants. No doubt this has an aesthetic impact on the novelistic form: what Forster identifies as "rhythm," or the immanent emergence of motifs, offers the novel a musical quality to forestall the abstracting and rigid principles of "pattern."

According to the OED, the word "broadcast" was not used to refer to radio transmissions until the early 1920s. It may be a mere coincidence that 1910, the year of *Howards End*'s publication, also marked the first daily radio broadcasts and the first wireless broadcast of opera (Enrico Caruso). Anxieties about technological broadcasting, such as Adorno's fear that the radio would soften the Fifth's immanently developed existential depth, are only retroactively in play with Helen's reveries. Still, Forster shares in Adorno's curiosity about the Fifth's formal sublimity in relation to its cultural mediation, signaled by that suggestive word. As Debra Rae Cohen, Michael Coyle, and Jane Lewty point out in their introduction to *Broadcasting Modernism* (2009), the term "encompasses all technologies, including the written word," producing textuality—aural or written—"as a transgressive signal, circulating at random beyond its original context."[25] Particularly before the radio, "broadcast" widely referred to the dissemination of knowledge and culture—retaining the agricultural overtones of the word "culture." A 1909 essay by J.A. Hobson suggests that the Liberal promise of "national culture" lies in "sowing knowledge broadcast in the common mind, to ripen afterwards in industrial efficiency."[26] The ambivalence in *Howards End* with respect to "sowing knowledge broadcast" unfolds as the sounds of Beethoven reappear in Bast's final reflections, before books are broadcast over and onto his head. Bast dies from a fatal arrhythmia while a sword is brandished at him: an image that, doubling Bast's umbrella with something edgier, recapitulates Beethoven's battle with the goblins, and reprises Nothung as well.

Thus, finally, the word "broadcast"—about a German composer battling with the Gothic—recalls anxieties about national expansion: about who shall inherit the earth. As in Wagner, the more one returns to nature, the more one is confronted by technology and conflict. Like the twilight of the gods in *Götterdämmerung*, the "end" of *Howards End* takes us back to the soil. The novel's somewhat emetic close, in which Helen takes Bast's and her love child back to the "big meadow," recognizes that their choice (and Forster's choice) "to make it all right in the end" by reclaiming the pastoral landscape remains fraught with instability. The child, who will inherit Howards End upon Margaret's death, will inherit also what Paul Wilcox (who's been off in Africa) refers to as the "picaninnies" on the establishment—a lingering trace of empire, filtered through Paul's husky uncouth racism, that threatens Margaret's and Helen's pastoral escape-hatch.

These colonial figures suggest that the conflicts of Beethoven's field have been broadcast over Howards End, and over *Howards End*. In chapter four, as Margaret's father expounds on the fate of Germany, he attributes the death of its poetry, philosophy, and music to "bigness," to a "Pan-Germanism" no better than British "Imperialism" (24). But Helen and Margaret find the intense formal development of Beethoven's Fifth, more than the "learned" Elgar, capable of broadcasting a musical narrative, whether as music alone or as battle music. As I discuss in my own chapter five, the ambivalence about British music bore one path toward provincial pastoralism, one toward cosmopolitanism. Of Elgar's First Symphony, Britten would later say, "only in Imperialistic England could such a work be tolerated" (Carpenter 70). In Forster, Elgar is associated with idle nationalism—not with the (potentially fatal) Pan-German bigness, nor the (potentially limiting) sense of musical detail, that keep Helen and Tibby attentive. Mrs. Munt, who "surreptitiously taps" along to Beethoven, chastises Margaret, "you mustn't run down our English composers" (30), but Englishness seems Elgar's only real virtue.[27]

Beethoven, unlike Elgar, seems for Forster's characters to engender the tension between an all-encompassing utopian bigness and a minute development of form. Modern music seemed, to Forster, to dilate this tension. Forster's interest in modernist music was sporadic; it may be that Britten's pacifism, Englishness, mildly dissonant diatonic idiom, and openly secret sexuality offered him a point of entry into the modernist musical scene.[28] Yet while Forster admits his difficulties with modern music, he acknowledges that what he hears as defects in a composition are integral to it: "A piece of contemporary music, to my ear, has a good many sudden deaths in it; the phrases expire as rapidly as the characters in my novel, the chords cut each other's throats, the arpeggio has a heart attack, the fugue gets into a nose-dive. But these defects—if defects they be—are vital to the general conception" (*TC* 121).[29] Even Beethoven's "magnificent victory" in the Fifth is balanced with a "magnificent death"—like the one that Adorno hears in the *Adieux* sonata as a "galloping" disappearance of meaning that carries a utopian promise of return. Forster's self-deprecating reference to the "sudden deaths" may refer also to his insouciantly killing off characters in *Where Angels Fear to Tread* and *Room with a View* (related, P.N. Furbank argues, to his boredom with heterosexual marriage plots [vol. 2, 132])—deaths in both cases associated with Beethoven. The treatment of Bast's heart attack, in recapitulating the Beethoven passage, recalls the defects that Beethoven stills without permanently solving: "Again and again must the drums tap, and the goblins stalk over the universe before joy can be purged of the superficial" (ch. 41). Leonard's plucky "conviction of innate goodness" and noumenal "joy" are threatened by the tapping drums and stalking goblins up until his own heartbeat gives out.

The disjunctive treatment of major characters' deaths in *Howards End* and *Passage* give bodily form to sonic "sudden deaths"—Beethoven's sublime noise, *Passage*'s echoing caves—that disrupt narrative shape. At the same time they convey the costs of noises, sublime (Beethoven) or mundane (telegrams, letters, bad investment advice), that are broadcast too profusely. In this way, Forster's writing offers an Adornian understanding of the defects and ruptures that assert themselves as vital to the structure of modern music; and, like Adorno, acknowledges the body as the site of this response. In "What I Believe," Forster posits an "aristocracy of the sensitive, the considerate and the plucky" (coincidentally, an ASCAP) to counterbalance the noxious influence of "Great Men," suggesting that such aristocrats should make themselves immune to political organization by embracing their own bodies: "I do not feel that my aristocrats are a real aristocracy if they thwart their bodies, since bodies are the instruments through which we register and enjoy the world" (73-4). Ultimately Forster emphasizes how his body facilitates an aristocracy of sympathy rather than of partisan allegiance: "Naked I came into the world, naked I shall go out of it! And a very good thing too, for it reminds me that I am naked under my shirt, whatever its colour" (76).

Forster's earlier writings on music and dance suggest that he was particularly sensitive to the possibilities of the ballet for this recuperation of aesthetic bodily experience. In a diary entry marking the Ballet's 1913 visit to the Covent Garden Royal Opera House, featuring Diaghilev productions of ballet and opera, Forster says little about the music itself, but recounts his awe at Leon Bakst's set designs and, not least, at the sight of Vaslav Nijinsky:

> Ballet—Nijinsky naked in *L'apres-midi d'un Faune*—a humorous and alarming animal, free from the sentimentality of my stories. . . . *Le sacre du printemps* and *Prince Igor* threw me into an intoxication greater than my youth's, so that I wanted to miss my train and have adventures all night. Yet at the back of it I watched

> myself which I did not [illegible]. There was a great deal to watch—mind on fire and body tinder—but the unwinking eye remained.[30]

Diaghilev's productions in London in the early 1910s shook up the British art scene. Performances of Debussy's *L'apres-midi* (likely the source of Stephen's "fitful" whole-tone fantasy), featuring Nijinsky's leotarded simulations of masturbation, elicited understandable shock. As Modris Eksteins explains, the 1911 Ballets Russes performance at George V's coronation, before an audience of "ambassadors and ministers, African kings, Indian chiefs, maharajahs and mandarins, and the cream of British society," led to the installation of a dance company in London, leading Diaghilev to proclaim that the Russian Ballet had "conquered the whole world" (26). Like both Diaghilev and Wagner, *Howards End* contemplates what sort of music will take over the world, while at the same time thinking about "another type" of person, "whom Nature favours—the Imperial. Healthy, ever in motion, it hopes to inherit the earth" (323). The movement of this "Imperial" type, as Jameson argues, accounts for the stylistic ruptures of *Howards End*, as empire exceeds the characters' purview and fragments perception; inversely, the echoes of *A Passage to India* reflect and broadcast the muddle at the heart of the metropole.

Ou-boum

Recalling Edmund Carpenter's and Marshall McLuhan's suggestion that the ears are "all encompassing," we can intuit why, for Forster, the body is so susceptible to resonance in Abbate's material and ideational senses. It is precisely because sound is so totalizing that *Howards End* immerses Helen in music's inescapable resonances; likewise, as *A Passage to India* subjects its Anglo-Indians to sonic muddles and musical sudden deaths, the hostile sound and soil seem to wash over them, physically and intellectually. Beethoven's Fifth itself is a series of intratextual echoes: maniacal repetitions and developments, from the inescapable four-note motif of the first movement to its oppressive goblinesque distortion in the third movement, and the constant triplet-plus-one figures (da-da-da-DUM) that permeate the finale. This is why, for Adorno, Beethoven is the great dialectician, his forms reinventing themselves in real time even as they try to accommodate a utopian, Schlegel- and-Schiller-like vision of unified brotherhood (whereas Brahms, Hanslick's consummate formalist, seemed to Adorno to lack that utopianism).

The "sudden" casualty in *Passage* is Mrs. Moore, who has been driven out of India by the echoes of the Marabar Caves and by her disgust with Adela Quested's false accusation that Aziz has raped her. (The Indian guide who leads her to the cave—an alternate accused—instructs her that "to shout is useless, because a Marabar Cave can hear no sound but its own" [171], a statement that primes Adela's panic about both her physical safety and her coherent subjectivity.) Mrs. Moore's death, too, derives from both symbolic and physical pressures of noise: not unlike Eliot, Mrs. Moore imagines that the Marabar Caves have collapsed all Western experience into the "far distant" "ou-boum" of an echo. This echo resonates and spreads as its disembodied presence seems to spread over her body: "the echo flourished, raging up and down like a nerve in the faculty of her hearing, and the noise in the cave, so unimportant intellectually, was prolonged over the surface of her life" (215). The Marabar Caves "[r]obbed infinity and eternity of their vastness" (an echo of the train in *Howards End*, which "rob[s]" the journey of "half its magic" [169]), making the land inassimilable to the mind and to the sensorium by reducing its sounds to indistinction. Mrs. Moore's faith in the infinite, and the somatic "surface" that marks the boundary between herself and the hostile soil of India, are both at the disposal of this echo, which jars her nerves and "miserable body" (*PI* 223).

Mrs. Moore's silencing is effected by an obvious plot contrivance: she dies on the High Seas, on her way back to England, and is buried in the Indian Ocean.[31] The Indians *within the novel* recognize it as a plot contrivance, a desperation to send off characters who might unsettle the narrative: they resent Mrs. Moore's absence at Aziz's trial, claiming that the one Briton sympathetic to the Indian plight has been silenced and shipped away. In these ways, *Passage* suggests a dialectical relation between noise and, on the other hand, the interpretation of noise through narrative or diegetic means. Mrs. Moore's name comes to stand in for the kinds of noise that Aziz's accusers can't live with and the subaltern can't live without: Mrs. Moore's symbolic force lies in her willingness to identify with specific Indian human beings and with the general "muddle" of India. But this, too, is an enabling fiction, notwithstanding Aziz's assertion that Mrs. Moore is an "Oriental" (21). Mrs. Moore has struggled with the echoes as much as anyone, and conversely, the colonized subjects in the novel are driven to reinterpret events beyond their purview.

"Muddle" is among Forster's favorite words: a key term of *Maurice*, where it intimates sexual confusion, and an even greater presence in *Pas-*

sage, where it seems the only term capable of describing India under the Raj. As Fielding leaves India and arrives in Venice, he finds a "harmony between the works of man and the earth that upholds them, the civilization that has escaped muddle." In Fielding we see a tension between Forster's own Paterian view of art, symbolized by Venetian beauty, and the productive, frictive incongruity between art and nature, which (as for Eliot) produces the muddle of British India.

But as Forster writes in his essay "London is a Muddle" (1932), citing the "O City City" passage from *The Waste Land*, "the muddle of London . . . need not be unpleasant" (*TC* 357). It appears that Forster also did not find the "muddle" of Indian music entirely "unpleasant," nor easy to distinguish from noise. In a 1921 letter written during his second visit to Dewas, Forster recounts an Indian celebration of a childbirth, a passage that resembles the Hindu birth of the god in *A Passage*:

> It began with fireworks and a discharge of rifles from the entire army in batches: then drums, trumpets, stringed instruments and singing. . . . The military band moaned Western melodies. . . . I am as far as ever from understanding Indian singing, but I have no doubt that I was listening to great art, it was so complicated and yet so passionate. The singer (man) and the drummer were of almost equal importance and wove round the chord of C . . . it was like Western music reflected in trembling water, and it continued in a single burst for half an hour.[32]

Forster hears in the music of colonized India an uneasy "reflection" of Western music (which, to Forster, is already erotically indeterminate), winding constellationally around one chord as it reflects and distorts the colonizer's harmonic order. Forster reiterates this experience in the last section of *Passage*, which depicts the celebration of a Hindu god being born. As if Helen's imagined "colour and fragrance" and sound were being "broadcast" over the landscape of India, *Passage* offers a synesthetic noise of sonic and visual confusion. The pillars of the temple "could scarcely be seen behind colored rags, iridescent balls, chandeliers of opaque pink glass, and murky photographs framed crookedly" (318), evoking a national confusion as well: "Noise, noise, the Europeanized band louder, incense on the altar, sweat, the blaze of lights" (319).

As I suggested in chapter one, the major crises of *Passage* are characterized by sonic confusion, an uncertainty about the limits of language's broadcast range. We hear, just to name a few examples, Professor Godbole's confounding sung "maze of noises" (77); Mrs. Moore's posthumous transmutation into an Indian goddess ("Esmiss esmoor," 251); Fielding's students reciting a poem in his honor after the trial, "the noise of which filled the lane with a crowd" (259); the Hindu festival in the final section, with the ensuing "tornado of noise" accompanying the Anglo-Indians' tumble into the water (354); and the echoes of the Marabar Caves, which addle Adela and kill off Mrs. Moore. Adela experiences these echoes as a sonic violation of her body, and is awoken from her stupor by the repeated "travestied" repetition of Mrs. Moore's name (250).

Sonically and etymologically linked to "mud," the term "muddle" underscores the narrator's thesis that "there is something hostile" in the "soil" of India. Its hostility, of course, responds to the hostility of an incursion. Just as Beethoven's sublime noise is entwined with the anxious, culturally inflected interpretations of its audience, the noises of India are inextricable from the efforts to interpret them. In a curious parenthetical side note, the narrator reveals the concept of "muddle" as a Western frame of reference: "they did not one thing which the non-Hindu would feel dramatically correct; this approaching triumph of India was a muddle (*as we call it*), a frustration of reason and form" (319, my emphasis); the narrator's ineffable frustration has to be mediated through the best English word he can find. The Indian muddles, then, are heard by the Brits as "travestied" and "Indianize[d]" echoes of Western names and expressions—reflections of Western music in trembling water. Godbole's song, a "maze of noises," is similarly interpreted as a colonial tension made immanent in the song's refusal to resolve:

> His thin voice rose, and gave out one sound after another. At times there seemed rhythm, at time there was the illusion of a Western melody. But the ear, baffled repeatedly, soon lost any clue, and wandered in a maze of noises, none harsh or unpleasant, none intelligible. It was the song of an unknown bird. Only the servants understood it. They began to whisper to one another. The man who was gathering water chestnuts came naked out of the tank, his lips parted with delight, disclosing his scarlet tongue. The sounds continued and ceased after a few moments as casually as they had begun—apparently half through a bar, and upon the subdominant. (85)

With yet another "unknown bird" that destabilizes its auditors, order disintegrates—Adela and Mrs. Moore have not tasted Fafner's blood and are not in step with India's natural entropy. Complete with the naked colonized body emerging from the water, Forster's narrator sentimentalizes the Hindu song "of an unknown bird"—another metaphorical birdsong that disintegrates order and "baffles" the imperial ear. This instability derives partly from the independence of Godbole's voice from his body; the attention is temporarily displaced from the singing body to the bodies of its auditors. In part it derives from the impersonal casualness with which "the sounds continued and ceased," diffusing Godbole's agency in producing the sounds, creating an "illusion of a Western melody" but destroying that illusion in the same breath. Godbole explains his own song as an invitation to Sri Krishna, in which he "take[s] the position of a milkmaid" and says to the god, "Come, come, come, come, come, come."[33] As Godbole produces a hymn, which finds its "rhythm" "destroyed" by the noise of electric lights (319–20), Forster succinctly, almost ideogrammically, condenses the choir's repetitive "chain of sacred sounds" into a miswritten inscription of backward desire: "God si love." Soon enough, we are told, the chain "broke rhythm, made a thick little blur of sound, and produced a new rhythm"—dilating this misbegotten inscription back into "Noise, noise, . . . noise, thunder," and "the tiny reverberation that was his soul" (320). The noise of the ritual, Godbole's "maze of noises," the echo itself—these alienating sounds replace the static idea of God as love, implanted by Esmiss Esmoor herself ("God. . . is . . . love" [53]), with a telescoping, metonymic rhythmic "chain," which gives voice to the "reverberat[ing]" noise of God as desire: "Come, come, come, come, come, come."

To the British characters within the novel, this rhythm confuses rather than transmits its messages, seeming purposelessly to stop and start. The song is a "maze of noises" not just because of its own immanent properties but because of an interpretive gap: Godbole's song communicates a halting and perhaps impossible desire between earthly and divine (God si love). The passage offers an "illusion of Western melody" but refuses to resolve, rhythmically or harmonically. Settling upon the subdominant (the "A" of "A-men"), the unease and ambiguity of Godbole's song—like that of the novel as a whole—introduces a resolution only to forestall it.

Similarly, the novel's last sentences both suggest and defer a possible resolution, displacing the basic structure of Godbole's song onto the choric landscape of India, whose constituents "said in their hundred voices, 'No, not yet,' and the sky said, 'No, not there' " (*PI* 362). The politics of *A Passage to India* with respect to empire have been thoroughly debated; Edward Said first called the novel's ending a concession to despair, part of a longstanding Western invention of Eastern alterity.[34] Yet whatever the precise nature of Forster's orientalism, his descriptions of the mud and the muddle can also be seen to reflect back on the disorientation of Western identity. As Homi Bhabha has argued, colonial mimicry—the "Indianized" "travesties" of English words and names—destabilizes the ground on which the colonizer's identity rests, revealing that identity, like language itself, to be constituted in difference.[35] Julia Obert notes, however, that Bhabha's metaphors (e.g., of the liminal) are primarily "visuospatial," and suggests that an auditory metaphor (like McLuhan and Carpenter's "all-encompassing" acoustic sphere) might better account for the political resonances of imperial space.[36] The novel's final dissonance formalizes the echo of the Marabar Caves: decoded in one way by Fielding and another by Aziz, the noise that emerges out of the caves can be synthesized only in a partial resolution.

Recalling Abbate's resonant echoes, we can hear the verbal and literary iterations of sound in the novel—the echoes of the caves, the echoing reverberation of *Esmiss Esmoor*—being materialized in Abbate's fleshly here and now, and in the bodies of Aziz and Fielding, as un-"moored" homoerotic energy seeking an attachment. They materialize in Adela's body as well, as a constant "buzzing noise" that disappears only after her retracted accusation. Adela's body has been affected not just by the shock of the caves, which she experiences as a rape, but by the discourse around her: being called ugly in the courtroom causes her body to "trembl[e]" with resentment. Forster's gestures to his "mind on fire, body tinder" in response to Debussy suggest that sound, though elusive, is felt as an impress on the body, which responds with a sensitive quiver. At the beginning of the trial scene, a disembodied voice emerges from the crowd to insult the accuser—a comment that "fell from nowhere, from the ceiling perhaps" (243), much as the sounds in the cave are ominous because they are immersive and invisibly sourced. Forster's attention to Adela's physical ugliness throughout the novel suggests that the echo has awakened a latent internal crisis, not just about Anglo-India but about her own physique. In describing the dissolution of her echo, Adela lets slip her unwellness "ever since that expedition to the caves, and possibly before it" (265).

Attentive to this kind of internal crisis, and well-versed in the "splitting" of the subject, Forster clarifies in "What I Believe" that while "personal relationships" may be the only thing "comparatively solid in a world full of violence and cruelty," "Psychology has split and shattered the idea of a 'Person,' and has shown that there is something incalculable in each of us, which may at any moment rise to the surface and destroy our normal balance" (68-9). It is the same hidden "goblin" that disturbs the great artist's fantasy in *Howards End*—the "panic and emptiness" interrupting Helen's *Fantasia*-like daydream of dancing elephants. Hence the fear about the impossibility of solid relationships in India reflects an anxiety about the relations internal to the trembling self. Mrs. Moore, in her late crankiness, feels "increasingly (vision or nightmare?) that, though people are important, the relations between them are not, and that in particular, too much fuss has been made over marriage; centuries of carnal embracement, yet man is no nearer to understanding man" (149). The echo exposes a false consonance in marriage—a carnal as well as existential disillusionment. Just as noise seems to disassemble language (including Mrs. Moore's married name), it casts a pall over the fuss that puts these bodies together.

For Aziz and Fielding, likewise, the final divorce seems to echo, in amplified form, the minor slips of their discourse, such as when a rumor of an affair between Fielding and Adela sows a discord: "Tangles like this still interrupted their intercourse. A pause in the wrong place, an intonation misunderstood, and a whole conversation went awry" (305). The voices of India, as at the end of *The Waste Land*, offer a choric materialization of desire—the "annual helter-skelter of April" producing "irritability and lust" (234)—as well as an effort on the part of the Indian landscape to expel those "foreigners" who find its sound and soil hostile. Notwithstanding his earlier claim that "Nothing embraces the whole of India," Aziz imagines a new cohesive India to exclude "foreigners of any sort! Hurrah! Hurrah for India! Hurrah! Hurrah!" (361). The protracted affectionate embrace and "half-kiss" between Aziz and Fielding—a settling on the subdominant, an unsettling of the subcontinent—suggests that a new India, and a solid personal relationship between these two men, will require an embrace of dissonance and distance.

Howards End, *A Passage to India*, and *Billy Budd* all query different manifestations of the hidden, "incalculable" inner person referenced in "What I Believe": this goblin can be accessed by musical noise, but resists having clear meaning attached to it, and therefore is deeply destabilizing to both local and global relationships. The Caves scene in some sense rehearses the Professor Godbole scene; we learn that "Mrs. Moore and Miss Quested had felt nothing acutely for a fortnight" after hearing Godbole's "queer little song," that they had "lived more or less inside cocoons, and the difference between them was that the elderly lady accepted her own apathy, while the younger resented hers" (146). Mrs. Moore's withdrawal into apathy—an Adornian retreat into critical negation—is sealed when she finally enters the Cave, which, when subjected to the scrutiny of the penetrating English, turns out to be another form of nothing. Though the narrator asserts that "the caves are readily described" (136), the description itself breaks that promise, for although one wall of the cave has "been most marvellously polished" (137), reflecting the lit flame of the tourist, their appearance beyond that is inscrutable: "Local report declares that these [hidden chambers] exceed in number those that can be visited—four hundred of them, four thousand or million. Nothing is inside them, they were sealed up before the creation of pestilence or treasure; if mankind grew curious and excavated, nothing, nothing would be added to the sum of good or evil" (138). "Local report" of the inaccessible caves constitutes another form of noise, more *rumori* and another song to the gods—the meaning of which has less significance than the fact of its being reported. If this noise reveals anything, it reveals Nothing but an empty sonic chamber. Similarly, while the Caves reveal Mrs. Moore's attachment to Western Christianity to be hollow at the core, the local report of Mrs. Moore disperses her name as un-moored noise across the landscape.

"Great is information," we are told in *A Passage to India*, "and she shall prevail" (211). Perhaps so, but rumor prevails in muddled form and "intercourse" is constantly interrupted. In *Peter Grimes*, the pervasiveness of "local report," and the mud of indiscrete disembodied sounds, become difficult to extract from the mud of the setting itself. Britten's operas show a similar dynamic. Though Forster writes in *Two Cheers* that the opera *Peter Grimes* lacked the "horizontality" and the "mud" of Aldeburgh in Crabbe's original poem, the domestic and natural settings of the opera seem constructed from rumor and gossip. In the hands of Britten and the leftist playwright Montagu Slater, the title character of *Peter Grimes* is always homesick (even when at home), a fact signaled by the mild dissonances signifying his inability to assimilate; in *Grimes*, Forster claims, "the community is to blame." Peter's dissonances, contrasted with the noise of rumor, leave him without any stable ground on which to stake his identity; though the opera offers Ellen Orford (a transplant from another Crabbe poem) as Grimes' best hope to stabilize himself, the implausibility of this union drives the opera's musical language.

Britten's training prior to *Grimes* involved brief experiments with noise-music; while *Grimes* and *Budd* employ no such techniques, Britten's collaborations with Auden, Isherwood, and Montagu Slater on leftist dramas and documentaries much advanced his development of a politically engaged musical language. A few points about Britten's early career are therefore in order.

Who Shall Inherit Britten?

A student of Frank Bridge and John Ireland, Britten disliked much of English music. About Walton he was ambivalent, finding *Façade* amusing and inventive but Walton's later works conservative and shoddy. A devotee of Alban Berg, with whom he wanted to pursue private studies (the RCM and his mother disallowed this), Britten was frustrated by the RCM's conservative Englishness. Even as of 1933, the RCM did not possess a copy of Schoenberg's two-decades-old *Pierrot Lunaire*, despite Britten's pleas (Carpenter 53). Britten's frustrations with Britain, and vice-versa, took on more political edge in later years. A lifelong pacifist, Britten's encounters with Auden, Isherwood, and Slater at the G.P.O. Film Unit in London amplified his left-leaning tendencies—not least, his distaste for the Empire. In an article entitled "England and the Folk-Art Problem," Britten rejected the "attempt to create a national music" as "tribal nationalism" (153), and found himself criticized by fellow British musicians for living abroad during wartime: as George Baker put it, "the Battle of Britain" was "a program in which Mr. Britten has no part" (qtd. in Carpenter 151). Britten's self-exile merged with his desire to find a niche as a gay man when, in 1939, he and Peter Pears moved to Brooklyn Heights to live with Auden, Isherwood, Carson McCullers, Golo Mann, Paul Bowles, and Gypsy Rose Lee, in a commune established by George Davis (144).[37] It was while in New York that the text of a Forster broadcast on George Crabbe, published in the *Listener*, made it into Britten's hands.

By the mid-1930s Britten had already written several successful works, but his career was in many respects launched by his work for the G.P.O. Under the auspices of the General Post Office, the G.P.O. Film Unit produced "educational films," temperately critical of social and economic injustices. As Carpenter explains, Britten was in desperate need of a job and "altogether appalled by the English musical scene" when he was hired to write the music for *The King's Stamp*, a short film about the design and manufacture of a postage stamp commemorating George V's Jubilee" (Carpenter 64–5). *The King's Stamp*, directed by Alberto Cavalcanti and John Grierson, struck Britten as "rubbish," but the act of working on the film taught him to compose quickly and adapt to less-than-ideal circumstances and resources (Carpenter 65–6). Thus Britten continued on his work for the G.P.O. by writing the music and overseeing the soundtrack to *Coal Face* (1935), Basil Wright's documentary on the coal-mining industry, and *Night Mail* (1936), on the British postal service.

In this brief but formative moment of his career Britten developed a politically conscious musical-dramatic technique. He worked with Randall Swingler, editor of the *Left Review*, and Slater, the playwright for the Left Theatre. He collaborated with Auden and Isherwood on productions for the Group Theatre, including *The Ascent of F6* (1937) and *On the Frontier* (1938). Paul Rotha's *Peace of Britain* (1936), temporarily stalled by the British Board of Film Censors for its opposition to military spending, exemplifies the one political cause—pacifism—with which Britten remained consistently affiliated. While Britten's major works engage little with noise-music of the Varèse or Antheil sort, his work for the G.P.O. helped him develop a musical technique for linking word, sound, and image, in a politically engaged way. In both *Night Mail* and *Coal Face*, Britten's music draws on hammers, metal, sandpaper, wind machine, metal chains, and "drain pipes with coal slipping down them," as well as technological manipulation (playing a tape backward).[38] Donald Mitchell suggests that at first glance Britten's orchestra more closely resembles "the sound-world of Varèse than Britten. . . . But what Britten was after was a kind of documentary realism, a musical factuality to accompany the images" (83). The music of *Coal Face* includes a male chorus intoning extensive catalogues of technical reports and industrial minutiae,[39] and Philip Reed explains that "every single noise heard on the soundtrack—while apparently 'natural' in origin—is, in fact, the product of Britten's detailed instrumentation."[40]

Both *Night Mail* and *Coal Face* feature Auden's verse, which posed several difficulties for Britten's composition and recording. A diary entry by Britten describes the verse as a "kind of patter" which required separate recording sessions, and which required a strict metronomic tempo (to aid his conducting Britten fashioned an "improvised visual metronome—flashes on the screen"). A celebration of the night mail's diffusion of "gossip, gossip from all the nations, / News circumstantial, news financial," the message of *Night Mail* is something like "Only connect!," the argument of Margaret's sermon to Henry Wilcox: "Mature as [Wilcox] was, she might yet be able to help him to the building of the rainbow bridge that should connect the prose in us with the passion. . . . Only connect! That was the whole of her sermon. Only connect the prose and the passion, and both will be exalted, and human love will be seen at its height. Live in fragments no longer" (186-7).

Rephrasing Friedrich Schlegel's proposed fusion of "poetry and prose, inspiration and criticism, the poetry of art and the poetry of nature," which, as Matthew Smith observes, anticipated the "collective form and utopian potential" at the political heart of Wagner (*Total* 14), Margaret Schlegel unsettles her previous critique of the "muddy" total art-work. She draws on a Wagnerian image, the "rainbow bridge" recalling Wotan's entry into Valhalla at the end of *Das Rheingold*: a very big house indeed, and a passage to the "Infinity" that Margaret associates with King's Cross (similar to the infinity whose buzzing emptiness is exposed by the Marabar echoes). For Bast, who initially refuses to discuss *Tannhäuser* because he is unsure how to pronounce it, Wagner implies gaps of cultural knowledge and class that also require bridging. These gaps are metaphorized spatially by the Westminster Bridge and Vauxhall Tunnel that Bast traverses on his way home from the Schlegels. Like *Night Mail*, *Howards End* seems to question the literal and metaphorical bridges that must be built for gossip, news, information, and official communications to be broadcast globally. The train in *Howards End* is imagined also as a "forcing-house for the idea of sex"—the "low rich purr" of the Great Western Express providing a ground-bass for intimate conversation even as it "rob[s]" the journey of "its magic."

If *Night Mail* and *Coal Face* accompany these bridged gaps with onomatopoetic noise-music, they prepare the music of *Grimes* and *Budd*, which require a musical language able to account for the muddle of an unspeakable eroticism and the noise of rumor.[41] While Britten's later work sublimates the noise of rumor into more "musical" expression, those noises make themselves known. Similarly, much as Attali argues that music performs a sacrificial function, Britten's operas tend to identify an outsider and narrate his expulsion.

Britten's Ninths: *Peter Grimes*, Dissonance, and the Art of Rumor

Arguing that "the community is to blame" for Grimes' death in the opera, Forster attributes that intervention to Slater's rewriting of Crabbe. Though Slater ultimately toned down his leftist class politics in *Grimes*, they certainly remain present: Grimes' lack of income partially motivates his refusal to marry Ellen (hence the need to keep acquiring boy apprentices), to ensure that she is marrying him for a reason other than "pity." Class tension thus tags on to Grimes' psychological self-doubt; indeed, Slater initially wished to cast Grimes as a sadomasochist, but Britten and Pears moderated this instinct in refocusing Peter's affection for Ellen. With this in mind, the introduction of Ellen into *Grimes* allows the audience to side *neither* with Peter *nor* with the drunk, womanizing, laudanum-addicted hypocrites around him in this "Borough," but instead to witness the process and effects of scapegoating and repression. As Stephen Arthur Allen points out, the "'confrontation' between Grimes and the Borough-as-protagonist . . . *never actually takes place*."[42]

It is Ellen who undergoes this confrontation, as the victim of the Borough's hypocrisy and of Peter's violence. Though Britten has been critiqued for his unsatisfactory treatment of women (not a problem in *Budd*), Ellen is arguably the boldest character in *Grimes*, to the extent that Edmund Wilson identified her as the opera's resident pacifist.[43] Yet I share Brett's inclination that *Grimes* is modern in its ability to promote identification with the unheroic title-character, whom the audience has "been socially conditioned to spurn."[44] The choice between Peter and Ellen ultimately is unnecessary: the hero and victim of the opera is the impossible *union* between Peter and Ellen, one of whom offers affection that is not returned, the other of whom cannot return the affection offered him. The influx of queer criticism on the opera bears out Edmund Wilson's assertion that Grimes "is always under the impression, poor fellow, that what he really wants for himself is to marry Ellen Orford [with a] 'whitened doorstep and a woman's care'" (162). Furthermore, Wilson suggests, what Grimes really wants is to convince the Borough that he is capable of elevating himself socially. The two desires amount to roughly the same thing: without marrying Ellen, Grimes is constitutionally incapable of according with community standards (as the chorus reiterates in Act II, "The Borough keeps its standards up" [222]).

The first scene of the opera resolves into the closest thing *Grimes* comes to a love duet, one that attempts to interpret social gossip and sublimate it into a kind of music rooted in an impossible domestic union. As the one woman willing to contravene the Borough, Ellen resists the strongly feminized presence of rumor. After being acquitted for the death of his second boy apprentice, Peter insists that he testify: "The case goes on in people's minds. The charges that no court has made will be shouted at my head" (Prologue, 25); in a section marked "Crowd hubbub," the chorus responds, "When women gossip the result is someone doesn't sleep at night!" (21).

Just as Peter is an outsider by virtue of his ill-fated encounters with his apprentices, Ellen is isolated by her affiliation with Peter. As Philip Rupprecht argues, theorizing (after Judith Butler) "hate speech" as illocutionary speech-act, the chorus in *Grimes* isolates Peter "in a display of intersecting legal and linguistic forces."[45] He notes that the choric repetitions of Peter's name, the first words of the opera (uttered in a legal inquest), reveal the very act of naming to be a social one. Peter himself has internalized this notion, correctly warning Ellen that she will "share the name of outlaw":

PETER: Where the walls themselves gossip of inquest!

ELLEN: But we'll gossip too, and talk and rest.

PETER: While Peeping Toms nod as you go, you'll share the name of outlaw too!

ELLEN: Peter, we shall restore your name, warmed by the new esteem that you will find . . .

PETER: Until the Borough hate poisons your mind! (Prologue, 25–6)

Ellen's line "We'll gossip too" is ambiguous: while promising an assimilation into the community, once Peter's "name" is "restore[d]," it also suggests a private space in which Ellen and Peter can gossip together, independent of the Borough's noise. Peter seems more cynical, noting that such a space is impossible "where the walls themselves gossip of inquest." The very material of the home, and in some respects the very material of the opera, is built on *rumori*.

In their duet, Peter and Ellen acknowledge that their association might be salvific for both of them: "My/Your voice out of the pain is like a hand that I can feel and know: Here is a friend, here is a friend" (26). Yet Britten's musical language makes this union impossible. The duet is driven by two commonly noted structural features, each of which renders the unease of Peter and Ellen's affection. The first is the duet's bitonality. Ellen sings in E major, Peter in f minor: two keys that have little to do with each other functionally, but which are linked enharmonically at the third (G#/A-flat), where both Ellen's and Peter's melodies tend to linger. Even in the unison passage, notated in Ellen's key of E, the melody shifts into f minor ("My voice") and back again, thanks to the intervention of the passage's second structural quirk: the use of minor ninths (the melodic interval one half-step greater than an octave). The passage resolves in E, a potential union anchored in Ellen's key, but that union feels tentative at best.

The interval of the minor ninth pervades *Peter Grimes*; Brett calls it "the interval most associated with Peter's loneliness and his private fantasies" ("Britten and Grimes" 996). The major ninth is equally conspicuous. Grimes' sublime aria "What harbour shelters peace," which precedes and is recapitulated in the opera's most famous orchestral passage (the "Storm" interlude), features a series of major ninths, framed by an ambiguous, strangely spaced orchestral chord (E-G-C#-F#-A). This chord, which contains an inversion of the tonic chord (E-C#-A), also seems to function as a diminished seventh chord (E-G-[B-flat]-[D-flat], with the B-flat omitted and the D-flat spelled enharmonically as C#. The diminished seventh tends to be ambiguous as a rule, an ambiguity that makes it an easy way to modulate, and Britten's use of it both suggests and problematizes Peter's resolution to marry Ellen. The text suggests that "Ellen" is his "harbour"—"her breast is harbour too/ When night is turned to day"—but the fuzzy tonal resolution suggests that this harbour is not at all peaceful. Stacked on the dominant (E), the chord suggests a resolution to the home base of A major; but a dominant chord would normally possess a G#, the leading tone that desires to resolve to the tonic. With a G rather than the G#, Britten's chord lacks this desire; while Grimes orally expresses a wish to consummate a union with Ellen, it is as if the musical language were a material force holding this desire back.[46]

The ambiguous dissonances and rhythmic quirks of *Peter Grimes* internalize and respond to the noise of a community: while on the one hand they illustrate Peter's and Ellen's internalizations of impossible affection, on the other hand they suggest the need for communities to accommodate marginal or subversive drives. Grimes' aria transitions into the storm at the center of the second scene, in which the characters consolidate in "Auntie's" pub. This scene features an outpouring of forced spontaneity: the character Ned Keene (a laudanum-selling quack) starts up a shanty, "Old Joe has gone fishing," to prevent the company from swarming on Grimes. Music hath charms to save Grimes for a time—the song turns quickly, ominously, into a round—yet the shanty is far from comforting, proceeding in 7/4 (like Tchaikovsky's 5/4 "waltz," one beat off), and containing a strange melodic back-and-forth between A and A-flat (fig. 6.1). Grimes uncomfortably joins in, singing his line in A major. These rhythmic and melodic quirks suggest an internal uncertainty about whether and how the collective can accommodate its "sensitive" character. Both Grimes' obsession and the chorus's invigilation make this impossible: as Grimes takes his third apprentice home, the chorus sings, "Home! You call that home?"

Grimes' home and harbour lie, inevitably, at the bottom of the ocean. In his final "mad scene," Grimes tracks back through the homes that have been offered him, repeating both "What harbour shelters peace," with its ninths, and "Old Joe." As Brett points out, whereas Grimes' "What harbour" passage is left unresolved in its first iteration, Grimes completes the phrase in

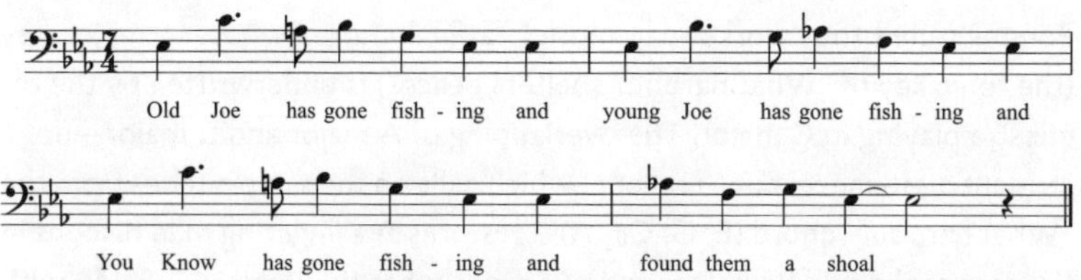

Figure 6.1 Excerpt from "Old Joe Has Gone Fishing," in Britten, *Peter Grimes: Vocal Score*, Op. 33. © Copyright 1945 by Boosey & Hawkes Music Publishers Ltd. Reprinted by permission of Boosey & Hawkes, Inc.

the mad scene. And the rhythms of "Old Joe" are smoothed out as Grimes acknowledges that his apprentice is dead at the bottom of the ocean: "You'll know who's gone fishing, when you bring in the shoal." The key of A-flat gives Grimes' final resolution a savagely layered irony. The consummations that Grimes sought but couldn't quite realize, in his love duet with Ellen and his "What harbour" aria in Act I, are finally materialized—as the ocean in which Peter and his apprentice are drowned. A-flat represents a half-step drop from Grimes' A-major "What harbour" aria, predicting Grimes' descent into madness and his impending drop to his "home" and "harbour"—a drop (A-flat vs. A-natural) also anticipated in the melodic quirk of "Old Joe." The A-flat enharmonically matches the absent leading tone that failed to drive home Grimes' aria; and, finally, it matches the pitch shared by Peter and Ellen in their "love duet." The note (G#/A-flat) that marks Peter's common bond with Ellen, and the absent drive of the leading tone in the "What harbour" aria (G# in the key of A), finally materializes as Grimes' descent into madness, and into the ocean—the great Baudelairean/Wagnerian/Eliotic primal mass of unconscious desire.

"The sea," as Eliot writes, "was calm." Whomever one identifies as the victim at the end of the opera, the order wins out, as its scapegoats are killed, silenced, or assimilated. Ellen herself is silenced at the end of the opera, after she offers one feeble "No!" to Balstrode's recommendation that Grimes sink his own ship. Yet the end of the opera questions whether and how, as the community reconsolidates, it might accommodate a dissonant counterpublic. The action suggests, not yet, not there; the chorus resumes its consonant hymns and daily rhythms. For what it's worth, however, the last word in the opera to be spoken by an individual (Auntie) is "rumour," dismissing the report of Grimes' boat "sinking out at sea." Once dismissed, this rumor gives way again to the daily patterns of daily life, the chorus singing what

Forster called the "work-a-day music": a final chorus whose A major key (the tonic key of "What harbour shelters peace") is underwritten by the orchestra playing in C major. The overlapping of A major and C major—not a strident dissonance, but a real one, which calls on the same pitches from the "What harbour" chord (E, G, C#, A)—gestures at a lingering mild discord in the reconsolidated Borough, and questions what the Borough will do with the next Grimes: the chorus will find a way to accommodate difference or, just as likely, will find a new scapegoat.

Billy Budd dramatizes the musically beautiful character scapegoated in the name of martial authority—a repression that turns back on the scapegoaters. In reworking the novel, Forster, Britten, and Eric Crozier smooth over much of the novel's emphasis on rumor, gossip, and epistemological uncertainty.[47] But in pacifying the novel's metageneric discourses, the opera explores the ideological functions of music: its ability to spellbind communities and still their noise. This function is explored through some of the opera's most sublime music: music that tries to lift the characters and audience out of immediately accessible onstage events.

The Spellbinding Forms of *Billy Budd*

The hints of homosexuality (specifically, pederasty) that shaped the early drafts of *Grimes* were, as Moffat explains, eventually revised out in favor of rendering Grimes as an "introspective" "neurotic" (281); and while Eric Crozier warned his collaborators against laying the "homosexual subtext" so thickly onto *Billy Budd*, the two found the idea irresistible. Britten's *Budd* illustrates and critiques what Melville's Vere describes as the "spellbinding" function of music: its ability to create order and fashion bonds of solidarity. As in *Grimes*, the opera's consonant choral music scenes reveal communal and musical order to rely not just on a heroic presence but on a scapegoat: the French, the mutinous, Billy himself. If in *Grimes* the community is to blame, in *Budd* the community is spellbound by choric consonance, which is disturbed but ultimately restored when its strong figure is scapegoated. *Billy Budd*'s most consonant music is its most unsettling: chords with no vertical dissonances, but no clear syntagmatic function, suggest the ruptures and scapegoats at the heart of sublime music.

Forster's interpretation of Melville's *Budd* in *Aspects of the Novel* emphasizes its musical qualities, elevating the story's significance from a local parable to universal "transcendence." For Forster, as Irene Morra writes, Melville's story had resonances in excess of its schematic allegories, making it a "prophetic" "song"—but a song "not without words," for those allegories (Budd as Christ) keep its verbal literariness in play, thereby failing to achieve the musical quality of Melville's more "difficult" books. For Forster, novelistic rhythm is shaped by a motivic presence capable of taking on a "life of its own" (like Dedalus's rhythmic apprehension of the whole), whereas "pattern" is a restrictive, externally binding (anti-Adornian) form. Melville's *Budd*, musical though it may be, has more pattern than rhythm, its literary shape externally imposed rather than emerging organically from the inside out.

The problems of aesthetic form, organic or "externally constructed" are inextricable from the novel's representations of *bodily* form in Melville's novel. In the first chapter, the narrator details the genre of person known as the "Handsome Sailor," whose "moral nature was seldom out of keeping with the physical make" (292). Billy's "moral nature" is guaranteed both by his "rustic beauty" (299) and by the "certain musical chime in his voice," the "veritable unobstructed outcome of the innermost man" (294). Melville's description of Billy's moral nature is thus tied to his "physical make" and to an inherent "musical" tendency, emerging rhythmically from the inside out. His characteristic flaw, the "one thing amiss in him," is an "occasional liability to a vocal defect," what Forster's Vere will call a "stammer in the divine": "under sudden provocation of strong heart-feeling his voice, otherwise singularly musical, as if expressive of the harmony within, was apt to develop an organic hesitancy, in fact more or less a stutter or even worse" (Melville 302). Billy Budd the character, like *Billy Budd* the novel, is a rhythmic construction whose external shape and vocal utterances are all organic manifestations of an inner life, as if his hesitancy stemmed from his heartbeat. Vere's final words in the novel, "Billy Budd, Billy Budd," are compared to the effect of a drug "which, soothing the physical frame, mysteriously operates on the subtler element in man" (382); the physical frame, the one thing capable of producing genuine, spontaneous utterances, is prone to the mysterious operations of rhythm.

The novel recognizes and develops the parallel between the shape of its characters' bodies and the shape of the novel itself. Billy's "organic hesitancy" is marshaled as evidence that he is not a "conventional hero" and that the story itself is "no romance" (302); at Billy's hanging, Melville imbricates the form of his body, the forms of military ritual, and the form of the novel itself. Seeing Billy's "form suspended in air," the sailors briefly threaten an "uncertain movement," in response to which Vere orders a beat-to-quarters an hour earlier than usual (379). He justifies this, as he justifies Billy's death, by disavowing the French Revolution: "'With mankind,' he would say, 'forms, measured forms, are everything; and this is the import couched in the story of Orpheus, with his lyre spellbinding the wild denizens of the wood.' And this he once applied to the disruption of forms going on across the Channel and the consequences thereof" (380). The beat to quarters, marked by a drumbeat and by the sacred music played by "a band on the quarter-deck," attempts to spellbind the forms of the sailors: not an organic hesitancy but a disciplinary measure of order. A different kind of narcotic from the one that produces Vere's final repetition of Billy's name, this one disciplines rather than liberates bodily response.

Melville attempts to account for both the music generated by individual bodies, and the music that controls those bodies, within the form of the novel itself—a form reliant on the art of rumor. Put another way, as the novel itself explores the relation between Forsterian rhythm (a pulse that emerges immanently from the text) and pattern (a frame delimiting interpretations of its content), the narrator and the presence of rumor are simultaneously at odds and in collusion. As rumor both constructs narrative and emphasizes its irregularities, it circulates unreliable discourse. The narrator finally asserts that the formal stability of the beat-to-quarters does not hold up in history: "The symmetry of form attainable in pure fiction cannot so readily be achieved" in documentation of fact, because "Truth uncompromisingly told will always have its ragged edges . . . less finished than an architectural final" (380–1). The sudden deaths of funny-looking art are an uncompromising sedimentation of truth's "ragged" violence, not to be covered over by Melville's narrator. The meaning of Vere's final utterance of Billy's name, for example, is conveyed by the medical attendant to the drumhead court officer, who has "kept the knowledge to himself" (382); hence the official accounts of this mutiny and execution, of Billy's suspended form and Vere's dying body, are "pure fiction," while the true account remains opaque.

Vere himself prefers history to fiction, having "nothing of that literary taste which less heeds the thing conveyed than the vehicle"—not because histories are true, but because they serve as mirrors to his own presuppositions, a "confirmation of his own reserved thoughts" that he had "vainly sought in social converse" (311). Unable to find his views confirmed in social discourse, he finds them in history and philosophy, which he uses as a "dike in the torrent of novel opinion" (312). Vere associates the French disruption of forms with "novel opinion" and, I would suggest, with the novel, a genre better able than history to account for "ragged edges." The contrast between fiction and history seems to undercut Claggart's accusation against Billy, which no one on board believes: it looks too symmetrical and finished to be true. Whereas actual mutiny resembles an organically rhythmic "distempering irruption of contagious fever in a frame constitutionally sound" (304), Claggart constructs a patterned plot of intellectual evil. Rumor, though unreliable, frays the edges of a too-coherent, binding narrative such as Claggart's. In adapting *Budd* for the stage, Forster and Crozier erase Melville's narrator and smooth over the book's emphasis on the "ragged edges" of events, silencing the novel's intriguing metageneric commentary. By replacing Melville's narrator with Vere himself, whom they give a framing solo epilogue and prologue, Forster and Crozier attempt to give Vere a redemptive roundness and a more sympathetic tenor than he possesses in Melville's novel.

For Forster, the notion that music could spellbind was not entirely conspiratorial, just as his notion of music's sublimity was not entirely cynical. As a searcher for the Wounded and Missing Department in Alexandria, Forster organized concerts and recitals for patients, performing both at the piano and as a Master of Ceremonies. Having successfully emceed at the Montazah Convalescent Hospital in 1917, Forster wrote to Edward Carpenter, "I was able to talk sense and quiet [the troops] because I loved them. . . . I felt that I had been burrowing under rubbish and touched something that was alive and had been trying to touch me. It is useless trying to touch something you don't want to touch" (qtd. in Furbank 34). In a letter to Carpenter, Forster's philosophical idol and gay icon, Forster was no doubt aware of the homoerotic echoes of his desire to "touch" the soldiers whom he loved. Yet Forster emphasizes the extent to which the concert touched *him*. The slight paternalism and vague eroticism of his efforts may comment retroactively on the crux of *Howards End*—the liberal impulse to educate and uplift—and proleptically on the "aristocracy of the sensitive." On one hand the genuinely sensitive effort to communicate about art offers a genuine intellectual and emotional thrill; on the other hand it is futile to "improve" people whom *you* don't really want to improve. Education, for Forster, requires some kind of affection for those being educated. In the opera, Vere's spellbinding of his soldiers is interlocked dramatically with his affection for those soldiers, much as his affection for Billy and his complicity with Billy's death are difficult to disentangle. As both the frame and the center of the opera, Vere embodies this ambiguity: he both acts and comments upon his own actions, produces music and listens to it.

Consonance Kills: Britten's *Budd*

Billy Budd itself stages the difficulty of interpreting music, dramatized in two scenes in which music and action are separated onstage. These sublime musical moments also signify acts of sublimation: of the noises of labor, or of unnamable desire. In these scenes, Britten's consonances do more than the dissonances to call into question Vere's military and narrative authority. In the first of these scenes (I.ii), Vere puts his ear to the floor to hear his sailors singing, demonstrating his genuine sympathy for his crew ("Starry Vere"). This scene follows directly from Vere's conversation with his lieutenants, which references the "Frenchified notions," "ideas," "bowing and scraping," "lingo," and "hoppity-skippity ways" (87–8) of the enemy. When a Lieutenant asks Vere if there is any "danger of French notions spreading this side," Vere responds, "great danger. There is a word which we scarcely dare speak." This word is identified as "Mutiny" in a B-minor triad: consonant order consolidates around the fear of "Frenchified notions." Ultimately, Billy himself is identified as a possible disruption of this order—a threat that Vere dismisses as he listens to the shipmen singing ("Blow her away! Blow her to hi-lo").[48] Whereas in the novel Vere's bookish "starriness" tends to distance him from his crew, in the opera it connects him to the crew: he uses his historical authority to *defend* Billy from suspicion of mutiny, after which he bends to listen, asserting that "Where there is happiness, there cannot be harm" (98).

The lieutenants are not persuaded. When Billy is sentenced to die, this first scene is narratively and thematically articulated with the second: the so-called "interview scene" (II.ii), in which Vere informs Billy of his verdict and sentence—offstage, behind a closed door. Here we have a kind of distorted phantasmagoria effect, in which the orchestral music has more presence than the actors themselves, though the chords image an interview between those two closeted bodies. Much of the critical attention to *Billy Budd* has been directed to this interview scene, accompanied by the opera's most striking and most consonant music: a series of thirty-four major and minor triads (the "interview chords"), with no dissonances (not even a seventh), no melody, and no clear harmonic direction. The interview chords gesture to the possibility of a redemptive erotic encounter; on one reading, the opera's entry into F major seems to mark Vere's entry into Billy, the discharge necessary to resolve his dissonant erotic attraction and prepare the restoration of order.

Yet without any dissonances to resolve, the chords are decentered and tonally adrift; this consonance, far from offering either a mystic or an erotic Wagnerian sublation, grows deeply alienating. Having no clear horizontal progression, and accompanying no onstage bodies, the chords halt narrative progress: though they assert the presence of symbolic meaning, they interrupt the production of syntactic meaning (an aggressive obstruction of, among other things, future-oriented narrative development). By alternating among groups of instruments (woodwinds, strings, brass), Britten obviates even the need for voice-leading from chord to chord. Without conceding too much to the antimodernist operagoer, this is an aggressively amelodic musical passage; even the possibility of melody is obstructed, as the drama derives from juxtapositions of dynamics and orchestration.[49] Many of the chords have no clear function in what appears to be the overarching key of F major (even that much is disputed), although each chord contains an F, an A, or a C. This ambiguous tonality, as Arnold Whittall suggests, enacts a "twisted" dialectic between love and war.[50] True to Britten's refusal to write a love duet, the closeted scene between Vere and Billy lacks any of the sinuous interchanges of voice—lacks any voice-leading at all, in fact—that one might expect of a redemptive or erotic climax. The interview passage binds the pair to a limited tonal range (F-A-C) while disallowing the pleasure of cadential satisfaction.

Hence despite Brett's claim that the chords suggest "unalloyed optimism" and Platonic beauty, this optimism is very much alloyed, not least by the dilemma at the heart of Forster's politics, "the compulsion to betray one's friend in order to save one's country."[51] Claire Seymour aptly identifies the "interview" passage as "the opera's own 'stammer'": a moment of expressive crisis at which both communal order and the myth of stable masculinity break down. The problem of identifying an erotic center in *Budd* is overdetermined: Billy's sensitive musicality, combined with his inarticulately divine "stammer," set up a figure open to being touched, while at the same time cloaking him in linguistic opacity—the dilemma of the open secret, "what we name by not naming, know by not knowing."[52] How Forster was to rewrite Billy, or how we are to reread him, is thus complicated by what Wayne Koestenbaum calls "the crossroads where anatomies and institutions collide," a collision he associates with the homosexual body: "Like voice, homosexuality appears to be taking place inside a body, when really it occurs in a sort of outerspace (call it 'discourse') where interiorities converge; the vocal body and the homosexual body . . . each is a looseleaf rulebook, a ledger of inherited prohibitions." Like Tiresias, whom Ed Madden places at the center of an array of "nervous" discourses about (and productive of) normative sexuality,[53] Billy is produced less as a "gay character" than as an exoskeletal "outerspace" of *rumori* and laws that coalesce into deadly consonances.[54] Koestenbaum, who identifies the throat as a "problematized zone" for the homosexual subject and for the operatic voice, helps to clarify the musical and/or beautiful sailor not as a static allegory of Christ-like innocence, but as a "cultural myth," like the pure voice, "as compelling, as naturalized, as hard to obtain distance from, as the myth of the sexual self" (226). The breakdown of Billy's voice creates an Eliotic glitch—a destabilizing noise in the outwardly coherent form of the impressed body, and in the binding consonances of the voiceless interview.

At one level, the sort-of-F-major interview passage prepares Vere's resolution of his own psychodrama. Vere announces that he has found "the love that passeth understanding": the same Biblical language that Eliot uses to resolve *The Waste Land* marks the opera's final resolution into B-flat major (of which F is the dominant). Britten gestures at the interview chords a final time as Vere announces, to the melody of "Billy in the Darbies," that he has found his own "anchor"—again, much like Grimes' search for his "harbour," except more tonally determinate: "I was lost on the infinite sea, but I've sighted a sail in the storm, the far-shining sail, and I'm content, I've seen where she's bound for, there's a land where she'll anchor forever, where she'll anchor forever." She is bound for B-flat, where the opera tentatively begins and confidently ends. The letter "B" being the German nomenclature for B-flat, Benjamin Britten frames the opera with Billy Budd's and his own initials (literarily connected, if only loosely, to the "British brawn and beef" glorified in the "Don't like the French" scene). Vere's memory and the sailor's scapegoated/eroticized body mediate one another in the opera's tonal language.

Yet just as Vere's devotion to order is troubled by the seemingly pure love music, and footnoted by his own psychological resolution, these consonances are tinctured by the sailors' collective chants in unison. Billy's final scene with the Dansker ("Dansker, goodbye!") echoes the ship's earlier unsuccessful pursuit of the French ("This is our moment!") (fig. 6.2). The scene approaches the Forsterian dilemma in a fashion both sentimental and satirical. On one level, it becomes clear that Billy has not betrayed his country

Figure 6.2 Excerpts from Britten, *Billy Budd: Vocal Score*, Op. 50. Chorus ("This is our moment"), two bars after II.i., rehearsal number 15. Billy ("Dansker, goodbye"), two bars after III.iii, before rehearsal number 12. © Copyright 1951 by Hawkes & Son (London) Ltd. Reprinted by permission of Boosey & Hawkes, Inc.

and the Dansker has not betrayed his friend. At the same time, by melodically echoing a scene of failed aggression, Billy parodies the need to impress persons into collectives, revealing its violence against both the person and the collective. The betrayal of one's friends, the opera suggests, *is* the betrayal of one's country.

Here the Dansker informs Billy that the sailors are now considering an actual mutiny in order to rescue Billy from his sentence. The sailors resist wordlessly to the same melody as Billy's farewell: a perfect fifth followed by a minor second—what Mervyn Cooke calls the "repression theme" (Fig. 6.3). This same melodic line characterizes their chant from the first act—"O heave away, heave." As the voices on deck rebel after Billy's hanging, they echo this theme in bitonal exchanges between E and B minor (Fig. 6.4). True to form, the lieutenants put away this revolt with relative ease—"Down all hands!", sung on a confident B-flat—and the music gradually winds down to B-flat major as Vere's final epilogue begins. This theme also permeates Vere's and the lieutenants' reference to the "Nore, the Floating Republic," in the "Don't like the French" scene, as well as the individual declamations of Billy ("Farewell, *Rights o' Man!*") and, in different form, Vere's declaration in the final scene ("Oh, what have I done?").

Vere's question, offered in the opera's Prologue as well, suggests that his own memory is reshaping the sailors' chant, and that the "repression theme" produced by the sailors is the product of his own repression. Its melodic parallels with the chant "O heave away" recall that Vere and Billy have been brought together only under the regime of impressment and the threat of an enemy "floating republic." If Vere's harbor shelters peace, he is nonetheless bound to repressive choric consonance; as Brett argues in "The Britten Era," Vere's epilogue, marked by an intensifying drumbeat, shows

Figure 6.3 Excerpts from Britten, *Billy Budd,* Op. 50. (a) Chorus ("O heave away heave"), I.i., rehearsal number 5. (b) Billy ("Farewell"), I.i, rehearsal number 33. (c) First Lieutenant ("The floating republic"), I.ii., rehearsal number 7. (d) Vere ("O what have I done"), Epilogue, rehearsal number 39. © Copyright 1951 by Hawkes & Son (London) Ltd. Reprinted by permission of Boosey & Hawkes, Inc.

that he is "so hopelessly contaminated by his role in killing other men . . . that his putative 'salvation' must be wishful thinking."[55] As with the rhythmic peroration at the end of *A Passage to India* ("the sky didn't want it . . . the horses didn't want it . . . No, not yet, . . . No, not there"), both the intensifying rhythmic drum and the horrifyingly contaminated consonances recalled in Vere's epilogue suggest that he, like Helen's marching goblins, has been impressed into a musical order too harmonious to be stable. It suggests moreover that Vere unconsciously seeks the restoration of psychological balance, threatened by what Forster calls the "incalculable" inner person, by assimilating into an order that would see him and that person extinguished. If the interview chords convey an unbalancing stammer in the opera's larger structure, they likewise suggest the spellbinding pull of solidarity that, as Forster knows, few will have the guts to betray.

Billy's final encounter with the Dansker is preceded by his final aria, adapted from the "Billy at the Darbies" ballad that ends Melville's novel. Melville's narrator notes that this poem is passed among the sailors them-

Figure 6.4 Excerpt from Britten, *Billy Budd,* Op. 50. Chorus and orchestra, II.iv, rehearsal number 30. © Copyright 1951 by Hawkes & Son (London) Ltd. Reprinted by permission of Boosey & Hawkes, Inc.

selves, thus granting it both the authenticity and the instability of nonofficial discourse. With fitting gallows humor, this poetic Billy exclaims, "'Tis me, and not the sentence they'll suspend!", speaking to the fatal "suspended sentence" of Billy's stammer and Vere's refusal to commute his death sentence. These failed speech-acts produce the "form suspended in air": the body of the handsome sailor, the hero and sacrificial lamb of the novella and opera bearing his name. The "suspension," a term also for a dissonance produced by a voice whose resolution is a beat or two delayed, suggests that the disruptions posed by the beautiful sailor must be purged; the body hanged there lingers as a suspended trace of illicit "musical" eroticism that threatens spellbinding illusions of nation and masculinity. The hint at the "suspended sentence," like the "stammer in the divine speech," rematerializes Billy's body as the "hoppity-skippity" infusion of desire, articulable only through coded repression or as a byproduct of ritual order.

Recall the last sentence of Forster's "What I Believe": "Naked I came into the world, naked I shall go out of it! And a very good thing too, for it reminds me that I am naked under my shirt, whatever its colour." Nathan Gunn's run of performances as Budd has garnered as many rave reviews of his shirtless physique as of his vocal technique. Neither Barthes, Eliot, Joyce, Adorno, Sitwell, Cocteau, Britten, nor Forster would be surprised to find the recorded voice of the "beautiful sailor" searching for a bodily source, for a humanity legible "under [one's] shirt, whatever its color." The ending of *Billy Budd* reinforces the spellbound community of the *Indomitable*, all wearing the same color, while dramatizing the scapegoated body at its center. Throughout the careers of Forster and Britten, as throughout modernist music and writing, the body moves and is moved by music that mediates the ideological noises of culture. Motivated by the pressures of imperial expansion and cultural consolidation, by the need to communicate unnamable erotic drives "when the walls themselves gossip of inquest," Forster and Britten channel the desires and ruptures of modernity into sublime noise: forms of music and writing whose aspirations toward formal cohesion remain critical of their own fractures. The end of *Budd*, at the end of what we now call modernism, reveals the resolution of fragmentation into unity, dissonance into consonance, to be no resolution at all.

Notes

Introduction

1. Conrad, "Preface," 132. Hereafter cited parenthetically.

2. Cowell, "The Joys of Noise," 249. Hereafter cited parenthetically.

3. See "The Musical Mystique," Taruskin's bilious review of Julian Johnson's *Who Needs Classical Music?*, Joshua Fineberg's *Classical Music, Why Bother?*, and Lawrence Kramer's *Why Classical Music Still Matters*.

4. Pater, *The Renaissance*, 86.

5. Barber, "Battle Music," 25. I found Barber's essay by way of Watkins, *Proof Through the Night*, 61. Both hereafter cited parenthetically.

6. See the first sentence of Adorno's *Aesthetic Theory* (1970): "It is self-evident that nothing concerning art is self-evident anymore, not its inner life, not its relation to the world, not even its right to exist." Hereafter cited parenthetically as *AT*.

7. Adorno and Horkheimer, *Towards a New Manifesto*, 39.

8. Proust, *Remembrance of Things Past*, vol. 2, 781.

9. McClary, *Feminine Endings*, 20. Hereafter cited parenthetically.

10. Mao and Walkowitz, "The New Modernist Studies," 437ff.

11. Taruskin, "A Myth of the Twentieth Century," 5-6.

12. See Jacques Rivière's 1921 review for *La Nouevelle Revue Francaise*, translated and reprinted in Truman Bullard, "The First Performance of Igor Stravinsky's *Sacre du Printemps*," vol. 2.

13. Preston, *Modernism's Mythic Pose*, 6. Preston refers specifically to Francois Delsarte's efforts to reunify body and spirit through new kinesthetic technique.

14. Eliot, "London Letter," 189.

15. Eliot, "*Ulysses*, Order, and Myth," 177.

16. On the *Rite* in context, see Eksteins, *Rites of Spring* and Ross, *The Rest is Noise*. Hereafter cited parenthetically.

17. Blackadder, *Performing Opposition*, xi. Hereafter cited parenthetically.

18. Reid, "Popular Theatre," 74-76, identifies the "normal noise" of social inter-

course; "ritual noise," such as applause; and the noise of "disturbance" that marks the breakdown of that ritual. Peter Bailey, "Breaking the Sound Barrier," 32, argues that rowdy audience behavior in Victorian London was a reaction against "respectability" in popular venues.

19. Marinetti, "The Variety Theatre," 256.

20. Tzara, "Dada Manifesto," 277.

21. Leavis, *New Bearings in English Poetry*, 73.

22. Russolo, *The Art of Noises*, 25. Hereafter cited parenthetically.

23. Schafer, *The Soundscape*, 202. Hereafter cited parenthetically.

24. Schafer, *The New Soundscape*, preface.

25. Banet-Weiser, "Preface," v. This essay prefaces a special edition of *American Quarterly* entitled *Sound Clash: Listening to American Studies*. For work in "sound studies," see Sterne, *Audible Past*; Thompson, *Soundscape of Modernity*; Picker, *Victorian Soundscapes*; Kahn, *Noise, Water, Meat*.

26. Martin Jay, *Downcast Eyes*, passim.

27. Attali, *Noise*, passim. Hereafter cited parenthetically. For a composer's perspective on noise in electronic and computer music, see Link, "Work of Reproduction."

28. Pound, *Hugh Selwyn Mauberley*, III.16. Hereafter cited parenthetically.

29. As David Cunningham writes, "Attali's mobilisation of a general concept of 'noise' needs to be read back into the temporal structure of experience . . . described by Adorno's philosophical conception of modernism." "Time for Dissonance and Noise," 68.

30. Adorno, "On the Contemporary Relationship" (1953), 144. Hereafter cited parenthetically as "Contemporary."

31. I loosely adopt this term from Bolter and Grusin, *Remediation,* which describes remediation as a process by which media "refashion prior media forms" (272–3).

32. Rainey, *Institutions of Modernism.* Hereafter cited parenthetically.

33. E.M. Forster, *Howards End*, 26. Hereafter cited parenthetically as *HE*.

34. McLuhan, *Understanding Media,* 8. On McLuhan and music—including the feedback loop between composer and audience—see Wilkey, "McLuhan and Meaning."

35. McLuhan and Carpenter, *Explorations in Communication*, 69.

36. Chion, *Audio-Vision*, 33.

37. Preface to Charlotte Eliot's *Savoranola* (1926), qtd. in Kenner, *The Mechanic Muse*, 9.

38. Lefebvre, *Rhythmanalysis*, xii.

39. Lukács, "Aesthetic Culture," 154.

40. Fussell, *Poetic Meter and Poetic Form*, 5. Fussell cites a similar assertion made by I.A. Richards, who praised Eliot's *Waste Land* for its "music of ideas" (Richards, *Principles*, 276).

41. Williams, *The Long Revolution*, 24.

42. See, for example, Sidran, *Black Talk*, 8; McClary, *Feminine Endings*, 23; Negus,

Popular Music in Theory, 222; DeNora, *Music in Everyday Life*, 86. I am not indifferent to the problems of the term "classical music," but I shall adopt it anyway; the alternative terms ("art music," "high music," etc.) do not strike me as improvements.

43. Both Bucknell, *Literary Modernism* and Albright, *Untwisting the Serpent* hereafter cited parenthetically.

44. See McClary, *Feminine Endings*; Williams, *Long Revolution*; Hutcheon and Hutcheon, *Opera: Desire, Disease, Death*; Taruskin, *Stravinsky and the Russian Traditions*; all hereafter cited parenthetically.

45. Middleton, *Studying Popular Music*, 35. Hereafter cited parenthetically.

46. Williams, *Culture and Materialism*, 39. Hereafter cited parenthetically as *CM*.

47. I apply the "shrinking island" trope, somewhat anachronistically, from Esty, *A Shrinking Island*; it will more directly apply to my chapter six.

48. On homologies between deconstruction and negative dialectics, see Jay, *Adorno*; Menke, *Sovereignty of Art*; Wilke, "Adorno and Derrida"; Subotnik, *Deconstructive Variations*; Kaufman, "Negatively Capable Dialectics"; and Jochen Schulte-Sasse's preface to Bürger, *Theory of the Avant-Garde*.

49. Quoted in McNeilly, "Culture, Race, Rhythm," 31. By 1919, McNeilly points out, Eliot attributed this unease to his status as a distinguished intellectual, with antennae too finely tuned for comfort.

50. Trilling, *E.M. Forster*, 118.

51. Sidran, *Black Talk*; Faulk, *Music Hall*; Jacques, *Change in the Weather*; Appel Jr., *Jazz Modernism*; Graham, *Great American Songbooks*. Hereafter cited parenthetically.

Chapter One. Orchestrating Modernity

1. Jameson, *The Political Unconscious*, 215.

2. Craft, *Stravinsky*, 53.

3. Abbate, "Wagner, Cinema, and Redemptive Glee," 200.

4. Terry Eagleton, "Contradictions," 35.

5. See Gramsci's argument that the Futurists "destroyed, destroyed, destroyed, without worrying if the new creations . . . were on the whole superior to those destroyed." "Marinetti the Revolutionary," 215.

6. "[After Attali], it seems, specialists in econometrics need no longer analyze their graphs—they need only listen to a given era's musical heartbeat to predict political upheavals." Nattiez, *Music and Discourse*, 47. Hereafter cited parenthetically.

7. Barthes, "Musica Practica," 153, his emphasis.

8. On Barthes in relation to the castrato, see Dame, "Unveiled Voices."

9. Since some languages possess no word for "music" (only for specific musical *practices*), Nattiez cautions that the shifting "schism between music and noise clearly illustrates the *mobility* of interpretants that separates 'musical' from 'nonmusical'" (54, his italics).

10. Hanslick, *On the Musically Beautiful*, 58, 68. Hereafter cited parenthetically.

11. Bernstein made a similar claim in his 1976 Harvard Lectures (reprinted as *The Unanswered Question*), using the "transformations" of Chomskyan linguistics to claim that music has a "purely musical meaning." I find Bernstein's use of Chomsky specious, but the claim of "purely musical meaning" has both precedents and successors.

12. This observation is indebted to Jonathan Neufeld; see, for example, his essay "Musical Formalism," a critique of the formalist aesthetics of Hanslick and Peter Kivy in relation to political performance. See also Hamilton, *Aesthetics and Music*, 81ff; Paddison, *Adorno's Aesthetics of Music*, 66ff.

13. Adorno, *Philosophy of New Music*, 31. Hereafter cited parenthetically as *PNM*.

14. Leppert, "Commentary," in Adorno, *Essays on Music*, 231–2.

15. Adorno, *Alban Berg*, 76.

16. Williams felt that *Ballet Mécanique* had "annihilated" the anxieties of urban noise: "when I actually came upon noise in reality, I found that I had gone up over it." Whitesitt, *Antheil*, 37. Jerz links this anecdote to Williams's "The Great Figure": "gong clangs/siren howls/and wheels rumbling." *Technology in American Drama*, 39. Both hereafter cited parenthetically.

17. See, for example, the discussion of Welles, Lazarsfeld, and Adorno in Jackie Orr's somewhat hypervigilant book *Panic Diaries.*

18. This formulation is indebted to Steggle, "Acoustics of Hell." Steggle cites T.S. Eliot's assertion, "I cannot feel that my appreciation of Milton leads anywhere outside the mazes of sound."

19. Ovid, *Metamorphoses*, trans. Dryden, 12.67–82. Hereafter cited by book and line.

20. Pound, *ABC of Reading*, 29.

21. Eliot, *The Waste Land*, II.102. Excerpts from *The Waste Land* hereafter cited parenthetically.

22. On rumor, noise, and gender, see Botelho, *Renaissance Earwitnesses*.

23. Picker, *Victorian Soundscapes*, 55.

24. Rainey, "The Creation of the Avant-Garde," 209.

25. On Lewis and Lukács, see Wollaeger, *Modernism, Media, and Propaganda*, 23ff.

26. See the discussion on "musical empathy" in Sherry, *Pound, Lewis, and Radical Modernism*, ch. 1.

27. Said, *Culture and Imperialism*, 49ff., compares Lukács's temporal emphasis on history to Gramsci's more territorial politics. Jed Esty, in *Unseasonable Youth*, claims that Lukács identifies, but fails fully to explore, the nation-state as the point of closure for the novel's temporality.

28. Lilienfield, "Music and Society in the 20th Century," 127.

29. On Lukács's relation to Bartók, see Frigyesi, *Bartók*, particularly 160ff.

30. These themes subtend Lukács's writing; see in particular his essays "The Ideology of Modernism" (1956) and "The Intellectual Physiognomy," 163ff.

31. Quoted in Laki, *Bartók and His World*, 12.

32. Paddison, *Adorno's Aesthetics*, 40. My account of Adorno on Bartók is deeply indebted to Paddison, 37ff. Hereafter cited parenthetically.

33. Williams, *Culture and Society*, 263–4, argues that while the term "organic" initially meant "mechanical" or "instrumental," critiques of modern industrialism led it to take on a holistic, agricultural connotation.

34. Jameson, "Beyond the Cave," 9.

35. On *Mandarin* as a "grotesque hybrid," see Brown, *Bartók and the Grotesque*, 131.

36. Monelle, *Linguistics and Semiotics in Music*, 3.

37. Osbert Sitwell, "A Few Days," 31.

38. Barthes, "The Grain of the Voice," 179, italics in original. Hereafter cited parenthetically.

39. Abbate, *In Search of Opera*, 10ff; Adorno, "Opera and the Long-Playing Record," 284.

40. Kreilkamp, *Voice and the Victorian Storyteller*, 182; Campbell. *Wireless Writing*.

41. Kahn, *Noise, Water, Meat*, 21. Hereafter cited parenthetically.

42. Schopenhauer, *World as Will*, vol. 1, 258. Hereafter cited parenthetically as *WWR*.

43. Magee, *Tristan Chord*, 128, argues that Schopenhauer "positively advocated" the political disillusionment that Wagner, by that point, was already experiencing. On *Das Rheingold* and Schopenhauer, see Berry, *Treacherous Bonds*, 60.

44. On Schopenhauer and Conrad, see Wollaeger, *Conrad*, 33ff. Hereafter cited parenthetically.

45. See Atrzert, "Schopenhauer and Freud."

46. Though it is hard to demonstrate that Baudelaire was directly engaged with Schopenhauer, Mestrovic argues that he "paved the way for . . . direct acceptance of Schopenhauer's philosophy into France." *The Coming Fin de Siècle*, 68. Eliot's favorite Schopenhauerian was Jules Laforgue, the short-lived French Symbolist poet. See Oser, *The Ethics of Modernism*, 46.

47. Baudelaire, "L'Homme et la Mer," *Flowers of Evil*, lines 5–8.

48. Qtd. in Thompson, *Soundscape*, 140. Hereafter cited parenthetically.

49. Suárez, *Pop Modernism*, compares Antheil to Eliot (135) and draws on the poem's various "modes of inscription," signification, and "textual mechanics" (122–3). Hereafter cited parenthetically.

50. Antheil, *Bad Boy of Music*. Hereafter cited parenthetically as *BBM*.

51. Carol Oja cites this passage, arguing that "the machine . . . freed composers to push beyond the limitations of acoustic instruments and human performers" (70). Hereafter cited parenthetically.

52. Stallybrass and White, *Politics and Poetics of Transgression*, passim. Hereafter cited parenthetically.

53. HaCohen, *Music Libel against the Jews*. Hereafter cited parenthetically.

54. Cowell, *Three Anti-Modernist Songs*, CD, Naxos, 2005.

55. Albright, ed., *Modernism and Music*, 103.

56. Eliot, "The Love Song of J. Alfred Prufrock," lines 96-7. Hereafter cited parenthetically.

57. Adorno, *Quasi Una Fantasia*, qtd. in Lydia Goehr, "Dissonant Works," 235.

58. Ringer, "Assimilation," 24. Hereafter cited parenthetically.

59. See Thomas Harrison, *1910*, 31. Like Ringer, Harrison draws on Schoenberg's status as a Jew, arguing that artists in 1910 sought "new modes of comprehension transcending the historical and stubborn dualities," particularly in the "hyphenated empire[s]" of Austro-Germany and Austro-Hungary.

60. Melnick, *Fullness of Dissonance*, 9. Hereafter cited parenthetically.

61. Adorno and Horkheimer, *The Dialectic of Enlightenment*, 120. Hereafter cited parenthetically as *DE*.

62. Orwell, "Politics and the English Language," 134.

63. Conrad, *Heart of Darkness*, 232. Hereafter cited parenthetically.

64. On modernist writing and dance, see Koritz, *Gendering Bodies*; Mester, *Movement and Modernism*; Preston, *Modernism's Mythic Pose*.

65. On Adorno and popular music, see Gracyk's *Rhythm and Noise*, ch. 6. Gracyk's study pursues Russolo's notion of the "noise-sound" to articulate rock music's innovations in timbre and dynamics.

66. Huxley, *The Perennial Philosophy*, 218.

67. Golston, *Rhythm and Race*, 17. Hereafter cited parenthetically.

68. Osbert Sitwell, *Penny Foolish*, 85.

69. Brecht's notes on *Threepenny Opera* (1929), entitled "The Literarization of the Theatre," speak of a "speaking-against-the-music" that defamiliarizes the written melody (45).

70. Stravinsky claimed in 1951 that his music was "best understood by children and animals" (something of a gimmick given the complex pitch relations of his music).

71. Eliot, "The Beating of a Drum," 11-2, asserts that poetry begins with a "savage beating on a drum," not only citing an origin, but identifying the "mimetic" Aristotelian function of rhythm.

72. Cowan historicizes Bücher's work as "part of a much broader medical mapping of the body as a network of organic 'rhythms'" by figures including Georg Simmel, Emil Jaques-Dalcroze, Hans Richter, Walter Ruttmann, and Fritz Lang. "The Heart Machine," 228. Hereafter cited parenthetically. On rhythm and labor management, see Rabinbach, *The Human Motor*.

73. Simmel, "The Metropolis and Mental Life," 52.

Chapter Two. Beating Obedient, Thinking of the Key

1. See Gunning, "Illusions Past and Future." For Marx, the phantasmagoria and the *camera obscura* served as material metaphors for false consciousness acting on

the perceptual apparatus (producing, respectively, a ghostly image and an upside-down refraction of the real object). Phantasmagoric effects pervade Wagner's work: Rhinemaidens clouded with steam produced by locomotive-boilers, Valkyries produced through magic-lantern effects, and stage-changes misted by colored smoke.

2. Cf. Lentricchia's study of modernism's disciplinary totalizing impulses in *Ariel and the Police*.

3. See Brooks's account of Eliot's "Thames Sisters" in "*The Waste Land:* An Analysis"; Chinitz's *T.S. Eliot and the Cultural Divide*; and Suárez's study of Eliot's "ragging" in *Pop Modernism*.

4. Wilson, "The Poetry of Drouth" (1922), 145.

5. Raymond Williams (*Drama: From Ibsen to Eliot* [1952]) praised *Sweeney's* rhythmic "ordering of sounds." On Williams, and on the street drill, see Tiwari and Tiwari, *Plays of T.S. Eliot*, 57. McNeilly, "Culture, Race, Rhythm," argues that *Sweeney* uses "presemantic rhythmic components of language" as a "radical form of cultural critique through a complex juxtaposition of high and low culture" (25).

6. J.M. Bernstein discusses this passage in *Against Voluptuous Bodies*, 210ff.

7. See Foster, *Adorno*, 161ff.

8. Paul Jones, "Technology is not the Cultural Form?", argues that though Williams refuses Adorno's all-encompassing terror of the culture industry, his embrace of homology "follows Adorno in rejectin[g] the affirmative dimensions of Benjamin's concept."

9. Dana, "Orchestrating *The Waste Land*," 268. Hereafter cited parenthetically.

10. Ruth Nevo, "*The Waste Land*," argues that the poem dislocates its own mythical orders: "its gaps and ellipses are the fountainheads of its significance, its disorder its order" (456).

11. As Stan Link writes, "As heard through noise, recordings isolate and contain their own authenticity that does not require verification from another source. Noise thus emancipates the perception of authenticity from the authority of any original" (39).

12. Kittler, *Gramophone, Film, Typewriter*, 44.

13. Harding, *Adorno and 'A Writing of the Ruins,'* 4–5.

14. Eliot, "The Music of Poetry," 32–3. Hereafter cited parenthetically.

15. Eliot, "Matthew Arnold," *The Use of Poetry*, 111. Hereafter cited parenthetically.

16. Levenson, *A Genealogy of Modernism*, 174.

17. Adorno, "Wagner's Relevance for Today," 587. Hereafter cited parenthetically as "Relevance."

18. Chinitz, *T.S. Eliot and the Cultural Divide*, 10.

19. Shaw, *The Perfect Wagnerite*, 17.

20. Huyssen, *After the Great Divide*, 36. Hereafter cited parenthetically.

21. Adorno, *In Search of Wagner*, 91. Hereafter cited parenthetically as *Search*.

22. Lukács, "The Ideology of Modernism," 189.

23. Bauer, "Adorno's Wagner," 81–2. The internal quotation is from *Dialectic of*

Enlightenment, 143. Miner, *Resonant Gaps* reads Adorno and Baudelaire as ambivalent toward Wagner's "vagueness" (51).

24. Adorno, "Selbstanzeige des Essaybuches 'Versuch über Wagner'" (1952), qtd. in Bauer 81.

25. Rainey, *Revisiting* The Waste Land, 51.

26. Eliot, "Marie Lloyd," 174. Hereafter cited parenthetically.

27. North suggests that Eliot's use of the Melanesians links cultural health with "unified popular culture," turning an anthropological lesson onto London. *Reading 1922*, 56. Michael North discusses the hypothesis, proffered by W.H.R. Rivers and Bronisław Malinowski, that the Melanesians had died by boredom; North weighs the contradictory possibilities that civilizations could be saved by anthropological knowledge, or that such knowledge could "so qualify faith in one's own society as to destroy it" (*Reading 1922* 54–5).

28. "[The phonograph] will be used to enable one to master a new air, the child to form its first songs, or to sing him to sleep." Edison, "The Phonograph and its Future," 533.

29. Eliot, "War-Paint and Feathers," 122.

30. Faulk, *Music Hall*, 51–2.

31. See Chinitz's "A Jazz-Banjorine, Not a Lute."

32. McLuhan, "Rhetoric of *The Waste Land*," 575.

33. On these "four Os" as a "left-hand rhythm," see Sigg, "Eliot as a Product of America," 21.

34. On Eliot and *Parade*, see Hargrove, "The Great Parade" and "T.S. Eliot and Popular Entertainment in Paris, 1910–1911."

35. Hauck, "Abortion and the Individual Talent."

36. See Huyssen, "Mass Culture as Woman," chap. 3 of *After the Great Divide*.

37. I am giving admittedly short shrift to the question of race here—Bell's essay is explicitly racist in several respects. See Michael North's discussion of Bell in *Dialect of Modernism*, 10, ch. 4 ("Pound and Eliot's Racial Masquerade"). On Adorno's own racial politics, see Leppert's edition of Adorno's *Essays on Music*, 531; Harding, *Adorno*, 102ff.; Wilcock, "Adorno, Jazz, and Racism." I hope it is clear that I do not share Adorno's distaste for jazz, but I reject the widespread notion that they express racist contempt for African-American musicians. Adorno attacked the culture industry's manipulation *of* black musicians for "coloristic" exotic effect ("On Jazz" [1936], 477).

38. On adaptation as "palimpsest," see Linda Hutcheon, *A Theory of Adaptation*, 33.

39. Rainey, *Annotated*, 105.

40. Eliot, *The Waste Land: A Facsimile*, 37.

41. Eliot, *The Waste Land: A Facsimile*, 30–1.

42. Eliot, "From 'Baudelaire,'" 236, my italics.

43. On Wagner's and Eliot's anti-Semitism, see Julius, *Eliot, Anti-Semitism, and Literary Form*, 101ff.

44. Showalter, "Syphilis," 105.

45. Lawrence Kramer, *Music as Cultural Practice,* 138.

46. Leppert, *The Sight of Sound*, xxvii. Hereafter cited parenthetically.

47. Smith, "Laughing at the Redeemer," 19, 10. Hereafter cited parenthetically.

48. Abbate, "Immortal Voices, Mortal Forms," 297.

49. On Eliot and media, see Suárez, Kreilkamp, Kenner, and Knowles, "Death by Gramophone."

50. See Cascone, "Aesthetics of Failure" and Sanglid, "Glitch," which draws on Adorno's phonograph essays.

51. Adorno, "Curves of the Needle," 274. Hereafter cited parenthetically as "Curves."

52. Adorno, "Form of the Phonograph Record," 280. Hereafter cited parenthetically as "Form." Adorno's ambivalent fascination with the phonograph, and with sound technologies in general, bears comparison to that of Béla Bartók, who used phonograph recordings of folkloric music to render its non-Western rhythms and tonalities more precisely. (See the brief discussion of Bartók in ch.1). Bartók wrote that Thomas Edison was "the father of modern folksong studies" (qtd. in Yates, "Percy Grainger, 265). Julie Brown writes that Bartók's interest in the phonograph and the radio was, as for Adorno, matched with a skepticism about the effects of mass-reproduced music on listening habits (*Bartók and the Grotesque*, 73).

53. Sterne, *The Audible Past*, 306–7.

54. Attali suggests that the record encodes not just sound, but "noise with a specific ritual function"—it encodes the time of production and of consumption, as "*people must devote their time to producing the means to buy recordings of other people's time*" (101, his italics).

55. I use the terms "phonograph" and "gramophone" interchangeably here. Albright, who argues that *Parade* is "constructed entirely around the rhythms of advertising," associates the ballet with Joyce, the "sometime copywriter" (*Untwisting* 190).

56. Cocteau, "The Eiffel Tower Wedding Party," 161.

57. On Futurism and the music hall, see Cheshire, "Futurism, Marinetti, and the Music Hall."

58. Kittler, "World-Breath: On Wagner's Media Technology." Hereafter cited parenthetically.

59. The Wagner passage is quoted in Levin, *Richard Wagner, Fritz Lang, and the Nibelungen*, 46.

60. Ed Madden, *Tiresian Poetics*, reads Tiresias as a figure of "cinematic" representation whose ambiguous body opens him, and the text, to conflicting "sexological" discourses.

61. In the *Tristan* lines initially quoted by Eliot ("Frisch weht der Wind / Der Heimat zu"), Kurwenal sings a song about a lost Irish love, in response to which the furious Isolde calls up her "feeble art" to effect her own "death by water": "To the

furious vortex/of raging tempests!" (I.i.). For a fuller account of Eliot in relation to *Tristan*, see Waldron, as well as Sloane, "Wagner's Arthurian Sources.'"

62. Katz discusses the McGurk Effect in *Capturing Sound*, 25.

Chapter Three. The Antheil Era

1. On Pound in relation to Marinetti, see Campbell, *Wireless Writing*, which argues that Pound "becomes part of a media network, whether in writing or over the wireless" (100).

2. Pound, "A Retrospect," 9. Hereafter cited parenthetically.

3. See Adams, "Are the *Cantos* a Fugue?". On Pound's musical aesthetics, see Bucknell, *Literary Modernism*; Adams, "Musical Neofism"; Adams, "The Soundscape of the *Cantos*"; Fisher, *Pound's Radio Operas*; and Henderson, "Pound and Music." All hereafter cited parenthetically.

4. Albright, *Quantum Poetics*, 151.

5. One finds the title spelled (even by Antheil himself) as "Mécanique" and "Méchanique," with and without the accents. I shall prefer "Mécanique" but preserve quoted spellings as they appear.

6. Lehrman, "The Ballet Mécanique Page."

7. Pound, "Antheil, 1924–1926," 315, his italics.

8. Albright, *Quantum* 214, observes this passage's obverse relation to "Mauberley" and its debts to Russolo. On the (non)programmatic elements in *Ballet Mécanique*, see Albright, *Untwisting* 237.

9. See Kenner, *Pound Era*, 317; on the pianola, see Marjorie Perloff, *Poetics of Indeterminacy*, 166–7.

10. Armstrong, "Player Piano," 1, his italics.

11. Pound, *Guide to Kulchur*, 170. Hereafter cited parenthetically as *GK*.

12. Pound, Canto LXV, p. 229. Excerpts from the *Cantos* will be cited by poem number and page, from the New Directions edition.

13. "We are undergoing an Antheil revival," writes Piccinini, Review. Cf. Oja, *Making Music Modern*; Cook, "Antheil's *Transatlantic*." The realization of *Ballet Mécanique* using automated instruments is documented in Frank's film *Bad Boy Made Good*. Rhodes' recent book *Hedy's Folly* garnered a review in the *New York Times* by American minimalist composer John Adams.

14. On these experiments, see Golston, *Rhythm and Race*, 65ff.

15. Cf. Edmund Wilson: "'Look at me!' [Pound] says in effect to his compatriots at home. 'See how cultured and cosmopolitan I have become since I've left America how different from you over there! I'll bet there's not a man among you who knows about Pratinas and Gaudier-Brzeska. I can read half a dozen languages! I am a friend of Francis Picabia!' But his sophistication is still juvenile, his ironies are still clumsy and obvious." *The Shores of Light*, 45.

16. Pound, "Arnold Dolmetsch," 38. Hereafter cited parenthetically.

17. Marjorie Perloff, *The Futurist Moment*, 189–90.

18. Coyle, *Ezra Pound, Popular Genres, and the Discourse of Genre*, 34. Hereafter cited parenthetically.

19. For example, Bucknell grasps Pound's "incoherent anti-Semitism" and economic values while emphasizing, after Pater and Mallarmé, music as textual surface.

20. Hoffa, "Pound and Antheil," 54, 60.

21. According to Erin Templeton, "Dear Ezzroar," Antheil's eventual turn to Hollywood solidified Pound's commitment to centralized patronage of the arts (a commitment found in the Malatesta *Cantos* and in Pound's Mussolinism).

22. Fisher, *Ezra Pound's Radio Operas*, 101.

23. Bush, *Ideographic Modernism*, finds in the ideogram a kinship with new means of storing data and with colonial discourses on the Orient.

24. Goble, *Beautiful Circuits*, 244. Goble builds on Alan Liu's claim that modernism offers "the spirit of industrialism in the formalist credo that form is integral with content," as it incoherently endorses "everything from art as a Duchamp ready-made to a New Critical verbal icon." *The Laws of Cool*, 79.

25. Strunk, *Elements of Style*, 122.

26. Man Ray credits Dudley Murphy; see Lawder, *Cubist Cinema*. Murphy was taken with Pound's "vortoscope," which used a shaving mirror in order to take "Vorticist-style photographs." Carpenter, *A Serious Character*, 281–2. Hereafter cited parenthetically.

27. Imbs, *Confessions*, 27. Hereafter cited parenthetically.

28. For more on Antheil's and Friede's reactions, see Whitesitt 29ff.

29. Benjamin, "Work of Art," 241. In *The Futurist Moment*, Marjorie Perloff grants Marinetti's fascism while contesting that futurism "inevitably pointed" toward fascism.

30. Pound, untitled, *The New Masses* (March 1927), rpt. in *Antheil and the Treatise on Harmony*, 139.

31. Pound, "Antheil (Retrospect)" (1924), 260. Hereafter cited parenthetically. The essay consists largely of quotations from Antheil's criticism of other composers.

32. Lewis, *Time and Western Man* (1927), 42. Hereafter cited parenthetically.

33. Antheil, "My Ballet Mecanique," 789–91, his italics. Hereafter cited parenthetically.

34. Bell and Lland. "Silence and Solidity."

35. Jaffé, *De Stijl*, 18–9.

36. Crary, "Spectacle, Attention, Memory," passim.

37. Jerz writes, "'Ballet Méchanique' and *Metropolis* confront technology as unavoidable, but . . . potentially empowering," such that "modern machinery retains all the primal frenzy of jungle drums." *Technology*, 40.

38. Rob Wallace, *Improvisation*, excavates a relationship between Pound's theories and African-American music, including his contributions to Nancy Cunard's

Negro anthology. See also North's discussion of Pound and Eliot's "racial masquerade" in *The Dialect of Modernism*.

39. On Pound, Lewis, and Bergson's "laws of musical empathy," see Sherry, *Radical Modernism*, 13.

40. For example, on Bergson and Leo Ornstein, see Oja, *Making Music Modern*, 17ff.

41. Quoted in Jerz, *Technology*, 37.

42. Kenner, *Mechanic Muse*, 41.

43. On the "spectacularly wrong" judgments in "Atheling's" writings, see Ingham, "Pound and Music," 241ff.

44. Pound, "Arnold Dolmetsch," 46. Hereafter cited parenthetically.

45. Pound, "*Vers Libre* and Arnold Dolmetsch," 439, his italics. Hereafter cited parenthetically.

46. Homer, *Odyssey* (trans. Lattimore), XII.190.

47. Quoted in Adams, "Are the *Cantos* a Fugue?", 38.

48. Debussy's relation to Wagner went through cycles of influence and *agon*, making Pound's association of Debussy with Wagner apt but complicated. See Holloway, *Debussy and Wagner*, and essays in Fulcher (ed.), *Debussy and his World*. *Pelléas* drew both comparisons to Wagner and triumphant declarations of Wagnerism's death (Donnellon, "Debussy," 46ff).

49. In addition to editing the *Ezra Pound and Music* volume, Schafer is among the first innovators of "soundscape" studies; his book *The Soundscape* contains sustained readings of the *Cantos*.

50. Liebregts, *Pound and Neoplatonism*, 203-4 offers a lucid account of Pound on Cavalcanti's "plastic."

51. Antheil, "Music Tomorrow," 123-6, his italics.

52. See Oja, *Making Music Modern*, 91ff.

53. Pound, "Cavalcanti," 150. Hereafter cited parenthetically. Eliot dates the essay "1910-1931."

54. T. Austin Graham argues that Pound's gesture to the "pornograph" [sic] in XXIX critiques the tawdry "mechanical music," which is corrupted by, and will not outlast, the cicadas' natural noise.

55. Letter to Agnes Bedford (April 1921), reprinted in Schafer (ed.), *Ezra Pound and Music*, 243.

56. Pound, "A Serious Artist," 51.

57. George Antheil, "Mother of the Earth," 227.

58. Michael Alexander, *Poetic Achievement*, 152.

59. Pound, "Henry James," 324. Hereafter cited parenthetically as HJ. Eliot is known to have said that James had a mind "so fine that no idea could violate it" ("Henry James," 151).

60. See, respectively, Campbell, *Wireless Writing*; and Tiffany, *Radio Corpse*.

61. Surette, *Birth of Modernism*, 16, 68ff, discusses the "nekuia" of the *Cantos* as rooted in occultism. Kuberski, *A Calculus of Ezra Pound*, 125, links Pound's nekuia to Adorno and Horkheimer's discussion of "the annulment of death" in *The Odyssey* (*DE* 76).

62. Douglas Mao, *Solid Objects*, 177.

63. Stauder, "Without an Ear," 258.

64. Bayard refers to Satie's "instanteneist" ballet *Relâche* ("Closed"; 1924). As an entr'acte to *Relâche*, Frances Picabia produced a film (*Entr'acte*) featuring Satie himself, as well as a funeral procession led by a camel. See Albright, *Untwisting*, 220ff. As an "entr'acte" to a ballet premised on a non-performance ("relâche"), the film bespeaks Satie's and Picabia's Dadaist inclinations.

Chapter Four. Joyce's Phoneygraphs

1. See Imbs, *Confessions*, 57.

2. Budgen, *James Joyce*, 182.

3. Ellmann, *James Joyce*, 558. Hereafter cited parenthetically as *JJ*.

4. See Paul Martin, "Mr. Bloom and the Cyclops." Martin performed his adaptation of the existing fragments of the opera at the 1996 International James Joyce Symposium; see Knowles, "Introduction," xxvii-xlii. Albright briefly mentions the *Mr. Bloom* project in *Untwisting*, 148, as does Kahn in *Noise, Water, Meat*, 126ff. Timothy Martin, "'Cyclops' as Opera," likens the episode's "alternation between . . . the straightforward narrative . . . versus the florid interpolations" to the operatic movement between aria and recitative (227).

5. See Antheil's letter to Pound in April 1925, reprinted in Piccinini, "*Non piu,*" 79.

6. Joyce, *Portrait*, 213. Hereafter cited parenthetically as *P*.

7. Quotations from Ulysses cited parenthetically, by chapter and line, as *U*.

8. See Weaver, *Joyce's Music and Noise*. Hereafter cited parenthetically.

9. On *Ulysses*' "phonographic" recording of noise, see Frattarola, "The Phonograph and the Modernist Novel," which describes "sound and peripheral noise as integral to the subjectivity of their characters" (147); Rice, "His Master's Voice and Joyce"; and Derrida, "Ulysses Gramophone."

10. See also Hall, "Joyce's Use of Da Ponte and Mozart's *Don Giovanni*"; Cope, "The Rhythmic Gesture"; Bowen, *Musical Allusions*; Wightman, "Szymanowski and Joyce"; Hodgart and Bauerle, *Joyce's Grand Operoar:*. On the "fugal" structure of "Sirens," see Cole, "Fugal Structure"; Levin, "The Sirens Episode as Music"; Zimmerman, "Musical Form as Narrator." Kenner writes, "Joyce embalms in cadences what Dublin embalms in music." *Dublin's Joyce*, 12.

11. Smith, "Structural Rhythm in *Ulysses*," 417.

12. The articles in the special section of *Modernism/Modernity* (2009) entitled "Joyce's Noises" include Margot Norris, on Joyce's 1929 recording of "Anna Livia

Plurabelle"; Maud Ellmann on aurality in *Ulysses;* and Vincent J. Cheng, on Joyce's prosody. The quotation is from Ellmann, 384.

13. Schneider, "Mediatization," argues that Joyce uses "Aeolus" and "Oxen of the Sun" to highlight the mediating properties of language.

14. McDonald, "The Strength and Sorrow of Young Stephen," reads consonance and dissonance as "mutually informing . . . categories," arguing that the sublimation of noise into dissonance privileges art as Joyce's best hope of confronting "the noise of [Ireland's] own politics" (381).

15. Danius, *The Senses of Modernism*, argues that *Ulysses* represents a modernist total artwork in the spirit of Wagner, but contends that Joyce privileges sight as the object of modernity's assault. Danius poses a connection between Joyce and Fernand Léger, the eye behind the *Ballet Mécanique* film (168).

16. In "'Toft's Cumbersome Whirligig,'" 154, Hampson uses the phrase "theatrical novel" to describe Flaubert's *Temptation of St. Anthony* in the context of "Circe's" "self-conscious theatricality."

17. See Martin, "Joyce, Wagner, and the Wandering Jew" and *Joyce and Wagner*. Hereafter cited parenthetically. Wagner's contempt for turning musical performances into social events led Joyce to ally him with "musical idealism" (*Joyce and Wagner* 1). Joyce grew impatient with the "Wagner cult," which he thought decadent and "[eighteen-]ninetyish" (32; see also Ellmann*, JJ* 112).

18. On "complex seeing," see Calico, *Brecht at the Opera*, 152ff.

19. Cocteau, "The Collaboration of 'Parade.'" Hereafter cited parenthetically.

20. Gilbert, *James Joyce's* Ulysses, 30, 177.

21. Danius, *Senses,* 167. Danius suggests that Joyce's novel, by attempting to dissociate sight and sound, demonstrates that the two "have to operate in tandem" (185).

22. See Reilly, "Joyce and Dublin Opera," and McCourt, "Joyce's Trieste." Reilly draws on Attali to argue that "Joyce's use of opera draws attention to its sophisticated cultural codes" and "institutional structure" (14); McCourt examines the politics of Trieste opera during Joyce's time there.

23. Joyce, "The Home Rule Comet," 159. Hereafter cited parenthetically.

24. Joyce, "Realism and Idealism," 173, hereafter cited parenthetically. The term translated as "realism" is *verismo*, a term also used for naturalistic Italian opera. Brown, "The Logic of Realism," cites *verismo* opera and Joyce's *Dubliners* in a Hegelian account of "realism."

25. Cf. Blake on Milton (1809): "Every time less than a pulsation of the artery / Is equal in its period & value to six thousand years" (quoted in Joyce, *Occasional*, 300n).

26. As S.L. Goldberg argues, "For Joyce the aesthetic symbol expresses both the 'naturalistic' world of external reality and the activity of the individual at the same time." *The Classical Temper*, 216.

27. Joyce, "James Clarence Mangan," 54. Hereafter cited parenthetically.

28. Joyce, "The Holy Office," hereafter cited parenthetically by line.

29. Yeats, "To Ireland in the Coming Times," lines 1–2. Hereafter cited parenthetically.

30. Both the excremental imagery and the poem's tetrameter suggest Joyce's debts to Swift, whose "excremental vision" would be discussed in John Middleton Murry's *Jonathan Swift: A Critical Biography*. See Anspaugh, "Powers of Ordure"; and Esty, "Excremental Postcolonialism."

31. Burns, *Gestural Politics*, 52–3. On Joyce's unbinding of linguistic authority, see McClean, "Wasted Words"; Garvey, "City Limits."

32. Kristeva, *Powers of Horror*, 23.

33. Pound, *Selected Letters*, 153.

34. Toop, *Sinister Resonance*, 140ff.

35. Spoo, "Rival Confessors in 'Chamber Music,'" 483.

36. Joyce, "Chamber Music," section I. Hereafter cited parenthetically.

37. Hepburn, "Noise, Music, Voice, *Dubliners*," 196.

38. Joyce, *Dubliners*, 109, 114. Hereafter cited parenthetically as *D*.

39. Owens, *Joyce's Painful Case*, 1, reads Duffy as a Catholic apostate who embraces, first, Schopenhauerian pessimism and, then, "Nietzschean nihilism."

40. O'Connor, "Joyce and Dissociated Metaphor," 373. Hereafter cited parenthetically.

41. In *Portrait* and *Ulysses*, Stephen associates the movement of rhythm with theatrical gesture—a wholly Wagnerian ideal. See Wagner, "The Art-Work of the Future," 101. See also Cope. As Boes argues, Joyce associates rhythm with the dialectical movement of history.

42. Gifford, *Joyce Annotated*, 218.

43. W.B. Yeats, *The Countess Cathleen*.

44. On the *Countess Cathleen* premiere, see Gifford, *Joyce Annotated*, 269, and Dean, *Riot and Great Anger*.

45. I accept Hall's argument that in *Ulysses* we should not just read da Ponte's words but should hear the musical accompaniment (79). "Là ci darem la mano" is performed, along with much of the music from *Ulysses*, on a CD entitled *Joyce Songs: James Joyce's Musical Dublin*.

46. Lenehan, of course, is a recycled character from "Two Gallants," in which he plays "a scale of variations idly along the railings" of the fence outside the Duke's Lawn (*D* 56)

47. Sicari reads the sound of MacHugh's teeth as a parody of naturalism. *Joyce's Modernist Allegory*, 70.

48. Knowles, "Introduction," xxx.

49. As Albright suggests, Picasso's costumes for *Parade*, with whorls suggestive of male genitalia, tell the audience something akin to "Go have sexual intercourse with yourself" (*Untwisting*, 189).

50. The relation between "Circe" and melodrama ("musical drama") also deserves

attention, in light of Bentley's suggestion that melodrama is the hypercorporeal "[n]aturalism of the dream life"—see *The Life of the Drama*, 205.

51. Wagner refers to *Zukunftsmusik* in his essay "Art and Revolution," and further develops the notion in "The Art-Work of the Future."

52. Martin notes a gesture to *Götterdämmerung* in "Circe's" reference to "the air of the bloodoath in The Dusk of the Gods" and Stephen's allusion to Siegfried's death (44; *U* 15.3651–3).

53. Tindall, *A Reader's Guide to "Finnegans Wake,"* 65. Hereafter cited parenthetically.

54. McLuhan and Fiore, *The Medium is the Massage*, 111. On McLuhan and the *Wake*, see Theall and Theall, "Marshall McLuhan and James Joyce."

55. Hayman, "*Tristan and Isolde*," reads the presence of *Tristan* in Joyce's *Wake*—in conversation with Pound—as a way out of fin-de-siècle decadence.

56. Marjorie Perloff, "Music for Words," hereafter cited parenthetically.

57. David Bernstein, "Music I," 69.

58. Cage, liner notes to *Roaratorio*, 19.

59. Cage, *X*, 57. Hereafter cited parenthetically.

60. Klein, "The Euphonium Cagehoused," 158.

Chapter Five. Performing Publicity

1. Edith Sitwell, *Taken Care Of*, 122. Hereafter cited parenthetically.

2. Pearson, *Façades*, 184–5. Hereafter cited parenthetically. Gyllian Phillips connects *Façade* to Maurice Ravel's and Georges Bizet's mediations of Spanish music, arguing that *Façade* makes an "ironic alliance between racial 'otherness,' darkness, and eroticism or desire." "'The Rhythm of the Visible World,'" 119, 127. Barringer claims that the *Façade* curtain imitated *Parade*'s "depersonalizing, automatic, mechanical" alienation of the audience. "Facades," 127.

3. Cevasco, *The Sitwells*, 5.

4. See Gottlieb, "Images, Technology, and Music"; and "Narrating Modernism," which reads *Façade* in relation to a variety of figures fascinated by technological mediations of voice.

5. See Madden, *Harlequin's Stick, Charlie's Cane*; Storey, *Pierrot*; Green and Swan, *The Triumph of Pierrot*; Watkins, *Pyramids at the Louvre*. Hereafter cited parenthetically.

6. Dunsby, *Schoenberg: Pierrot Lunaire*, 6–7.

7. Letter from Aldous Huxley to Julian Huxley, 1917, repr. in *Letters of Aldous Huxley*, 132.

8. Honneth, "Communication and Reconciliation," 50–1. Hereafter cited parenthetically.

9. Osbert Sitwell, "A Few Days in an Author's Life," 31.

10. Driver, "'Façade' Revisited," 8.

11. Podrom, "Influence? Or Intertextuality?," 205–16.

12. See Lloyd, *Walton: Muse of Fire*, 57–8.

13. *Pall Mall Gazette* 13 June 1923, quoted in Lloyd, *Walton: Muse of Fire*, 45.

14. Quoted in Glendinning, *Edith Sitwell*, 77. Osbert refers to the Bloomsbury Group as a "Junta" in *Left Hand,* 19. Hereafter cited parenthetically.

15. Lewis, *The Apes of God*, 354–5.

16. Stoppard, *Artist Descending a Staircase*, scene 2. Lewis's attitudes toward the radio were ambivalent. As Alexander Ruch explains, Lewis saw the BBC's potential to provide broad-based cultural patronage (not least, of his own work), but resented the "ghettoization" of high culture initiated by the corporation's need to differentiate listening publics ("The Best in the Worst," *passim*).

17. Mansell, "Sound and Cultural Politics," 119.

18. For notable exceptions, see Gottlieb and Barringer.

19. See Silver, "Jean Cocteau and the *Image d'Epinal*," hereafter cited parenthetically.

20. O'Brien, "Pantomime," 113. Hereafter cited parenthetically.

21. Glendinning, *Sitwell*, 60. See also Gilpin, "Hardy to Auden," 541; Green and Swan, *Triumph*, 246.

22. Wagner, "On Actors and Singers," 182; Craig, "The Actor and the Über-Marionette," 74. There is more to be said on the role of puppet-theater in modern art (including Conrad, Eliot, and Laforgue), and about Craig's antagonisms with the Ballets Russes (about which, see Garafola, *Diaghilev*, 47).

23. Edith Sitwell, "Façade," *Collected Poems*, hereafter cited parenthetically by poem and line number.

24. Walkowitz, *Cosmopolitan Style*, 4. Hereafter cited parenthetically.

25. Gubar, *Racechanges*, 140ff.

26. Phillips, "Something Lies" 71; Bryant, "Sitwell." Both hereafter cited parenthetically.

27. Brecht, "Alienation Effects," 91. Hereafter cited parenthetically.

28. Quoted in Green and Swan, *Triumph*, 42. On the Sitwells' "dandy-aesthete culture," which "imposes on everything a style that defies the 'mature' values of his father and mother," see Green, *Children of the Sun*, 7.

29. Anderson, *Powers of Distance*, hereafter cited parenthetically.

30. Quoted in Richards, *Imperialism and Music*, 73. (The etymology of "Jingoism" is G.W. Hunt's "Macdermott's War Song" [1878].)

31. Lloyd, *Walton: Muse of Fire*, 5–6.

32. "Hugh Allen, the organist of New College, had played a piano reduction of *Petrushka* to the young chorister, and "when on holiday in Oldham Walton had . . . made a 'horrible din' by playing through *Le Sacre du Printemps* and Bartók's *Allegro Barbaro*." Coggrave, "Sacred Music," 23.

33. Letter to Louisa Walton, 8 Oct. 1916, in Walton, *Selected Letters*, 11.

34. Osbert Sitwell, *Laughter*, 171. Hereafter cited parenthetically.

35. Glenn Watkins, *Proof through the Night*, 42–3. Watkins informs much of my account of the relationship between the Great War and national musical styles.

36. Susana Walton, *Behind the Façade*, 50.

37. On Walton's relief, see Pearson, *Façades*, 134.

38. Stanford, "Music and the War," *Interludes*, 106.

39. Cox, "Towards the National Song Book," argues that a "growing feeling of imperial nationalism" culminated in the 1906 publication of C.V. Stanford's *National Song Book*, which served to bolster Stanford's own civic values and to "tame and refine the working class" (251).

40. Dent, "Landscape with Figures," 1041.

41. Ralph Vaughan Williams, "Should Music Be National?," 6. Hereafter cited parenthetically.

42. Osbert Sitwell, "A Few Days," 21–3 discusses his conflict with Moncrieff (presented as "Mr. X"), who mocks the Sitwells in "a queer-bastard Catholic-Socialist-ultra-Conservative paper."

43. For notable exceptions, see the essays in Stewart Craggs, ed., *William Walton*.

44. W.S. Gilbert, *Patience*, Act I, 168.

45. On *japonisme* in Gilbert and Sullivan's *Mikado*, see Carolyn Williams, *Gilbert and Sullivan*, 255ff.

46. Richard Greene, *Edith Sitwell*, 248. Hereafter cited parenthetically.

47. Edith Sitwell, "Some Notes on my Own Poetry," xv. Hereafter cited parenthetically.

48. Sacheverell Sitwell, *Liszt*, 112.

49. *Selected Letters of Edith Sitwell*, p.52. Greene points to a draft of a brief sketch of Sitwell's in which a pianist named Barbados strikes the piano so brutally that the piano-tuner has to give it first aid (177).

50. On Meyerhold and Taylorism, see McCarren, *Dancing Machines*; Pitches, *Science and Stanislavsky*. Meyerhold "had his audiences march around the foyer before assaulting them . . . with his *Gesamtkunstwerk* of movement and kinetic power." Stites, *Revolutionary Dreams*, 161.

51. See McCarren, *Dancing Machines*, 130.

52. Rudnitsky, *Russian and Soviet Theater*, 93. See also Moody, "Meyerhold."

53. Kennard, *Masks and Marionettes*, 1. Hereafter cited parenthetically.

54. It was as "impersonal yet recognizable types" that Harlequin and Pierrot "appealed to the classical Cubists of 1917/21." Theodore Reff, "On Harlequin and Pierrot," 140.

55. Anderson, "Pierrot," 338. For masked *commedia* actors, emotion "must be shown not through the face but through gesture." Luciano, *Mask of Comedy*, 3. On

the mask's intensification of voice, see Kennard, 4. On masks in modernist musical theater, see Sheppard, *Revealing Masks*.

56. Schoenberg, Foreword to *Pierrot Lunaire*, 38, his italics.

57. See Stravinsky, quoted in Green and Swan, 201.

58. Adorno, "Über einige Arbeiten Arnold Schönbergs," quoted in Frisch, "Music and Jugendstil," 160. Martin Green and John Swan write, similarly, that *Pierrot* transmutes the *commedia* figure's stylized triviality into "an almost too animal and immediate expression of spiritual emotions" (201). On the relations between Schoenberg's music and text, see Dunsby, *Schoenberg*; Stadlen, "Schoenberg's Speech-Song"; Hines, *Collaborative Form*.

59. With *Pierrot*, "the artistic conventions of the past, rejected by Expressionism as inauthentic, are . . . restored and vindicated through the spirit of irony." Alan Lessem, "Schönberg," 436.

60. Giraud, "Pierrot Lunaire," 56.

61. *Sprechstimme* "simulate[s] speech—not for the sake of simplicity or any naturalistic effect, but in order to heighten the artificiality, the eeriness of the music." Albright, *Modernism and Music*, 37.

62. Latham, "Listening to the Talking Cure" and Scrimshaw, "Non-cochlear Sound" are both found in the excellent recent volume *Sound, Music, Affect* (2013).

63. Bernays, *Biography of an Idea*, 102. Hereafter cited parenthetically. For an additional discussion of the Ballets Russes' publicity campaigns, see Garafola, *Diaghilev's Ballets Russes*, 203–4.

64. Osbert Sitwell, *Sing High! Sing Low!* (London: Macmillan, 1977), 170.

65. Reed, "Design for (Queer) Living," 389–90.

66. Margaret Dean-Smith, "Hornpipe (ii)."

67. Laurence, *Lily Briscoe*, 34, in view of Frankfurt School critiques of "kitsch," claims that Bloomsbury aesthetes saw chinoiserie not as a fetish but as "training for the eye." Laurence reads Strachey's closet drama *Son of Heaven* as a "literary 'chinoiserie,'" fascinated with the "extravagant theatricality" of the Chinese court, and with Victoria's "gender play" (171–2).

68. Rudy, *Electric Meters*, 83.

69. Quoted in Picker, *Victorian Soundscapes*, 125.

70. Edith Sitwell, *Fire of the Mind*, 187.

71. Osbert Sitwell, "The Edwardians; the Rich Man's Feast," rpt. in *Penny Foolish*, 80–1.

72. Cocteau, "Collaboration," 140.

73. Cocteau, "Fragments from 'Igor Stravinsky and the Russian Ballet,'" 42, his italics.

74. Eric Bentley, *In Search of Theatre*, 49.

75. Pelfrey and Hall-Pelfrey, *Art and Mass Media*, 109.

76. On the *image d'Epinal* and World War I, see Winter, *Sites of Memory*, 127.

77. Sacheverell Sitwell, Preface to Cyril Beaumont, *A History of Harlequin* (1926), xvi. He also praises the Harlequins of Gino Severini, who painted the screen for *Façade*'s later performances.

78. Gubar, *Racechanges*, 139.

79. Pollock, *Differencing the Canon*, 267–8. See McNelly, "Nature, Women, and Claude Levi-Strauss."

Chapter Six. Aristocracy of the Dissonant

1. Compare Schoenberg's assertion that consonances can be introduced into atonal music, but only if they are treated carefully—consonance in atonal music, that is, must be prepared and controlled to no lesser extent than dissonance in tonal music. Britten was ambivalent about Schoenberg, but a great admirer of Berg.

2. This specific phrase is used to describe *Grimes* in Brett, "Salvation at Sea," 73; the concept is developed throughout the essays collected in *Music and Sexuality in Britten*.

3. On the homoerotics of Schubert's and Tchaikovsky's music, see McClary, *Feminine Endings*.

4. Quoted in Brett, "Musicality, Essentialism, and the Closet," 20. Hereafter cited parenthetically.

5. Moffat, *The Great Unrecorded History*, 195. Hereafter cited parenthetically.

6. On the latter, see Avery's discussion in *Radio Modernism*.

7. Britten's obituary in *The Times*, run adjacent to an op-ed on homosexuality, made no allusion to his sexuality and only barely mentioned Pears (Gill, *Queer Noises*, 20).

8. Forster, *Maurice*, 195.

9. On homosexuality and nation in *Maurice*, see Hartree, "A Passion"; and Bailey, "Heroes and Homosexuals."

10. Britten, *Billy Budd: Vocal Score*, I.ii., 90. Hereafter cited parenthetically by act, scene, page, and (as applicable) rehearsal number.

11. Crompton, *Byron and Greek Love*, 4.

12. Gill, *Queer Noises*, 18.

13. Forster, "What I Believe," 67. All passages from *Two Cheers* hereafter cited parenthetically as *TC*.

14. Sedgwick, *Epistemology of the Closet*, 93.

15. Whitesell, "Britten's Dubious Trysts," 653. Hereafter cited parenthetically.

16. On Britten's interest in the East, see Brett, "Eros and Orientalism"; Cooke, *Britten and the Far East*; Sheppard, *Revealing Masks*.

17. Lew, "A New and Glorious Age," hereafter cited parenthetically.

18. Lee Edelman, *No Future*, 25.

19. Warner, *Publics and Counterpublics*, 95–6.

20. Victoria Moon Joyce, "What's so Queer about Composing?", 43.

21. Anderson, *Imagined Communities*, 149.

22. Fillion, *Difficult Rhythm*, xvii. Hereafter cited parenthetically.

23. Firchow, "Germany and Germanic Mythology in *Howards End*," claims that the Beethoven passage "is really based on Wagner's Ring cycle" (66). DiGaetani points out that a similar "rainbow bridge" fantasy appears in Forster's "Celestial Omnibus." *Wagner and the Modern British Novel*, 94.

24. Jameson, "Modernism and Imperialism," 45, 50. Hereafter cited parenthetically.

25. Cohen, Coyle, and Lewty, *Broadcasting Modernism*, 3.

26. Hobson, *The Crisis of Liberalism*, 110–1.

27. Carpenter suggests that only after meeting Auden did Britten start criticizing music on political as well as aesthetic grounds.

28. Forster's writings on Mozart and Wagner focus little on the music, more on the symbolic and mythical content: "What I Believe" briefly discusses the Nibelunglied. Forster's friends Goldsworthy Lowes Dickinson and E.J. Dent were both Mozart devotees; Dent's translations of the libretti to Mozart's operas were particularly important in the establishment of opera in England.

29. Matz, "'You Must Join My Dead,'" links Forster's abandonment of the novel to his affair with Mohammed el Adl.

30. E.M. Forster, Locked Journal, entry dated 24 July 1913. Thanks to Patricia Maguire for helping me with Forster's handwriting.

31. Forster, *A Passage to India*, hereafter cited parenthetically as *PI*. Furbank suggests that Forster's representations of India are informed by his experiences in Egypt.

32. Forster, *Hill of Devi*, 118.

33. Moran, "'Come, Come,' 'Boum, Boum,'" argues that the phrase "come, come" exemplifies what *Aspects of the Novel* calls "easy rhythm," motivically recurring without "harden[ing] into a symbol."

34. Said refers to the "disappointing conclusion" of *Passage*, remarking on "the pathetic distance still separating 'us' from an Orient." *Orientalism*, 244.

35. See Bhabha, *The Location of Culture*, 85ff.

36. Obert, "Cultural Capital of Sound."

37. See Tippins, *February House*.

38. See Carpenter, *Britten* 67, and Mitchell, *Britten and Auden*, 83–6. Hereafter cited parenthetically.

39. Wright, "Britten and Documentary," 779.

40. Reed, "Britten in the Cinema: *Coal Face*," 76.

41. On Britten's much-understudied work for the GPO, see Reed, "Britten in the Cinema"; and Reed, "The Incidental Music of Benjamin Britten."

42. Allen, "He Descended into Hell," 91, his emphasis.

43. Wilson, "An Account of 'Peter Grimes.'" On Britten's treatment of women, see Ellen McDonald, "Women in Benjamin Britten's Operas."

44. Brett, "Britten's Dream," 263.

45. Rupprecht, *Britten's Musical Language*, 74.

46. Brett argues that this passage juxtaposes Grimes' major ninth, "signifying his visionary side," with "an inversion of a motive associated with the Borough at the inquest scene," hinting at "the process of 'internalization'" (*Music and Sexuality* 61).

47. For a deconstruction of Melville's multiple narrative discourses, see Johnson, "Melville's Fist."

48. Claire Seymour, *Operas of Benjamin Britten*, 143, argues that as Claggart identifies the sailor, he disrupts Vere's tonal stability, "shatter[ing] Vere's confident B major protests" with "good reports" of Billy's beauty.

49. "There is . . . nothing that comes within any text-book definition, however broad, of melody." John Culshaw, qtd. in Whittall, "Twisted Relations," 155.

50. Arnold Whittall, in "Twisted Relations," claims that Britten's "technical dialectics" enact a tension between love and war, as the interview passage effects dialectical tensions between "chromatic" and "diatonic" harmonizations of the F, A, and C, and uses each triad to destabilize the tonal "environment" of F major (159). Hereafter cited parenthetically. On the interview passage, see also Brett, "Salvation at Sea," Hindley, "Love and Salvation," Hindley, "Britten's 'Billy Budd,'" argues that the movement between F and C represents a plagal cadence (F is the subdominant of C) rather than an authentic cadence (C is the dominant of F), and finds the plagal cadence being given "equal prominence" in Vere's epilogue ("Budd" 119). This may take on extra frisson given Godbole's closure on the subdominant.

51. Whittall, "Twisted Relations," 152.

52. Koestenbaum, "The Queen's Throat," 212. Hereafter cited parenthetically.

53. Madden, *Tiresian Poetics*, 64, 119ff. Madden builds also on Koestenbaum's account in *Double Talk* of *The Waste Land*'s homoerotics.

54. According to Annmarie Jagose, queer theory "turns identity inside out, and displays its supports exoskeletally." *Queer Theory*, 132.

55. Brett, "The Britten Era," 102.

Bibliography

Abbate, Carolyn. "Immortal Voices, Mortal Forms." In *Analytical Strategies and Musical Interpretation: Essays on Nineteenth- and Twentieth-Century Music*. Edited by Craig Ayrey and Mark Everist, 288–300. Cambridge: Cambridge University Press, 1996.

——. *In Search of Opera*. Princeton, NJ: Princeton University Press, 2003.

——. "Wagner, Cinema, and Redemptive Glee." *Opera Quarterly* 21 (Autumn 2006): 597–611.

Adams, Stephen. "Are the *Cantos* a Fugue?" In *Literature and Music*. Edited by Nancy Anne Cluck, 36–43. Provo, UT: Brigham Young University Press, 1981.

——. "Musical Neofism: Pound's Theory of Harmony in Context." *Mosaic* 13, no. 2 (1980): 49–69.

——. "The Soundscape of the *Cantos*: Some Ideas of Music in the Poetry of Ezra Pound." *Humanities Association Review* 28 (1977): 167–88.

Adorno, Theodor. *Aesthetic Theory*. Translated by Robert Hullot-Kentor. Minneapolis: University of Minnesota Press, 1998.

——. *Alban Berg: Master of the Smallest Link*. Translated by Christopher Hailey and Juliane Brand. Cambridge: Cambridge University Press, 1994.

——. "The Curves of the Needle." Translated by Thomas Y. Levin. Reprinted in *Essays on Music*. Edited by Richard Leppert, 271–76. Berkeley: University of California Press, 2002.

——. "The Form of the Phonograph Record." Reprinted in *Essays on Music*, 277–82.

——. *In Search of Wagner*. Translated by Rodney Livingstone. 2nd ed. London: Verso, 2005.

——. *Minima Moralia: Reflections on a Damaged Life*. Translated by E.F.N. Jephcott. London: Verso, 2005.

——. "On Jazz." Translated by Jamie Owen Daniel. Reprinted in *Essays on Music*, 470–92.

——. "On the Contemporary Relationship between Philosophy and Music." Reprinted in *Essays on Music*, 135–58.

——. "Opera and the Long-Playing Record." Translated by Thomas Y. Levin. Reprinted in *Essays on Music*, 283–6.

——. *Philosophy of New Music*. Translated by Robert Hullot-Kenter. Minneapolis: University of Minnesota Press, 2006.

——. "The Radio Symphony." Reprinted in *Essays on Music*, 251–69.

——. "Wagner's Relevance for Today." Translated by Susan H. Gillespie. Reprinted in *Essays on Music*, 584–602.

Adorno, Theodor, and Max Horkheimer, *The Dialectic of Enlightenment*. Translated by John Cumming. New York: Continuum, 1972.

——. *Towards a New Manifesto*. Translated by Rodney Livingstone. London: Verso, 2011.

Albright, Daniel, ed. *Modernism and Music: An Anthology of Sources*. Chicago: University of Chicago Press, 2004.

——. *Quantum Poetics: Yeats, Pound, Eliot, and the Science of Modernism*. Cambridge: Cambridge University Press, 1997.

——. *Untwisting the Serpent: Modernism in Music, Literature, and Other Arts*. Chicago: University of Chicago Press, 1999.

Alexander, Michael. *The Poetic Achievement of Ezra Pound*. Edinburgh: Edinburgh University Press, 1998.

Allen, Stephen Arthur. "'He Descended Into Hell': Peter Grimes, Ellen Orford, and Salvation Denied." In *The Cambridge Companion to Benjamin Britten*. Edited by Mervyn Cooke, 81–94. Cambridge: Cambridge University Press, 1999.

Anderson, Amanda. *The Powers of Distance: Cosmopolitanism and the Cultivation of Detachment*. Princeton, NJ: Princeton University Press, 2001.

Anderson, Benedict. *Imagined Communities: Reflections on the Origin and Spread of Nationalism*. London: Verso, 1983.Anderson, John D. "Pierrot: Dramatic and Literary Mask." In *Fools and Jesters in Literature, Art, and History: A Bio-Bibliographical Sourcebook*. Edited by Vicki K. Janik, 336–42. Westport, CT: Greenwood Press, 1998.

Anspaugh, Kelly. "Powers of Ordure: James Joyce and the Excremental Vision(s)." *Mosaic* 27, no. 1 (1994): 73–100.

Antheil, George. *Bad Boy of Music*. New ed. New York: Samuel French, 1990.

——. [Stacey Bishop, pseud.] *Death in the Dark*. London: Faber and Faber, 1930.

——. "Mother of the Earth." *Transatlantic Review* (musical supplement) 2, no. 1 (1927–8): 227.

——. "Music Tomorrow." *Transition*, December 1927, 123–6.

——. "My Ballet Mecanique, What It Means." *Der Querschnitt* 5, no. 9 (1925): 789–91.

——. *The Shape of the War to Come*. New York: Longmans, Green, and Co., 1940.

Appadurai, Arjun. *Modernity at Large: Cultural Dimensions of Globalization*. Minneapolis: University of Minnesota Press, 1996.

Appel, Alfred Jr. *Jazz Modernism: From Ellington and Armstrong to Matisse and Joyce*. New Haven: Yale University Press, 2004.

Armstrong, Tim. "Player Piano: Poetry and Sonic Modernity." *Modernism/Modernity* 14, no. 1 (2007): 1–19.

Arnold, Matthew. "Dover Beach." Reprinted in *The Oxford Book of English Verse*. Edited by Christopher Ricks, 453. Oxford: Oxford University Press, 1999.

Atrzert, Stephan. "Schopenhauer and Freud." In *A Companion to Schopenhauer*. Edited by Bart Vandenabeele, 317-32. West Sussex: Blackwell, 2012.

Attali, Jacques. *Noise: The Political Economy of Music*. Translated by Brian Massumi. Minneapolis: University of Minnesota Press, 1985.

Avery, Todd. *Radio Modernism: Literature, Ethics, and the BBC, 1922-38*. Aldershot: Ashgate, 2006.

Bailey, Peter. "Breaking the Sound Barrier." In *Hearing History: A Reader*. Edited by Mark Smith, 23-35. Athens: University of Georgia Press, 2004.

Bailey, Quentin. "Heroes and Homosexuals: Education and Empire in E.M. Forster." *Twentieth-Century Literature* 48, no. 3 (2002): 324-47.

Banet-Weiser, Sarah. "Preface." *American Quarterly* 63, no. 3 (2011): v-vi.

Barber, Cecil. "Battle Music." *The Musical Times* 59, no. 899 (1918): 25-6.

Barringer, Tim. "Façades for *Façade*: William Walton, Visual Culture, and English Modernism in the Sitwell Circle." In *British Music and Modernism, 1895-1960*. Edited by Matthew Riley, 125-46. Surrey: Ashgate, 2010.

Barthes, Roland. "The Grain of the Voice." *Image-Music-Text*. Translated and edited by Stephen Heath, 179-89. New York: Hill and Wang, 1977.

———. "Musica Practica." *Image-Music-Text*, 149-54.

Baudelaire, Charles. *"Flowers of Evil" and Other Works/"Les Fleurs du Mal" et Oeuvres Choises*. Translated and edited by Wallace Fowlie. New York: Dover, 1992.

Bauer, Karin. "Adorno's Wagner: History and the Potential of the Artwork." *Cultural Critique* 60 (2005): 68-91.

Bell, Ian, and Meriel Lland. "Silence and Solidity in Early Anglo-American Modernism: Nietzsche, the Fourth Dimension, and Ezra Pound, Part One." *Symbiosis* 10, no.1 (2006): 47-62.

Benjamin, Walter. "On Some Motifs in Baudelaire." Translated by Harry Zohn. Reprinted in *Illuminations*. Edited by Hannah Arendt, 155-200. New York: Schocken, 1968.

———. "The Work of Art in the Age of Mechanical Reproduction." Reprinted in *Illuminations*, 217-51.

Bentley, Eric. *In Search of Theatre*. New York: Atheneum, 1975.

———. *The Life of the Drama*. New York: Atheneum, 1991.

Bernays, Edward L. *Biography of an Idea: Memoirs of Public Relations Counsel Edward L. Bernays*. New York: Simon and Schuster, 1965.

Bernstein, David W. "Music I: To the Late 1940s." *The Cambridge Companion to John Cage*. Edited by David Nicholls, 63-84. Cambridge: Cambridge University Press, 2002.

Bernstein, J.M. *Against Voluptuous Bodies: Late Modernism and the Meaning of Painting*. Palo Alto: Stanford University Press, 2006.

Bernstein, Leonard. *The Unanswered Question: Six Talks at Harvard*. Cambridge, MA: Harvard University Press, 2006.

Berry, Mark. *Treacherous Bonds and Laughing Fire: Politics and Religion in Wagner's Ring*. Aldershot: Ashgate, 2000.

Bhabha, Homi K. *The Location of Culture*. London: Routledge, 1982.

Blackadder, Neil. *Performing Opposition: Modern Theater and the Scandalized Audience*. Westport, CT: Praeger, 2003.

Boes, Tobias. "*A Portrait of the Artist as a Young Man* and the 'Individuating Rhythm' of Modernity." *ELH* 48 (2008): 767-85.

Bolter, Jay David, and Richard Grusin. *Remediation: Understanding New Media*. Cambridge, MA: MIT Press, 2000.

Botelho, Keith. *Renaissance Earwitnesses: Rumor and Early Modern Masculinity*. New York: Palgrave, 2009.

Bowen, Zack. *Musical Allusions in the Works of James Joyce: Early Poetry through Ulysses*. Albany: SUNY Press, 1974.

Brecht, Bertolt. "Alienation Effects in Chinese Acting." Reprinted in *Brecht on Theatre*. Translated and edited by John Willett, 91-100. New York: Hill and Wang, 1964.

——. "The Literarization of the Theatre." Reprinted in *Brecht on Theatre*, 43-7.

Brett, Philip. "The Britten Era." In *Decomposition: Post-Disciplinary Performance*. Edited by Sue-Ellen Case, Philip Brett, and Susan Leigh Foster, 95-110. Bloomington: Indiana University Press, 2000.

——. "Britten's Dream." In *Musicology and Difference: Gender and Sexuality in Music Scholarship*. Edited by Ruth Solie, 259-80. Berkeley: University of California Press, 1993.

——. "Eros and Orientalism in Britten's Operas." In *Queering the Pitch: The New Gay and Lesbian Musicology*. 1st ed. Edited by Philip Brett, Elizabeth Wood, and Gary C. Thomas, 235-56. London: Routledge, 1994.

——. "Musicality, Essentialism, and the Closet." In *Queering the Pitch*, 9-26.

——. "Salvation at Sea: *Billy Budd*." Reprinted in *Music and Sexuality in Britten: Selected Essays*. Edited by George E. Haggerty, 70-80. Berkeley: University of California Press, 2006.

Britten, Benjamin. *Billy Budd: Vocal Score*. Edited by Erwin Stein. London: Boosey and Hawkes, 1961.

——. *Peter Grimes: Vocal Score*. Edited by Erwin Stein. London: Boosey and Hawkes, 1945.

Brown, Julie A. *Bartók and the Grotesque: Studies in Modernity, the Body, and Contradiction in Music*. Aldershot: Ashgate, 2007.

Brown, Marshall. "The Logic of Realism: A Hegelian Approach." *PMLA* 96, no. 2 (1981): 224-41.

Bryant, Marsha. "Sitwell Beyond the Semiotic: Gender, Race, and Empire in *Façade*." *Tulsa Studies in Women's Literature* 26, no. 2 (2007): 243-67.

Bucknell, Brad. *Literary Modernism and Musical Aesthetics: Pater, Pound, Joyce and Stein*. Cambridge: Cambridge University Press, 2002.

Budgen, Frank. *James Joyce and the Making of "Ulysses."* Bloomington: Indiana University Press, 1960.

Bullard, Truman C. "The First Performance of Igor Stravinsky's *Sacre du Printemps*." PhD diss., University of Rochester, 1971.

Bürger, Peter. *Theory of the Avant-Garde*. Translated by Michael Shaw. Minneapolis: University of Minnesota Press, 1984.

Burns, Christy L. *Gestural Politics: Stereotype and Parody in Joyce*. Albany: SUNY Press, 2000.

Bush, Christopher. *Ideographic Modernism: China, Writing, Media*. Oxford: Oxford University Press, 2010.

Cage, John. Liner notes to *Roaratorio*. Ars Acustica. WERGO 6303-2. CD. 1994.

——. *X: Writings '79–82*. Middletown: Wesleyan University Press, 1983.

Calico, Joy. *Brecht at the Opera*. Berkeley: University of California Press, 2008.

Campbell, Timothy. *Wireless Writing in the Age of Marconi*. Minneapolis: University of Minnesota Press, 2006.

Carpenter, Humphrey. *Benjamin Britten: A Biography*. New York: Scribner, 1993.

——. *A Serious Character: The Life of Ezra Pound*. New York: Delta, 1988.

Cascone, Kim. "The Aesthetics of Failure: 'Post-Digital' Tendencies in Contemporary Computer Music." *Computer Music* 24, no. 4 (2000): 12–18.

Cevasco, G.A. *The Sitwells: Edith, Osbert, and Sacheverell*. Boston: Twayne, 1987.

Cheng, Vincent J. "'The Twining Stresses, Two by Two': The Prosody of Joyce's Prose." *Modernism/Modernity* 16, no. 2 (2009): 391–9.

Cheshire, David F. "Futurism, Marinetti, and the Music Hall." *Theatre Quarterly* 1, no. 3 (1971): 54–8.

Chinitz, David. "A Jazz-Banjorine, Not a Lute: Eliot and Popular Music before *The Waste Land*." In *T.S. Eliot's Orchestra: Critical Essays on Poetry and Music*. Edited by John Xiros Cooper, 3–24. New York: Garland, 2000.

——. *T.S. Eliot and the Cultural Divide*. Chicago: University of Chicago Press, 2003.

Chion, Michel. *Audio-Vision: Sound on Screen*. Translated by Claudia Gorbman. New York: Columbia University Press, 1994.

Cocteau, Jean. "The Collaboration of 'Parade.'" In *The Cock and the Harlequin*. Translated by Rollo H. Myers, 53–7. London: Egoist Press, 1921.

——. "The Eiffel Tower Wedding Party." Reprinted in *The Infernal Machine and Other Plays*. Translated and edited by Dudley Fitts, 151–78. New York: New Directions, 1963.

——. "Fragments from 'Igor Stravinsky and the Russian Ballet.'" In *The Cock and the Harlequin*, 41–3.

Coggrave, John. "Sacred Music." In *William Walton: Music and Literature*. Edited by Stewart R. Craggs, 22–33. Aldershot: Ashgate, 1999.

Cohen, Debra Rae, Michael Coyle, and Jane Lewty, ed. *Broadcasting Modernism*. Gainesville: University Press of Florida, 2009.

Cole, David W. "Fugal Structure in the Sirens Episode of *Ulysses*." *Modern Fiction Studies* 19 (1973): 221-6.

Conrad, Joseph. *Heart of Darkness*. Edited by Cedric Watts. Oxford: Oxford University Press, 1990.

——. "Preface to *The Nigger of the 'Narcissus*.'" Reprinted in *Modernism: An Anthology of Sources*. Edited by Vassiliki Kolocotroni, Jane Goldman, and Olga Taxidou, 131-4. Chicago: University of Chicago Press, 1998.

Cook, Susan. "George Antheil's *Transatlantic*: An American in the Weimar Republic." *The Journal of Musicology* 9, no. 4 (1991): 498-520.

Cooke, Mervyn. *Britten and the Far East: Asian Influences in the Music of Benjamin Britten*. Woodbridge: Boydell and Brewer, 2001.

Cope, Jackson. "The Rhythmic Gesture: Image and Aesthetic in Joyce's *Ulysses*." *ELH* 29, no. 1 (1962): 67-89.

Cowan, Michael. "The Heart Machine: 'Rhythm' and Body in Weimar Film and Fritz Lang's *Metropolis*." *Modernism/Modernity* 14, no. 2 (2007): 225-48.

Cowell, Henry. "The Joys of Noise." Reprinted in *Essential Cowell: Selected Writings on Music*. Edited by Dick Higgins, 249-52. Kingston, NY: McPherson, 2001.

——. *Three Anti-Modernist Songs*, CD, Naxos, 2005.

Cox, Gordon. "Towards the National Song Book: The History of an Idea." *British Journal of Music Education* 9, no. 3 (1992): 239-53.

Coyle, Michael. *Ezra Pound, Popular Genres, and the Discourse of Genre*. University Park: Pennsylvania State University Press, 1995.

Craft, Robert. *Stravinsky: The Chronicle of a Friendship 1948-1971*. London: Gollancz, 1972.

Craggs, Stewart, ed. *William Walton: Music and Literature*. Aldershot: Ashgate, 1999.

Craig, Edward Gordon. "The Actor and the Über-Marionette." In *On the Art of the Theatre*. Edited by Edward Gordon Craig, 54-94. London: Browne's Bookstore, 1912.

Crary, Jonathan. "Spectacle, Attention, Memory." *October* 50 (1989): 96-107.

Crompton, Louis. *Byron and Greek Love: Homophobia in Nineteenth-Century England*. Berkeley: University of California Press, 1985.

Cunningham, David. "A Time for Dissonance and Noise: On Adorno, Music, and the Concept of Modernism." *Angelaki* 8, no. 1 (2003): 61-74.

Dame, Joke. "Unveiled Voices: Sexual Difference and the Castrato." In *Queering the Pitch*, 139-53.

Dana, Margaret E. "Orchestrating *The Waste Land*: Wagner, Leitmotiv, and the Play of Passion." In *T.S. Eliot's Orchestra*, 267-94.

Danius, Sara. *The Senses of Modernism: Technology, Perception, and Aesthetics*. Ithaca: Cornell University Press, 2002.

Dean, John FitzPatrick. *Riot and Great Anger: Stage Censorship in Twentieth-Century Ireland*. Madison: University of Wisconsin Press, 2004.

Dean-Smith, Margaret. "Hornpipe (ii)." In *Grove Music Online* (2008), www.oxfordmusic online.com/subscriber/article/grove/music/13367.

DeNora, Tia. *Music in Everyday Life*. Cambridge: Cambridge University Press, 2000.

Dent, Edward J. "Landscape with Figures." *The Athenæum*, 17 October 1919, 1041.

Derrida, Jacques. "Ulysses Gramophone: Hear say yes in Joyce." Reprinted in *A Companion to James Joyce's "Ulysses."* Edited by Margot Norris, 69–90. Boston: Bedford, 1998.

DiGaetani, John Louis. *Richard Wagner and the Modern British Novel*. Madison, NJ: Fairleigh Dickinson University Press, 1978.

Donnellon, Déirdre. "Debussy as Musician and Critic." In *The Cambridge Companion to Debussy*. Edited by Simon Trezise, 43–60. Cambridge: Cambridge University Press, 2003.

Driver, Paul. "'Façade' Revisited." *Tempo* 133/134 (1980): 3–9.

Dunsby, Jonathan. *Schoenberg: "Pierrot Lunaire."* Cambridge: Cambridge University Press, 1992.

Eagleton, Terry. "Contradictions of Modernism." In *Modernity, Modernism, Postmodernism.* Edited by Manuel Barbeito, 35–44. Santiago de Compostela: Universidade de Santiago de Compostela, 2000.

Edelman, Lee. *No Future: Queer Theory and the Death Drive*. Durham, NC: Duke University Press, 2004.

Edison, Thomas A. "The Phonograph and its Future." *The North American Review* 126, no. 262 (1878): 527–36.

Eksteins, Modris. *Rites of Spring: The Great War and the Birth of the Modern Age*. Boston: Houghton Mifflin, 2000.

Eliot, T.S. *The Annotated "Waste Land" with Eliot's Contemporary Prose*. Edited by Lawrence Rainey. 2nd ed. New Haven: Yale University Press, 2006.

——. "The Beating of a Drum." *The Nation & the Athenæum* 34 (6 October 1923): 11–2.

——. "From 'Baudelaire.'" Reprinted in *Selected Prose of T.S. Eliot*. Edited by Frank Kermode, 231–7. New York: Harcourt, 1975.

——. "From 'Henry James.'" Reprinted in *Selected Prose of T.S. Eliot*, 151–2.

——. "London Letter, September 1921." Reprinted in *The Annotated "Waste Land,"* 188–91.

——. "The Love Song of J. Alfred Prufrock." Reprinted in *The Complete Poems and Plays, 1909–1950*, 3–7. New York: Harcourt, 1962.

——. "Marie Lloyd." Reprinted in *Selected Prose of T.S. Eliot*, 172–4.

——. "Matthew Arnold." *The Use of Poetry and the Use of Criticism: Studies in the Relation of Criticism to Poetry in England*, 95–112. Cambridge, MA: Harvard University Press, 1986.

——. "The Music of Poetry." Reprinted in *On Poetry and Poets*, 17-33. London: Faber and Faber, 1985.

——. "Portrait of a Lady." Reprinted in *The Complete Poems and Plays,* 8-11.

——. "Tradition and the Individual Talent." Reprinted in *Selected Prose of T.S. Eliot,* 37-44.

——. "*Ulysses*, Order, and Myth." Reprinted in *Selected Prose of T.S. Eliot*, 175-8.

——. "War-Paint and Feathers." *The Athenœum*, 17 October 1919, 1036.

——. *The Waste Land: A Facsimile and Transcript of the Original Drafts including the Annotations of Ezra Pound*. Edited by Valerie Eliot. London: Harvest, 1971.

Ellmann, Maud. "Joyce's Noises." *Modernism/Modernity* 16 (April 2009): 383-90

Ellmann, Richard. *James Joyce*. Oxford: Oxford University Press, 1982.

Esty, Joshua [Jed]. "Excremental Postcolonialism." *Contemporary Literature* 40, no. 1 (1999): 22-59.

——. *A Shrinking Island: Modernism and National Culture in England*. Princeton, NJ: Princeton University Press, 2004.

——. *Unseasonable Youth: Modernism, Colonialism, and the Fiction of Development*. Oxford: Oxford University Press, 2011.

Faulk, Barry. *Music Hall and Modernity*. Athens: Ohio University Press, 2004.

Fillion, Michelle. *Difficult Rhythm: Music and the Word in E.M. Forster*. Champaign: University of Illinois Press, 2010.

Firchow, Peter E. "Germany and Germanic Mythology in *Howards End*." *Comparative Literature* 33, no. 1 (1981): 50-68.

Fisher, Margaret. *Ezra Pound's Radio Operas: The BBC Experiments, 1931-1933*. Cambridge, MA: MIT Press, 2002.

Forster, E.M. *The Hill of Devi*. Orlando: Harvest, 1953.

——. *Howards End*. Edited by Douglas Mao. New York: Longman, 2010.

——. Locked Journal, Modern Archive Centre, King's College, Cambridge.

——. *Maurice*. New York: Norton, 1981.

——. *A Passage to India*. London: Harcourt, 1984.

——. *Two Cheers for Democracy*. New York: Harvest, 1951.

Foster, Roger. *Adorno: The Recovery of Experience*. Albany, NY: SUNY Press, 2008.

Frank, Ron, director. *Bad Boy Made Good: The Revival of the "Ballet Mécanique."* DVD. Albany: Electronic Music Foundation, 2006.

Frattarola, Angela. "The Phonograph and the Modernist Novel." *Mosaic* 43, no. 1 (2010): 143-59.

Frigyesi, Judit. *Béla Bartók and Turn-of-the-Century Budapest*. Berkeley: University of California Press, 2000.

Frisch, Walter. "Music and Jugendstil." *Critical Inquiry* 17, no. 1 (1990): 138-61.

Fulcher, Jane F., ed. *Debussy and his World*. Princeton, NJ: Princeton University Press, 2001.

Furbank, P.N. *E.M. Forster: A Life*. 2 vols. London: Secker and Warburg, 1978.

Fussell, Paul. *Poetic Meter and Poetic Form*. Rev. ed. New York: McGraw-Hill, 1979.

Garafola, Lynn. *Diaghilev's Ballets Russes*. New York: Da Capo, 1998.

Garvey, Johanna X.K. "City Limits: Reading Gender and Urban Spaces in *Ulysses*." *Twentieth-Century Literature* 41, no. 1 (1995): 108–23.

Gifford, Don. *Joyce Annotated: Notes for "Dubliners" and "A Portrait of the Artist as a Young Man."* Berkeley: University of California Press, 1982.

Gilbert, Stuart. *James Joyce's "Ulysses": A Study*. New York: Vintage, 1958.

Gilbert, W.S. *Patience; or, Bunthorne's Bride.* Reprinted in *The Complete Plays of Gilbert and Sullivan*, 157–200. New York: Norton, 1976.

Gilpin, George H. "1898–1945: Hardy to Auden." In *The Columbia History of British Poetry*. Edited by Carl Woodring and James S. Shapiro, 532–53. New York: Columbia University Press, 1994.

Glendinning, Victoria. *Edith Sitwell: A Unicorn among Lions*. London: Weidenfeld and Nicolson, 1981.

Giraud, Albert. "Pierrot Lunaire." Translated by Stanley Applebaum. In *Verklärte Nacht and Pierrot Lunaire*. New York: Dover, 1994.

Goble, Mark. *Beautiful Circuits: Modernism and the Mediated Life*. New York: Columbia University Press, 2010.

Goehr, Lydia. "Dissonant Works and the Listening Public." In *The Cambridge Companion to Adorno*. Edited by Thomas Huhn, 222–47. Cambridge: Cambridge University Press, 2004.

Goldberg, S.L. *The Classical Temper: A Study of James Joyce's "Ulysses."* London: Chatto and Windus, 1961.

Golston, Michael. *Rhythm and Race in Modernist Poetry and Science*. New York: Columbia University Press, 2008.

Gottlieb, Lynette. "Images, Technology, and Music: The Ballets Suédois and *Les mariés de la Tour Eiffel*." *Musical Quarterly* 88, no. 4 (2005): 523–55.

———. "Narrating Modernism: Technology and the Changing Voice of Musical Collaboration, 1909–1959." PhD diss., SUNY Buffalo, 2002.

Gracyk, Theodor. *Rhythm and Noise: An Aesthetics of Rock*. Durham, NC: Duke University Press, 1996.

Graham, T. Austin. *The Great American Songbooks: Musical Texts, Modernism, and the Value of Popular Culture*. Oxford: Oxford University Press, 2012.

Gramsci, Antonio. "Marinetti the Revolutionary." Reprinted in *Modernism*, edited by Kolocotroni, 214–5.

Green, Martin. *Children of the Sun: A Narrative of "Decadence" in England after 1918*. New York: Basic Books, 1976.

Green, Martin, and John Swan. *The Triumph of Pierrot: The Commedia Dell'Arte and the Modern Imagination*. New York: Macmillan, 1986.

Greene, Richard. *Edith Sitwell: Avant-Garde Poet, English Genius*. London: Virago, 2011.

Gubar, Susan. *Racechanges: White Skin, Black Face in American Culture*. Oxford: Oxford University Press, 1997.

Gunning, Tom. "Illusions Past and Future: The Phantasmagoria and its Specters," www.MediaArtHistory.org, 2004.

HaCohen, Ruth. *The Music Libel against the Jews*. New Haven: Yale University Press, 2012.

Hall, Vernon Jr. "Joyce's Use of Da Ponte and Mozart's *Don Giovanni*." *PMLA* 66, no. 2 (1951): 78-84.

Hamilton, Andy. *Aesthetics and Music*. London: Continuum, 2007.

Hampson, R.G. "'Toft's Cumbersome Whirligig': Hallucinations, Theatricality, and Mnemotechnic in V.A. 19 and the First Edition Text of 'Circe.'" In *Reading Joyce's "Circe."* Edited by Andrew Gibson, 143-78. Amsterdam: Editions Rodopi, 1994.

Hanslick, Eduard. *On the Musically Beautiful: A Contribution towards the Revision of the Aesthetics of Music*. Translated by Geoffrey Payzant. Indianapolis: Hackett, 1986.

Hargrove, Nancy D. "The Great Parade: Cocteau, Picasso, Satie, Massine, Diaghilevand T. S. Eliot." *Mosaic* 31, no. 1 (March 1998): 83-106.

——. "T.S. Eliot and Popular Entertainment in Paris, 1910-1911." *Journal of Popular Culture* 36, no. 3 (2003): 547-88.

Harrison, Thomas. *1910: The Emancipation of Dissonance*. Berkeley: University of California Press, 1996.

Hartree, Anne. "'A Passion that Few English Minds have Admitted': Homosexuality and Englishness in E.M. Forster's *Maurice*." *Paragraph* 19, no. 2 (1996): 127-38.

Hauck, Christina. "Abortion and the Individual Talent." *ELH* 70, no. 1 (2003): 223-66.

Hayman, David. "*Tristan and Isolde* in *Finnegans Wake*: A Study of the Sources and Evolution of a Theme." *Comparative Literature Studies* 1, no. 2 (1964): 93-112.

Henderson, Archibald. "Pound and Music: The Paris and Early Rapallo Years." PhD diss., University of California at Los Angeles, 1983.

Hepburn, Allan. "Noise, Music, Voice, *Dubliners*." In *Bronze by Gold: The Music of Joyce*. Edited by Sebastian D.G. Knowles, 189-212. New York: Garland, 1999.

Hindley, Clifford. "Britten's 'Billy Budd': The 'Interview Chords' Again." *Musical Quarterly* 78, no. 1 (1994): 99-126.

——. "Love and Salvation in Britten's 'Billy Budd.'" *Music & Letters* 70, no. 3 (1989): 363-81.

Hines, Thomas. *Collaborative Form: Studies in the Relations of the Arts*. Kent: Kent State University Press, 1991.

Hobson, J.A. *The Crisis of Liberalism: New Issues of Democracy*. London: P.S. King, 1909.

Hodgart, Matthew, and Ruth Bauerle. *Joyce's Grand Operoar: Opera in "Finnegans Wake."* Champaign: University of Illinois Press, 1996.

Hoffa, William Walter. "Ezra Pound and George Antheil: Vorticist Music and the Cantos." *American Literature* 44, no. 1 (1972): 52-73.

Holloway, Robin. *Debussy and Wagner*. London: Eulenberg, 1979.

Homer. *The Odyssey*. Trans. Richmond Lattimore. New York: Harper and Row, 1967.

Honneth, Axel. "Communication and Reconciliation: Habermas' Critique of Adorno."

In *The Frankfurt School: Critical Assessments*, Vol. 6. Edited by Jay Bernstein, 40–55. London: Routledge, 1994.

Hutcheon, Linda. *A Theory of Adaptation*. London: Taylor and Francis, 2006.

Hutcheon, Linda, and Michael Hutcheon. *Opera: Desire, Disease, Death*. Lincoln: University of Nebraska Press, 1999.

Huxley, Aldous. *Letters of Aldous Huxley*. Edited by Grover Smith Huxley. London: Harper and Row, 1969.

——. *The Perennial Philosophy*. New York: Harper, 1970.

Huyssen, Andreas. *After the Great Divide: Modernism, Mass Culture, Postmodernism*. Bloomington: Indiana University Press, 1986.

Imbs, Bravig. *Confessions of Another Young Man*. New York: Henkle-Yewdale, 1936.

Ingham, Michael. "Pound and Music." In *The Cambridge Companion to Ezra Pound*. Edited by Ira B. Nadel, 236–48. Cambridge: Cambridge University Press, 1999.

Jacques, Geoffrey. *Change in the Weather: Modernist Imagination, African American Imaginary*. Amherst: University of Massachusetts Press, 2009.

Jaffe, Aaron. *Modernism and the Culture of Celebrity*. Cambridge: Cambridge University Press, 2005.

Jaffé, Hans. *De Stijl*. Translated by R.R. Symonds. New York: Harry N. Abrams, 1971.

Jagose, Annmarie. *Queer Theory: An Introduction*. Melbourne: Melbourne University Press, 1996.

Jameson, Fredric. "Beyond the Cave: Demystifying the Ideology of Modernism." *The Bulletin of the Midwest Modern Language Association* 8, no. 1 (1975): 1–20.

——. "Modernism and Imperialism." In *Nationalism, Colonialism and Literature*. Edited by Fredric Jameson, Edward Said, and Terry Eagleton, 43–68. Minneapolis: University of Minnesota Press, 1990.

——. *The Political Unconscious: Narrative as a Socially Symbolic Act*. Ithaca: Cornell University Press, 1981.

Jay, Martin. *Adorno*. Cambridge, MA: Harvard University Press, 1984.

——. *Downcast Eyes: The Denigration of Vision in 20th-Century French Thought*. Berkeley: University of California Press, 1994.

Jerz, Dennis. *Technology in American Drama, 1920–1950: Soul and Society in the Age of the Machine*. Westport, CT: Greenwood, 2003.

Johnson, Barbara. "Melville's Fist: The Execution of Billy Budd." *Studies in Romanticism* 18, no. 4 (1979): 567–99.

Jones, Paul. "The Technology Is Not the Cultural Form?: Raymond Williams's Sociological Critique of Marshall McLuhan." *Canadian Journal of Communication* 23, no. 4 (1998), www.cjc-online.ca/index.php/journal/article/view/1058/964.

Joyce, James. "Chamber Music." Reprinted in *The Portable James Joyce*. Edited by Harry Levin, 629–48. New York and London: Penguin, 1976.

——. *Dubliners*. Edited by Robert Scholes and A. Walton Litz. Rev. ed. New York: Viking, 1996.

———. *Finnegans Wake*. New York: Viking Press, 1939.

———. "The Holy Office." Reprinted in *The Portable James Joyce*, 657–60.

———. "The Home Rule Comet." Reprinted in *Occasional, Critical, and Political Writing*. Edited by Kevin Barry, 155–9. Oxford: Oxford University Press, 2000.

———. "James Clarence Mangan." Reprinted in *Occasional, Critical, and Political Writing*, 53–60.

———. *A Portrait of the Artist as a Young Man*. Edited by Jeri Johnson. Oxford: Oxford University Press, 2000.

———. "Realism and Idealism in English Literature." Reprinted in *Occasional, Critical, and Political Writing*, 163–82.

———. *Ulysses*. Edited by Hans Walter Gabler. New York: Vintage, 1986.

Joyce, Victoria Moon. "What's So Queer about Composing? Exploring Attali's Concept of Composition from a Queer Perspective." *Popular Music and Society* 21, no. 3 (1997): 35–59.

Joyce Songs: James Joyce's Musical Dublin, RTE Lyric FM (2004).

Julius, Anthony. *T.S. Eliot, Anti-Semitism, and Literary Form*. Cambridge: Cambridge University Press, 1996.

Kahn, Douglas. *Noise, Water, Meat: A History of Sound in the Arts*. Cambridge, MA: MIT Press, 2001.

Katz, Mark. *Capturing Sound: How Technology Has Changed Music*. Berkeley: University of California Press, 2010.

Kaufman, Robert. "Negatively Capable Dialectics: Keats, Vendler, Adorno, and the Theory of the Avant-Garde." *Critical Inquiry* 27, no. 2 (2001): 354–84.

Kennard, Joseph Spencer. *Masks and Marionettes*. New York: Macmillan, 1935.

Kenner, Hugh. *Dublin's Joyce*. New York: Columbia University Press, 1987.

———. *The Mechanic Muse*. Oxford: Oxford University Press, 1987.

———. *The Pound Era*. Berkeley: University of California Press, 1973.

Kittler, Friedrich. *Gramophone, Film, Typewriter*. Translated by Geoffrey Winthrop-Young and Michael Wutz. Palo Alto: Stanford University Press, 1999.

———. "World-Breath: On Wagner's Media Technology." Translated by Friedrich Kittler and David Levin. In *Opera Through Other Eyes*. Edited by David Levin, 215–38. Palo Alto: Stanford University Press, 1994.

Klein, Scott. "The Euphonium Cagehoused in Either Notation: John Cage and *Finnegans Wake*." In *Bronze by Gold*, 151–70.

Knowles, Sebastian D.G. "Death by Gramophone." *Journal of Modern Literature* 27, no. 1/2 (2003): 1–13.

———. "Introduction." In *Bronze by Gold*, xxvii–xlii.

Koestenbaum, Wayne. "The Queen's Throat: (Homo)sexuality and the Art of Singing." In *Inside/Out: Lesbian Theories, Gay Theories*. Edited by Diana Fuss, 205–34. London: Routledge, 1991.

Koritz, Amy. *Gendering Bodies/Performing Art: Dance and Literature in Early Twentieth-Century British Culture.* Ann Arbor: University of Michigan Press, 1995.

Koss, Juliet. *Modernism after Wagner*. Minneapolis: University of Minnesota Press, 2010.

Kramer, Lawrence. *Music as Cultural Practice, 1800–1900*. Berkeley: University of California Press, 1990.

Kreilkamp, Ivan. *Voice and the Victorian Storyteller*. Cambridge: Cambridge University Press, 2005.

Kristeva, Julia. *Powers of Horror: An Essay on Abjection*. Translated by Leon S. Roudiez. New York: Columbia University Press, 1982.

Kuberski, Philip. *A Calculus of Ezra Pound: Vocations of the American Sign*. Gainesville: University Press of Florida, 1992.

Laki, Péter. *Bartók and His World*. Princeton, NJ: Princeton University Press, 1995.

Latham, Clara. "Listening to the Talking Cure: *Sprechstimme*, Hypnosis, and the Sonic Organization of Affect." In *Sound, Music, Affect: Theorizing Sonic Experience*, 101–116. Edited by Marie Thompson and Ian Biddle. New York and London: Bloomsbury, 2013.

Laurence, Patricia. *Lily Briscoe's Chinese Eyes: Bloomsbury, Modernism, and China*. Columbia: University of South Carolina Press, 2003.

Lawder, Standish D. *The Cubist Cinema*. New York: New York University Press, 1975.

Leavis, F.R. *New Bearings in English Poetry*. London: Chatto and Windus, 1932.

Lefebvre, Henri. *Rhythmanaysis: Space, Time, and Everyday Life*. Translated by Stuart Elden and Gerald Moore. London: Continuum, 2004.

Lehrman, Paul D. "The Ballet Mécanique Page," http://antheil.org.

Lentricchia, Frank. *Ariel and the Police: Michel Foucault, William James, Wallace Stevens*. Madison: University of Wisconsin Press, 1987.

Leppert, Richard. "Commentary." in Adorno, *Essays on Music*, 213–50.

——. *The Sight of Sound: Music, Representation, and the History of the Body*. Berkeley: University of California Press, 1993.

Lessem, Alan. "Schönberg and the Crisis of Expressionism." *Music & Letters* 55, no. 4 (1974): 429–36.

Levenson, Michael. *A Genealogy of Modernism*. Cambridge: Cambridge University Press, 1986.

Levin, David. *Richard Wagner, Fritz Lang, and the Nibelungen: The Dramaturgy of Disavowal*. Princeton, NJ: Princeton University Press, 1998.

Levin, Lawrence. "The Sirens Episode as Music: Joyce's Experiment in Prose Polyphony." *James Joyce Quarterly* 3, no. 1 (1965): 12–24.

Lew, Nathaniel Geoffrey. *A New and Glorious Age: Constructions of National Opera in Britain, 1945–1951*. Ann Arbor: University Microfilms, 2001 [UMI 3044555].

Lewis, Wyndham. *The Apes of God*. Santa Rosa: Black Sparrow Press, 1981.

——. *Tarr*. New York: Knopf, 1918.

——. *Time and Western Man*. Edited by Paul Edwards. Santa Rosa: Black Sparrow Press, 1993.

Liebregts, Pieter. *Ezra Pound and Neoplatonism*. Cranbury: Rosemont, 2004.

Lilienfield, Robert. "Music and Society in the 20th Century: Georg Lukács, Ernst Bloch, and Theodor Adorno." *International Journal of Politics, Culture, and Society* 1, no. 2 (1987): 120–46.

Link, Stan. "The Work of Reproduction in the Mechanical Aging of an Art: Listening to Noise." *Computer Music Journal* 25, no. 1 (2001): 34–47.

Liu, Alan. *The Laws of Cool: Knowledge Work and the Culture of Information*. Chicago: University of Chicago Press, 2004.

Lloyd, Stephen. *William Walton: Muse of Fire*. Woodbridge: Boydell Press, 2001.

Luciano, Eleonora. *The Mask of Comedy: The Art of Italian Commedia*. Louisville: JB Speed Art Museum, 1990.

Lukács, György. "Aesthetic Culture." Reprinted in *The Lukács Reader*. Translated and edited by Arpad Kadarkay, 146–59. Oxford: Blackwell, 1995.

——. "The Ideology of Modernism." Reprinted in *The Lukács Reader*, 187–209.

——. "The Intellectual Physiognomy." Reprinted in *Writer and Critic*. Edited by Arthur D. Kahn, 149–88. New York: Grosset and Dunlap, 1970.

Madden, Ed. *Tiresian Poetics: Modernism, Sexuality, Voice, 1888–2001*. Cranbury, NJ: Rosemont, 2008.

Madden, Robert David. *Harlequin's Stick, Charlie's Cane: A Comparative Study of Commedia Dell'arte and Silent Slapstick Comedy*. Bowling Green: Bowling Green University Popular Press, 1975.

Magee, Bryan. *The Tristan Chord: Wagner and Philosophy*. New York: Henry Holt, 2000.

Mansell, James G. "Sound and the Cultural Politics of Time in the Avant-Garde: Wyndham Lewis's Critique of Bergsonism." In *Wyndham Lewis and the Cultures of Modernity*. Edited by Andrzej Gasiorek, Alice Reeve-Tucker, and Nathan Waddell, 111–26. Farnham: Ashgate, 2011.

Mao, Douglas. *Solid Objects: Modernism and the Test of Production*. Princeton, NJ: Princeton University Press, 1998.

Mao, Douglas, and Rebecca Walkowitz. "The New Modernist Studies." *PMLA* 123, no. 3 (2008): 737–48.

Marinetti, F.T. "The Variety Theatre." Reprinted in *Modernism*, edited by Kolocotroni, 253–6.

Martin, Paul. "'Mr. Bloom and the Cyclops': Joyce and Antheil's Unfinished 'Opéra Méchanique.'" In *Bronze by Gold*, 91–104.

Martin, Timothy. "'Cyclops' as Opera." *James Joyce Quarterly* 38 (2001): 227–30.

——. *Joyce and Wagner: A Study of Influence*. Cambridge: Cambridge University Press, 1991.

——. "Joyce, Wagner, and the Wandering Jew." *Comparative Literature* 42, no. 1 (1990): 49–72.

Marx, Karl. *Capital*. Translated by Ben Fowkes. 3 vols. London: Penguin, 1992.

Matz, Jesse. "'You Must Join My Dead': E.M. Forster and the Death of the Novel." *Modernism/Modernity* 9, no. 2 (2002): 303–17.

McCarren, Felicia. *Dancing Machines: Choreographies in the Age of Mechanical Reproduction*. Palo Alto: Stanford University Press, 2003.

McClary, Susan. *Feminine Endings: Music, Gender, and Sexuality*. Minneapolis: Minnesota University Press, 1991.

McClean, Clara D. "Wasted Words: The Body Language of Joyce's 'Nausicaa.'" In *Joycean Cultures, Culturing Joyces*. Edited by Vincent John Cheng, Kimberly J. Devlin, and Margot Norris, 44–58. Newark: University of Delaware Press, 1998.

McCourt, John. "Joyce's Trieste: *Città Musicalissima*." In *Bronze By Gold*, 33–57.

McDonald, Ellen. "Women in Benjamin Britten's Operas." *Opera Quarterly* 4, no. 3 (1986): 83–101.

McDonald, Michael Bruce. "The Strength and Sorrow of Young Stephen: Toward a Reading of the Dialectic of Harmony and Dissonance in Joyce's *Portrait*." *Twentieth-Century Literature* 37, no. 4 (1991): 361–89.

McLuhan, Marshall. "Pound, Eliot, and the Rhetoric of *The Waste Land*." *New Literary History* 10, no. 3 (1979): 557–80.

——. *Understanding Media: The Extensions of Man*. Cambridge, MA: MIT Press, 1994.

McLuhan, Marshall, and Edmund Carpenter. *Explorations in Communication: An Anthology*. Toronto: Beacon, 1960.

McLuhan, Marshall, and Quentin Fiore. *The Medium Is the Massage*. San Francisco: Jerome Agel and HardWired, 1996.

McNeilly, Kevin. "Culture, Race, Rhythm: *Sweeney Agonistes* and the Live Jazz Break." In *T.S. Eliot's Orchestra*, 25–47.

McNelly, Cleo. "Nature, Women, and Claude Levi-Strauss." *Massachusetts Review* 26 (1975): 7–29.

Melnick, Daniel C. *Fullness of Dissonance: Modern Fiction and the Aesthetics of Music*. Rutherford: Fairleigh Dickinson University Press, 1994.

Menke, Christoph. *The Sovereignty of Art: Aesthetic Negativity in Adorno and Derrida*. Translated by Neil Solomon. Cambridge, MA: MIT Press, 1999.

Mester, Terri A. *Movement and Modernism: Yeats, Eliot, Lawrence, Williams, and Early Twentieth-Century Dance*. Fayetteville: University of Arkansas Press, 1997.

Mestrovic, Stjepan G. *The Coming Fin de Siècle: An Application of Durkheim's Sociology to Modernity and Postmodernism*. 2nd ed. London: Routledge, 2011.

Middleton, Richard. *Studying Popular Music*. Buckingham: Open University Press, 1990.

Miller, Tyrus. *Late Modernism: Politics, Fiction, and the Arts Between the World Wars*. Berkeley: University of California Press, 1999.

Miner, Margaret. *Resonant Gaps: Between Baudelaire and Wagner*. Athens: University of Georgia Press, 1995.

Mitchell, Donald. *Britten and Auden in the Thirties: The Year 1936*. London: Faber and Faber, 1981.

Moffat, Wendy. *The Great Unrecorded History: A New Life of E.M. Forster*. New York: Farrar, 2010.

Monelle, Raymond. *Linguistics and Semiotics in Music*. Chur, Switzerland: Harwood, 1992.

Moody, C. "Vsevolod Meyerhold and the 'Commedia dell'arte.'" *Modern Language Review* 73, no. 4 (1978): 859–69.

Moran, Ronald. "'Come, Come,' 'Boum, Boum': 'Easy' Rhythm in E.M. Forster's *A Passage to India*." *Ball State University Forum* 9 (1968): 3–9.

Morra, Irene. "'A Song Not Without Words': Singing Billy Budd." *Literature and Musical Adaptation*. Edited by Michael J. Meyer, 7–27. Amsterdam: Rodopi, 2002.

Nattiez, Jean-Jacques. *Music and Discourse*. Translated by Carolyn Abbate. Princeton, NJ: Princeton University Press, 1990.

Negus, Keith. *Popular Music in Theory: An Introduction*. Middletown: Wesleyan University Press, 1996.

Neufeld, Jonathan. "Musical Formalism and Political Performances." *Contemporary Aesthetics* 7 (2009), http://hdl.handle.net/2027/spo.7523862.0007.010.

Nevo, Ruth. "*The Waste Land*: Ur-Text of Deconstruction." *New Literary History* 13, no. 3 (1982): 453–61.

Norris, Margot. "The Music of Joyce's Vernacular Voices." *Modernism/Modernity* 16 (April 2009): 377–82.

North, Michael. *The Dialect of Modernism: Race, Language and Twentieth-Century Literature*. Oxford: Oxford University Press, 1994.

——. *Reading 1922: A Return to the Scene of the Modern*. Oxford: Oxford University Press, 1999.

Obert, Julia. "The Cultural Capital of Sound: *Québécité's* Acoustic Hybridity." *Postcolonial Text* 2, no. 4 (2006), http://postcolonial.org/index.php/pct/article/view/493/353.

O'Brien, John. "Pantomime." In *The Cambridge Companion to British Theatre, 1730–1830*. Edited by Jane Moody and Daniel O'Quinn, 103–14. Cambridge: Cambridge University Press, 2007.

O'Connor, Frank. "Joyce and Dissociated Metaphor." In *A Portrait of the Artist as a Young Man: Text, Criticism, and Notes*. Edited by Chester G. Anderson, 371–7. New York: Viking, 1968.

Oja, Carol J. *Making Music Modern: New York in the 1920s*. Oxford: Oxford University Press, 2000.

Orr, Jackie. *Panic Diaries: A Genealogy of Panic Disorder*. Durham, NC: Duke University Press, 2006.

Orwell, George. "Politics and the English Language." Reprinted in *In Front of Your Nose: 1945–1950*. Edited by Sonia Orwell and Ian Angus, 127–39. Boston: David R. Godine, 2000.

Oser, Lee. *The Ethics of Modernism: Moral Ideas in Yeats, Eliot, Joyce, Woolf and Beckett*. Cambridge: Cambridge University Press, 2007.

Ovid. *Metamorphoses*. Translated by John Dryden. Edited by Samuel Garth. London: Wordsworth, 1998.

Owens, Cóilín. *James Joyce's Painful Case*. Gainesville: University Press of Florida, 2008.

Paddison, Max. *Adorno's Aesthetics of Music*. Cambridge: Cambridge University Press, 1993.

Pater, Walter. *The Renaissance: Studies in Art and Poetry*. Edited by Adam Phillips. Oxford: Oxford University Press, 1998.

Pearson, John. *Façades: Edith, Osbert, and Sacheverell Sitwell*. London: Macmillan, 1976.

Pelfrey, Robert, and Mary Hall-Pelfrey. *Art and Mass Media*. New York: Harper and Row, 1985.

Perloff, Marjorie. *The Futurist Moment: Avant-Garde, Avant Guerre, and the Language of Rupture*. Chicago: University of Chicago Press, 1986.

——. "Music for Words Perhaps: Reading/Hearing/Seeing John Cage's *Roaratorio*." In *Postmodern Genres*. Edited by Marjorie Perloff, 193–228. Norman: University of Oklahoma Press, 1989.

——. *Poetics of Indeterminacy: Rimbaud to Cage*. Evanston: Northwestern University Press, 1981.

Perloff, Nancy. *Art and the Everyday: Popular Entertainment and the Circle of Erik Satie*. Oxford: Oxford University Press, 1993.

Phillips, Gyllian. "'The Rhythm of the Visible World': Music, Text, and Performance in Selected Writings of Edith Sitwell, Gertrude Stein, and Virginia Woolf." PhD diss., University of Western Ontario, 1996.

——. "'Something Lies Beyond the Scene [seen]' of *Façade*: Sitwell, Walton, and Kristeva's Semiotic." In *Literature and Musical Adaptation*, 61–80.

Piccinini, Mauro. "'Non più andrai farfallone rumoroso'—'You Will Go No More, Noisy Butterfly': Joyce and Antheil." *Journal of Modern Literature* 26, no. 1 (2002): 73–89.

——. Review of *George Antheil: Symphonies and Other Works*. *American Music* 22, no. 1 (2004): 197–202.

Picker, John. *Victorian Soundscapes*. Oxford: Oxford University Press, 2003.

Pitches, Jonathan. *Science and the Stanislavsky Tradition of Acting*. London: Routledge, 2006.

Podrom, Cyrena N. "Influence? Or Intertextuality? The Complicated Connection of Edith Sitwell with Gertrude Stein." In *Influence and Intertextuality in Literary History*. Edited by Jay Clayton and Eric Rothstein, 205–16. Madison: University of Wisconsin Press, 1991.

Pollock, Griselda. *Differencing the Canon: Feminist Desire and the Writing of Art's Histories*. London: Routledge, 1999.

Pound, Ezra. *ABC of Reading*. New York: New Directions, 1934.

——. "Antheil, 1924-1926." Reprinted in *Ezra Pound and Music: The Complete Criticism*. Edited by R. Murray Schafer, 314-5. London: Faber and Faber, 1977.

——. *Antheil and the Treatise on Harmony.* New York: Da Capo, 1968.

——. "Arnold Dolmetsch." Reprinted in *Ezra Pound and Music*, 46-7.

——. *The Cantos of Ezra Pound*. New York: New Directions, 1995.

——. "Cavalcanti." Reprinted in *Literary Essays of Ezra Pound*. Edited by T.S. Eliot, 149-200. New York: New Directions, 1954.

——. "George Antheil (Retrospect)." Reprinted in *Ezra Pound and Music*, 253-65.

——. *Guide to Kulchur*. New York: New Directions, 1970.

——. "Henry James." Reprinted in *Literary Essays of Ezra Pound*, 295-338.

——. "Hugh Selwyn Mauberley." Reprinted in *Personae: The Shorter Poems of Ezra Pound*. Rev. ed. Edited by Lea Baechler and A. Walton Litz, 183-225. New York: New Directions, 1990.

——. "Les Millwin." Reprinted in *Personae*, 93.

——. "A Retrospect." Reprinted in *Literary Essays of Ezra Pound*, 3-14.

——. *The Selected Letters of Ezra Pound, 1907-1941*. New York: New Directions, 1971.

——. "A Serious Artist." Reprinted in *Literary Essays of Ezra Pound*, 41-57.

——. "*Vers Libre* and Arnold Dolmetsch." Reprinted in *Literary Essays of Ezra Pound*, 437-50.

Preston, Carrie. *Modernism's Mythic Pose: Gender, Genre, Solo Performance*. Oxford: Oxford University Press, 2011.

Proust, Marcel. *Remembrance of Things Past*. Translated by C.K. Scott-Moncrieff and Terence Kilmartin. 2 vols. New York: Vintage, 1982.

Puchner, Martin. *Stage Fright: Modernism, Anti-Theatricality, and Drama*. Baltimore: Johns Hopkins University Press, 2002.

Rabinbach, Anson. *The Human Motor: Energy, Fatigue, and the Origins of Modernity*. Berkeley: University of California Press, 1990.

Rainey, Lawrence. "The Creation of the Avant-Garde: F.T. Marinetti and Ezra Pound." *Modernism/Modernity* 1, no. 3 (1994): 195-220.

——. *Institutions of Modernism: Literary Elites and Public Culture*. New Haven: Yale University Press, 1999.

——. *Revisiting "The Waste Land."* New Haven: Yale University Press, 2007.

Reed, Christopher. "Design for (Queer) Living: Sexual Identity, Performance, and Decor in British Vogue, 1922-1926." *GLQ* 12, no. 3 (2006): 389-90.

Reed, Philip. "Britten in the Cinema: *Coal Face*." In *The Cambridge Companion to Britten*. Edited by Mervyn Cooke, 54-77. Cambridge: Cambridge University Press, 1999.

——. "The Incidental Music of Benjamin Britten: A Study and Catalogue Raisonné of His Music for Film, Theatre and Radio." PhD diss., University of East Anglia, 1987.

Reff, Theodore. "On Harlequin and Pierrot in Picasso's Work after 1917." In *Canto d'Amore: Classicism in Modern Art and Music, 1914–1935*. Edited by Gottfried Boehm, Ulrich Mosch, and Katharina Schmidt, 140. London: Merrell Holberton, 1996.

Reid, Doug. "Popular Theatre in Victorian Birmingham." In *Performance and Politics in Popular Drama: Aspects of Popular Entertainment in Theatre, Film and Television, 1800–1976*. Edited by David Bradby, Louis James, and Bernard Sharratt, 65–89. Cambridge: Cambridge University Press, 1980.

Reilly, Seamus. "Joyce and Dublin Opera, 1888-1904." In *Bronze By Gold*, 3–32.

Rhodes, Richard. *Hedy's Folly: The Life and Breakthrough Inventions of Hedy Lamarr, the Most Beautiful Woman in the World*. New York: Vintage, 2011.

Rice, Thomas J. "His Master's Voice and Joyce." *European Joyce Studies* 18 (2003): 149–66.

Richards, I.A. *Principles of Literary Criticism*. London: Routledge, 2001.

Richards, Jeffrey. *Imperialism and Music: Britain 1876–1953*. Manchester: Manchester University Press, 2001.

Ricks, Christopher. *T.S. Eliot and Prejudice*. London: Faber and Faber, 1988.

Ringer, Alexander L. "Assimilation and the Emancipation of Historical Dissonance." In *Constructive Dissonance: Arnold Schoenberg and the Transformation of Twentieth-Century Culture*. Edited by Juliane Brand and Christopher Hailey, 23–34. Berkeley: University of California Press, 1997.

Ross, Alex. *The Rest is Noise: Listening to the Twentieth Century*. New York: Macmillan, 2007.

Ruch, Alexander. "'The Best in the Worst of All Possible Worlds': Corporate Patronage in Wyndham Lewis's Late Work." In *Wyndham Lewis and the Cultures of Modernity*. Edited by Andrzej Gasiorek, Alice Reeve-Tucker, Nathan Waddell, 145–62. Surrey: Ashgate, 2011.

Rudnitsky, Konstantin. *Russian and Soviet Theater 1905–1932*. Translated by Roxanne Permar. Edited by Lesley Milne. New York: Harry N. Abrams, 1988.

Rudy, Jason. *Electric Meters: Victorian Physiological Poetics*. Athens, OH: Ohio University Press, 2009.

Rupprecht, Philip. *Britten's Musical Language*. Cambridge: Cambridge University Press, 2001.

Russolo, Luigi. *The Art of Noises*. Translated by Barclay Brown. New York: Pendragon, 1986.

Said, Edward. *Culture and Imperialism*. New York: Vintage, 1993.

——. *Orientalism*. Rev. ed. New York: Vintage, 1994.

Sanglid, Torben. "Glitch—The Beauty of Malfunction." In *Bad Music: The Music We Love to Hate*. Edited by Christopher Washburn and Maiken Derno, 257–74. London: Routledge, 2004.

Schafer, R. Murray, ed. *Ezra Pound and Music: The Complete Criticism*. London: Faber and Faber, 1977.

——. *The New Soundscape: A Handbook for the Modern Music Teacher*. New York: Associated Music Publishers, 1969.

——. *The Soundscape: The Tuning of the World*. Rochester, VT: Destiny Books, 1993.

Schneider, Ulrich. "Mediatization in 'Aeolus' and 'Oxen of the Sun.'" In *Joyce, Modernity, and Its Mediation*. Edited by Christine van Boheemen, 15–22. Atlanta: Rodolpi, 1989.

Schopenhauer, Arthur. *The World as Will and Representation*. 2 vols. Translated by E.F.J. Payne. Mineola: Dover, 1958.

Scrimshaw, Will. "Non-cochlear Sound: On Affect and Exteriority." In *Sound, Music, Affect: Theorizing Sonic Experience*, 27–44. Edited by Marie Thompson and Ian Biddle. New York and London: Bloomsbury, 2013.

Sedgwick, Eve Kosofsky. *Epistemology of the Closet*. Berkeley: University of California Press, 1990.

Seymour, Claire. *The Operas of Benjamin Britten: Expression and Evasion*. Rochester, NY: Boydell, 2004.

Shakespeare, William. *Complete Works*. Edited by David Bevington. New York: Harper Collins, 1992.

Shaw, George Bernard. *The Perfect Wagnerite: A Commentary on the Niblung's Ring*. New York: Dover, 1967.

Sheppard, Anthony. *Revealing Masks: Exotic Influences and Ritualized Performance in Modernist Music Theater*. Berkeley: University of California Press, 2001.

Sherry, Vincent. *Ezra Pound, Wyndham Lewis, and Radical Modernism*. Oxford: Oxford University Press, 1993.

Showalter, Elaine. "Syphilis, Sexuality, and the Fiction of the Fin de Siècle." In *Sex, Politics, and Science in the Nineteenth-Century Novel*. Edited by Ruth Bernard Yeazell, 95–108. Baltimore: Johns Hopkins University Press, 1990.

Sicari, Stephen. *Joyce's Modernist Allegory: "Ulysses" and the History of the Novel*. Columbia: University of South Carolina Press, 2001.

Sidran, Ben. *Black Talk*. New edition. New York: Da Capo, 1983.

Sigg, Eric. "Eliot as a Product of America." In *The Cambridge Companion to T.S. Eliot*. Edited by A. David Moody, 14–30. Cambridge: Cambridge University Press, 1994.

Silver, Kenneth E. "Jean Cocteau and the *Image d'Epinal*: An Essay on Realism and Naiveté." In *Jean Cocteau and the French Scene*. Edited by Arthur King Peters, 81–105. New York: Abbeville Press, 1984.

Simmel, Georg. "The Metropolis and Mental Life." Reprinted in *Modernism*, edited by Kolocotroni, 51–9.

Sitwell, Edith. "Façade." Reprinted in *Collected Poems*, 110–58. London: Duckworth Overlook, 2006.

——. *Fire of the Mind: An Anthology*. Edited by Elizabeth Salter and Allanah Harper. London: Michael Joseph, 1976.

——. "Some Notes on my Own Poetry." Reprinted in *Collected Poems*, xv–xlvi.

——. *Taken Care Of.* New York: Atheneum, 1965.

Sitwell, Osbert. "A Few Days in an Author's Life." In *All at Sea: A Social Tragedy in Three Acts for First-Class Passengers Only*, 21–9. London: Duckworth, 1927.

——. *Laughter in the Next Room*. London: Macmillan, 1949.

——. *Left Hand, Right Hand!* London: Macmillan, 1949.

——. *Penny Foolish: A Book of Tirades and Panegyrics*. 2nd ed. Freeport: Books for Libraries, 1967.

——. *Sing High! Sing Low!* London: Macmillan, 1977.

Sitwell, Sacheverell. *Liszt*. New York: Philosophical Library, 1956.

Sloane, Patricia. "Richard Wagner's Arthurian Sources, Jessie L. Weston, and T.S. Eliot's 'The Waste Land.'" *Arthuriana* 11, no. 1 (2001): 30–53.

Smith, Mack. "The Structural Rhythm in *Ulysses*: Dominant to Love to Return." *Twentieth-Century Literature* 30, no. 4 (1984): 404–19.

Smith, Matthew Wilson. "Laughing at the Redeemer: Kundry and the Paradox of *Parsifal*." *Modernist Cultures* 3, no. 1 (2007): 5–25.

——. *The Total Work of Art from Bayreuth to Cyberspace*. London: Routledge, 2007.

Spoo, Robert. "Rival Confessors in 'Chamber Music': Meaning and Narrative in Joyce's Lyric Mode." *James Joyce Quarterly* 26, no. 4 (1989): 483–98.

Stadlen, Peter. "Schoenberg's Speech-Song." *Music & Letters* 62, no. 1 (1981): 1–11.

Stallybrass, Peter, and Allon White. *The Politics and Poetics of Transgression*. Ithaca: Cornell University Press, 1986.

Stanford, Charles Villiers. "Music and the War." In *Interludes: Records and Reflections*, 102–24. London: John Murray, 1922.

Stauder, Ellen Keck. "'Without an Ear of his Own': Pound's Janequin in Canto 75." *Quaderni di Palazzo Serra* 15 (2008): 257–77.

Steggle, Matthew. "*Paradise Lost* and the Acoustics of Hell." *Early Modern Literary Studies* 7, no. 1 (2001), www.chass.utoronto.ca/emls/07-1/stegmil2.htm.

Sterne, Jonathan. *The Audible Past: Cultural Origins of Sound Reproduction*. Durham, NC: Duke University Press, 2003.

Stites, Richard. *Revolutionary Dreams: Utopian Vision and Experimental Life in the Russian Revolution*. Oxford: Oxford University Press, 1991.

Stoppard, Tom. *Artist Descending a Staircase*. Reprinted in *Plays Two*, 109–56. London: Faber and Faber, 1997.

Storey, Robert. *Pierrot: A Critical History of a Mask*. Princeton, NJ: Princeton University Press, 1978.

Strunk, William. *The Elements of Style*. Edited by E.B. White. 4th ed. London: Penguin, 2008.

Suárez, Juan A. *Pop Modernism: Noise and the Reinvention of Everyday Life*. Chicago: University of Chicago Press, 2007.

Subotnik, Rose Rosengard. *Deconstructive Variations: Music and Reason in Western Society*. Minneapolis: University of Minnesota Press, 1996.

Surette, Leon. *The Birth of Modernism: Ezra Pound, W.B. Yeats, T.S. Eliot, and the Occult*. Quebec: McGill-Queens University Press, 1993.

Symons, Arthur. *The Symbolist Movement in Literature*. Rev. ed. New York: E.P. Dutton, 1919.

Tamplin, Ronald. "*The Tempest* and *The Waste Land*."*American Literature* 39, no. 3 (1967): 352–72.

Taruskin, Richard. "The Musical Mystique: Defending Classical Music against Its Devotees." *The New Republic*, 22 October 2007.

——. "A Myth of the Twentieth Century: *The Rite of Spring*, the Tradition of the New, and 'The Music Itself.'" *Modernism/Modernity* 2, no. 1 (1995): 1–26.

——. *Stravinsky and the Russian Traditions: A Biography of the Works through Mavra*. 2 vols. Oxford: Oxford University Press, 1996.

Templeton, Erin E. "'Dear Ezzroar,' 'Dear Anthill': Ezra Pound, George Antheil and the Complications of Patronage." In *Musical and Literary Modernism: Critical Essays and Comparative Studies*. Edited by Robert McParland, 66–86. Newcastle: Cambridge Scholars Publishing, 2006.

Theall, Donald, and Joan Theall. "Marshall McLuhan and James Joyce: Beyond Media." *Canadian Journal of Communication* 14, no. 4 (1989): 46–66.

Thompson, Emily. *The Soundscape of Modernity: Architectural Acoustics and the Culture of Listening in America, 1900–1933*. New edition. Cambridge, MA: MIT Press, 2004.

Tiffany, Daniel. *Radio Corpse: Imagism and the Cryptaesthetic of Ezra Pound*. Cambridge, MA: Harvard University Press, 1998.

Tindall, William York. *A Reader's Guide to "Finnegans Wake."* Syracuse: Syracuse University Press, 1996.

Tippins, Sherrill. *February House: The Story of W.H. Auden, Carson McCullers, Jane and Paul Bowles, Benjamin Britten, and Gypsy Rose Lee, Under One Roof in Brooklyn*. New York: Houghton, 2005.

Tiwari, Subha, and Maneesha Tiwari. *Plays of T.S. Eliot*. New Delhi: Atlantic Publishers, 2007.

Toop, David. *Sinister Resonance: The Mediumship of the Listener*. New York: Continuum, 2010.

Trilling, Lionel. *E.M. Forster: A Study*. Norfolk, CT: New Directions, 1943.

Tzara, Tristan. "Dada Manifesto." Reprinted in *Modernism*, edited by Kolocotroni, 276–80.

Wagner, Richard. "The Art-Work of the Future." Reprinted in *"The Art-Work of the Future" and Other Works*. Edited and translated by W. Ashton Ellis, 69–214. Lincoln: University of Nebraska Press, 1993.

——. "On Actors and Singers." Reprinted in *Actors and Singers*. Edited and translated by William Ashton Ellis, 157–228. Lincoln: University of Nebraska Press, 1995.

——. *Siegfried*. Vocal reduction score by Karl Klindworth. Brussels: B. Schott's Söhne, 1871.

Waldrep, Shelton. *The Aesthetics of Self-Invention: From Oscar Wilde to David Bowie*. Minneapolis: University of Minnesota Press, 2004.

Walkowitz, Rebecca. *Cosmopolitan Style: Modernism Beyond the Nation*. New York: Columbia University Press, 2007.

Wallace, Rob. *Improvisation and the Making of American Literary Modernism*. New York: Continuum, 2010.

Walton, Susana. *Behind the Façade*. Oxford: Oxford University Press, 1988.

Walton, William. *Façade Entertainments*. Edited by David Lloyd-Jones. Oxford: Oxford University Press, 2002.

——. *Selected Letters of William Walton*. Edited by Malcolm Hayes. London: Faber and Faber, 2002.

Warner, Michael. *Publics and Counterpublics*. New York: Zone, 2007.

Watkins, Glenn. *Proof Through the Night: Music and the Great War*. Berkeley: University of California Press, 2003.

——. *Pyramids at the Louvre: Music, Culture, and Collage from Stravinsky to the Postmodernists*. Cambridge, MA: Harvard University Press, 1994.

Weaver, Jack. *Joyce's Music and Noise: Theme and Variation in His Writings*. Gainesville: University Press of Florida, 1998.

Wenner, Melinda. "Hedy Lamarr: Not Just a Pretty Face." *Scientific American*, 3 June 2008.

Whitesell, Lloyd. "Britten's Dubious Trysts." *Journal of the American Musicological Society* 56, no. 3 (2003): 637–94.

Whitesitt, Linda. *The Life and Music of George Antheil, 1900–1959*. Ann Arbor: UMI Research Press, 1983.

Whittall, Arnold. "'Twisted Relations': Method and Meaning in Britten's *Billy Budd*." *Cambridge Opera Journal* 2, no. 2 (1990): 145–71.

Wightman, Alistair. "Szymanowski and Joyce." *The Musical Times* 123, no. 1676 (1982): 679–81.

Wilcock, Evelyn. "Adorno, Jazz, and Racism: 'Über Jazz' and the 1934–7 British Jazz Debate." *Telos* 107 (1996): 63–80.

Wilke, Sabine. "Adorno and Derrida as Readers of Husserl: Some Reflections on the Historical Context of Modernism and Postmodernism." *boundary 2* 16, no. 2/3 (1989): 77–90.

Wilkey, Jay. "Marshall McLuhan and Meaning in Music." *Music Educators Journal* 56, no. 1 (1969): 54–8.

Williams, Carolyn. *Gilbert and Sullivan: Gender, Genre, Parody*. New York: Columbia University Press, 2011.

Williams, Ralph Vaughan. "Should Music Be National?" In *National Music and Other Essays*. Edited by Michael Kennedy, 1–11. Oxford: Oxford University Press, 1987.

Williams, Raymond. *Culture and Materialism*. 2nd ed. London: Verso, 2005.

——. *Culture and Society, 1780–1950*. New York: Columbia University Press, 1983.

——. *Keywords: A Vocabulary of Culture and Society*. Rev. ed. Oxford: Oxford University Press, 1985.

——. *The Long Revolution*. Orchard Park: Broadview, 2001.

Wilson, Edmund. "An Account of 'Peter Grimes' from 'London in Midsummer.'" Reprinted in *Benjamin Britten: Peter Grimes*. Edited by Philip Brett, 159-62. Cambridge: Cambridge University Press, 1983.

——. "The Poetry of Drouth." Reprinted in *The Waste Land*. Edited by Michael North, 140-45. New York: Norton, 2001.

——. *The Shores of Light*. Reprinted in *Literary Essays and Reviews of the 1920s & 30s*. New York: Library of America, 2007.

Winter, Jay. *Sites of Memory, Sites of Mourning: The Great War in European Cultural History*. Cambridge: Cambridge University Press, 1995.

Wollaeger, Mark. *Joseph Conrad and the Fictions of Skepticism*. Palo Alto: Stanford University Press, 1990.

——. *Modernism, Media, and Propaganda: British Narrative from 1900 to 1945*. Princeton, NJ: Princeton University Press, 2007.

——. "Reading *Ulysses*: Agency, Ideology, and the Novel." In *Joyce and the Subject of History*. Edited by Wollaeger, Victor Luftig, and Robert Spoo, 83-104. Ann Arbor: University of Michigan Press, 1996.

Wright, Basil. "Britten and Documentary." *The Musical Times* 104, no. 1449 (1963): 779-80.

Yates, Michael. "Percy Grainger and the Impact of the Phonograph." *Folk Music Journal* 4, no. 3 (1982): 275-85.

Yeats, W.B. *The Countess Cathleen*. London: T.F. Unwin, 1899.

——. "The Peacock." Reprinted in *The Collected Poems of W.B. Yeats*, 121.

——. "To Ireland in the Coming Times." Reprinted in *The Collected Poems of W.B. Yeats*. Edited by Richard J. Finneran, 50-1. New York: Simon and Schuster, 1996.

Zimmerman, Nadya. "Musical Form as Narrator: The Fugue of the Sirens in James Joyce's *Ulysses*." *Journal of Modern Literature* 26, no. 1 (2002): 108-18.

Index